PLANNING IN POSTMODERN TIMES

THE RTPI Library Series

**Editors: Cliff Hague, Heriot Watt University, Edinburgh, Scotland
Robin Boyle, Wayne State University, Michigan, USA
Robert Upton, RTPI, London, UK**

Published in conjunction with The Royal Town Planning Institute, this series of leading-edge texts looks at all aspects of spatial planning theory and practice from a comparative and international perspective.

The series

- explores the dimensions of spatial planning and urbanism, in relation to people, place, space and environment;

- develops the theoretical and methodological foundations of planning;

- investigates the relationship between theory and practice;

- examines the contribution of planners to resolving social, economic and environmental concerns.

By linking planning to disciplines such as economics, anthropology, sociology, geography, environmental and urban studies, the project's inherent focus on sustainable development places the theoretical and practical relationships between social, economic and environmental issues in their necessary spatial context.

Planning in Postmodern Times
Philip Allmendinger, University of Aberdeen, Scotland

Sustainability, Development and Spatial Planning in Europe
Vincent Nadin, Caroline Brown and Stefanie Dühr, UWE, Bristol, UK

Planning for Crime Prevention
Richard Schneider, University of Florida, USA, and Ted Kitchen, Sheffield Hallam University, UK

PLANNING IN POSTMODERN TIMES

PHILIP ALLMENDINGER

London and New York

First published 2001
by Routledge, 11 New Fetter Lane, London EC4P 4EE
Simultaneously published in the USA and Canada by Routledge, 29 West 35th Street, New York, NY 10001

Routledge is an imprint of the Taylor & Francis Group

© 2001 Philip Allmendinger

Typeset in 9.5/13.5pt Akzidenz Grotesk Regular by Wearset, Boldon, Tyne and Wear
Printed and bound in Great Britain by Clays Ltd, St Ives plc

British Library Cataloguing in Publication Data
A catalogue record for this book is available from the British Library

Library of Congress Cataloging in Publication Data
Allmendinger, Philip, 1968–
      Planning in post modern times / Philip Allmendinger.
         p.cm. -- (The RTPI library series)
      Includes bibliographical references and index.
      1. City planning. 2. Postmodernism--Social aspects. I. Title. II. Series.

      HT166 .A616 2000
      307.1'216--dc21   00-037779
ISBN 0–415–23422–0 (PPC)
ISBN 0–415–23423–9 (PB)

CONTENTS

Preface   **VII**

01   Rethinking planning: the legacy of the Enlightenment   **1**

02   What is the postmodern?: social theory   **25**

03   What is the postmodern?: new times   **55**

04   Is planning a modern project?   **91**

05   Responses to new times: different paradigms for a new planning 1   **121**

06   Responses to new times: different paradigms for a new planning 2   **155**

07   The scope for a new postmodern planning: theory   **189**

08   The scope for a new postmodern planning: practice   **227**

09   Conclusions   **257**

Bibliography   **263**

Index   **278**

PREFACE

Most of this book was written while I was staying in Nürnberg. This beautiful city was once a centre of art and literature, but is better known now as being related to one of the most dismal episodes in human history. During this period totality ruled over difference and extreme technical-bureaucracy and rationality borne of the Enlightenment exposed the darker side of modernity. There is a degree of irony that this book is about ways in which land use planning can incorporate difference in ways other than those traditionally associated with modernity.

Following the fragmentation of social theory in the wake of Kuhn and others, planning theory followed a wider shift in the social sciences generally in seeking to balance an understanding of reality as socially constructed with the need to maintain overarching principles such as justice. Postmodern thinking has played an important role in exposing the less desirable aspects of modernity and has brought to the fore new understandings of the discursively created subject (Foucault), the role of cultural influences in ordering society (Baudrillard) and the breakdown in transcendental meaning (Lyotard). However, it has played a very minor if non-existent role as a basis for an alternative, despite its claim to be 'after'-modern.

This is mainly due to the postmodern penchant for relativity – the lack of 'closure', the 'anything goes' mentality that is a powerful pin-prick to the generalising and stultifying but does little as a contribution to any alternative understanding or basis for society. But this need not be the case. In this book, I explore ways in which a postmodern understanding and approach to planning can be developed that maintains elements of difference and diversity while attempting to underpin them with processes and principles that allow communities to agree and move forward together.

Some may argue that the result is not postmodern at all. There is some truth in this. However, when it comes to attempting to construct or even think about basic tools such as methodologies, postmodern thinking is far too abstract. What I attempt to do in this book is use the principles of postmodern thought while drawing upon other fields of thinking to supplement it. The result is a mixture of different traditions of thought that maintain the tenets of postmodern thinking while providing a realistic alternative to other current schools of thinking in planning theory.

Necessarily, such an endeavour builds upon the thoughts and works of many beyond those cited throughout the book. Thanks must first go to the city of Nürnberg and its many cafés and bars that provided a wonderful environment in which to work. Steven Tiesdell and Yvonne Rydin kindly provided support and comments on an earlier draft as did two anonymous referees. Huw Thomas, as usual, was generous with his time in supplying many thoughts and questions on the content. I have tried to incorporate or respond to their points where possible. The rest, as they say, is mine.

CHAPTER 1

RETHINKING PLANNING: the legacy of the Enlightenment.

INTRODUCTION

It seems that hardly a day goes by without a conflict in land use planning emerging in the headlines somewhere. Whether it is the latest in a line of corruption scandals, rural people concerned about the loss of greenfield land, protesters living in trees to halt new road building, bureaucratic nightmares making 'innocent' people jump through hoops or the loss of town centre shops, planners are in one way or another 'to blame'. Planners may cry 'foul!' at such accusations, claiming that it is the political process that is to blame, or that they cannot control everything. It is not them that make decisions but others. This myth of professional neutrality still peddled in some quarters (see Greed, 1996). But fifty odd years on from the inception of our current planning system, why do we still have homelessness, car choked cities, damp infested tower blocks, and environmental degradation? While planners cannot be held responsible for the crimes of others, they must surely take some blame and ask themselves 'why?'.

There are a number of critiques of planning that point to various causes of this failure. The political right claim that there is 'too much' planning. The left naturally point to an altogether different cause. Planning has not tackled the root causes of urban problems because it was never meant to:

> the scope, content and direction of planning are shaped by political struggles, at various spatial scales, in which the protagonists (and lines of cleavage) arise from the conflicts of interest endemic in capitalist society (H. Thomas, 1999: 27).

Planning exists to help the market and support capitalism, not challenge and supplant it. Whatever the reason there is a growing disenchantment with the outcomes of planning. Partly this is due to the trend of an increasingly politicised population challenging government and partly because it is clear that planning has lost its way. Keeble set the direction of planning as being

> the art and science of ordering the use of land and the character and siting of buildings and communication routes so as to secure the maximum practicable degree of economy, convenience and beauty (1952: 9).

This mission statement pervaded both the self-image of planners and the view from the outside that there was a technical solution that a planner could provide. Nearly half a century on the Royal Town Planning Institute still sees the role of planners as 'to advance the art and science of Town Planning for the benefit of the public' (RTPI, 1999). This is against a massively different backdrop from that which existed in 1947. For example, there is widespread distrust over public authority most recently highlighted in the Scott Inquiry on arms sales to Iraq, the Macpherson inquiry into police inaction over the murder of Stephen Lawrence, the cover up of BSE, the gerrymandering in Westminster Council and the 'cash for questions' outcry. These cases have demonstrated a culture of secrecy, personal benefit being advanced over public good and general incompetence at the heart of government. Planners and councillors have not been immune to the growing distrust of professional officials and elected representatives. At a variety of times over the past few years both professional planners and councillors have been accused and, in some cases, found guilty of corruption and malpractice. The issue of malpractice is a contestable area, as in cases such as North Cornwall where the term was used to cover a departure from national guidelines. Corruption, on the other hand, is a more clear-cut issue. A recent case has involved the indictment of five local councillors after one developer bragged that he 'bought and paid for' their support (*Planning*, 5th November 1999: 5). As well as the more blatant cases of offering money in return for support or favourable decisions, the planning regime has also been encouraged to engage in what is euphemistically termed planning gain or planning obligations. While this is undoubtedly a useful mechanism to extract public benefits from private profit it has undoubtedly led, for example, to developers such as supermarkets trying to outbid each other for permission (Healey, et al., 1995). It is not surprising, therefore, if the public perception is of the planning system 'buying' and 'selling' permissions particularly if negotiations over planning gain are kept out of the public realm (Thomas, 1997).

The growing general distrust of public officials, whether right or wrong, is challenging the very idea of professions. The whole apparatus of planning was built around the notion of a benevolent elite working towards common goals:

> in planning, the assertion that the purpose of planners and the planning process is to provide a future which will be of benefit to us all is a belief which is integral to the practice of the activity of planning (B. Evans, 1995: 55).

Such a belief derived from the early writings on the subject and the philanthropic movements that saw improving the good of the working classes as their goal. The planner's role in this, as Davies (1972) famously pointed out, was as an 'evangelistic bureaucrat':

> we the citizens are forced to give up more and more of the areas of decision-making to a group of powerful, highly trained officials possessing, it would appear, a range of quasi-magical potencies (1972: 3).

This perspective has been reinforced through different mechanisms in the post-war period including the idea of value neutrality that underpinned classic planning textbooks such as Lewis Keeble's *Principles and Practice of Town and Country Planning* (1952) and the dominance of the systems and rational approaches to planning that dominated practice during the 1960s and 1970s. The legacy of such an elitist self-image lingers today. Campbell and Marshall (1998) conclude from their survey of planners in 1996 that, overall, their primary obligation was to the concept of professional autonomy and independent professional judgement.

It is hardly surprising that in a world very different from that which saw the genesis of the modern movement the concept of an apolitical profession acting in the public good no longer seems appropriate. While the world has changed dramatically, it seems that the planning profession remains the same. Planners either feel no need to change or, like a rabbit in a car's headlights, they do not know in what direction to move. My feeling is that the reason for the current malaise has more to do with the latter situation. However, this is not to say that all that is required is a new direction for planning. The idea of a profession is founded on some form of elitist and privileged knowledge that serves a public interest. But an increasingly fractured and fractious public means that such an interest cannot be 'read off' automatically – there is not one interest but many.

So the idea of planning as a profession is central to its current problems. There have been various critiques of planning as a profession and I do not want to engage too much with them here (see Reade, 1987, B. Evans, 1993, 1995, 1997). In addition, Brian McLaughlin also pointed to the role of planning courses in perpetuating the idea of an elitist profession. He considered them a form of indoctrination into a planning profession rather than a critical reflection on the needs of people and cities.

> Far too much planning education is little more than a series of descriptive anecdotes – about developments, conflicts, regulatory regimes, and the like – but with little or no attempt at theoretical analysis and explanation (McLaughlin, 1994: 1114).

His recommendation was for undergraduate planning degrees to be replaced by courses designed to allow students to critically reflect upon spatial and policy issues. Similarly, Grant (1999) claims that the idea of planning as a profession is no longer sustainable.

> in recent years, the roles of the older professions have yielded to deregulatory pressures that have come both from Government and from within the professions themselves (1999: 21).

The pressure to open up professions and increase competition has led to the lifting of some statutory monopolies such as solicitors' conveyancing. There has also been a blurring of the distinction between different professions including those concerned with land and property. Common concerns such as urban regeneration cut across traditional boundaries leading to some to call for a greater fluidity in professional disciplines:

> We urgently need more people with expertise in urban design, planning and property development within central and local government. Career training for relevant professions currently lacks a sufficient inter-disciplinary dimension (Urban Task Force, 1999: 10)

As Gunder and Fookes (1997) point out, part of the attack on the idea of planning as a profession was an element of a broader growth in anti-planning thinking throughout the 1980s and 1990s from both the left and right. But even in a period of intense pressure to deregulate, planning as a practice and a profession survived. There are two reasons for this. The first revolves around planning's flexible and amorphous nature. Cullingworth (1997) commented on the 50th anniversary of the British planning system that it has not really changed all that much. This is true to the extent that there is still a planning system that has development plans and development control at its core. What has changed, however, are the processes and priorities of planning, changes that were allowed because of the loose legislatory framework that permitted significant alteration without recourse to new legislation. During one of the most turbulent eras for planning, Thatcher governments of the 1980s were able to introduce potentially radical changes such as the B1 Use Class and Circular 22/80 without primary legislation. There was no new planning Act to replace the extant 1971 Act until 1990. Planning has not changed because it does not need to – the accommodation of change is built into a flexible system. Second, planning has survived because of an unintentional role it has developed, a role I would term 'The Three Ps': Protecting Property Prices. It seems that society is now a land use planning junkie. It cannot do without it. After 50 years it has become institutionally embedded within so many legal and institutional systems such as housing finance or retail investment that it commands support not because it promotes collective change, but precisely because it does not. This is why the Thatcher governments could not alter planning – it underpinned the exclusionary desires of their natural constituency and appealed to the self-interested nature of shire voters.

So, all is not well with planning but is propped up because of support from property interests and a lack of a realistic alternative. And while planners continue to benefit from their status as professionals there is a lack of impetus to change the status quo. How can we approach such a rethink? As Muller (1998) rightly points out, the notion that there is a single paradigm for planning is unsupportable. Instead he identifies and welcomes a plurality of models that can be used *à la carte* depending on the political, social, economic and physical conditions of certain environments. The problem with such an approach is not in its concept of a plurality of competing positions, but in its lack of critical reflection upon them. Different paradigms imply fundamentally different conceptions of interests, methodologies, power and outcomes. In a world where powerful interests can choose from a selection of competing paradigms for planning there is a danger, if not inevitability, that public intervention in land will continue to favour such interests. There is also an issue of certain paradigms being out of step with the broad changes within society. The current favoured paradigm, collaborative planning, is based upon a revised modernist notion of consensus. But, the argument of this book is that society is shifting to new or *post*modern times which both favour and require different conceptions of planning not founded in eighteenth-century ideals. Economic, cultural and political globalisation, as well as their manifestations, have led to changed sensibilities, outlooks and expectations. In such a world the plurality of positions and values means that it is difficult to impose one particular view and justify it over others. This fragmentation has had a significant impact upon social theory and planning. The traditional view of planning saw it based upon 'the neutrality of observation and the givenness of experience; the ideal of unequivocal language and the independence of data from theoretical interpretation; the belief in the universality of conditions of knowledge and criteria for theory choice' (Bohman, 1996: 2). In place of this we have, instead, a recognition of indeterminacy, incommensurability, variance, diversity, complexity and intentionality in some routes of theoretical development – traits that question the very notion of 'planning'. One outcome has been the emergence and re-emergence of a multitude of post-empirical theoretical perspectives that include collaborative planning, neo-pragmatism and postmodern interpretations, all of which, to greater or lesser degrees, perceive planners as fallible advisors who operate like everybody else, in a complex world where there are no 'answers' only diverse and indeterminate options. Different routes out of this indeterminacy are being followed. Some theorists are trumpeting the collaborative approach and others neo-pragmatism, public choice theory or a multitude of other ways forward. What is needed is an approach that is flexible enough to allow different paradigms to exist that can challenge dominant thinking and the protectionist interests that currently prop planning up. The subject of this book is to rethink planning in a way that will address issues such as those highlighted above and provide such a framework. Like other post-positivist positions it is based on the need to move away from the epistemic notion of planning; that is, the claim and assumption that planning is based on scientific knowledge born of modernity. However, I argue that other routes that lead away from the idea of planning as a modernist enterprise do not adequately address the problems of planning. In which case, in what direction can planning go? Some,

such as Bell (1973), Tofler (1981) and Naisbitt (1984) have attempted to characterise these changes as being founded on the shift from a production-based to an
information-orientated society. As information and services have become dominant
in western societies so we have also experienced wider implications such as
increased diversity, a loss of local distinction and greater divisions between the
information-rich elites and those who have become the new proletariat left to
provide services for them. Others, such as Hall and Jaques (1989), point to a
seismic change in the economic foundations of society that are terms post-Fordism
or neo-Fordism (Aglietta 1979, 1982). Post-Fordists claim that the marked change
in the nature of production has involved a move away from the mass-production
characteristics of classic Fordism to a more flexible and specialised niche function
based around specialisation in specific localities. Again, like the information society
theorists, this shift has wider political and cultural significance as flexible production requires flexible and multi-skilled workers leading to a breakdown of class and
class-based politics and the rise of single issue politics and, in the cultural sphere, the
rise of individualism.

In contrast, neo-Fordists deny this shift in the basis of capital. What we are
witnessing is another attempt by capital to overcome one of its periodic crises. The
mass production and consumption of the last manifestation of capital that emerged
on the back of Fordism and Taylorism has exhausted itself and is now looking for
the next impetus for growth. This is what they term 'neo-Fordism' or the globalisation of Fordist strategies which has seen production shift to cheap labour areas in
the developing world and the rise of flexible specialisation as an attempt to challenge organised labour. Both interpretations agree on the existence of something
'new', that localism and diversity are now important considerations though are
sometimes reductionist in their interpretation of wider and social cultural change
emanating from changes in the economy.

Finally, the third broad interpretation of change is that of postmodernism or
post-modernity. Unlike the other two schools, postmodernism provides no simple
summary of its analysis of change or its view of the future. The different theories of
change – the information society, post-Fordism and postmodernism – overlap one
another. While the differences may be more than emphasis, common themes do
emerge. First, all accept some idea of change. All focus on decentralisation, diversity and a renewed emphasis on localities. But rather than positing a reductionist
explanation based on the dynamics of the economy or information, postmodernism
takes a much broader world view that, if anything, focuses on the cultural. In doing
so it subsumes the other perspectives and provides (ironically) a meta-theory of
change. Both the information society and post/neo-Fordist ideas are still wedded
to the Enlightenment ideal of progress and rationality. Postmodernism seeks both
to challenge this and provide alternatives that offer a framework to accommodate

difference (including different planning paradigms) and a way forward itself. Like the other two perspectives on change, it says as much about its proponents and opponents as it does about the world itself. But, postmodernism is not simply about providing an explanation for cultural change, it is also in some guises a highly original (if eclectic) re-interpretation of the past and present, as well as, in some cases, proffering a radical prescription for the future. Unlike the information school or the post-Fordists it has a more varied and eclectic basis than simply a largely left- and/or right-wing approach. Depending on your reading, it is both, none or some. It can be radical, conservative or just plain daft depending on who you read and how it is read. For example, Sayer is annoyed with the postmodern for dressing up anti-foundationalism in new clothes and ignoring the fact that it has been around long before the postmodern became fashionable (1993: 322). As such, it is provocative and is the ideal basis for a radical evaluation of planning. As Jameson (1992: 48) puts it:

> I ... wonder whether any other concept can dramatise the issues in quite so effective and economical a fashion.

Turner (1990: 1) also finds the postmodern a source of potentially radical thought:

> there can be an important alliance between progressive politics (in gender issues, multicultural alternatives to racism, in ecology movements and cultural criticism) and postmodernism.

Like other areas of public policy, planning is trying to come to terms with these changes. The land use planning system in the UK is a product of an earlier time, a period and approach that emerged from the Enlightenment and has been termed modernity. Leonie Sandercock sums up the situation thus:

> In the post-war rush to turn planning into an applied social science much was lost – the city of memory, of desire, of spirit, the importance of place and the art of place-making, the local knowledges written into the stones and memories of communities. Modernist architects, planners, engineers – Faustian heroes all – saw themselves as experts who could utilise the laws of development to provide societal guidance. The hubris of the city-building professions was their faith in the liberating potential of their technical knowledge and their corresponding belief in the ability to transcend the interests of capital, labour, and the state, and to arrive at an objective assessment of 'the public interest' (1998: 4).

The planning system was created at a specific niche in history when consensus was required between many disparate interests. As a result the legislation and procedures of the system were produced in such a way as to both make the objectives vague and malleable, and also to allow a great deal of change to be made by Westminster without recourse to primary legislation. As such the system has adapted through a combination of 'mend and make do' without significant rethinks over its relationship to societal needs and its own purpose. Significant advances in our thinking concerning such modern enterprises as planning have emerged in the past 30 years or so. Some have sought to provide a neo-modernist vision based on consensus that provides a nightmare of control and consensus, though under the guise of 'difference'. The problem with such approaches is that they accept the increasingly pluralistic nature of society and even pay lip-service to it but then argue that, in the face of such difference, the most important imperative is to search for consensus. For some, the challenge is to

> imagine a *deliberative democratic politics* that recognizes and respects plurality and difference while being no less committed to *learning and acting together*, a politics that helps us to clarify critically the truth of our possibilities for human betterment, helping us to *listen, learn and act* – even as we know full well that some people along the way will be lying through their teeth (whether out of fear or out of greed) (Forester, 1998: 215).

Another route that has been less travelled is the approach that takes a postmodern perspective though this masks a multitude of positions and critiques. Theoretically, this is the most underdeveloped path and has mainly been used to expose some of the inherent contradictions, drawbacks, potential and real problems with planning that echo the feeling of different times. As Flyvbjerg (1998a, 1998b) has hinted, in current theoretical circles the difference between the neo-modern and postmodern approaches basically comes down to whether you follow a Habermasian concern with Kantian universalism or whether you feel a focus on difference *à la* Foucault et al. is more appropriate. Although the Habermasians have been making most of the running (due in no small measure to the left-leaning liberalism of his followers in the planning world) they have attempted to co-opt the concerns of Foucault (usually in their acknowledgment of difference) while ignoring the fundamentally different implications of both schools. As Kuhn or Rorty might put it, these two schools inhabit different *Weltanshauung* that do not comprehend the position of the other. While some of the postmodern directions imply a nihilistic 'no planning', this is not the case with all – particularly the usefulness of critique of postmodern social theory. But, more constructively (and to a much lesser degree), postmodern think-ing also points the way to the possibility of a new and emancipated planning, one that work with, rather than against, these different times. It also provides a frame-work that runs with the grain of the zeitgeist. This is not to say that postmodernity provides all the answers. As I go on to argue, there are serious difficulties with postmodern social theory if it is to be interpreted as a basis for a rethought planning. In particular, it lacks a methodology, regards agreement as 'terroristic' and is too relativistic in its attitude towards values. This does not mean we need to discard it, but rather explore how it can be modified to be practical *and* radical.

So, at the heart of the book are the issues of modernity and postmodernity. It seems almost impossible to pick up a newspaper, listen to the radio or even write something without the term postmodern being used. But as many authors have pointed out, there is significant disagreement and difference in the use and therefore understanding of the term. Part of the problem is that we have a natural tendency to feel that we are living in new and different times. It is simply alluring. In a political climate of 'New Labour, New Britain' the word 'new' denotes something good and desirable. We want to feel that we are different and better than what went before, or that the march of history is in a positive direction. This is part of the problem with the terms modernity and postmodernity. Modern is an equally-emotive term that conjures up images of progress. Postmodern is almost a reinforcement of that – 'ultra' or 'extra' modern. These confusions arise even before we start to analyse what is meant by different users of the terms. This is because any journey through the post- or late-modern landscape of contemporary society should first try to locate itself in relation to its 'post': what is 'modernity'? It is only from this position that one can be begin to build an understanding of what we mean by modern, postmodern and late modern.

We also need an analysis that goes beyond the idea of modernity and post-modernity as merely epochs. It is worth stating here that I am not convinced we live in 'postmodern times' in its broadest sense. Modernity is inextricably bound up with capitalism and there is little doubt that any differences we do experience are ultimately subject to its dynamics. We do live in an era where sensibilities are significantly different and in some areas the classical modern manifestations are breaking down, e.g., in art and politics. But such changes have been around and ongoing for a long time. The postmodernism I recognise is one of attitude. The contribution of many shifts in our understanding of representation, foundational thought and truths that have been brought under the umbrella of postmodernism are a useful tool in shining a strong and revealing light on the practices and assumptions of contemporary life. And such contemporary life, including planning, is deeply sub-merged in the practices of modernity. To me, the term postmodern represents an eclectic shift in attitude and understanding about modernity but, following Lyotard (1984: 79), from *within* modernity. So, the postmodern is no more or no less than this: in its origin it is a manifestation, in its use it is reflective.

But, as usual, things are not that straightforward (that's postmodernism for you!). The problem is that there is a complex mixture of views on both modernity and postmodernity that is not simply a semantic exercise. At the heart of the maelstrom of perspectives is a mixture of normative and prescriptive thinking that means any debate is ultimately irreconcilable. Many Marxist-inspired writers, for example, cannot accept what they see as postmodernism's nihilism and rejection of grand theories, as to do so would obviously undermine the possibility of their privileged analysis and solution. Then again, some of the most perceptive analyses of the postmodern have come from Marxists or ex-Marxists (e.g. Jameson, Harvey, Lyotard, Foucault and Baudrillard). Postmodern writers, on the other hand, perceive such grand theories as anathema (or 'terroristic') and useless in an increasingly fragmented world (the irony is that such a belief sounds suspiciously like a 'grand theory' itself). Other 'layers' of seeming confusion are added in that both modernists and postmodernists claim to be working towards similar broad ends: emancipation, freedom, tolerance, etc. At the same time, some who are critical of modernity (e.g., Nietzsche and Weber) cannot also be seen as 'postmodernists' while others who would undoubtedly benefit from the breaking down of some of the consequence of modernity (e.g. feminists) do not subscribe to the relativisms of postmodernity and its ambivalent attitude towards existing power structures. Further issues relate to the relationship between the Enlightenment and modernity, terms that are often used synonymously but have distinct consequences and meanings.

So there is a need to step back a little to provide some clarity. Just as the question 'what is modernity?' proceeds 'what is postmodernity?' so we must first step back even further and address the issue of 'what is the Enlightenment?'.

MODERNITY AND THE ENLIGHTENMENT

To contrast the Enlightenment and modernity is like making the distinction between a bomb going off and the damage caused in its wake. Although some see the Enlightenment as simply a tendency towards a new form of critical inquiry and the application of reason, this is an understatement. Just like the terms it was to create, the Enlightenment is, in Porter's (1990) view, hard to pin down and a constantly shifting entity. Its most important feature was the move from a theological world to a secular one. This entailed a

> Rational form of social organisation and rational modes of thought (which)
> promised liberation from the irrationalities of myth, religion, superstition, release
> from the arbitrary use of power as well as from the dark side of our human
> natures (Harvey, 1990: 12).

Its main exponents were an eclectic collection of thinkers who

> shared a general commitment to criticising injustices and exposing the
> inefficiencies of the *ancien régime*; to emancipating man, through knowledge,
> education and science, from the chains of ignorance and error, superstition,

theological dogma, and the dead hand of the clergy; to instilling a new mood of
hope for a better future . . .; and to practical action for creating greater
prosperity, fairer laws, milder government, religious tolerance, intellectual
freedom, expert administration, and not least, heightened individual awareness
(Porter, 1990: 5).

This is not to say that disagreements did not occur however. Although various
dates (depending on different emphases) can be advanced for this shift (see Smart
(1993)), there is broad agreement that the start of the eighteenth century witnessed the birth of a broad movement that could be termed 'the Enlightenment'. I
use the term 'movement' in an even looser sense than it is normally employed. This
is because, as Hamilton has summarised, the Enlightenment involved

- A characteristic bundle of ideas
- An intellectual movement
- A communicating network of intellectuals
- A set of institutional centres
- A publishing industry with an audience
- An intellectual fashion
- A zeitgeist
- A history and geography (1990: 22).

This amorphous nature of the Enlightenment movement masked a number of different emphases from its leading lights or *philosophes* including Descartes, Comte,
Voltaire, Kant, Rousseau, Hume and others. 'Heroes' of the Enlightenment were
those figures such as Isaac Newton who could lift minds above the 'ignorance' of
dogma and tradition in the world to a new and objective sphere. This was not only
in the field of natural sciences. Enlightenment thinkers

tried to apply the scientific style of thinking to the regions of the aesthetic,
social and political theory (Gay, 1969: 126).

Rationality and reason were elevated, science was seen as the leading or universal
basis for thought and progress and

the attainment of knowledge would lead very directly to human freedom, to a
liberation from both drudgery and the dangers associated with eking an
existence out of the natural environment (Cloke et al., 1991: 188).

This fusion of critical rationality with 'progressive' ideals has led Habermas to characterise the period as a 'project' whose aims were to develop 'objective science,
universal morality and law, and autonomous art according to inner logic' (quoted in

Harvey, 1990: 12). But it is important to point out that Enlightenment thinkers were not simply rationalists. They believed in a pre-Marxist form of praxis, i.e, the fusion of theory and practise. The contrast with the pre-modern period (which Kellner (1989) has termed the 'middle ages') could not have been greater. Compared to the biblical view of the cosmos summed up in Genesis and the doctrine that accompanies it, the Enlightenment was characterised by

- Reason
- Empiricism
- Science
- Universalism
- Progress
- Individualism
- Tolerance
- Freedom
- Uniformity of human nature
- Secularism (Hamilton, 1992: 21).

These factors provided the building blocks of modernity, a movement we can identify as a broad outcome of the Enlightenment that has driven the emergence of certain distinctive features or social characteristics of western existence in the past two centuries (Hall, 1992: 6). Such features include the nation–state, modern capitalism, liberalism and democracy, all of which underpinned the French and American constitutions and heralded the 'modern period'. In addition to these characteristics, Giddens (1990) identifies three main differences between pre-modern and modern times. First, there is the pace of change. While pre-modern societies may have been considerably more dynamic (and in some cases were characterised by periods of extraordinary progress such as the Renaissance), the rapidity of change brought about by modernity has been exceptional. In a selective and enormously-optimistic view, Isaacson has concluded that in this century alone, humankind has

> split the atom, ... launched airplanes and landed on the moon, concocted a general theory of relativity, devised the transistor and figured out how to etch millions of them on tiny microchips, discovered penicillin and the structure of DNA, ... bombed Guernica, ... developed cinema and television and wired the world (1998: 30).

Second, there is the scope of change. Much has been written on the globalisation of society and it is now a truism to say that we live in a 'global village' where change is pandemic. Harvey's (1990) image of 'time-space compression' captures this feeling and reality of 'closeness' where people produce and consume on a global scale. Finally, there is the intrinsic nature of modern institutions which, in most cases, are not found in pre-modern societies. For example, the political system of the nation–state is a particularly modern phenomenon that evolved from the pre-modern city states. However, it is interesting to note that the Henley Centre predict that cities will replace countries as the basic units of international power in the twenty-first century. Unconsciously echoing Umberto Eco's focus on the return of the medieval in *fin de siécle* western societies, they consider that city states will hold greater sway in trade and diplomacy as they increasingly compete to attract international capital (The *Independent on Sunday*, 12th April 1998).

While it may be relatively simple to define modernity in terms of what it is not (i.e., what went before) it is far more difficult to ascribe a positive meaning beyond broad generalities. This can be demonstrated through the various extremes of definition. For Giddens modernity refers to

> modes of social life or organisation which emerged in Europe from about the seventeenth century onwards and which subsequently became more or less world-wide in their influence (1990: 1).

While, according to Docherty, modernity concerns progress and freedom that aims at:

> human emancipation from myth, superstition and enthralled enchantment to mysterious powers and forces of nature through the progressive operations of critical reason (1993: 5).

Berman takes a more poetic stance that introduces an important dark undercurrent or dialectic:

> To be modern is to find ourselves in an environment that promises adventure, power, joy, growth, transformation of ourselves and the world – and, at the same time, that threatens to destroy everything we have, everything we know, everything we are (1982: 15).

Finally, for Bauman, modernity was the path to the horrors of the twentieth century:

> the Holocaust was not the antithesis of modern civilisation and everything (or so we like to think) it stands for. We suspect (even if we refuse to admit it) that the Holocaust could merely have uncovered another face of the same modern society whose other, so familiar, face we so admire. And that the two faces are perfectly comfortably attached to the same body (1989: 7).

What the four views above tell us is that there is by no means agreement on the content, objectives and influence of modernity. More importantly, however, both Berman and Bauman raise what has been termed the 'dark side' of modernity. One such dark side is its 'dynamic of change'. Modernity was and is, above all, a source for change. For Marxists, its inherent change was a capitalist one.

> The emergent social order of modernity is capitalistic in both its economic
> system and its other institutions. The restless, mobile character of modernity is
> explained as an outcome of the investment–profit–investment cycle which,
> combined with the overall tendency of the rate of profit to decline, brings about
> a constant disposition for the system to expand (Giddens, 1990:11).

Giddens discerns a more complex origin than capitalism to the dynamic of change and the basis of the dark side. First, there is the separation of time and space. In the pre-modern world, time and space were inextricably linked – 'when' was almost always connected to 'where'. The spread in the use of mechanical clocks and the standardisation of social time led to the separation of time and space and a situation where place is increasingly affected by events beyond the locale. This distanciation fed the dynamic of modernity by allowing the disembedding of social systems (see below) which facilitated the development of organisations (including the modern state) and bureaucracies through more detailed control and observation of the population.

Second, there is the disembedding of social systems by which Giddens means the 'lifting out' of social relations and their restructuring across time and space. Two specific mechanisms are at work here. First, is the creation of symbolic tokens (e.g., money) which can be exchanged without specific regard to the characteristics of individuals that handle them allowing the exchange of 'anything for anything anywhere'. Because it is a universal commodity, money is also an agent of time–space distanciation allowing global transactions at any time. Second, experts (as Weber predicted) have come to dominate social and material systems. We now depend on experts in many fields to provide access to specialised knowledge, e.g. doctors and engineers. Like money, expert systems are disembedding mechanisms because they remove social relations from their immediate locale.

Finally, there is the reflexive ordering and reordering of social relations. In pre-modern societies tradition had an important role in structuring and influencing time and space as questions such as 'why?' and 'how?' usually had answers in Christian or other doctrines. In modern societies the role of doctrine in providing answers is greatly diminished. Far greater weight is given to the input of information that arises as a consequence of action. Reflecting upon action and knowledge (e.g., how can I make more of this product?) replaces the more stable reference of tradition and thereby posits a high level of uncertainty into modern life. However, unlike the natural sciences, greater reflection on knowledge and action feed into that action and are likely to alter it and thereby shift the original subject. There thus arises a situation that could be likened to a dog chasing its own tail. Reflection is constantly trying to make sense or add knowledge to a subject area but in doing so changes that subject thereby leading to more reflection.

The complex causes of modernity's restlessness are a matter of dispute and one that need not concern us too much. What we can conclude is that modernity sought and succeeded to change society through innovation, novelty and dynamism (Berman, 1982). But such change was not absolute as in Marx's dialectic or teleological view of progress. Modernity's revolutions were and are incessant and have inexorably led to the individualisation, secularisation, industrialisation, cultural differentiation, commodification, urbanisation, bureaucratisation and rationalisation of the modern world (Kellner, 1989).

This revolutionary basis of modernity was largely ignored by the founding thinkers of the Enlightenment who wanted to move society forward and break free of religious dogma, opening up the 'truth' of science. But this was only for the few (including, naturally, the educated elite). As Porter points out, the experience of limited democracy had not been particularly attractive to the *philosophes*. Parliaments in Europe had tended to be filled with self-serving elites, and the mass of the population were largely illiterate and superstitious. There was no great desire from the elite for increases in the franchise for the mass of the population, nor was the revolutionary shift in thinking perceived as a threat to the established social order. Change would come gradually and affect only 'men of influence'. What they failed to see was that the empiricism and scientific progress they valued provided a motor for much wider change. And it is this tension between the perceived advantages and worthy aims of modernity and its inherent disruptive element that provides the main hiatus between the broadly pro-modern and the critical-modern. According to many writers (including Marx, Durkheim and latterly Habermas) while we should accept and welcome the positive aspects of modernity we must also see it as a double-edged sword and seek to change its destructive or dark side (for Marx it was capitalism, for Habermas the dominance of instrumental rationality). Others (e.g. Giddens (1990)) have painted a more positive view and, while accepting some of the criticisms of those who point to modernity's less desirable outcomes, maintain that the benefits have far outweighed the drawbacks and those who seek to criticise have exaggerated their position. Both sets of arguments accept the creative and destructive dynamic of modernity.

It is crude and simplistic to paint a homogenous picture of the Enlightenment. Following Jameson (1984), Harvey (1990) has identified different periods – the latest of which is the much debated 'late' or postmodern. I discuss the postmodern later in the book, though some of the foundations of this turn can be found in what has been termed modernity's dark side. Essential to the idea of modernity, as I have discussed above, was the belief that everything is destined to be speeded up, dissolved, displaced, transformed and/or reshaped (Hall, 1992: 15). 'The only secure thing about modernity is insecurity, its penchant for totalising chaos' (Harvey, 1990: 11). The idea presented is of modernity's never-ending process of fragmentation and rupture. This process is not linear and modernity becomes more troubled the more it seeks to change. Various writers have identified this as its 'dark side' including Nietzsche and Weber. The former saw the supposed objective basis of the 'new world order' and the search for truth through reason as nothing more than a 'will to power'. The latter claimed that the 'triumph' of the Enlighten-ment was based on instrumental rationality which would lead to the fragmentation of knowledge, an 'iron cage of bureaucracy' through commodification and the growth of specialised knowledge and experts leading to a 'crushed' human spirit. One outcome of this perpetual change is the increasingly schizophrenic experi-ences of living in a modern world. Following Lacan, Jameson argues that we lose a sense of continuity, a growing depthlesness of living which is profoundly disturbing as everything from consumer durables to societal values are increasingly ques-tioned and replaced.

Criticism of the Enlightenment has existed as long as the Enlightenment itself. Edmund Burke opposed the French Revolution claiming it had replaced one despotic regime with another. He went on to make another valid point in Porter's view, that most of the leading Enlightenment thinkers had never held any political office and were 'armchair' revolutionaries. Part of the reason for this lack of 'real' engagement was the limited opportunities to actually gain experience of government in the aristocracy-laden governments of France and the UK. Second, as mentioned earlier, there was a distinct distrust of the masses – a distrust that led to a more limited view of democracy than has developed in the twentieth century. Another source of criticism came from the Romantics such as Blake who talked of the 'dark satanic mills', criticising the leading *philosophes* as 'evil geniuses' for ignoring imagination, feeling, history and tradition (Porter, 1990: 2).

These early criticisms made little real impact on the 'juggernaut' of modernity (Giddens, 1990). It was Nietzsche who provided the intellectual stimulus to others who built on his concerns with the Enlightenment Project. Two influential writers on this darker side were Adorno and Horkheimer who, in their 1944 work *Dialectic of Enlightenment* (1979) set themselves the task of unmasking the 'totalitarian' nature of modernity. As Docherty (1993) points out, like many aspects of modernity their problem is not with the theory of the Enlightenment, but its practice. The abstrac-tion from nature of all that was messy by science into formal categories was seen by the founding thinker of modernity as its main strength. However, according to Adorno and Horkheimer, this had drawbacks:

From now on, matter would at last be mastered without any illusion of ruling or
inherent powers, of hidden qualities. For the Enlightenment, whatever does not
conform to the rule of computation and utility is suspect (1979: 6)

The world had been reduced to one form of reasoning that excludes all others.
Everything that could be is transformed into mathematical abstractions, and everything that cannot is ignored or suppressed. The struggle to understand and control
nature through instrumental rationality leads inevitably to the control of free will, the
diminution of human emancipation, individual responsibility and initiative. Although
Marxists, Adorno and Horkheimer considered this an even greater threat to
mankind than class repression.

Because of the dominance of instrumental rationality, the world is reproduced
in a distorted form, creating an illusion of the power of scientific knowledge over
nature. However, Docherty concludes that:

It is important to stress that this is an illusion. This kind of knowledge does not
give actual power over nature, for that in nature which is unnameable to its
formal or conceptual categories simply escapes consciousness entirely. What it
does give in the way of power is, of course, a power over the consciousness of
others who may be less fluent in the language of reason (1993: 6).

This tension between different forms of reason is something that the defenders of
modernity and Habermas, in particular, fully accept. Scientific reason and rationality
have come to dominate other ways of conceiving the world and, as a result, the
Enlightenment has betrayed the (limited) emancipatory goals it set itself by replacing religious with scientific dogma. More fundamentally, Adorno and Horkheimer's
analysis also points to the distancing of human reason from the world and the cir-
cularity of scientific rationality being a self-confirming but inevitably unengaged
process with the material world. Far from engaging with the world and proving a
secular, universal and human-centered motor for progress, it provides only a ritual
of thinking that disengages from the political and non-abstracted nature of the
world. The political (that is, questions of values) is sucked into this abstracted and
instrumentally-rational environment. Difference and subtlety are reduced through
this levelling process of abstraction while fact and value are separated, with the
former being seen in the service of values – values that were assumed to be universal (Hamilton, 1990: 43).

As a number of critics of modernity have pointed out, the internalisation of
issues such as the separation of facts and values would inevitably lead to questions
concerning 'who decides?' and 'who possessed superior reason?'. But modernity
had become, in Lyotard's (1984) famous phrase, a 'meta-narrative' with a globalis-
ing and teleological determinism that discounted such questions as minor irritations

to the 'juggernaut' of instrumental reason (Giddens, 1990). The historicity that underpinned it did not allow for dissension, 'The victors in history thus proceed in triumphal procession, bearing with them the spoils of their victory, including those documents which record, legitimise and corroborate the necessity of their victory' (Docherty, 1993: 11). The direct consequence of suppressed histories is the masking of the dark side of modernity and the rationalisation of any process that comes within its remit. Slavery, for example, continued following the American Revolution regardless of the 'modern' basis of the Constitution and was defended using Enlightenment reason. Similarly, the terrors of the French Revolution and the massive inequalities of modern capitalism can all be traced back to the influence of the Enlightenment. The anarchy, disorder and 'will to power' identified by Nietzsche was no more that an aberration in the 'belief in linear progress, absolute truths and rational planning of ideal social orders under standardised conditions of knowledge and production' (Harvey, 1990: 35). According to some, the unease at the ethical vacuum and prioritised instrumental rationality of modernity reached its zenith in the gas chambers of Auschwitz. Building on the unease of Adorno and Horkheimer, Zigmund Bauman argues that modernity is no more than a process, a process that can serve good or evil in equally rational ways. The history of the Holocaust was, to Bauman, fully in accordance with the thrust of modernity.

> Structurally, the gas chambers are driven by the same presiding principles that were taken for granted as the positive aspects of modernity: the principles of rational efficiency. The structure of thought which facilitates the possibility of the Holocaust is inscribed in the philosophical structure of Enlightenment itself, for the drive towards a rational society has been controverted into a drive towards rationalism itself, a rationalism which can be used for fascist as well as emancipatory ends (Docherty, 1993: 13).

These issues point to the difficulty in ascribing the Enlightenment or modernity either a homogenous character or a generally beneficial legacy. Enlightenment *philosophes* claimed that there was a single universal standard of justice governed by natural law and a single uniform human nature endowed with the same attributes and desires (Porter, 1990: 51). But history has frequently demonstrated that this claim has not been translated into practice. Instead, other Enlightenment ideas such as reason have been used to subjugate people. Adorno and Horkheimer (1979) have argued that reason has often been associated with absolutism and repression. The myth of Christianity was supplanted by a similar scientific fable including that of economics. Adam Smith's laissez-faire economics might have led to great strides in freedom from feudal society but equally led to the justification of a different form of exploitation. Freedom might have been an Enlightenment ideal but it was a freedom that had a human price.

The complexity and ambiguity of the Enlightenment legacy led to a number of criticisms, though it was not until the term postmodern was coined that the idea of the modern as an epoch and set of ideas began to be seriously questioned.

THE EMERGENCE OF THE POSTMODERN

There is a complex early accretion of the term postmodern that demonstrates its origin from a variety of spheres which led Turner (1990) to conclude that there is great difficulty in finding an adequate periodisation of modernity and postmodernity. Before I attempt to map out this contested landscape it is first necessary to be clear about what I mean by the different terms I shall use throughout the rest of the book. The difficulties of definition are explored in more detail in the next chapter but suffice to say here that it is important to recognise the different cultural contexts and uses of the terms postmodern and postmodernity in different parts of the world. For example, an understanding of pluralism and diversity will differ between the United States and the more centralised states of Europe. Also, the rise of fascism *and* communism in Europe has provided a particularly acute sense of history that means that (with a broad brush) German social theorists have been less willing to explore the relativisms of postmodernity than, say, the French, and have defended the 'unfinished project' of modernity against what they see as the conservative and irrationalist critique of the postmodernists (Habermas, 1987). Further, the meanings of the modern and the postmodern vary between different social science traditions (Smart, 1993) which is partly to do with the struggle to gain intellectual control over the concept (Featherstone, 1988).

It is usual when discussing the postmodern to make a distinction between *object* or *epoch* and *attitude*. The former is taken to be a concern with an age of postmodernity or how complex social, economic and cultural changes have made things different. Post-industrial theorists would fall into this category with their focus on origins and directions of change. The postmodern of attitude concerns social theory, or how we might think about our world. The most influential contributions to this have undoubtedly been the so-called 'French' school of thinkers including Foucault, Derrida, Baudrillard and Lyotard. From these two broad approaches we can identify three areas of concern that comprise the postmodern. First is the distinction between the modern and the postmodern in epochal terms. This is a difference to what went before and is linked to post-industrial themes concerning the emergence of new forms of industrial processes, cultural manifestations and attitudes. It emphasises a complex mixture of changes that cannot be reduced simply to a development of what went before, a change in consumer lifestyles, mass communication or dominant tastes and fashion (Kellner, 1983) that comprise a dramatic break that warrants the term 'post'. Second, there is the concern of social theory and philosophy which amounts to an attack on modernist abstract, ahistorical and totalising theory. In particular, there is a suspicion of foundational truths, over-arching master theories and rationality so beloved of positivism towards a more open and relativistic approach. Finally, the postmodern encompasses a critique of the subject and representation: the idea that we can represent reality through language. Instead, postmodernism (or more accurately, poststructuralism) argues for a more decentered view that we can never represent reality and instead must accept a never-ending chain of signifiers. This posits a discursive model of many accepted 'realities'.

I shall be focusing upon the social theory aspect of the postmodern in this book as my aim is to explore a new planning. However, it is inevitable that because of the large degree of overlap other aspects will be touched upon. I discuss both epoch and attitude in greater detail in Chapters 2 and 3. Here, I want to give a broad history of the term and identify some important aspects as a prelude to the greater detail later on. The term itself has been identified as having a multitude of origins (Smart, 1993). Best and Kellner (1991: 5) trace its first usage back to the English painter John Watkins Chapman who spoke of postmodern painting around 1870 when trying to describe a form of painting more modern than the avant-garde French impressionism. In historical circles the postmodern was used in the early part of the twentieth century to describe the collapse of contemporary European culture. Arnold Toynbee employed it to identify a distinctive historical break with the 'modern' period which he defined as running from 1475–1875. By the 1950s however, the term had gained a new currency and popularity. Changes to and in society were recognised as being more than merely cultural. Significant shifts in the economic base of western economies were beginning to drive the kind of change identified by Kumar (1995) as post-industrial. The collapse of distinctive localities and the rise of globalised culture – 'time-space compression' as Harvey (1990) or 'time-space distanciation' as Giddens (1990) puts it – led to a new manifestation of the postmodern. But there were already complaints about the vagueness of the term:

> At some unmarked point during the last twenty years we imperceptibly moved out of the Modern Age and into a new, as yet nameless, era (Ducher, quoted in Best and Kellner, 1991: 7).

But for Ducher the change was more than simply cultural. It involved perceptions, knowledge, certainties and technology. Others pointed to what was to become in the late 1980s the 'end of history' thesis of Francis Fukuyama (1989) by focusing on the convergence towards liberal democracy. But, modernity's 'dark-side' also became the focus of attention through the Frankfurt School's critiques of rationality, again adding to the general sense of change. If anything, the advances in science and technology throughout the 1950s and 1960s which were largely a result of modernity's rationality created more, not less, certainty. Modernity was producing more varied, consumer-orientated goods which were in turn creating more demand for the same further fragmenting markets and consumers.

Again, historians such as Geoffrey Barraclough (1964) pointed to differences between 'then' and 'now' – a break had occurred that warranted the label 'postmodern'. The cultural dimensions of this new epoch began to be explored more in art and literature. In architecture the high modernism of Le Corbusier, Bauhaus and Mies van der Rohe was replaced by a celebration of more playful, popular juxtapositions of styles. This clear embodiment of the Enlightenment tradition were unsuccessful attempts to create 'machines for living'. It has now

> become commonplace in postmodernist circles to favour a reintroduction of multivalent symbolic dimensions into architecture, a mixing of codes, an appropriation of local vernaculars and regional traditions (Huyssen, 1984: 14–15).

Such postmodern styles seemed to express *tout court* the entire postmodern concern with anti-authoritarianism and the eclecticism and playfulness that was happening in society and that architects wanted to expand. Kumar (1995: 106) believes that postmodern architecture seeks

> to break down modernist distinctions between 'high' and 'low' culture, 'elite' and 'mass' art. In place of the autocratic imposition of a monolithic taste it accepts a diversity of 'taste cultures', whose needs it tries to meet by offering a plurality of styles.

During the late 1960s and early 1970s social theorists began to explore the wider aspects of this new sensibility. Post-industrial theorists such as Bell (1973, 1976) explored what he saw as the motors for this change as well as the nihilistic and negative social consequences. Thus, as Best and Kellner (1991: 15) point out, by the 1980s we witnessed two distinct cultural discourses in the postmodern: a positive celebration of difference and pluralism, and a negative critique of its associated ills. Irving Howe and Clement Greenberg saw the postmodern as a capitulation to kitsch and commercialism while Harry Levin and Lionel Trelling saw it as little more than hedonism and a threat to social values (Kumar, 1991: 107). But these were lone voices against the dominant movement of culture at the time. Modernity was associated with everything that was wrong in society: racism, sexism, inequality, authority, etc. But as Antonio and Kellner (1991) rightly point out, this emphasis on the repressive and dark sides of modernity is one-sided, for modernity had its own internal critiques from Nietzsche onwards. It is this argument that led to the claim of Habermas and others that postmodernity was, in reality, little more than nascent modernity. I return to these arguments in Chapters 2 and 3. The debates over whether the postmodern is a cultural manifestation of the post-industrial, or merely a latent element and reaction against the modern, rumble on and seem to take up an inordinate amount of academic time. What is clear is that these cultural and economic discourses were largely *reactions* to change, i.e. they tried to comprehend a wider social shift that we could broadly term post-industrial. But more fundamental and proactive thinking on social theory emerged largely in France throughout the 1970s and 1980s that was to have a profound influence on the postmodern debate.

The French influence grew directly out of the experience of left-leaning academics following the national crisis of 1968. Best and Kellner (1991: 17) point to the rapid industrialisation following the war as the dynamic for a host of new social theories that sought to explain the transformations in culture and society. These new social theories were put down to the effects of post-industrial society as elsewhere, but a host of new theories emerged to account for increasing consumerism and its effect on society. The dominant discourses of Marxism, existentialism and phenomenology began to look vulnerable in the post-industrial landscape and its hinterland. Structuralism in particular, with the emphasis on objectivity, rigour and truth was challenged by Derrida and others who argued for a more relativistic and infinite relationship between signified and signifier. Meaning was not stable but changing and unable to be pinned down. Foundational knowledge and its truth claims were also attacked, though by using earlier critiques provided by Nietzsche, Heidegger and Wittgenstein. Truth was replaced by interpretation, objectivity with subjectivity. While this re-thinking was going on, it became clear that the French state and its institutions were part of the problem, not the solution. Still stuck in the high modernist, top-down, paternalistic tradition they became a focus for grievances in 1968 in national strikes and protests. As Best and Kellner (1991: 23) conclude:

> The May 1968 upheaval contributed in significant ways to later developments of postmodern theory. The student revolts politicized the nature of education in the university system and criticized the production of knowledge as a means of power and domination ... the students also analyzed the university as a microcosm of a repressive capitalist society and turned their attention to 'the full range of hidden mechanisms through which a society conveys its knowledge and ensures its survival under the mask of knowledge: newspapers, television, technical schools and the *lycée*'.

It was this shift in understanding that sensitised philosophers such as Foucault, Lyotard and Baudrillard to the limits of Marxists analysis and pushed them in new directions to examine the nature of knowledge in post-industrial society. The concept of the autonomous subject was also challenged as attention began to be paid to the influence of power and language upon its construction. The overall result was to embrace difference and shun totality and the monolithic and crude class-based politics of Marxism. Although these trends were to lead to the two distinct though related fields of post-structuralism and postmodernism, I treat both as coming under the heading of the postmodern.

The rest, as they say, is history. Or, in the case of the postmodern, a non-teleological, discursively-created though contextually sensitive will to power. Here are the origins of the postmodern though its significance, development and interpretation has been a far wider phenomenon, particularly in the United States and the English-speaking world. Ironically, many of the French theorists that provided such a fillip to the whole broad movement deny they are postmodern and even attack the concept (Baudrillard excluded). The term can be 'read' differently, as 'anti' modern, as a rupture with it, or simply as a reflective, differential modern. So much for the development. What does it *mean*? What I now do in the following chapter is provide summaries of some of the main positions before I attempt to tackle what I interpret it to be.

CHAPTER 2

WHAT IS THE POSTMODERN?: social theory

INTRODUCTION

> *'What are you up to?' I cried.*
> *'I?' said Adrian, steering me expertly into a passing coffee house. 'I am in the*
> *business of buying you a coffee. Espresso? Cappuccino? Latte?'*
> *'Latte isn't coffee,' I said. 'It's the Italian word for milk.'*
> *'They are so behind the times in your part of the world,' said Adrian. 'You'll be*
> *telling me next that post-modernism hasn't reached the provinces yet.'*
> *'I'm not sure if it has or not,' I said.*
> *'What exactly is it when it's at home?'*
> *'Well, it's the stage that culture reaches when it does more borrowing than*
> *creating. At least, I think it is. Pop records created from other records ... novels*
> *that revisit other novels ... films which interpret one period in terms of another*
> *... lives of people which might be biographies and might be novels ...'*
> *'Was the film* Time Bandits *post-modernist then?'*
> *'I expect so,' said Adrian, vaguely.*
> (Miles Kington, *The Independent,* 15th May 1998).

Any exploration of the postmodern usually commences with a vain attempt at answering the question 'what is the postmodern?' I shall be no different. Before I attempt to answer the question however, I would like to digress and set out how the postmodern itself precludes any simple answer to this. The postmodern is such a multifaceted phenomenon that it is difficult, if not misleading, to ascribe any specific meaning. In fact, to do so would not be postmodern at all. For, according to many authors, the postmodern at its most essential is a celebration of difference and a suspicion of foundation and truth. So even before I attempt a definition, I encounter a paradox. I want to convey some essence of what I feel the postmodern is, but in doing so I will inevitably be using the modernist tools of foundational thought; trying to pigeonhole something, to give it a 'completeness' and boundaries. This paradox emerges from the most-used definition: the postmodern is, in Lyotard's (1984) phrase, 'an incredulity towards meta-narratives'. In other words, a scepticism or suspicion towards theory or totality. Lyotard's much-quoted phrase is the basis of many answers to the question, 'what is the postmodern?'. But, as I pointed out in Chapter 1, this definition sounds like a meta-narrative itself. So, in the spirit of this, we should logically be suspicious of Lyotard's meta-narrative and consequently suspicious of the postmodern. Lyotard is not alone in falling into a trap of his own setting. Foucault announces the end of the role of the intellectual in speaking 'truth to power' as Rabinow puts it (1984: 23). Like Lyotard, this is based on Foucault's desire to historicise and problematise accepted 'truths' and unmask the 'will to power' behind notions such as 'liberty' and 'truth'. But how can Foucault make such sweeping pronouncements and on what basis is his knowledge superior in this regard? Derrida has taken Foucault to task for attempting to escape the rationality he seeks to critique. Any such attempt is doomed as he will inevitably become caught up in the very terms and structures we seek to escape. How can we communicate 'unreason' without using 'reason'? This raises problem number one. Problem number two follows on from this and though on the face of it seems to address problem one, in fact only adds to it. The logic of suspicion towards meta-narratives is to emphasise instead plurality and difference. Indeed, without a hint of irony, Lyotard actually calls for a law of difference to ensure this. If this is so, then any definition of the postmodern will be as legitimate as the next as there is no overall theory or meta-narrative against which to assess it. If every definition is correct, then every definition must also be incorrect as there can never be any absolute. If we apply this to the field of ethics or politics then how can progress or action be undertaken? How can we ensure that difference is maintained? This is a problem that Lyotard realised and found the only way to overcome it was to fall back on modernist prescription: to ensure difference we have to force it. Similarly, Foucault (according to Baudrillard) found the logic of his critique of modernity too troubling as it pointed to a world of relativity and nihilism. This is, of course, judging the postmodern by modern standards and as Kumar (1995) points out, we should really judge it by its own standards. Whether we choose to do this or not says more about us than it does about postmodernism. For example, do you believe that there is no such thing as truth, i.e. an objective, black and white right and wrong? Most people would say 'yes'. But truth is a slippery concept. If asked, 'do you always tell the truth?', I suspect most people would say 'no'. There are times when we need to hide the truth though this does not mean that we are 'bad' or not committed to the truth as an ideal. The postmodern perspective relativises truth (there is no 'right' or 'wrong') and even goes as far as denying truth actually exists. So, for most people, it is anathema. But here's the rub: the postmodern is so diverse that when applying standard critical tests such as 'is this theory true?' and coming to the conclusion that it is not, then another equally postmodern theory can be pointed at that either backs up, denies or alters the first theory so as to invalidate the question. Take Foucault's view of power as a seamless web that flows and has no locus (outlined further on in this chapter). Does power operate in this way? Foucault says so, but Baudrillard says it ignores important cultural influences. Power is far more plural than Foucault has allowed for. The 'truth' in this case is twofold.

First, that both are correct and incorrect (in my view) and second, that 'testing' such an idea is impossible anyway. But another more fundamental issue arises: the postmodern actually revels in the confusion of all that arises when we apply Enlightenment logic. As Kumar rightly says:

> Earnest examinations of the fit between theory and reality are met with an ironic smile. Contradiction and circularity, far from being regarded as faults in logic, are in some versions of postmodern theory actually celebrated (1995: 103).

I do not want to make too much of a logical deconstruction of the postmodern. The point I am trying to make is the difficulty in tackling the question, 'what is the post-modern?'. My attempt therefore has not started well, or even got off the ground. Indeed, I will not even attempt to answer it until the next chapter because I will make a distinction between the postmodern as *social theory* and the postmodern as *new times*. Postmodern as *social theory* is a broad, largely French-inspired attempt to analyse the impacts of modernity, its underlying assumptions and implications within changed times. But it is also a way to think about contemporary life in terms of a postmodern sensibility as well as alternatives to modern ways of thinking. The postmodern as *new times* is an equally eclectic school that is closely allied to the post-industrial and information society and post/neo-Fordism theses briefly discussed in Chapter 1. Although related in some ways and different in others ways to the social theory field, they point with different emphases to overall change within society that some term postmodern. This is particularly so with the sensibility aspect of the new times school.

Berger (1998:12) believes that you cannot separate the postmodern as social theory and the postmodern as new times (though he does not employ these terms directly). I believe this is not only possible but necessary particularly if one is trying to reflect on an institution such as planning. Books and articles on the post-modern tend to conflate the two or focus on the sensibility of new times. For example, Charles Jencks captures the blend of both social theory and sensibility in his definition of the postmodern:

> The Post-Modern Age is a time of incessant choosing. It's an era when no orthodoxy can be adopted without self-consciousness and irony, because all traditions seem to have some validity. This is partly a consequence of what is called the information explosion, the advent of organised knowledge, world communication and cybernetics. It is not only the rich who become collectors, eclectic travellers in time with a superabundance of choice, but almost every urban dweller. Pluralism, the 'ism' of our time, is both the great problem and the great opportunity: where Everyman becomes a Cosmopolite and Everywoman a Liberated Individual, confusion and anxiety become ruling states of mind and

ersatz a common form of mass-culture. This is the price we pay for the Post-
Modern Age, as heavy in its way as the monotony, dogmatism and poverty of
the Modern epoch. But, in spite of many attempts in Iran and elsewhere, it is
impossible to return to a previous culture and industrial form, impose a
fundamentalist religion or even a Modernist orthodoxy. Once a world
communication system and form of cybernetic production have emerged they
create their own necessities and they are, barring a nuclear war, irreversible
(1989: 7).

Ironically, Jenks' definition of the postmodern employs the teleological view more
reminiscent of modernity. Regardless of this general conflation of different aspects,
it is important to distinguish between the two as they can be mutually exclusive, i.e.
you can sign up to the thesis that we are living in new (or different) times without
buying the idea of postmodern social theory. Similarly, it is perfectly possible to
argue that modernist social theory is dogmatic and reductionist and a more 'postmodern' multivalent approach is required without accepting the 'new times' thesis.
As I argue in this chapter, many of the writers on postmodern social theory (e.g.,
Lyotard and the early Baudrillard) also reflect and conflate both theory and sensibility in an almost 'Catch-22' situation. Lyotard starts off by reflecting on new or postmodern times and then develops theories that both explain it and provide ways of
making even more difference which will presumably require a further development
or refinement of theory. Soloman has raised the 'chicken and egg' question over
the postmodern. He believes that the postmodern is a certain intellectual adaptation to conditions of modern life (1998: 42). How far has life imitated or influenced
art? So, to answer the question, 'what is the postmodern?' we need to recognise
that there are two sub-questions: 'what are the main themes of postmodern social
theory?' and 'are we living in new (postmodern) times?'

Having said this, I am wary of falling into what is a natural tendency to
abstract and simplify, to round off and contrast and instead, following Foucault (as I
shall set out) I attempt to 'problematise' the situation and argue that there cannot
be a 'neat' resolution to the question 'what is postmodernism?' In this chapter, I
attempt to minimise (I can never totally avoid) abstraction by selecting and sum-
marising some writers who have contributed in different ways to the 'condition' of
postmodernity as social theory and thereby leave them to speak on their own. In
doing this I am conscious that (i) my choice is arbitrary and reflects my own prejudices and (ii) some of the writers deliberately and explicitly rejected the label postmodern.

LYOTARD

Like many writers on the postmodern, Lyotard has a long history of engagement with ideas from a variety of sources. He recanted his earlier Marxist orientation in the late 1970s and his contribution to the postmodern debate can be distilled down to two books, The *Postmodern Condition* (1984) and *The Differend* (1988) (first published in 1979 and 1983 respectively). Lyotard's engagement with the postmodern is based on wide foundations that can be traced to Saussurian struc-turalism, Derridian post-structuralism, Wittgenstein's 'language games', Kuhn and Feyerabend's work on paradigmatic shifts in scientific thought and a less obvious but no less influential debt to Nietzschean and Weberian analysis. As Haber (1994) rightly points out, central to Lyotard's postmodernism is the link between linguistic structural analysis and the self. Like Derrida, Lyotard emphasises the ubiquity of language and the significance of semiotics. Objects and events already have meaning and to understand this meaning we must focus on the conventions which give objects currency, i.e., discourse. The Saussurian concept of signifier and signified and the relative autonomy of language in relation to reality imply that signifiers have meaning not in relation to a signified, but to each other. 'Warm' gets its meaning from others words or signifiers such as either 'day' or 'embrace' for example. Consequently, the relation between signifier and signied is arbitrary and can be endlessly altered or interpreted leading to what has been termed the 'death of the author'. No transcendental meaning can be ascribed to a signifier. The implications of Saussure's insight and Lyotard's transfer to the self is of infinite possibilities, interpretations and selves with no possibility of closure – no end, no absolute definitions and no totality.

These concerns runs through Lyotard's work which emphasises above all the need to challenge existing interpretations of the status quo and release difference. As he puts it:

> The postmodern would be that which, in the modern, puts forward the unpresentable in presentation itself; that which denies itself the solace of good forms, the consensus of a taste which would make it possible to share collectively the nostalgia for the unattainable; that which searches for new presentations, not in order to enjoy them but in order to impart a stronger sense of the unpresentable (Lyotard, 1983: 68).

Drawing on the work of Alan Touraine and Daniel Bell, Lyotard argues in *The Post-modern Condition* that postmodernity has emerged through the conditions of advanced capitalism. Knowledge has been transformed into a commodity in the post-industrial landscape where its nature and use will 'change', though Lyotard does not make clear how. Focusing on science and following Nietzsche, Lyotard claims that this commodification of knowledge has led science to abandon its search for 'truth' and replace it with a search for 'power'. In addition (and this time drawing on Weber and latterly Habermas) science has come to see instrumental rationality as the only form of legitimate reason. This is all familiar ground but Lyotard's point of departure concerns the role of narratives, the ways in which science claims its legitimacy and has attempted to suppress and ridicule other forms of reason. Contrasting traditional narrative (i.e. spoken), rules and rituals Lyotard claims that they are bound up in self-legitimacy – they need no exterior justification; they just 'are' and no argument or proof is required. However, though science considers such forms of reason 'barbaric' and bases itself on its own transcendental status, there are two problems. First, science cannot ultimately justify itself without recourse to such narratives. Second, transcendental or over-arching meta-narratives have all been shown to be no more than 'language-games' themselves.

Again, following Wittgenstein, Lyotard traces what he sees as the decline of over-arching theories, or 'meta-narratives' as he terms them. Since the Second World War such grand narratives have declined in their importance (though why is not fully explained) to be replaced by what he terms *petit récits* or small narratives that focus on the micro-politics of everyday life. Grand narratives such as Marxism no longer have legitimacy. The only area of life where such meta-narratives continue to exist is in the field of science which considers itself above such basic narratives or language-games. The Enlightenment legacy privileged scientific rationality above other forms of reason and, according to Lyotard, science still tries to legitimise its own rules through reference to such narratives. As Connor puts it:

> Science is therefore no longer held to be valuable and necessary because of the part it plays in the slow progress towards absolute freedom and absolute knowledge. With this loss of confidence in the metanarratives ... comes the decline of general regulatory power in the paradigms of science itself, as science discovers the limits of assumptions and procedures for verification, encountering paradoxes and throwing up questions ... that are undecidable, that is, not questions that have no answer, but questions that can be shown in principle to be unanswerable (1997: 27).

The result of these undecidables is the fragmentation of science into specialisms that aim not at the search for truth but at 'performativity'. Such performativity in science seeks verifiable facts and research that reproduces the opportunity for more research that backs up previous work. As well as the search for transcendental truths (which still justify science as a privileged area of knowledge) we have localised and specialised language-games that justify themselves – much as the narratives dismissed by science as 'primitive' do. The two traditional meta-narratives that provide the legitimacy for science are firstly, that knowledge is produced for its own sake and secondly, that it leads towards human emancipation.

There are two outcomes of this. First, is the 'paradox of science'. It seeks to promote its own form of reason and dismiss others (such as narratives) while it is itself dependent upon such 'barbaric' narratives for its own justification.

> Scientific knowledge cannot know and make known that it is the true
> knowledge without resorting to the other, narrative kind of knowledge, which
> from its point of view is no knowledge at all. Without such recourse it would be
> in the position of presupposing its own validity and would be stooping to what it
> condemns: begging the question, proceeding on prejudice. But does it not fall
> into the same trap by using narrative as its authority? (Lyotard, 1984: 29).

Second, and more importantly, postmodern science (which exists alongside the more traditional and modern science) that has its justification in localised 'language-games' becomes not just a description of the inherent failure of science's own paradox, but also a prescription *tout court* of how society should proceed. Postmodern science seeks its legitimation in narrative and consequently 'truth' is to be found there:

> Postmodern science − by concerning itself with such things as undecidables,
> the limits of precise control, conflicts characterised by incomplete information,
> 'fracta', catastrophes, and pragmatic paradoxes − is theorising its own evolution
> as discontinuous, catastrophic, non-rectifiable, and paradoxical. It is changing
> the meaning of the word knowledge, while expressing how such a change can
> take place. It is producing not the known, but the unknown. And it suggests a
> model of legitimation that has nothing to do with maximised performance, but
> has its difference understood as paralogy (Lyotard, 1984: 60).

Postmodern science does not seek transcendental truths but that which is not or cannot be represented, preventing consensus on meta-narratives. Emancipation for Lyotard will be achieved through dissensus, resistance, questioning, challenges, play and invention, such systems are 'one(s) in which a statement becomes relevant if it "generates ideas", that is, if it generates other statements and other rule games' (Lyotard, 1984: 64). Consensus or the search for it and one voice, is nothing short of 'terror' in its demand to 'Adapt your aspirations to our ends − or else' (Lyotard, 1984: 63). Because of the centrality of incommensurate 'language games' Lyotard rejects Habermas' notion of 'ideal speech', replacing it instead with his pagan politics or radical pluralism. His own infinite language game seeks to encourage paralogy, not homology. The only rule of Lyotard's game is that no one can be excluded, 'Let us wage war on totality; let us be witness to the unpresentable; let us activate these differences' (Lyotard, 1984: 82).

Lyotard is aware of many of the issues that immediately spring from his politics (if not his analysis). If we cannot judge in the world of paralogy, how can we act or decide what is 'just' or 'unjust'? The answer he proposes is to replace a politics of reason with a politics of opinion. As a consequence, justice cannot be grounded in absolutes, but multiplicity. The consequences of such a rule are troubling even for Lyotard:

> This is where there is an essential political problem ... rule by convention would require that one accept, let's go to the bottom of things right away, even Nazism. After all, since there was near unanimity upon it, from where could one judge that it was not just? This is obviously very troublesome (Lyotard, 1985: 74).

Haber (1994) claims that this concern means Lyotard is entrenched in the old paradigms which have the need for some kind of universalising principle. Clearly, he does not have the courage of his convictions when it comes to accepting the logic of his own arguments. His solution is to use what Haber terms the 'Kantian Ideal' (1994: 26). According to this, each language game provides its own legitimacy through the requirement that no position can be challenged as inferior. The sovereign realm of each language game cannot judge any other. As a number of authors have pointed out, Lyotard's prescription (or enforcement) of a multiplicity rule puts him in the position that he seeks to avoid: 'At one and the same time Lyotard wants to combine a radical commitment to otherness with a universalistic principle of constraint' (Haber, 1994: 33).

These themes and some of the issues raised by Lyotard's pagan politics are addressed in his second major contribution to the postmodern, *The Differend* (1988). As Connor puts it, '(*The Differend*) is his attempt to make out, not so much an ethical system, as a set of ethical possibilities, in terms of the structure of address and communication within language itself' (1997: 37). Lyotard builds on his earlier post-structuralist analysis and emphasises that phrases are political: choosing one word or sentence over another is a deliberate act. The act of choosing is designed to make a point, to sell an idea, to 'win' an argument:

> Phrases and the linking of phrases are artificial and strategic. This is always the case, since language is a differential system, phrases and linkages always and necessarily exclude other possible phrases and linking of phrases (repress and suppress difference) (Haber, 1994: 18–19).

This choice will inevitably result in silencing other (possible) voices.

> In the differend, something asks to be put into phrases and suffers from the injustice of not being able to be instantly put into phrases. This is when human beings who thought they could use language as an instrument of

> communication learn through a feeling of pain which accompanied silence (of
> pleasure which accompanied the invention of a new vision), that they are
> surrounded by language (Lyotard, 1984a: 16–24).

The idea of the differend comes from the resolution or lack of it concerning the conflict of such phrases. When conflict emerges between two discourse or phrase regimens, as Lyotard terms them, then a differend emerges. The idea is not to try and resolve them, but to celebrate them, witness them and look for where resolution has taken place while pointing to suppressed or silenced voices.

The Postmodern Condition and The Differend provide the basis of Lyotard's main contribution to the postmodern and like most aspects it has not been without criticism. His lack of engagement with detail in his analysis of science mean that it is difficult to tie down exactly what he is basing his arguments on. But even at Lyotard's superficial level, his claims are at the least suspect. While science is in some respects being commodified (as are the social sciences and other areas of life) and while quantum mechanics and chaos theory are questioning some of its foundational truths, there has not (even in the 20 or so years since Lyotard wrote The Postmodern Condition) been a breakdown of science's objective consensus. His ideas on this seem to be based on a watered-down Kuhn and Feyerabend that lack the persuasive force of either.

Another issue has been advanced by Eagleton (1996) who challenges Lyotard's claim that modern capitalism is the motor behind the increases in diversity he identifies in the postmodern as well as the increases in inequality. If this is so, Eagleton argues, we should be wary of embracing Lyotard's paralogy/diversity as, to do so, we may be encouraging increases in inequality as well as cultural difference. How do we know whether difference as an outcome of postmodern practices is not accompanied by other, less desirable aspects if all we have to judge is difference itself? A further issue lies in the practical aspects of Lyotard's paralogy. In everyday situations, people are liable to declare a judgement on what is 'just' and 'unjust'. Following Lyotard we could conclude that this breaks his law of multiplicity. If we cannot judge, then how can we decide? Lyotard is caught between his distaste for the 'we' and the implications of the 'I'. As such he is forced back to the totality and foundationalism he seeks to undermine. Many authors believe that Lyotard's theory of multiple justice does not address questions of power. Lyotard fails to see structures of race and gender as important in social structure but even more troubling is that, through his emphasis on difference per se, he would not recognise such all embracing categories as legitimate.

Jameson (1984a: xvi) has claimed that Lyotard's postmodernism and his pagan politics have a lot in common with the original aims of the Enlightenment thinkers, and Bertens (1995) argues that he is not the radical voice many have seen. His entry into the postmodern has been read by some as being little more than a radical form of pluralism, a form that is intrinsically 'safe'. The problems with his approach do not detract from either his influence upon the debate or his challenge to the status quo. The emphasis on the linguistic self, the role of master-narratives and the suspicion of foundational truths have been a powerful influence on the broad thrust of the postmodern. But, beyond this influence, it has been left to others to address some of the gaps Lyotard undoubtedly creates.

FOUCAULT

Attempting to capture the essence of Foucault is a slippery and difficult business, not least because he deliberately attempted to evade capture:

> I am no doubt not the only one who writes in order to have no face. Do not ask who I am and do not ask me to remain the same (quoted in McNay, 1994: 1).

This deliberate obfuscation is compounded by the changing emphasis between some of Foucault's earlier and later works, particularly the change between a negative and positive view of power:

> When I wrote Madness and Civilisation, I made at least an implicit use of this notion of repression. I think indeed that I was positing the existence of a sort of living, voluble and anxious madness which the mechanisms of power and psychiatry were supposed to have come to repress and reduce to silence. But it seems to me now that the notion of repression is quite inadequate for capturing what is precisely the productive aspect of power (quoted in McNay, 1994: 30).

Nevertheless, Foucault has had a profound and lasting effect on postmodern thought. Like Lyotard he has a deep distrust of universal truths and global theorising. But, as Rabinow (1984) points out, he does not refute 'meta-narratives' but merely tries to historise and problematise them. The result is that Foucault disputes claims of an external position of certainty or understanding that is beyond a historically-constituted reality. Two main themes run through his work: power and the subject. He rejected the uni-directional state or class-orientated power struggle of Marxist or Enlightenment thinking, instead exploring a more subtle exercise of power as 'flows' with no locus or closure. In a similar analysis, he also rejected the Enlightenment view of a sovereign, rational, reflective subject preferring instead a discursive perspective of the individual created through dominant discourses and subject to normalising power regimes. These two themes developed throughout his writings though they were substantially refined. Consequently, I shall trace the main themes and their development throughout Foucault's work.

Madness and Civilisation and *The Birth of the Asylum* focused on the cultural constructions of madness and a critique (shadowing the Frankfurt School and Adorno and Horkheimer) of Enlightenment rationality. Prior to the Enlightenment, madness and reason were integrated – there was little or no judgement of madness as 'inferior', it was seen simply as a different (and sometimes privileged) view on life and reason. With the coming of the Enlightenment and the dominance of instrumental rationality, a fundamental change occurs with regard to the mad. Madness comes to be seen as a form of deviance and disruption.

> By a strange act of force, the classical age was to reduce to silence the mad whose voices the Renaissance had just liberated, but whose violence it had already tamed (Foucault, 1965: 38).

The effect, in Smart's (1993: 20) view, was the emergence of a 'monologue of reason' and three critical consequences. First was the growth in exclusion as a means of 'treating' madness. Second, was the confluence of medicine and madness which were two previously distinct spheres. Medicine developed as a mediation between reason and unreason which was a change that eventually led to the disciplines of psychiatry and psychology. Finally, following the first two developments and, by far the most insidious aspect according to Foucault, was the shift from physical confinement to a balance between physical control and self-restraint. 'Codes of conduct' developed that involved self-restraint through routinised and systematic life-styles with an ever-present knowledge of punishment for transgression. The result is a history of the other, or an 'archaeology of science' where madness is the historically constituted other of reason. Foucault's early work on madness uses

> a comparative, historical approach [which] highlights both that madness has no presocial essence and also that there is nothing natural or inevitable about strategies through which, in modern society, the mad are confined and socially excluded (McNay, 1994: 17).

The division between reason and unreason clearly reflects Foucault's concern with questioning the teleological and progressive view of history and Enlightenment thought/reason. As such he seeks to problematise many of the classifications, assumptions and bases of knowledge in modern society. Foucault does not draw any wider conclusions from his study of madness but the wider implications are clear: the reader should be suspicious of foundational truths, the status of others in society and questions over progress, especially in sciences. As he says of madness:

> Madness is much more historical than is usually believed, and much younger too (quoted in McNay, 1994: 17).

Clearly Foucault is challenging the Enlightenment basis of objective knowledge by tracing thought systems back to social rather than abstract foundations and, as such, the conclusions to be drawn are that truth is also suspect. Foucault's earlier work highlighted the themes that he was to develop, though they have been subject to substantial criticism. Midelfort (1980) has attacked Foucault's over simplification and romanticism of the rise of the mad in medieval Europe. Like the critics of the Enlightenment covered in Chapter 1, Foucault can be accused of over-egging the dark side of Modernity. This is something that he admits to, particularly the discontinuities or historical breaks (Best and Kellner, 1991: 44). He assumes a causal relationship between the ascendancy of Enlightenment rationality and the confinement of the mad which he later accepted was a result of his under-developed notion of power employed in *Madness and Civilisation* – something that he was to refine in his two next studies, *The Order of Things* and *The Archaeology of Knowledge*.

In *The Order of Things* (1970) Foucault turns his attention to the discursive foundations and formations of thought, widening his critique of reason and unreason to scientific thinking generally. As Smart (1993: 32) puts it, Foucault's aim was to

> uncover the laws, regularities, and rules of formation of systems of thought in the human sciences which emerged in the 19th century.

Foucault identifies three distinct periods (the Renaissance, classical and modern age) each with its own episteme. An episteme is a set of relations within one of these periods that unites discursive practices. Each of these periods has a different episteme which differs dramatically from the preceding one, questioning the general assumption of a gradual progression and refinement of scientific and human knowledge, and providing the space within which to think 'otherness' and non-linear and/or events. This 'disruptive' method was termed 'archaeological' by Foucault and stands in direct opposition to the more traditional Enlightenment-inspired teleological approach to history that privileges the self-reflective autonomous subject. According to Best and Kellner (1991: 43) discontinuity is no longer seen as a blight on the historical narrative and stigmatised in principle. The more traditional focus of history depends on a totality or abstraction that obscures more than it reveals.

> Beneath these abstractions are complex interrelations, a shifting plurality of decentered, individualised series of discourses, unable to be reduced to a single law, model, unity or vertical arrangement (Best and Kellner, 1991: 43).

In its place is posited a more socially-constructed and discursive subject – the episteme – that explains why one way of thinking or saying has been chosen over another. Its aim is to break down reductionist, total, abstract and teleological views of history. But this is not to replace them with plurality for plurality's sake à la Lyotard. Instead it is a disassembling and reconstruction that may, in the end, lead to a similarly-totalised history if that is what is appropriate: continuities in history may well exist. Foucault is obviously gunning for the more pernicious forms of Enlightenment reason here and is mirroring (at a distance) Feyerabend's work on the juxtaposition of reason-based scientific knowledge and other ways of thinking and knowing. But his conclusions have far wider significance, particularly in undermining the progressive nature of human development though questioning the autonomous, sovereign individual and instead pointing to a decentered and multiple locus of knowledge in a disrupted and discursively-constructed world. Like madness, subjects are not pre-discursive entities. The episteme, according to McNay (1994: 62), is an *a priori* set of rules that determines what can and cannot be said – leading Sartre to accuse him of creating an idealist account of knowledge that determines what can and cannot be said. But Foucault provided the most devastating critique of his own work himself when he later reformulated the relationship between power and knowledge to be more than the reductionist account portrayed in *The Order of Things*. Such a reductionist approach precluded alternative knowledges arising and the possibility of other factors outwith the episteme influencing it.

Criticism of an over-reliance on discursive knowledge formation in *The Order of Things* led to Foucault introducing a refinement in *The Archaeology of Knowledge* that served to emphasise further what could be seen as postmodern concerns. In place of the episteme, Foucault introduced the archive which he perceived as a system of discursive formation which admits a more open system of regularities than the 'closed' episteme. Unlike the episteme, the archive seeks to include historical influences that can be more influential in the longer term than other fleeting aspects. To a certain extent Foucault is attempting to create a truism (however vague) to back up his earlier concerns with truth itself – or its more problematic nature.

> The notion of the discursive formation is used to problematise the self-evident unity of such discourses (McNay 1994: 66).

Nevertheless, Foucault is still claiming that the discursive realm still influences the non-discursive. In *The Archaeology of Knowledge* it is the discursive realm that has priority in that it determines non-discursive elements (McNay, 1994: 70). This claim has been widely criticised. Dreyfus and Rabinow (1982) claim that non-discursive formations must have pre-dated discursive and that it is clear that the former does exert a strong influence on the latter. As Best and Kellner (1991: 45) put it:

a more adequate analysis would ultimately have to focus more directly on practices and institutions to situate discourse within its full social and political context.

Foucault attempted to do this in his later work, particularly in *Discipline and Punishment* and the shift to what he termed (following Nietzsche) a genealogical method. The starting point for archaeology and genealogy are the same: the disassembly of universal truths of history, the exposure of local, lost voices and the potential for infinite productions of meaning against the limited and regulated scope for discourse. However, Foucault places more emphasis on the economic, political and institutional influences upon discourse formation including a reformulated view of power. As in *The Archaeology of Knowledge* Foucault problematises history through genealogy.

> Events are inserted into universal explanatory schemas and thereby given false unity.

and

> Far from being teleologically governed, the historical processes that give rise to the emergence of events are in fact discontinuous, divergent and governed by chance (quoted in McNay, 1994: 88–9).

From this comes Foucault's reformulated theory of power as permeating all relations in the never-ending struggle to define history. The reductionist views of power (e.g. class based) are rejected and replaced by two related aspects. First, power as a non-centred strategy that flows and entails automatic resistance. Second, power as a normalising force which disciplines behaviour and sets 'norms'. On the first aspect, Foucault claims that

> Power must be analysed as something which circulates, or rather as something which only functions in the form of a chain. It is never localised here or there, never in anybody's hands, never appropriated as a commodity or piece of wealth. Power is employed and exercised through a net-like organisation. And not only do individuals circulate between its threads; they are always in the position of simultaneously undergoing and exercising this power (Foucault, 1980: 48).

This view of power is contra to the Enlightenment perspective of a uni-directional economic or juridical force and opens up important positive views of power relations. This leads Foucault to see power as an ordering force, i.e. channelling and shaping rather than restricting and impeding. The primary medium for this is Foucault's second insight: power as a normalising force. In *Discipline and Punishment* (1979) Foucault demonstrates how normalising power has influenced and shaped the subject through institutions such as prisons, schools and hospitals, utilising

timetables for constant imposition and regulation of activity, surveillance
measures to monitor performance, examinations such as written reports and
files to reward conformity and penalise resistance and normalising judgement to
impose and enforce moral values such as the work ethic (Best and Kellner,
1991: 47).

The goal of this use of power (which has replaced the more visible and violent
forms of subject repression found in the pre-Enlightenment period) is the normali-
sation of the subject – the elimination of all social and psychological irregularities.
Again, drawing heavily on Nietzsche, Foucault links power with knowledge – the
will to knowledge cannot be separated from a will to power. As Best and Kellner
(1991: 50) point out, this linkage

> is symptomatic of the postmodern suspicion of reason and emancipatory
> schemes advanced in its name.

The subject in Foucault's view of power remains discursively constituted but the
discourses have a much more sophisticated and polymorphous origin including the
pernicious effects of normalising power.

Sarup (1998) claims that Foucault is much more concerned with analysing
issues of power and dominance rather than prescribing or suggesting an alternative politics of resistance. However, it is possible to tease out Foucault's alternatives.

> Free political action from all unitary and totalising paranoia. Developing action,
> thought, and desires by proliferation, juxtaposition, and disjunction, and not by
> subdivision and pyramidal hierarchisation (quoted in Best and Kellner, 1991:
> 54).

Foucault's alternatives are based on his analysis of knowledge/power and the
subject. The normalising role of power in the production of the subject needs to be
stripped away and (unlike the Marxist approach) this does not require class consciousness or revolution. Power relations are contingent and fragile and the exposure of their normalising force is seen as sufficient to provide the impetus for
change. To enable this, Foucault called for a 'plurality of autonomous struggles
waged throughout microlevels of society' (Best and Kellner, 1991: 56). This is a
postmodern concept of micropolitical resistance to (increasingly) centralised
power. Release from the normalising and disciplining aspects of power is, for Fou-
cualt, liberation. Any other strategy, such as institutional change, class conflict or
even a consensus-based approach à la Habermas fail to appreciate the nature of
power relations. As power is decentred and plural, it follows that political struggle
should be too.

> A Foucauldian postmodern politics, therefore, attempts to break with unifying and totalising strategies, to cultivate multiple forms of resistance, to destroy the prisons of received identities and discourses of exclusion, and to encourage the proliferation of difference of all kinds (Best and Kellner, 1991: 47).

In a passage written generally, though surely applicable to planning, Foucault says:

> It seems to me that the real political task in a society such as ours is to criticise the workings of institutions which appear to be both neutral and independent; to criticise them in such a manner that the political violence which has always exercised itself obscurely through them will be unmasked, so that one can fight them (quoted in Best and Kellner, 1991: 57).

However, Foucault never really engages in a postmodern politics and this can be seen as one of the many criticisms that have been aimed at him. Sarup in particular has picked on his vagueness and the lack of methodological protocols that would allow, for example, one archaeological analysis to be judged against another. This vagueness runs through his work and often leaves important questions left unanswered: who is the struggle offered above against? Why should power always produce resistance? Poulantzas (1978) has picked up this question of resistance and tried to unpick its implications, arguing that Foucault is actually saying that resistance is an essential element of humanity, as is the choice not to resist or to obey. But undoubtedly this is not developed by Foucault to anyone's satisfaction. Neither is the dismissal of ontological concentrations and effects of power in institutional, state and economic forms. Such concentrations and their effects undoubtedly exist, but for Foucault they are ignored in favour of his micro-political focus. Similarly ignored, according to Habermas (1987), in Foucault's one-sided analysis is the positive side of the Enlightenment which has brought the opportunity to criticise itself through advances in liberty and choice. Finally, echoing the point made at the beginning of the chapter, Foucault can be accused of inconsistency in his criticism and use of totalising statements.

Notwithstanding these points, it is undeniable that Foucault provides powerful analyses of monolithic perceptions of power relations, as well as other accounts that ignore power altogether. He also adds important insights to the critical Enlightenment perspective of other postmodernists with an acute appreciation of the normalising impacts of power relations. Although he discounted himself as a postmodernist per se, he highlights and adds to the general thrust of postmodern concerns.

BAUDRILLARD

If Derrida has been accused of seeking to peel away but not destroy the meaning of the Enlightenment and modernity, then Jean Baudrillard has no such delicacy. Instead he emphasises the dystopian and nihilistic implications of modernity, particularly in its later phases. He argues that capitalism has led to a technological explosion, the death of 'authenticity' and its replacement with a precession of simulacra that bear no relation to any reality whatever. The consequence is the hyperreal, a state where all referentiality and meaning are lost. Modernity 'thus produces the Other of the real – fantasy – to legitimise the normativity of its own practices' (Docherty, 1993: 14).

> Disneyland is presented as imaginary in order to make believe that the rest is real, when in fact all of Los Angeles and the America surrounding it are no longer real, but of the order of the hyperreal and of simulation (Baudrillard, 1983: 25).

As a consequence of the precession of simulacra and the loss of referentiality, there comes a loss of critical distance where the mass of people can no longer decide for themselves what is 'real or unreal', 'right or wrong'. Although Norris (1985) has criticised Baudrillard for his ultimate disenchantment with the concepts and categories of Enlightenment thought, Bertens (1995: 158) believes that he provides important new insights into the 'discursive organisation that the media impose on the social field' and raises our awareness to its repressive potential. Baudrillard has therefore emerged as one of the most important and high profile postmodern thinkers who, unlike many other writers trapped under the postmodern 'umbrella', accepts the label.

Baudrillard's early work in *The System of Objects* (1968) and *The Consumer Society* (1970) explore what he sees as the new social order of consumption from a neo-Marxist perspective, replacing the central tenets of use and exchange value with semiotic value. The post-war explosion in consumerism and products has in turn led to the development of new values, modes of behaviour and relations to objects and to other people (Kellner, 1989: 10) replacing Marxist-inspired class-based classification and structuring systems. Objects, such as consumer durables, now confer status through socially-constructed signification.

> We are surrounded today by the remarkable conspicuousness of consumption and affluence, established by the multiplication of objects, services and material goods, all of which constitutes a sort of fundamental mutation in the ecology of the human species. Strictly speaking, these affluent individuals are no longer surrounded by other human beings as they were in the past, but by objects (Baudrillard, 1970: 17).

Consumption should not be understood as meeting needs but (building on struc-turalism) as a system of inexhaustible floating signifiers. Thus,

> He [Baudrillard] argues that the commodity has now become a sign in the
> Saussarian sense, with its meaning arbitrarily determined by its position in the
> self-referential system of signifiers. Consumption, then, must not be understood
> as the consumption of use-values, but primarily as the consumption of signs
> (Sarup, 1993: 162).

This adds an important cultural dimension to Marxian critique of political economy, criticising the standard view of consumption as satisfaction of needs and, in doing so, distancing himself from the Marxist dialectic of the inevitability of socialist revolution. As Kellner (1989: 18) points out, if everything in society can now be seen as a commodity to be bought and sold separate from any fixed meaning, then there can be no individual transcendence towards the consciousness requisite for concerted group revolt. This places the former Marxist in an ambivalent position *vis-à-vis* Marxism itself. Baudrillard's attempts to update Marxist thought into a neo-Marxian framework have the effect of undermining it and adding a powerful addi-tion. His insightful neo-Marxism points to the propensity of society to develop a tautological relationship with the individual by both socially-creating the meaning of needs and simultaneously meeting them. At the same time, he is clearly moving away from Marxist analysis and its 'inevitable' implications. However, his final break with Marxism comes in his next work, *The Mirror of Production* (1975), which fore-closes on the possibility of combining Marxist political economy with semiotics. Building on his own analysis of use and exchange value under a system of signs, he argues that, as both use value and needs are socially constructed (i.e. by capitalism itself) then they cannot be used as a stick with which to beat the iniqui-ties of capitalism. Further, he criticises Marx for not escaping the logic of capitalism and accuses Marxism of not being a radical critique but capitalism's highest form of justification (Sarup, 1993: 162). Marxism merely reproduces the primacy of pro-duction which is itself a product of capitalism. This critique within a socially-constructed system 'closes off' more radical alternatives (Kellner, 1989: 40). Baudrillard was, in Sarup's (1993: 164) words, moving

> From a radical position on the Left ... towards a right-wing post-structuralist
> and post-modernism.

Baudrillard's rejection of Marxism and his embracing of postmodern perspectives led him to attack other reductionist theories (mirroring Lyotard and Foucault) in *On Seduction* (1979). As an alternative to the class-based revolutions of Marxism, Baudrillard develops his own concept of resistance based on a politics of dif-ference.

> Against the values and practices of capitalist society, Baudrillard is searching for
> a form of life in radical opposition to the dominant types of exchange, use and
> sign value in productivist societies (Kellner, 1989: 45).

He therefore proposes a form of symbolic exchange which is neither use value nor exchange value. Symbolic exchange includes:

> The exchange of looks, the present which comes and goes, prodigality, festival
> – and also destruction (which returns to non-value what production has erected,
> valorised) (quoted in Best and Kellner, 1991: 116).

This is Baudrillard's attempt to subvert or overcome the influence of capitalism by focusing on the practicalities of everyday life. He concentrates on the marginalised micro-politics of groups such as blacks and gays who he sees as pursuing their own needs over the dominant capitalistic culture. Here Baudrillard is close to the micro-political emphasis of Lyotard and Foucault, though this is as close as he would get. During the 1980s Baudrillard moved on to the manifestations and implications of what he accepted as the postmodern world in his most famous works on hyper-reality and simulacra.

Baudrillard's work throughout the 1980s and beyond is based on his interpretation of the continued influence of media and culture in shaping society and, as such, he moves centre stage in the postmodern debate. Moving beyond Marxism he begins to develop his own social theory based on semiotics and the ubiquitous and pervasive influence of signs. In *L'échange symbolique et la mort* (1976) production as the organising force of society is replaced by the influence of media, technology, information, computers. We have moved from a metallurgic to semiurgic society where signs now constitute the new social order. But within this new social order there is an increasing excess of information and increasingly weaker links between signs and the signified. The boundary between image and reality has now imploded leading to what he terms the hyper-real where we can no longer actually tell what is real and what is simulation.

> Simulation is no longer that of a territory, a referential being or a substance. It is
> the generation of models of a real without origins or reality: a hyperreal
> (Baudrillard, 1983: 2).

The recent examples from accusations of 'faking' television programmes help illustrate this breakdown between the real and the unreal. Carlton Television in the UK were accused of faking an interview with Fidel Castro and faking another programme about drug-smugglers. The BBC admitted re-filming supposedly spontaneous scenes in another documentary and Channel 4 owned up to using actors to recreate situations that were presented as being filmed surreptitiously. As one newspaper report noted at the time:

> Life is no longer exciting enough for television producers. Confessional chat
> shows, docu-soaps, and now, it seems, award-winning investigations are no
> longer factual programmes. Instead, our TV screens are proffering us real life –
> but with a twist. Non-fiction is served up, mixed with fiction (The *Independent*,
> 7th May 1998: 18).

Indeed, the hyper-real is actually more real than the real. It is an aspiration, a dream, an image. Signs or simulacra are now reality. There is no referent or grounding upon which you can contrast and compare. This goes beyond simple nostalgia for 'the good old days' or security, and allows instead the development of wilful nostalgia – the (mis)use of signs as a tool of power. Myths and images take on a potentially powerful role in the creation of simulacra – e.g. planned 'good', unplanned 'bad'.

Baudrillard (1983) argues that signs do not hide the truth, but the fact that there is none. Truth means different things to different people so there cannot be one truth, but a multitude of truths. He feels that truth and reality are lost under a sea of signs:

> Reality no longer has the time to take on the appearance of reality: it captures
> every dream even before it takes on the appearance of a dream (1983: 152).

Simulacra, or the hyper-real simulation, are organised under a 'code' or 'codes'.

> Society contains codes and models of social organisation and control which
> structure the environment and human life (Kellner, 1989: 80).

Where this code comes from is unclear but Baudrillard uses the example of interior design manuals, exercise video-cassettes, cookbooks and newspapers that all structure activities of everyday life. In planning we could see a link with the work on planning doctrine (Alexander and Faludi, 1996). While there is an element of choice the scope of choice and range of options are predetermined. Consequently, all radical change is curtailed – there is choice to provide alternatives but the choices are binary in nature, thereby ruling out exploration and the avant-garde. There is also an in-built system of deterrence against instability and anything other than binary oppositions. Scandals, such as Watergate with its accusations of wrong-doing and corruption, hide the fact that it is the system as a whole that is corrupt and thereby strengthen the system.

But the analysis of a semiurgic society alone would not warrant the title of 'Postmodern High Priest' for Baudrillard. As Kellner (1989: 131) points out, in his earlier works Baudrillard tended to cite Foucault positively and there are some broad similarities between Foucault's epistémes and Baudrillard's codes. But from the late 1970s Baudrillard moved away from a general alignment with Foucault towards a more avant-garde, nihilistic, cynical and apolitical position thereby abandoning his previous commitment to developing a politics of symbolic exchange and transgression. Baudrillard's disenchantment with Foucault seems to originate from his own journey from a materialist analysis and position, through the general reaction against the failed revolution in Paris in 1968, to a more contemporary and questioning phase as we have seen above. Foucault took a broadly similar route though Baudrillard claims that when Foucault travelled he turned back, becoming disenchanted or afraid of the logic and final destination of his journey. This is a criticism that can equally be aimed at Lyotard. Baudrillard had no such qualms. *Forget Foucault* (1987, original 1977) claims that Foucault's theories of power are now obsolete in the new social era. Power is no longer anchored in institutions but in signs and codes, simulations and the media – it can be feigned, masqueraded and simulated (Kellner, 1989: 133). As such, Baudrillard claims that it is impossible to chart the trajectories and structures of power. We cannot therefore ground any oppositional politics in Lyotard's or Foucault's micro-level as power is more dispersed and plural than either can imagine – there is nothing we can put our finger on to struggle against. This shift places Baudrillard in an exposed and nihilistic position.

> If being nihilist is to privilege this point of inertia and the analysis of this irreversibility of system to the point of no return, then I am a nihilist (Baudrillard, quoted in Best and Kellner, 1991: 126).

For Baudrillard, the journey from which he refuses (unlike Foucault) to return means that society, our postmodern society, is devoid of meaning and grounded theories. This leads Best and Kellner to describe it as a nihilism without joy, without energy, without hope for a better future. The world has 'done' everything, everything has been achieved and all that is left is to play with the pieces.

> The postmodern condition is thus for Baudrillard a play with all forms of sexuality, art and politics, combining and recombining forms and possibilities, moving into the time of transvestism (Best and Kellner, 1991: 137).

Baudrillard has had many followers and critics and a number of consistent themes from both. He has been praised for adding valuable, often brilliant, insights into Marxism and our understanding of contemporary society particularly with regard to capturing the essence of the media-driven age. But undoubtedly there are difficulties too. Perhaps the biggest criticism that can be levelled at Baudrillard regards his level of abstraction and consequent under-theorising. It is difficult if not impossible to grasp anything concrete in his work. Unlike Foucault, who based his analyses upon detailed historical data, Baudrillard has increasingly depended upon opinion and simplification to the point of parody. In his attacks on Foucault he has a point that Foucault ignores the influence and role of culture, media and signs in his theory of power, but Baudrillard equally ignores the disciplining nature of power highlighted by Foucault. Best and Kellner accuse him of seeing what he wants to see: the media images and polyculturalism of America while failing to notice or choosing to ignore the poverty, class, racial and gender divisions that still divide modern societies:

> If he were merely expressing opinions or claiming to present a possible perspective on things, one would be able to enjoy his pataphysical meanderings, but Baudrillard's writing is increasingly pretentious, claiming to describe 'the real state of things', to speak for the masses, and to tell 'us' what we really believe (1991: 139).

Baudrillard then is critiquing the breakdown of totalising thought with his own meta-narratives, which all seem to be dystopian visions. Regardless of these sound criticisms there can be no getting away from the relativist nihilism Baudrillard describes and prescribes for postmodern society. As Hebdige rather depressingly puts it:

> Post-modernity is modernity without the hopes and dreams which made modernity bearable (1988: 195).

JAMESON

The landscape of Marxist or left-wing engagement with the postmodern can be broadly split into a number of groups. First are those who have attempted to rubbish the idea of postmodernism (e.g. Eagleton and Habermas). Second are those who have attempted some kind of integration of radical left-wing politics and postmodernism and abandoned it (e.g. Foucault and Lyotard). Finally, there is Baudrillard who attempted to refine Marxism by integrating semiotics, though ended up moving beyond it to an extreme postmodern position. Fredric Jameson adds an important fourth position that has influenced other significant contributions such as David Harvey's. He manages both to successfully integrate the postmodern within Marxist analysis and provide a convincing Marxist explanation for it. According to his view, postmodernity is the cultural logic of late capitalism (Jameson, 1984). There are some broad similarities in his analysis with elements of the post/neo-Fordist perspective, i.e. attempting to explain what appear to be radically different times by reference to the meta-narrative of economic determinism.

> every position on postmodernism in culture ... is ... an implicitly or explicitly political stance on the nature of multi-national capital today (Jameson, 1984: 55).

In developing this position Jameson draws heavily on Ernest Mandel's *Late Capitalism* (1975). Mandel argues that what we are witnessing is a more advanced, sophisticated and pure capitalism that has extended its logic to a far greater number of areas and has even managed to invade cultural aspects of life. Jameson's adoption of this thesis to reformulate Marxism and envelop the postmodern challenge of Baudrillard and others throws a lifebelt to left-wing analysis, and provides the basis for a more constructive Marxist engagement with the postmodern.

Jameson's starting point, like the post/neo-Fordists, Baudrillard and Lyotard, is to explore the changes in society: the 'new times' of postmodernity. But unlike Baudrillard and Lyotard he puts these new experiences and situations down to yet another manifestation of capitalism which has replaced the old modernist forms of thinking and knowing. The postmodern for Jameson is a cultural one. In postmodern times there has been a breakdown of the distinction between high and low culture as well as a commodification leading to a loss in 'critical distance' where culture can be used to attack capitalism. In addition (and echoing Baudrillard and Lyotard), Jameson identifies a number of manifestations of this cultural malaise, including the 'death of the subject' by virtue of the radical fragmentation and dispersal into a 'disorientating hyper-space'. Although there are significant similarities in his analysis to other postmodern thinkers there are also some important differences. The most important difference (and crucial to his reductionist argument) is the maintenance of meta-theories within his postmodern. Like Baudrillard's code, meta-narratives for Jameson are now less visible (Adam Smith's 'invisible hand' of capitalism takes on a new significance) though are still there directing change. This is of course crucial to his maintenance of economic reductionism which he posits as *the* main directing force or meta-narrative. But this is not the only aspect of his Marxist thinking that is cast in a new light. History is still a class struggle for Jameson and not the epistemic shifts of Foucault. While this conception may seem archaic, Jameson's use of Williams' (1977) distinctions between emergent and dominant cultural forms

> provides a more adequate account of postmodernism as a historical rupture
> than do radical postmodernists such as Baudrillard or Lyotard (Best and Kellner,
> 1991: 186).

There are continuities and discontinuities within the postmodern according to Jameson which again provide the basis for his argument concerning its logical link to modernity and its dominant structuring force of capitalism. Similarly, postmodern culture may or may not dominate over more modern forms depending on the sphere and whether it is emergent or dominant. Other more important pre- or modern influences may exist. But the postmodern emphasis on *a priori* difference excludes the possibility or inevitability of continuities between the modern and the postmodern and Jameson's totalising claim that it is all simply a cultural manifestation of capitalism. But Jameson can also be too totalising himself in claiming that postmodernism is a cultural dominant by not analysing those areas where it is clearly more of a continuity from modernity or unrelated to either modern or postmodern roots.

Like other left-leaning attempts to create a new politics as found in Foucault, Lyotard and (the early) Baudrillard, Jameson also theorises a response. The disorientation and fragmentation felt by people under the postmodern cultural maelstrom undermines collective action and consequently radical action. To overcome this Jameson calls for a new politics where individuals are able to 'map' or perceive their position within society – much in the same mould as Marx's concept of class consciousness. This could be achieved through 'cognitive mapping' though this is not explored enough to provide a clear idea of how it would work. As Best and Kellner (1991: 189) also point out, if postmodernity is merely a tool of capitalist logic, surely it could disarm such concepts? And if capitalism is so diverse and ingrained it is difficult to imagine how narratives such as novels could map the whole and position the subject. Not surprisingly, Jameson criticises other attempts to focus on micro-politics as merely 'playing with the pieces' and that, following post-structuralist thinking, the world is unrepresentable. But the details and practicalities of Jameson's strategies is unclear beyond a 'politics of alliance' that would bring together disparate groups or individuals with some common interests following a realisation of the inequity of their position. Jameson's north American perspective begins to show through clearly as it is easy to recognise the pluralistic nature of that society against, say, the more homogenised and centrally-directed situation of the UK. He recommends learning from the experiences of marginalised groups such as women and blacks that will provide an inventory of experiences of how to create alliances and push at the boundaries of the state. Although each group has different aims and experiences it is possible to demonstrate the logic behind their grievances as being found (still) within capitalism.

Best and Kellner (1991) are critical of Jameson's ambiguity concerning his new-left politics and questions of how such an alliance would emerge seem unclear. But fundamental is their criticism of the tensions between privileging Marxism as the master-discourse and the primacy of individualism in a renewed class-politics. More traditional Marxist class-based politics are still central to Jameson's vision of socialism but his means of a politics of alliance seem to undermine the notion of classes. The tensions within Jameson's work between traditional class-based politics and the existence of fragmented non-class aligned groups is overcome by Laclau and Mouffe's attempt to interpret postmodernism from a left-wing perspective.

LACLAU AND MOUFFE

Rather than the esoteric writings of Baudrillard and Lyotard and the born-again Marxism of Jameson, Laclau and Mouffe provide a much more practical and pragmatic orientated engagement with the postmodern. Like Jameson they attempt to rethink left-of-centre politics in 'new times' but direct their efforts not necessarily to saving Marxism but to providing a practical alternative to the right-wing hegemony that has been in the ascendancy throughout the west over the past two decades. It is this hegemonic growth that seems to have mirrored, influenced and built on the postmodern concerns with individualism and fragmentation. For Laclau and Mouffe, such aspects are not naturally allied with the right; they too have a place in a renewed left-wing alternative.

They are critical of the reductionist Marxist logic that excludes the evident plurality of society and still clings instead to crude class-based analysis. However, unlike the binary nature of much of the modern/postmodern debate in Marxist circles they do not either fully reject/accept either a modern (Marxist) or postmodern (relativist) position. Instead they plough a middle course (much in the same way, though with different emphasis and analysis, as Richard Rorty) taking and rejecting elements of both to provide the basis for what they term

> the emergence of collective action, directed towards struggling against
> inequalities and changing relations to subordination (1985: 153).

Their main departure from Jameson is their rejection of meta-narratives, including Marxism, and their attempt to move beyond it towards a more pragmatic, though left-leaning politics. However, they do accept the 'new times' thesis of growing commodification, dispersal and fragmentation. With this growing fragmentation comes the emergence of different political and social alignments that undermine the monolithic Marxist emphasis on class. In place of the *a priori* productivist logic they embrace the postmodern and post-structuralist concept of the discursively-created subject. However, it is not exclusively so. There are structural influences upon this discursively-created self including the logic of capital. This leads to points of common interest where overlapping concerns mean that there are concentrations of similarities, e.g., gender, age, ethnic origin. The basis for a new postmodern socialist politics would be to create linkages between these 'nodes' of interest.

The object of their radical and pluralist postmodern socialism remains capitalism but their aim is not the more traditional socialism of the Marxist tradition. Instead, they pursue a pluralistic democracy that builds upon existing liberal democracy (1985). As Best and Kellner (1991: 198) point out, their rejection of classical Marxist analysis of power while maintaining its logic and implications as the enemy leaves their pursual of radical democracy power blind (much in the same way as Foucault). Without a strategy to overcome existing power relations, their pluralistic politics is too passive in the force of what they identify as a repressive and inequitable system. Further, the dynamics of recent hegemonic discourses under the New Right have shifted the goal by defining concepts such as democracy in an anti-collectivist and individualistic way. It is here in the semiotic and discursive world of liberal society that the battle for meaning must be fought.

Criticism of Laclau and Mouffe's approach has been aimed at its abandonment of essentialism and its replacement with a nihilistic and relativistic notion of values such as democracy. Laclau and Mouffe's response has been two-fold. First, arguing that progressive values can be defined and legitimised through pragmatic language games. Second, they then avoid the problems that Lyotard found himself in with this move by claiming that not all positions are equally valid on the basis of moral tradition. Unlike Lyotard they cannot be accused of inconsistency on this embrace of modernity/postmodernity as they have always maintained that they are attempting to find a modern and postmodern way forward (Laclau, 1988).

> One of the valuable lessons of Laclau and Mouffe's work is to show that postmodern theory does not entail a rejection of modern political commitments to freedom, democracy and mass political struggle (Best and Kellner, 1991: 200).

But Best and Kellner's criticism that Laclau and Mouffe can be accused of abstracting Marxist thinking too far (1991: 203) seems to be missing the point. Even if Marx never actually said history was teleological, his dialectic certainly implied it. Laclau and Mouffe seem more concerned with building on the ruins of Marxist analysis rather than providing a watertight critique of it and it is this blend of anti-essentialism and pluralism that is their main project. What is more credible (though still open to criticism itself) is Best and Kellner's objection to the emphasis on agency and contingency in Laclau and Mouffe's employment of discourse. Their middle-way between essentialism and relativism does not adequately account for concentrations of power or the existence of deterministic structures. Instead, all influences are given equal weight. This 'all is equal' *weltanschauung* ignores power structures, manipulation, dis-information and all the other nefarious practices of life. It is not enough, as Best and Kellner point out, to label all social practices as discursive because this does not help analysis of or resistance to 'real' nodes of power and influence such as the state or the economy.

THE MAIN THEMES OF POSTMODERN SOCIAL THEORY

Regardless of the very broad range of thinking from the admittedly limited, though arguably representative, selection of thinkers, five main themes emerge to give a synthesis from the analysis in Chapter two.

1 THE BREAK-DOWN OF TRANSCENDENTAL MEANING

This is not a new or particularly postmodern theme as it goes back at least as far as Nietzsche. However, Lyotard, Baudrillard and Foucault all build on the post-structuralist rejection of stable signifiers and emphasise instead the infinity of meaning. But in Lyotard's case this lack of transcendental meaning also manifests itself in what he terms an 'incredulity towards meta-narratives' or grand theories. For Lyotard, reductionist theories no longer represent the world (if they ever did). Grand narratives of science, reason and progress have been replaced by a plethora of goals, styles and methods. However, Foucault is more open minded on this, preferring 'suspicion' to an obituary, he still seeks to 'problematise' rather than dismiss them entirely. Jameson's postmodernism still has a place for the grand narratives, though he accepts the need for a more pluralistic and flexible interpretation. For all this suspicion there is still no convincing theory of why such narratives have lost their meaning and force. This is compounded by the ease and comfort with which they rush to fill the death of such over-arching theories with ones of their own (see theme 3 below).

2 THE DISCURSIVELY-CREATED SUBJECT

Foucault's brilliant exegesis of madness exposed its lack of a pre-social essence. In doing so, he questioned scientific rationality and Enlightenment 'truths'. History and the self are more likely to lie outside linear and teleological perspectives of the self and history that favour rational, autonomous individuals. Laclau and Mouffe base their own radical politics on a similar basis though add other, more structural influences to make up for Foucault's failure to see the influences of the non-discursive such as the state or economy. The influence of non-discursive spheres is one of the main weaknesses in the discursive perspective on history and the self. One way Foucault and Baudrillard try to explain it is through the existence of an amorphous cultural map labelled the 'code', 'episteme' or 'archive'. However, Jameson plumps instead for old-fashioned economic determinism and thereby denies the discursive–non-discursive link.

3 THE ROLE OF CULTURAL INFLUENCES IN ORDERING SOCIETY

Baudrillard's code and Foucault's episteme are tools to help explain why, in such a fragmented and discursively-created world, there are still common threads and values. The episteme is a set of discursively created rules that explain why one way of thinking or saying has been chosen over another. The influences upon these rules vary and can (and have) changed over time. But their main role is to limit possibilities and maintain discipline. These two functions were developed in Baudrillard's code which he argued created stability within an increasingly unstable world. These sets of rules look uncomfortably like the kind of reductionist logic and meta-narrative they all seek to question. The influence upon such codes is predominantly cultural and media driven, which leads to the development of a symbiotic relationship emerging: society created the media and through the predominance of signs the media is increasingly influencing and creating society. Less and less connection and engagement with a world outside of media images is made as external reality, according to Baudrillard, is lost.

4 FRAGMENTATION AND DISPERSAL

All the thinkers in Chapter 2 point to an increasingly fragmented and dispersed world where the 'old rules' no longer apply. This is linked in many ways to the 'new times' theses though less specifically. Lyotard's new times are based heavily around the 'information society' ideas of Bell and Touraine. But the theory of fragmentation is most forcefully advanced by Baudrillard to the point of a 'hyper-real' leading to the development of new ethics and values. 'We can no longer make sense of the pieces' seems to be both Baudrillard and Jameson's interpretations. But Jameson advances a far more hopeful and less nihilistic counter-strategy that is based on his belief in fragmentation being both a threat and an opportunity. For Laclau and Mouffe, fragmentation leads to different political alignments that undermine the emphasis on class.

5 FOUCAULT AND BAUDRILLARD'S POWER

Closely linked in some ways to the fragmentation of society is Foucault's concept of dispersal and disciplining power. Challenging the uni-directional characteristics of economic determinism, Foucault analyses power as 'flowing' at every level of society, thereby focusing his attention upon more micro-political rather than structural constraints. But there is an element of 'structural' control in this in the form of his normalising and disciplining role for power through, for example, institutional and discursive practices. Baudrillard's view at first accorded with this but his later radical postmodernism based on extreme fragmentation rejected Foucault's perspective as being too simplistic: power is more dispersed than even he realises and there is no hope of tracing it.

PRESCRIPTIONS AND ALTERNATIVES

Most postmodern writers such as Foucault or Lyotard would cringe at the prospect of the word 'prescription' as a description of their own strategies of resistance or social theory. To do so would potentially re-create other systems of distorted power. The real alternatives should ideally emerge from local, micro-political processes. Baudrillard would, of course, reject it outright as hopeless. But all offer some kind of counter-strategy against either the 'insidious' effects of modernity, the naïve and dated analysis of Marxism or the right-wing embrace of individualism. Throughout these strategies, some common themes emerge.

1 A MICRO-POLITICS OF ANALYSIS

The over-riding theme of postmodern thinking is to base any analysis of change at a micro-political level. The death of meta-narratives naturally points to the micro. For Foucault, the micro is where power is embedded and it is here where any analysis of, for example, exclusion should be focused. For Baudrillard and Lyotard too (though both in different ways) there was a clear emphasis upon the micro as an arena that should be the focus of any analysis of politics. The curious absence of any real engagement with macro-level structuring from the three former Marxists (Lyotard, Foucault and Baudrillard) is countered by Jameson and Laclau and Mouffe who balance any focus by fusing micro and macro levels of influence. But one thing is clear, the postmodern as social theory is predominantly a micro-level phenomenon.

2 A MICRO-POLITICS OF RESISTANCE

Lyotard's strategy of resistance, his 'Pagan Politics', is the most well known among the postmodern for both its simplicity and its inherent contradictions. It is basically comprised of two strategies. First, there is an opposition or dissensus that seeks to encourage people to say 'no'. But it also seems to prohibit a search for consensus or agreement – a 'yes'. Second, it seeks to not only encourage this but (falling back on his Kantian ideal) actually enforce it, thereby precluding any possible agreement. As I set out in Chapter 2, this radical pluralism seems to be conflated with absolute relativism and consequently undermined his attempts by accusations of being impartial. Foucault similarly proffers a localised micro-strategy but does not want to provide any rules or proposals that may add to the disciplining or domi-nating layers of extant power. Instead, his is a more passive 'something will emerge' approach that depends on a realisation rather than a strategy of active revelation. Baudrillard's earlier attempts to counter hegemonic semiotics depended on a rather vague and implausible strategy of symbolic exchange which no doubt left capitalism shaking in its boots. But the most realistic strategies emerge from

Jameson and Laclau and Mouffe. For Jameson, the fragmented postmodern land-scape could be mapped and various overlapping interests combined to form a poli-tics of alliance. How this would occur is not so clear and it seems to depend a good deal on the Marxist strategy of emerging consciousness. Laclau and Mouffe's approach is similar in its attempt to connect 'nodes' of interest but seeks to achieve this through a strategy of 'deepening' democracy that at least provides some clue as to how consciousness will be achieved. For them, there are still meta-narratives. Modernist notions such as freedom, democracy, etc. can be improved by postmodern social theory.

This is an outline of some of the main contributions to postmodern social theory. I now turn in Chapter 3 to the other aspect of the postmodern – new times.

CHAPTER 3

WHAT IS THE POSTMODERN?: new times

INTRODUCTION

It is obvious from Chapter 2 that there is a plurality of positions within the postmodern space of social theory. But it is possible to identify broad groupings. The two
most obvious to emerge are undoubtedly the nihilistic extremes of Baudrillard and
Lyotard and the more constructive, critical postmodernisms of Jameson, Laclau
and Mouffe, and Foucault. Another important distinction that emerges is between
those who attempt to formulate new theories of knowledge (e.g. Foucault and
Lyotard) and those who are concerned with the 'experience', manifestations and
implications of the postmodern as found in the economy or society (e.g.,
Baudrillard and Jameson). The postmodern is therefore quite clearly not going to
be easy to put a fix on.

The previous chapter provides us with some themes which direct us to the
broad area of interest concerning the postmodern as social theory but it does not
provide a comprehensive picture by any means. It also presents the postmodern as
an ahistorical phenomenon when there are serious arguments to the contrary
which I will explore in more detail below. Finally, and most importantly, it provides a
variety of ways to proceed if we are to build a postmodern planning. Unfortunately,
they are all (nearly) mutually exclusive and therefore we need to consider this in
more depth, particularly because the extreme postmodernists such as Baudrillard
and Lyotard deny the possibility or desirability of any form of social intervention at
all – their postmodern planning would be no planning. However, the postmodern is
not confined to social theory and much of what passes for it can actually be more
accurately described as a feeling or sensibility of difference – the postmodern as
new times. Building on the previous chapter this chapter aims to try and answer
the question 'what is the postmodern?' by focusing on this sensibility.

THE POSTMODERN AS NEW TIMES

I set out in Chapter 1 the broad outlines of the three areas of thinking that have
influenced and have been influenced by the feeling that we are living in new or
postmodern times – that of the post-industrial or information society, the broad
concerns of post-Fordism and the postmodern of sensibility. I argued there, that
there is significant overlap between all the analyses of change. But there has been

an additional impetus to these two schools of thought that point to the conclusion that we are living in new or certainly different times. The first is the *fin de siècle* sensibility of the millennium. The second are the implications of the 'end of history' thesis following the collapse of communism in Eastern Europe. This confluence of changed sensibilities points towards 'newness' (Allmendinger and Chapman, 1999). But as Smart (1993) retorts, the lifting of the threat of global catastrophe has been replaced by the spectre of local conflicts – the Balkanisation of regions not merely in the former Yugoslavia, as well as the growing nationalism of Scotland and Australia and the anti-Federal sentiments in the US. Similarly, conflict on a global scale has been replaced by more 'micro'-level threats such as terrorism. New times, new worries? Just like Nietzsche's double-edged sword of modernity, the 'new world order' that was supposed to rise in the wake of the Gulf War seems to involve new world *dis*order. Smart (1993) (perhaps over-deterministically) considers this symbiotic relationship to be inevitable.

> Order and disorder are inextricably connected, they are simultaneously
> constituted and spiral in a double helix-like fashion around the axis of modernity.
> Hence the perpetual preoccupation with the elimination or reduction of forms of
> disorder through the engineering or management of orderliness in modern
> forms. A preoccupation which is regenerated and reconstituted through the
> realisation that ordering interventions seems to promote disorders, to precipitate
> effects or 'unintended consequences' of disorder (41–2).

These sensibilities, which could be termed difference *and* similarity, underscore contemporary life. Explanations vary, but I shall focus on the three broad schools mentioned above. The basic premise of all these schools is that we are living in different/new/postmodern times, though the degree and origin of this difference varies. Whether these times are termed *new*, *late* or *post modern* is irrelevant. The question is, are they different enough to warrant a re-examination of planning, and do they help in our search for a planning of difference? All three fields of thought are inconclusive (not surprisingly) though all point to (at the very least) some difference, though with strong continuities from the modern.

THE INFORMATION SOCIETY

One of the main approaches to dissecting modern society is through the key of information to the extent that it now seems to be a truism that information and its means of transmission and processing through computers have radically altered the ways we live. The influence and dominance of information and electronics on modern society cannot be denied. Nevertheless, as a number of recent critiques have pointed out, there are significant differences between quantitative and qualitative studies on the impact of the information society that undermine or at least question some of the claims about its effects. There are also serious questions over whether an information society exists and if it can be regarded as a break from what went before or merely a continuation of existing trends. Whatever the position, it is generally agreed that two broad though related inputs have fed into the idea of an information society. The first was in the late 1960s and early 1970s that arose from the early implications of computers and telecommunications. This combined with what appeared to be significant changes in the economic base of society and, in particular, the shift from predominantly manufacturing-based to service-orientated economies. The other major spur to the information society thesis emerged in the late 1980s and early 1990s from the second generation of changes that accompanied the internet and the convergence of digital media technology. Beyond these broad generalities lies a minefield of claim and counter-claim.

> In an extensive and burgeoning literature concerned with the 'information age' there is little agreement about its major characteristics and its significance other than that – minimally – 'information' has achieved a special pertinence in the contemporary world' (Webster, 1995: 2).

Regardless of this disagreement, Webster (1995) identifies five broad meanings behind the term 'information society'.

1 TECHNOLOGICAL

This is the most common meaning for the information society and refers to the massive technological changes that have occurred in the past 30 years or so and their impact upon society. Computer technology is beginning to permeate all corners of society affecting change as a consequence.

2 ECONOMIC

The 'economics of information' concerns itself with the size and growth of information industries and seeks to measure its contribution to GNP. The basic argument is that if the contribution of information industries to society is growing then it is possible to claim that there is an emergence of an information society. The study of the economics of information has led some to claim that knowledge has become the foundation of the modern economy.

3 OCCUPATIONAL

Another motor to the information society thesis is the change in occupations largely from manufacturing work to service-orientated employment. Large-scale

restructuring of traditional heavy industries and the growth in 'white collar' information-orientated work have led to the situation where 'only a shrinking minority of the
labour force toils in factories ... and the labour market is now dominated by
information operatives who make their living by virtue of the fact that they possess
the information needed to get things done' (Stonier, quoted in Webster, 1995:
14).

4 SPATIAL

The organisation of time and space have been equally affected by the emergence
of an information society. This has occurred through the growth in networks of
information that link formerly disparate locations leading to 'time–space compression' as Giddens terms it. Such an effect has led to a growth in the immediacy of
change and the breakdown of local variation as globalisation of information has
taken its toll.

5 CULTURAL

The various permeations of change that society has experienced in the past 20
years or so can be put down to a variety of causes (as the other two categories of
change in this chapter point out). Not surprisingly, the information society theorists
put these cultural changes down to the increase in the amount and quality of
information through various media – the signification of the explosion in culture and
media through television, PCs, personal communication, etc. that herald the emergence of an 'information society'.

    These five factors form the basis of different interpretations of the idea of an
'information age': their common thread is the argument that it is different from what
went before. None of these ideas are without criticism as I will explore later. But
although they differ in their interpretation and emphasis, they received a broad
thrust of respectability and coherence from the writings of the biggest proponent
of an information society, Daniel Bell (1973). Bell was one of the first to attempt to
map this changing landscape of technology, its interaction with society and its trajectory. He termed what he found a 'post-industrial' age that to him described the
significance of these changes in the shift from a 'goods-producing society' to a
service society. Against a backdrop of massive change and uncertainty about its
significance and direction, Bell provided a route map in his *The Coming of Post-
Industrial Society* (1973). He argued that what he terms the post-industrial society
(though this is used interchangeably with 'information society') has emerged due to
the increased importance of information. Such information has not only increased
in quantitative terms but also *qualitatively* – it is a different kind of knowledge.
Society has moved through certain phases, argues Bell: pre-industrial, industrial
and now post-industrial. Each period has been characterised by different forms of

production – industrial by manufacturing and post-industrial by services. Information now rivals or even replaces industry and physical goods in the economy. By the mid 1970s about 47 per cent of the workforce worked as what Bell termed information workers while 28 per cent were employed in industry, 22 per cent in the service sector and 3 per cent in agriculture (Bell, 1980). In our post-industrial society, services now dominate. The key to understanding why post-industrial society has emerged lies with increases in productivity. As industrial society increased productivity it released resources in the form of workers and money to purchase luxury goods, as well as services such as education and health which can now be afforded by society. The logic of this process is that, eventually,

- few people will be employed in manufacturing as automation and productivity increases
- production will continue to increase
- increases in national wealth will lead to increased service employment (Webster, 1995: 35).

The new post-industrial nature of society is founded upon information.

> My basic premise has been that knowledge and information are becoming the strategic resource and transforming agent of post-industrial society . . . just as the combination of energy, resources and machine technology were the transforming agencies of industrial society (Bell, 1980: 531).

As information is central to this society Bell argues that professionals will come to dominate it. Such professionals will change society through the increased use of rationalisation, thereby minimising or eradicating uncertainty while increasing the efficacy of service provision such as health. As the effectiveness of such services increase, society will become more communally rather than individually orientated.

Bell's work has been highly influential and has been developed by Toffler (1981), Naisbitt (1984) and Stonier (1983) among others. According to Naisbitt, the centralised hierarchies of the industrial era were being undermined by the more eclectic, flatter and neutralised structures of the post-industrial society which would in turn begin to break down other hierarchies of society. Others, such as Stonier went further in predicting a more egalitarian land of plenty where workers are freed from the drudgery and leisure time is increased. The nation-state seems to be another arena of flux. In an application of the dialectic logic (as opposed to empirical evidence) that underpins much of the thinking on the post-industrial or information society, the proponents of change infer a shift from the space- and time-bound limits of agrarian and industrial societies to a decline in the nation–state accompanied by a growing nationalism.

It's easy to scoff at such utopian claims of the post-industrialists such as Bell and Toffler with the benefit of hindsight (though some authors seemed wildly hopeful even well into the 1980s and beyond). Many of the earlier interpretations of change were based on the wishful projection of inadequate base information. Do the trends highlighted by Bell and others add up to a new society? I will examine criticisms of the five main pillars of information society theorists before turning to Bell himself.

There is voluminous criticism of the notion of a new information society based on new technology alone.

> There has been a surfeit of gee-whiz writing that, awed by the pace and
> magnitude of technological change, naively tells us that 'the Computer
> Revolution ... will have an overwhelming and comprehensive impact, affecting
> every human on earth in every aspect of his or her writing' (Webster, 1995: 8).

Despite the visibility of this technology and its supposedly widespread impact there is little in the way of firm evidence to explain what makes this technological society different. At what point is a society 'industrial' or 'informational based' on the diffusion of technology? A second common objection to this technology-led view is that it is determinist, 'technology changes the world' in other words. As Webster points out, why is technology seen as aloof from the social realm? (1995: 10). It is, in fact, part of that realm which dictates where and how technology should develop (for military purposes, for example).

Nowhere has the idea of an information society been challenged more than in the economic and occupation realms. The various claims that this society or that is now an information society is founded on a number of subjective assumptions regarding what is or what is not an information worker. The problem is that different assumptions lead to different conclusions concerning the significance of information employment and this is compounded by the recognition that all areas of work involve information to greater or lesser degrees. An electronic engineer, for example, may spend different proportions of her time either designing or overseeing the production of a new circuit board – how would this be incorporated into a distinction between manufacturing and service employment?

Finally, the increase of information through multi-media technologies and the impact upon culture have been equally criticised along the same lines as the 'how much information does it take to change society?'. Like the post-Fordist and post-modern theses discussed later, the information society approach points to the cultural changes and puts it down purely to the availability and transfer of information. Quantity is again being confused with quality. How, asks Webster, can we distinguish this change in society from, say, the 1920s, other than purely as a matter of degree of difference?

The broad charge against the bases of the information society are that they fail to identify criteria against which to objectively measure their claim that we are now in an information society. They tend to point to a feeling of change or depend upon subjective criteria that, when reinterpreted, may produce different and contrary results. Similar critiques can be made of Bell's arguments concerning the shift to an information age. His model of progression appears, at the least, to be a crude case of historicism and teleological thinking as it encapsulates his belief in the onward progress of society towards a better future. His idea of a more caring society based on professionals who have the good of the community at heart seems to have been undermined by the experience of the Thatcher years, as does his concept of Keynesian economic management replacing laissez-faire thinking.

Bell's thesis is based on the idea of a separate and identifiable break with industrial society which naturally is a victim of similar critique to the broad information society proponents, i.e., at what point have we entered an information society? But another criticism has been levelled at Bell by Kumar (1995) and others who claim that what Bell identifies as a new age is in fact the continuation of other long-term trends that can be traced back to the consequences of the previous industrial revolution and the dynamics of capitalism in particular. Kumar (1995) also points to evidence that undermines or at least seriously questions the claims of a new cultural and social world as a result of the 'growth of information'. Far from an increase in the skills and knowledge of workers per se, as Bell claims, there has actually been an overall decrease. Contrary to the information society providing a social Utopia, it is clear that it is capitalist-driven as technology is merely being put to use in increasing profitability. The conclusion that he comes to is that while significant, the information society does not add up to a major new social order and has, in effect, speeded up processes already at work:

> The imperatives of profit, power and control seem as predominant now as they have ever been in the history of capitalist industrialism (Kumar, 1995: 154).

It has also been argued by Kumar (1995) that the growth of service sector employment which is seen by the information society protagonists as a consequence of the technological revolution is actually a feature of Taylorism: the office has become industrialised as well as the factory floor. Further, the proportion of workers employed in services was comparatively high throughout the nineteenth century and has remained between 45–50 per cent up to 1980 (Webster, 1995: 41). Figures like this help refute the idea that service growth is dependent upon increases in manufacturing productivity. Instead of arguing, as Bell does, that service employment grows as manufacturing employment declines, we can argue that

> What one sees ... is that a good deal of service sector work is engaged, not in consuming the wealth created by industry, but in assisting its generation (Webster, 1995: 43).

Bell's idea of a post-industrial, information-based society seems to follow the undoubted explosion in information but does not adequately theorise its significance or basis. As both Webster and Kumar argue, a more probable basis is a continuation rather than radical break to a new age. The growth in information can be directly attributed to the development of capitalism. Capitalism is not fixed, but dynamic and the information-based production phase is merely one of a number of phases over time. This is not to deny that there are indeed changes in culture and society as a direct consequence, but it is to bring such changes within a capitalist logic much as Jameson does. Some of the consequences are strikingly similar to the change in sensibilities identified by cultural postmodernism commentators. The undermining of hierarchy, the emphasis on the individual who is empowered by the availability of information and choice, the challenge to collective values and the explosion in images and signs through mediums such as television are all direct consequences of the information society. Thus while the early information society theorists over-egg the significance of change based on their own limited evidence, recent experience points to notable and potential developments often contrary to earlier expectations. However, neither theorists nor empirical experience provides a convincing analysis of the basis of some of the cultural manifestations of change as a result of technology.

While influential, the information society theorists have come in for a good deal of criticism. In the past few years the idea of an information age has been given increased impetus from the explosive growth in the internet and multi-media technology. In particular, there is the inevitability of greater connection capacity that will lead to the emergence of 'real time' communication, i.e., live pictures and sound, between individuals connected by contemporary technology.

> The same switches used to send a TV show to your home can also be used to
> send a video from your home to any other – paving the way for video phones ...
> The same system will allow anybody with a camcorder to distribute videos to the
> world (Elmer-Dewitt quoted in Poster, 1998: 258).

Though less theoretical thinking has accompanied these developments, the evidence of impacts is more visible and the implications of this growth in multi-media are currently being felt throughout the world. The critics of Bell and others make a convincing case for rejecting their analysis, though fail to substitute their own explanation of the growth in information and its impact. This is especially so given the recent developments in digital technology and the growth of the internet, neither of which really figured in Bell's analysis. But this renewed interest is focusing on both the trajectory of these developments and also some of the less progressive attributes. Three issues highlight this. First, there is the unequal access to the technology that is driving the growth in the internet and multi-media. It is disproportionately dominated by middle-class white males while large sectors of society are being left behind in this emerging new motor of society with the possibility that an information under-class will emerge which undermines the potential for a great levelling plurocracy envisaged by Masuda and other information society theorists:

> We are moving towards the twenty-first century with the very great goal of building a Computopia on earth (1985: 633).

Second, and related to the first wave of post-industrial society theorists discussed earlier, a number of recent cases have highlighted the redundancy and problematic nature of the nation–state where the internet is concerned. Information available in one country freely may be prohibited in another but the ease of access and the lack of a national origin on host addresses means that there are, in effect, no borders. There was recently an attempt by the German government to sue the American internet provider Compuserve for providing access to pornography on the internet, something that under the American First Amendment is permitted. Another question that arises is 'who is culpable in such cases?', the service provider, the site author or the telecommunications company that transmitted the data? One result is that nations are being forced to examine their laws to provide some form of common law as regards the internet, though

> Nation–states are at a loss when faced with a global communication network. Technology has taken a turn that defines the character of power of modern governments (Poster, 1998: 260).

Finally, there is the biggest issue for capital: the free and easy access to data that will increasingly involve prime products such as audio and video. There is already concern in the music industry about the piracy of music over the internet. The irony is that the introduction of the digital medium in the form of CDs in the early 1980s is exactly the medium that links computers and allows potentially infinite copies to be made. Like nation–states, big business is now running to catch up with the technological changes.

Interestingly, the last few years have seen some of the predictions of techno-logical growth come true, though with startlingly different consequences. Society *has* undoubtedly changed as a result of technology and in particular the greater use of computers. Nevertheless,

> The acceptance of the growing importance of IT, even an information revolution, is one thing, the acceptance of the idea of a new industrial revolution, a new kind of society, a new age, is quite another (Kumar, 1995: 17).

Whilst I agree with this sentiment, there is undoubtedly a change of some sort going on. Whether this is an effect of the growth in new technology or a cause of the dynamics of captialism is important to our understanding of a changing world, but of equal importance is a direction for that change. Does the information society theses help explain change to society? Not in their present form. They fail to adequately theorise it but nevertheless not even Webster or Kumar dismiss the idea of change of some kind, only that it is a clear break with what went before. There are also arguments and more recent changes that point to developments in the growth of information and its use that are beginning to represent significant changes but not of a new society. A different society that has echoes of familiar themes such as inequality appears to be emerging with its basis firmly in the dynamic of late capitalism.

FORDISM AND POST-FORDISM

In a similar and related development of the new times thesis there has been a (mainly Marxist) interpretation of the changes in the regime of accumulation and the wider implications for society throughout the 1970s and 1980s. Amin summarises it as a debate

> about the putative transition from one dominant phase of capitalist development
> in the post-war period to another thirty to fifty year cycle of development based
> upon very different economic, societal and political norms (1994: 3).

Fordism is a term that loosely refers to the mass production and Taylorist approach to management introduced by Henry Ford that emerged as a dominant regime of accumulation in the 1920s and 1930s up until roughly 1973 (Filion, 1996) and was characterised by an era of intensive accumulation and monopolistic regulation of the economy (Amin, 1994: 9). The oil crisis of 1973 heralded a turning point for Fordism with the higher expenditure on energy leading to higher production costs, world-wide economic slow down, reduced political expenditure and an undermining of the effects of Kenynesian demand management. In place of the Fordist regime of mass and standardised production, common values and a belief in science and progress came the emergence of small, specialist, high-tech and flexible production that helped undermine many of the cultural and social norms of Fordism. This change involved

> A shift to the new 'information technologies'; more flexible, decentralised forms
> of labour process and work organisation; decline of the old manufacturing base
> and the growth of the 'sunrise', computer-based industries; the hiving off or
> contracting out of functions and services; a greater emphasis on choice and
> product differentiation, on marketing, packaging and design, on the 'targetting'
> of consumers by lifestyle, taste, and culture rather than by categories of social

class; a decline in the proportion of the skilled, male, manual working class, the rise of the service and white-collar classes and the 'feminization' of the work force; an economy dominated by multinationals, with their new international division of labour and their greater autonomy from national state control; and the 'globalisation' of the new financial markets, linked by the communications revolution (Hall, 1988: 24).

The initial interpretation of these changes analysed them as a post-Fordist form of accumulation and production (Hall, 1988, Hall and Jaques, 1989) and, like the information society theorists, post-Fordist thinkers claim that changes in the economic sphere have wider implications particularly (and emphasising the left-leaning dominance of this school) in the realm of potentially breaking the stranglehold of capitalist determinism and logic. This hopeful spin is tempered by a more sombre realisation. It is no coincidence that many of the economic and social characteristics of post-Fordism have emerged in parallel with the ascendancy of right-wing and neo-liberal ideologies in the west (Harvey, 1990, Hall and Jaques, 1989) and, as such, the prospects for a renewed socialist project seem unlikely.

Amin (1994) identifies three broad positions within the post-Fordist debate. First, there is the *regulation approach* emanating from writers such as Aglietta (1979), Lipietz (1997) and Boyer (1990) that aim to 'encapsulate and explain the paradox within capitalism between its inherent tendency towards instability, crisis and change, and its ability to coalesce and stabilize around a set of institutions, rules and norms which serve to secure a relatively long period of economic stability' (Amin, 1994: 7). Thus the regulation school sought to both explain and project the future of capitalism against the backdrop of the seismic changes that had occurred in the mid 1970s and concentrated their efforts upon the embedding of social practices rather than the teleographic outcome of economic 'logic'. Two central ideas emerged to account for this. First is the *regime of accumulation*, or the informal rules, norms and ethics that maintain relationships within the economy and include, for example, patterns of consumption and demand, profit sharing and management theory. Second, is the *mode of regulation* which are the more formal rules and regulations that set out relationships between the different actors in the economy, including government, institutions, trade unions, etc. Changes in these two key concepts explain the changes and dynamics of different regimes of accumulation. Consequently, regulation theorists do not speak of post-Fordism as such because Fordism has gone through a number of different regimes, of which the post-1973 period is simply one of many. Similarly, different national contexts have different forms of accumulation – there is not one. Additionally, changes in the regime of accumulation or the mode of regulation do not imply a sudden rupture with the past but more of an evolution that contains new and similar elements:

classic Fordism continues to exist alongside changes identified by Hall and Jaques and others. What the 1970s witnessed was a periodic crisis of Fordism and not its demise.

Amin terms the second school *neo-Schumpeterian* given its basis in cyclical analysis and entrepreneurial capitalism. There is significant overlap between the neo-Schumpeterian analysis and that of the regulation school, particularly in its use of similar paradigms of accumulation and regulation. But the neo-Schumpeterian view is more dependent upon the post-industrial/information society emphasis on technology as the driving force behind the periodic crises of capitalism. Crises are resolved by technological or innovative break-throughs that initiate further techno-logical and social demands and thereby create the conditions for further sustained growth. Innovations and technology are not confined to new products but could also include changes such as improved understanding of manufacturing processes like those initiated under Fordism. Under this view, Fordism involved a regime of mass production and consumption which was challenged by the emerging techno-economic paradigm from the mid-1970s onwards. The shift between the mature, mass producing technologies and their social manifestations, and the newer spe-cialised production techniques enabled by technological advances accounts for the crisis of capitalism and its resolution.

Finally, there is the *flexible specialisation* approach as argued by Sabel (1982) and Piore (Piore and Sabel, 1984) among others. Amin considers this approach to be less theoretically founded than the other two and less concerned with the deterministic elements of economic theory. The key to understanding the changes in Fordism lie in the distinction between mass production and flexible specialisation – the former based on semi-skilled workers and the latter on more skilled workers. Both approaches have existed since the industrial revolution to fulfil different needs in the market. At the turn of the nineteenth century the mass production element was more dominant and 'crowded out' the more bespoke goods. However, what happened during the 1970s was that the flexible special-isation tenet became more dominant through the prevailing demands for cheap and differentiated goods which was reinforced by the widespread embracing of this concept by industry generally. Technology became available that enabled flex-ible and specialised production to meet the demand for less mass produced goods. The shift towards flexibility was as much social and political as determined by the inherent nature of capitalist development, and the social determinant for dif-ference certainly echoes the broad themes of fragmentation and rupture identified by the social theorists in the previous chapter and the sensibility of change dis-cussed further on in this chapter.

Each of the three schools has been subject to detailed scrutiny and criticism. Adherents to each school tend to criticise the other for their interpretation of

Fordism and the relationship between Fordism and Taylorist approaches. For example, Jessop (1994) identifies nine forms of Fordism building on the work of Tickel and Peck. The regulation school has also been accused of being reductionist in its portrayal of capitalism as having some sort of teleological logic when history demonstrates that rather than an unfolding logic, a more realistic view would emphasise discontinuity and struggle. As opposed to the economic determinism of the regulation school, neo-Schumpterians have been accused of favouring a technological reductionism. While technological change has been influential throughout history, other more important factors have often led the way such as social change in attitudes or cultural shifts in consumption. Many of the criticisms aimed at the information society theorists are equally applicable. In particular, experience demonstrates that recessions and down-turns in the economy can equally apply when there are technological break-throughs such as in the early 1980s and 1990s. The over-simplification and confusion of cause and effect have also been criticisms of the flexible specialisation school. Like the presentation of Fordism as homogenous, the dualism of flexible specialisation versus mass production is also seen as a caricature. As Jessop (1994) and others have also pointed out, there has been a high degree of diversity within Fordism that does not correspond to the neat binary oppositions of either mass production or flexible specialisation.

Regardless of the different interpretations, the broad analysis of post-Fordism points to change of some kind.

> All the approaches discussed . . . are rooted in different conceptual traditions,
> and . . . generalize at different levels of analysis. Reading across the approaches,
> however, there emerges a considerable degree of consensus as regards the
> nature, dynamic and crisis of the passing era (Amin, 1994: 16).

Equally, regardless of the criticism of technological determinism and economic reductionism, the emergence of the information society and post-Fordist parallel is no coincidence – the ability of firms to adapt to meet more eclectic and changeable demands to a large degree depends upon information technology and computerisation. Also, like the information society theorists, post-Fordism also concentrates on a disintegration and disorganisation within firms but also between firms. Rather than the Fordist and Marxist interpretation that on the whole theorises firms growing larger to maintain profitability, post-Fordists see the changes in firms as now favouring smaller, fragmented and specialised structures. Firms themselves become flexibly specialised using techniques such as computer-aided design and manufacture and by employing a small core of highly-skilled workers to change products quickly to meet changing demands.

Lash and Urry (1987) consider the broad changes in the economy as the emergence of 'disorganised capital' that undermines many of the theories and understandings of Fordist/Marxist analysis. Identifying many of the themes that were later to be developed by Giddens (1990) (see below), and attempting to explain some contemporary trends, they argue that this latest phase in capitalism has led to decentralised and globalised capital. This has had the effect of (among other things) dealigning class politics and a dissolving of corporatist industrial relations and the emergence of a new service class with its own distinctive values. The general upshot is a fragmentation and pluralisation of society and a distinctive new culture that heralds the end of traditional political opposition and requires a more sensitive analysis and reformulation of left-wing politics. Echoing Jameson and Laclau and Mouffe, they perceive a new set of interests emerging around which people can rally. Such groupings or 'nodes' of interest or collective identities will be unrecognisable from the previous manifestations given the radically different nature of this new form of disorganised capital.

The links between the changes in the form of accumulation and its effects on wider social and cultural aspects of life have been developed by others who draw on the interpretation of Lash and Urry. Hall and Jaques argue that, just as Fordism affected social life through its emphasis on de-skilling and regulation, so post-Fordism has a similar, though different impact:

> The transition, then, is not epochal – not in the sense of the classic transition
> from feudalism to capitalism, but as fundamental and far-reaching as, say, the
> transition in the closing stages of the 19th century from the 'entrepreneurial' to
> the advanced or organised stage within capitalism (Hall and Jaques, quoted in
> Kumar, 1995: 51).

The manifestations of this change are many and Kumar (1995: 52) has summarised them into three broad categories. In the *economy*, the shift from Fordism to post-Fordism includes the rise of the global economy and a consequent reduction in the importance of the nation–state. The rise of flexible specialisation, decentralisation and dispersal of production, flatter hierarchies, increased part-time working and shorter contracts. In *politics and industrial relations* we have witnessed a fragmentation of social class, a decline of national class-based politics and voting and the rise of single issue movements and the 'floating' voter. Unions have declined in size and significance as have mass parties. In *culture* there has been an increase in individualist modes of thought, entrepreneurship and an end of universal modes of thought and representation, a fragmentation of values and a more popularist approach to culture.

It is undeniable that capitalism is changing and that these changes are having a consequent impact upon other areas of life. It is the significance that is debatable. Like the post-industrial interpretations, it is more probable, as the post-Fordists argue though with different emphases, that what we are witnessing is another twist in the shape of capitalism. But we must not divorce the arguments of either view from the important fact that all the different interpretations are also arguing about the future of Marxism and its relevance in the late twentieth century. The post-Fordist analysis effectively undermines much of the relevance of Marxist analysis and as such there are other important interests at stake. Its strength is that it points to the strong economic foundations of much of the changes occurring as well as the over-spill into the social and cultural spheres.

We can see the parallels between the broad post-Fordist interpretation of change and some of the postmodern concerns in social theory, e.g., the emphasis on the local through social embedding of relationships and rules, and the rejection of grand theories such as economic or Marxist orthodoxy in favour of more contingent and complex determinants. What the broad post-Fordist interpretation does not do is provide a convincing non-economic analysis of change. Can we say that Madonna was a product of Fordism or post-Fordism? Neither can it escape its teleological and deterministic origins in logic of economics or Marxism. Some, such as David Harvey or Stuart Hall, attempt to interpret post-Fordism as being the motor behind cultural change. There is little doubt that changes in capitalism have influenced wider social and cultural practices. But they cannot adequately account for all the change that comes under the rubric of new times. While the different theories point to diversity and change, they are founded upon monolithic and monocausal theory that allows for no other determinant. Non-economic and reductionist interpretations of change are often called feelings or sensibility and it is to that interpretation of new times that I now turn.

SENSIBILITY

If post-industrialists and post-Fordists have a clear economic origin for the claims concerning new times, then the final broad collection of interpretations are more eclectic and without such definite basis. This is roughly what I mean by sensibility. Two broad aspects stand out. The first is the chronologically-based argument on the growth of difference or the postmodern of period. The second is the more aesthetic experience of difference in various fields including architecture, the arts, the media, politics, etc. Again, like most of the postmodern 'story', there is significant overlap between the two; for example, the emergence of postmodern architecture is both a chronological phenomenon and an aesthetic experience. Both aspects can and are analysed together and independently as part of the postmodern sensibility.

There has been a much longer experience of the postmodern in art and aesthetics than in social theory which really emerged post 1968 (Benko, 1997).

The term itself can be traced back to a number of different fields, many of which, as Best and Kellner point out, anticipated the ideas of current and more contemporary usage. Jones, et al. (1993) highlight a broad shift in thinking that was identified by Karl Mannheim in 1927. The rise of modern instrumental rationalism that accompanied the industrial revolution in the late eighteenth century created two broad schools of social and political thought: rationalistic and conservative. The latter were not only concerned with preservation of the status quo but also emphasised local particularity and diversity as well as rejecting teleological views of history and being suspicious of instrumental rationality. Jones, et al. imply obvious parallels here with the broad themes of postmodern thinking 200 years later and perhaps this accounts for Habermas' accusations of the postmodern as 'neo-conservatism'. Another precursor to current postmodern concerns can be found in the so-called romantics who sought to reclaim the sentimental, lost histories and methods suppressed by modernity. Through the mixing of

> literary genres, fusing of poetry and prose, and attempts to syncretize criticism,
> philosophy, science, history, and art, along with its tendency towards the
> progressive and infinite, [it] led to the production of varied forms of texts whose
> penultimate expression was the fragment (Jones, et al, 1993: 4).

Such fragments sought no overall meaning other than that which the reader gave. It was not until the post second world war era that the term postmodern began to be used to mean a definite shift in thinking and feeling that marked something new. Rosenberg and White (1957) built on the foundations provided by Toynbee to describe something different about society where western culture, industrialisation and urbanisation reduces diversity (the 'difference' here is ironically a growing sameness). Similarly, Drucker (1957) tries to pin down this feeling of difference while Mills (1959) believes that the modern age has been left behind:

> our basic definitions of society and of self are being overtaken by new realities
> (quoted in Best and Kellner, 1991: 8).

At this stage in the history of the postmodern the general view was that it was both ambiguous and transient. It reflected a diaspora of feelings and questions that heralded the beginning of something new – more often than not forged in the technological advances of the post-war world. But what exactly was new and its implications were not clear. Various fields began to simultaneously reflect upon and develop this new sensibility of change under the rubric of the postmodern. In architecture, Robert Venturi published *Complexity and Contradiction in Architecture* which discussed the pastiche of Las Vegas 'style' (1966). Susan Sontag wrote a number of influential essays including *Notes on Camp* that both enthused about the potential and 'release' of non-rationalist structures while criticising the straight-jackets of form and content characteristic of modernity. But as Best and Kellner (1991: 11) point out, the most prolific celebration and popularisation of literary postmodernism has been undertaken by Ihab Hassan. In various works from 1971 to 1987 he has charted the experiments and developments in 'anti-literature' characterised by a 'revulsion' against the western self. Hassan saw in modernism the principle of 'Authority' and in post-modernity, the principle of 'Anarchy'. The latter involved a tendency towards 'indeterminancy', a compound of pluralism, eclecticism, randomness and revolt (Kumar, 1995: 108). During the 1970s the postmodern began to gain a new ascendency particularly as the social theory of Foucault, Baudrillard and Lyotard began to challenge more orthodox thinking. But many aspects of the new sensibility that had previously existed in isolation from each other or from any form of unifying movement started to develop a consciousness. As Handy describes it:

> Baby-boom intelligentsia, in order to justify years spent watching The Jetsons
> and Batman, start thinking of those wasted years as cultural-historical research
> (1998: 55).

The most clearly-articulated shift to the postmodern undoubtedly came in architecture. In 1977 Charles Jencks published his *The Language of Postmodern Architecture* while in 1975 Philip Johnson's AT&T building in New York brought postmodern architecture to the attention of a wider non-architectural audience. Common terms and styles between the different aesthetic genres began to point towards something that represents more than an isolated or transient movement: pastiche, irony, cynicism, popularism and playfulness defined and described disparate developments in the arts. These developments were not without their critics (see below) but perhaps the most important contribution they made were the generally positive and opportunistic view of the new cultural and aesthetic shifts that led the way for the development of the postmodern during what has undoubtedly been 'its' decade: the 1980s:

> The cultural discourses ... shared certain epistemological perspectives with
> later postmodern theoretical discourse which emphasised difference, otherness,
> pleasure, novelty, and attacked reason and hermeneutics (Best and Kellner,
> 1991: 15).

One cannot forget, however, the extent to which, as Turner puts it:

> [The] meanings of modern and postmodern vary between different social
> science and humanities traditions (1990a: 4).

Nevertheless, there is a broad-based consensus covering roughly *what* has changed and *when*. For Benko (1997: 7) the post-1968 cultural world saw a shift from order to anarchy, organised activity to play, deconstruction replaces creation and individual liberty takes precedence over collective values in fields as diverse as architecture, cinema, music, dance, philosophy, psychoanalysis, theology, historiography, literature and literary criticism.

We can all point to examples of manifestations of this new postmodern aesthetic in different media. Indeed, it is now an academic industry to do so. But the postmodern seems to have developed even beyond this. For Berger, it is about surface, no depth, *'staying cool in the face of an increasingly chaotic world is the essence of the new postmodern attitude'* (1998: 50). It's now more than an avant-garde reaction, it's a way of coping with the times. This raises the possibility of the postmodern as sensibility merging with the manifestations of postmodern as new times in an almost symbiotic way. The latter raises the problems of technological determinism, chaos and insecurity while the former provides a cultural and social basis for reaction. For Hardy, the postmodern is anything that's 'sort of old but sort of new, a little bit ironic, or kind of self-conscious – like movies that steal bits from old movies' (1998: 52). Even postmodern irony now creeps into the definition of the postmodern.

> It's [the postmodern] culturespeak, shorthand for *Stuff That's Cool Now*. It's the postmodern (you know what I mean) version of *groovy*, except that using it makes you sound smart (Handy, 1998: 52).

In place of the modern emphasis on unity, we have an abandonment of the search for unity. There is instead textuality, arbitrariness, interpretation, pastiche, juxtaposition, that all take place in the present. So, where can we see/feel/experience this? Just about everywhere apparently. For Soloman, the postmodern spirit pervades everything 'from an Andy Warhol soup can to the music of Talking Heads' (1998: 36). It has manifestations in film, architecture, fast food restaurants, shopping malls, the Internet, jokes, fashion, sport and museums to name a few. I will briefly explore two examples.

Miller and Reed (1998) have argued that baseball has lost its grand modern narratives of the American Dream – the working-class work ethic of economic and material success. The turning point, they argue, was the 1994 baseball strike where the 'working class hero' was revealed as being more about greed and self-promotion, individuality and anti-authoritarianism. In place of modern, more heroic values has risen

> a sense of limits, of relativity, of varied styles and goals, and skepticisms about progress and perfectability (1998: 26).

Part of the reason for this shift has been the role of TV (Miller and Reed make some loose parallels with Baudrillard's theories of simulacra). The audience for baseball through TV now includes fans who have never seen a 'live' game (the implication being that these are in some way less 'pure' than the 'real' fan). Baseball has shifted from an idealistic modern game to the progressively profit-orientated postmodern media event.

Not being a fan of baseball I will have to take Miller and Reed's account at face value, though if we see baseball as sport writ large then parallels can be drawn with soccer, tennis or other sports. The details may be different but the broad trends are similar – from amateur ethics of fair play to professional spectacles of merchandise and money. But to what degree is their portrayal of the two baseballs accurate or merely a product of a simplistic binary opposition or even nostalgia? Did the 'working class', modern heroes of the sport play for nothing but the love of the game? To what extent was the American Dream a reality or product of an idealistic goal? American politicians still talk of an 'American Dream' (which was, after all, about the meta-narratives of 'life, liberty and the pursuit of happiness'). How far have the means and ends of these changed or have they simply been implemented differently? It could be argued that what Miller and Read point to is nothing more than difference or change but with strong consistencies between their modern and postmodern. This raises an argument I shall develop later which has two main strands. First, that there are strong continuities between the modern and the postmodern and second, that some of the features now termed postmodern were actually part of the modern and previously termed the avant-garde.

Berger (1998) has explored the postmodern world of art museums or galleries as a consequence of both the breakdown of high and pop-art and the postmodern spectacle of consumption and entertainment. In modern times, museums used to be places were society showed the best and most inspiring of paintings and sculpture. Now, in the postmodern sensibility,

> Art is happening on streets, TV sets, movie theatres, and theme parks ...
> certainly not in those dreadful places that make me feel hurt (Granley, quoted in
> Berger, 1998: 89).

As art has changed, the role of the museum has also changed. From a modernist interpretation of high-art and high-art museums to a postmodern situation of popular multifarious art and a corresponding pluralism of places where art is exhibited and consumed. As Berger puts it:

> They are no longer quiet, no longer dull, no longer essentially repository
> institutions devoted essentially to preserving the cultural canon and the
> aesthetic status quo. They have become absorbed, like so many other aspects
> of contemporary society, with the culture of entertainment (1998: 97).

Now there are exhibitions of the comic strip, multi-media interfaces, 'live' demonstrations that combine information with entertainment. Berger's descriptions certainly sound a chord with general experience. It does seem that there are now countless museums or 'experiences' as they seem to be increasingly called. But surely what he describes (however accurately) points to the difficulty is ascribing a clear definition of the term 'post' – it seems that we still have museums, only that they are different in terms of their exhibits and means. Maybe the art is more postmodern than the museums themselves? On the other hand, one could argue, as Kumar does, that the act itself has not changed:

> it is difficult to see in what way there has been any real departure from modernism. The antinomian, anarchic, anti-systemic character of postmodernism seems at one with the form and the spirit of much of what we understand as modernism, especially that aspect of it associated with the theory and practice of the avant-garde (Kumar, 1995: 109).

The interdeterminancy of the claim to a distinctive and different postmodern culture are clearer in some fields than others. In architecture it is much easier to point to the playful juxtaposition of styles than it is to argue that MTV is more postmodern than *I Love Lucy*. This is not to deny the existence of difference, only to question the degree of change. So the postmodern as sensibility like the information society and post-Fordist interpretation of new times provides some indicators of change, points to some clear differences (and continuities) but flounders on its ability to identify something distinctly post in the culture per se that is not either limited or could not be explained by the tensions and manifestations of capitalism and modernity. These objections are not new or particularly devastating to the postmodern. But they do raise some important questions that critics of the postmodern consider to be significant enough to seriously question the whole postmodern project.

CRITICISM OF THE POSTMODERN

The postmodern social theory and new times challenge to modernity has itself not gone unchallenged. Its defenders and the critics of the postmodern are legion (if somewhat eclectic) but here I shall focus on Giddens, Habermas, Harvey and Eagleton who all seek to defend modernity as the basis of their left-leaning optimism for a 'new' and emancipatory society. Rejecting the postmodern conclusions (though admitting to some of the analyses) they wish to preserve or rediscover the foundationalist basis of centre-left politics and as such have a defensive and begrudging tone, as if having to defend the unfinished 'project' of the Enlightenment is an unnecessary distraction. For example:

> [Habermas] directs fierce criticism at any intellectual development, whether it
> occurs in art, science, social theory or whatever, where Enlightenment concepts
> (order, reason) and ambitions (emancipation, progress) are seemingly
> dismantled for no purpose other than that of perverse negation (Cloke et al.,
> 1991: 189).

Similarly, Eagleton rants about the trivialisation of important issues and the loss of the 'big picture' where

> morality [is] about adultery rather than armaments, sexual deviancy rather than
> starvation (1996: 70).

However, one of the benefits of the postmodern critiques has been to force modernity's defenders to engage with their detractors and to (reluctantly) accept some of their arguments. Although a harsh (and amusing) critic of the postmodern, Eagleton, for example, maintains that

> It has put the skids under a number of complacent certainties, prised open
> some paranoid totalies, contaminated some jealously protected purities, bent
> some oppressive norms and shaken some rather frail looking foundations
> (1996: 27).

Other than a broad defence there are three main arguments of the 'pro' modernists. First, that modernity's critics have got it wrong. The contrasts with the premodern period are misleading and inaccurate and their position is unduly pessimistic and inchoate. Further, what they identify as evidence of modernity's 'death' is in reality no more than a consequence of modernity. Second, while modernity has a 'sombre' (as opposed to 'dark') side (and while some of the critiques of the critical-moderns are accepted), modernity is (and must be) redeemable. Besides, the postmodern itself is as much a double-edged sword as modernity, bringing with it both hope and despair. Third, we are stuck with modernity, whether we like it or not, so let's make the best of it rather than trying to destroy it.

As outlined in Chapter 1, criticism of modernity and the Enlightenment has been ongoing for most of this century through, for example, the work of the Frankfurt School: The postmodern in many ways built on that from the late 1960s onwards so it is surprising therefore that it is not until the early 1980s that a rigorous (mainly left-wing) defence of modernity as well as a counter attack on the postmodern is forthcoming. There are two main reasons for this. First, although criticism of modernity has a long history it is not until the 1970s that a more coherent picture emerges that brings together disparate strands of thinking and presents a more coherent critique. The date 1973 was a particular watershed as the ramifications of the oil crisis (the undermining of Keynesian orthodoxy and the start of the neo-liberal ascendancy) met the blossoming of technological changes in the economy and society in a world becoming disenchanted with Marxist-socialism. The spectre of postmodernism provided not only a critique, but in some cases also emerges as an alternative and with this alternative comes a concrete challenge to the values and forms of modernity. Perhaps the delay in reaction to the challenge came from the make-up of many postmodern thinkers who, by and large, came from a left-leaning position. Disenchanted with the dashed hopes of potential revolutions in 1968, the totalitarian nightmares of Soviet-style socialism and the seemingly impervious nature of western capitalism many left-wing intellectuals started to search for alternatives:

> If the the more abstract questions of state, class, mode of production, economic justice, had proved for the moment too hard to crack, one might always shift ones attention to something more intimate and more immediate, more sensuous and particular (Eagleton, 1996: 17).

Such an alternative seriously challenges the foundational nature of theory including, importantly, historical materialism or Marxist-based approaches. It is perhaps not surprising therefore that Marxists like Eagleton should feel bitterness towards the 'weakness' of former Marxists such as Lyotard and Baudrillard for abandoning 'the faith'. There is an irony however. Although Marxist-inspired thinkers sought major changes in the mechanisms of the Enlightenment and modernity (particularly its capitalist basis) they have been forced to become one of its main defenders against anti-foundationalist challenges to their own privileged analysis.

The main argument of the pro-modernists is to dismiss the postmodern critiques as being no more than an aspect of modernity or a reaction to a specific (unwelcome) aspect of it. For Habermas and Harvey, modernity was always dynamic and pushing at new boundaries and barriers and frontiers. What has happened, according to Habermas, is that aesthetic modernity has reacted against the invasion of its domain by instrumental rationality. According to Habermas' interpretation, the original aim of the Enlightenment was to

> develop objective science, universal morality and law, and autonomous art, according to their own inner logic. At the same time, this project intended to release the cognitive potentials of each of these domains to set them free from their esoteric forms (1981: 9).

The pervasive spread of instrumental rationality due to its underpinning of capitalism from science into other fields such as art is modernity's 'dark side'.

I have included Jameson under the postmodern social theorists in Chapter 2 but he could equally be seen to occupy an anti-postmodern position because of his influence upon other Marxist-inspired defenders who are less inclined to take a positive view of postmodernism. As I argued earlier, Jameson (1984) follows a similar line to Habermas and seeks to claim postmodernity as modernity's own. His is the most daring attempt by Marxists to build on what he sees as the postmodern world without abandoning the meta-narrative of Marxism. But beyond his own heavily-used contribution to the pro-modern movement in the early 1980s, he has undoubtedly influenced other Marxist -inspired attempts to hold back the postmodern tide. Harvey (1990) for one, follows Jameson's 'late modern' path and also argues that modernity itself is behind the phenomenon of postmodernity and the postmodern critics are merely unmasking its latent logic and manifestations. Using more classical Marxist imagery, Harvey sees modernity and its associated capitalism going through another 'crisis', and this crisis is what the postmodernists are using as the basis for their criticisms. Like Habermas, he accepts that there are some progressive and reactionary aspects to the criticisms. However, the progressive merely helps us in pointing out where modernity failed or fell short of the mark while the reactionary seeks only to destroy. Harvey has generated a great deal of critical acclaim for his work (both good and bad). For example, Pile and Rose (1992) castigate it for its smugness and refusal to admit gender and race into the centrality of social relations and its universalising assumptions and prescriptions. Pile and Rose's uncontained anger at Harvey could equally be applied to the other defenders of modernity and derives in large part from the materialist basis of his analysis. This does raise an interesting aspect of the modern/postmodern debate that, despite its subtleties below the surface, it does tend to fall into a binary (modern) confrontation. I tackle this question in more detail below. Richard Rorty provides a useful 'way in' to the (highly abstracted) 'two camps' and effectively criticises both as missing the point. Against the pro-modern he argues that Habermas and others feel the need to defend modernity and the Enlightenment because not to do so would betray the philosophical foundationalism that goes back to Descartes:

> The preservation of the Platonic ideas that our most distinctively human faculty was our ability to manipulate 'clear and distinct' ideas, rather than to accomplish feats of social engineering, was Descartes' most important and most unfortunate contribution to what we now think of as 'modern philosophy' (Rorty, 1985: 170).

Habermas' defence of modernity is for the sake of foundational philosophy, not modernity and masks the fact that his different types of reason have not made a significant difference to society, but political discourses (by which Rorty means pragmatic and progressive events and situations) have.

> It is, after all, things like the formations of trade unions, the meritocratization of
> education, the expansion of the franchise, and cheap newspapers, which have
> figured most largely in the willingness of the citizens of the democracies to see
> themselves as part of a communicative community (1985: 169).

As the pro-modern protestations are themselves without foundation because
reason never had much impact upon modernity, then the postmodern criticisms
must also be less than relevant. The objectives of the Enlightenment have
been met regardless and despite of the role played by foundationalists such
as Habermas and Giddens and critical-modernists such as Nietzsche, Adorno,
Horkheimer, Foucault, et al. However, going beyond his criticism of both camps,
he does draw on elements of both to define his own position. From the post-
structuralists he takes the concept of multiple selves set out by Foucault
and Derrida above. Moral choices are merely the fact that we belong to
multiple communities simultaneously. From the modernists he lifts Habermas'
'ideal speech' and 'undistorted communication' but puts these down to liberal politics rather than the necessary defence of the lifeworld. Though Rorty can be rightly
criticised for his somewhat smug vision of the benefits of western liberalism and
their universal application, he does provide an important counter position that provides an alternative to the binary oppositions of the critical- and pro-modern
camps.

The problem with the analyses of Habermas and Harvey is that they are
prisoners of their own position. Forced to defend foundational thought, modernity
(and by association capitalism) from a stand point that also wants to see it
undermined and eventually overthrown, they at best sound prickly and at worst dis-
missive and unconvincing. However, in an extremely thorough defence of modernity, Giddens (1990) provides a more reflective and balanced view that goes
further than Habermas and Harvey in his interpretation of the 'sombre side' and
rejects his interpretation of the spread of instrumental rationality into other spheres.
For Giddens, the 'sombre' sides of modernity are the outcome of the very forces
upon which society has progressed – e.g., dull, repetitive and degrading labour
and environmental degradation are all the flip side of increased choice and economic, social and political welfare. He also goes on to criticise some of the foundational perspectives of the critics of modernity. Weber's view concerning the
iron cage of bureaucracy, for example, is wide of the mark in late modernity
where organisations have to be spontaneous and flexible to survive. In place of the
image of the Holocaust, Giddens argues we should instead consider modernity a
juggernaut:

> a runaway engine of enormous power which, collectively as human beings, we
> can drive to some extent but also threatens to rush out of control and which

could rend itself asunder. The juggernaut crushes those who resist it, and while it sometimes seems to have a steady path, there are times when it veers away erratically in directions we cannot foresee. This ride is by no means unpleasant or unrewarding, it can often be exhilarating and charged with hopeful anticipation. But as long as the institutions of modernity endure we shall never be able to control completely either the path or the pace of the journey. In turn, we shall never be able to feel entirely secure, because the terrain across which it runs is fraught with risks of high consequence. Feelings of ontological security and existential anxiety will coexist in ambivalence (1990: 139).

Criticising the postmodern sentiments on a broad scale, Giddens argues that modernity has not witnessed the loss of community or the infringement of the Habermas 'system' into the 'lifeworld'. Instead, modernity has created a complex relationship between both familiarity and estrangement that defies simple explanation. But further, and building on the ironic emphasis of postmodernity, Giddens seems to scorn the 'revelation' of a 'nostalgia' mode. People are aware of their life choices that involve a shifting balance between the 'advances' afforded by modernity (e.g., time-saving consumer durables) and the 'one foot in the past' feeling that drives the retro look. This paradox is a natural consequence of modernity, not an indication of its decadence. Instead of a one-way street of increasingly restricted opportunities and scenarios, Giddens claims that modernity creates a two-way street that emphasises a complex disembedding and re-embedding of social relations.

The self-same processes that lead to the destruction of older city neighbours and their replacement by towering office-blocks and skyscrapers often permit gentrification of other areas and a recreation of locality (1990: 142).

Similarly, in place of the postmodern focus on impersonality, we have a dynamic of intimacy and impersonality, a situation that is not too different from pre-modern times. Relationships can be maintained over great distances through telecommunications and while we still and will always depend on 'experts', people know far more than they did and can, if they wish, become even more knowledgeable in those areas. The question is not 'are we living in new times?', but 'how should we react?', or how best can we ride the juggernaut to minimise the danger but maximise the opportunities? The answers Giddens (1990: 135) provides are a neat summary of the positions we all face and the difference between the critical- and pro-modern stances.

- Progressive acceptance. Surviving while accepting that so much is outside our control that the most we can hope for are temporary gains.
- Sustained optimism. To persist with the attitudes of the Enlightenment and have faith in its reason.

- • Cynical pessimism. The resorting to black humour and nihilism.
- • Radical engagement. Practical contestation towards perceived sources of danger to reduce or transcend impacts.

As opposed to the view that the postmodern is modernity in a dynamic state, there is an eminent and large body of opinion that argues that much of what has been proclaimed as postmodernity is an 'add on' to modernity, dependent upon it (Kumar, 1995: 109, Best and Kellner, 1991, Wollen, 1993), or at the very least significant and largely consistent with it:

> postmodern thought is clearly traceable from modern 'bloodlines' (Dear, 1997: 49)

Even Lyotard, in a much overlooked (ignored?) argument claims that the postmodern (which he rejects as a description of new times) is no more that modernist avant-garde:

> modernism has allowed itself to become ossified, bureaucratised and commercialised. It no longer challenges and threatens, as it should. Post-modernism is the form modernism takes when it has lost its revolutionary elan. It is the aspect of modernity that constantly reminds it of its essentially subversive and disruptive purpose (quoted in Kumar, 1995: 110).

For Lyotard, a 'work can become modern only if it is first postmodern. Post-modernism thus understood is not modernism at its end but in its nascent state, and this state is constant' (1984: 79). In other words, the postmodern is the constant cutting edge or vanguard of the modern – every period has some form of the postmodern emphasising a 'sameness with difference' as Jones, et al. (1993: 2) term it.

> It [the postmodern] shadows modernism. Modernism lurks in its sequel, haunts it. The very fact that a phenomenon is called 'postmodern' – that it differs from modernism by nothing more than a prefix – pays tribute to the power of modernism's cultural force field and suggests that postmodernism might be no more or less than an aftermath or hiatus (Gitlin, 1998: 63).

Gitlin goes on to claim that modernism tore up unity and postmodernity has been enjoying the shreds in an orgy that will be resolved with a new form of social and economic order. In the mean time we have to live with the confusion and stress of the postmodern: 'Postmodernity is modernity without the hopes and dreams which made modernity bearable' (Hebdige, 1988: 195). To back up the argument that every era has its own postmodern, Turner claims that the 'Baroque crisis' in Spain and France during the first half of the eighteenth century was initiated by transformations in the world economy leading to cultural crises or individualism and commercialism that heralded the industrial revolution. Artwork of the time 'celebrated artificially, mixing high and low culture, and playfully manipulated kitsch to produce, through its own version of the culture industry, a mass culture' (1990a: 9). The transformations eventually heralded capitalism and modernity implying that we are in some sort of transition now.

Within this evolutionary and cyclical development (a teleological view that postmodernists would naturally reject) there will be counter voices or voices of dissent just as modernity had. Therefore we should expect and welcome the tensions and questions that arise. Best and Kellner (1991: 257) claim that there are theorists within the modern tradition who are critical and reflective about overly-totalising and positivist currents in modern theory, while a whole tradition of modern theory including Marx, Dewey and Weber call for theory to be reflective and self-critical. In addition, some modern theory recognises differentiation and fragmentation (see Chapter 7). These traditions are largely ignored by the overly dogmatic view of modern theory as totalising and positivist. But Eagleton (1996) goes further than this and argues that postmodernists conflate and confuse terms, including, for example, hierarchy and elitism. What is actually wrong with hierarchy, he asks, when everybody subscribes to some form of hierarchy of values? The multifarious nature of postmodern society means that such thinking about what is 'better' or 'worse' is obsolete according to many postmodern social theorists. Such theories belong to the past. But, as many have argued, there are difficulties in presenting an epochal break. Although Jencks puts the start of postmodernity at 3.32 pm on 15th July, 1972 when the modernist Pruitt-Igoe scheme was demolished, Antonio and Kellner (1994) highlight the complex constituents of modernity and postmodernity.

Part of the problem is the stark or binary nature of much of the debate which precludes the questions concerning overlaps and continuities raised above. Table 3.1 follows many authors and presents a (typical) set of oppositions with regard to the modern/postmodern hiatus.

Pile and Rose (consciously) fall into the modernist trap of presenting modernity and postmodernity as false oppositions to each other to demonstrate the resulting binary nature of the debate. As they put it:

> can postmodernists dismiss the claims of modernist critical theory and still play
> a critical role, and can modernists dismiss the claims of the postmodernists and
> still be critical? (1992: 129).

Similarly, Mommaas (1996) warns against pitting the modern against the postmodern while Berg (1993) is concerned about the construction of modernism and postmodernism as unified, monolithic essences situated in opposition to each other. He goes on to argue that in some ways the binary nature of the debate

Table 3.1 The (allegedly) false oppositions of modernity and postmodernity

Modernism	Postmodernism
Purpose	Play
Hierarchy	Anarchy
Mastery	Exhaustion
Distance	Participation
Centring	Decentring
Genre/boundary	Text/intertext
Metaphor	Metonymy/synecdoche
Grand narrative	Local narrative
Master code	Idiolect
Reading	Writing
Phallus	Androgyny
Paranoia	Schizophrenia
Origin/cause	Difference/trace
Determinancy	Interdeterminancy
Transcendence	Immanence
The 'one'	The 'many'
Clarity	Ambiguity
Community	Dissemination
Explosion	Implosion
Production	Simulation
Centre	Margin
Transparency	Opacity
History	Genealogy
The real	The hyperreal
Foundationalism	Nihilism

Source: Pile and Rose (1992): 128

could be inhibiting (though not a waste of time) and 'old hat'. Although Benko pits modernity against the postmodern in some kind of fight to the death, engaged in 'a headlong flight from the present. Each represents an attempt to impose a new cultural regime' (1997: 1) do we have to 'choose' between the postmodern and the modern? And it is not simply modernists who portray the situation in a binary light. Eagleton, for example, argues that for all its talk of plurality, the postmodern operates on strict binary codes of opposition that include a multitude of moral prescriptions:

> hybridity is preferable to purity, plurality to singularity, difference to self identity (1996: 28).

This point is picked up by Wilder (1998) who argues that the binary opposites of modernity and postmodernity inevitably lead to 'missed information' that exists between the two extremes. This is driven by the digital nature of much of the postmodern technology and culture which mirrors what Kosko (1994) describes as the logical positivist inheritance from modernity and specifically, the scientific emphasis of the Enlightenment. The main thrust of the argument about new times has been the liberating effects of technology but it could also be argued that digitial technology can actually reduce choices by presenting a bivalent representation of a multivalent reality.

So where do these criticisms leave the postmodern? Undoubtedly there are many salient points. But here are three main criticisms of the critics themselves. First, they tend to present the postmodern as a straw man and mostly portray it in a grotesque and narrow way, as a monolithic essense and more often than not focusing on the extreme postmodern thinkers such as Baudrillard as representative. This is understandable to a degree, as some of the postmodern is based on a style that is rather easy to caricature or ridicule. Lemert sums this up well:

> It is true that there is stupid theory done in the name of postmodernism just as there is stupidity done in the name of social psychology or cultural studies or economics. Opponents of postmodernism, of which there are very many, seize upon the unexceptional stupidity of *some* things postmodern in order to mock the thing itself. This amounts to the same as judging the Russian people by the failures of the Soviet regime or, for that matter, judging the merits of sin by the unexceptional fact that preachers commit it in spite of their theories (1997: x).

There needs to be some serious engagement with the broad spectrum of ideas. As we saw in Chapter 2, the postmodern of Laclau and Mouffe cannot be described as being closely related other than by name and some broad concerns to that of Baudrillard. Yet it is the latter and some of the more extreme forms of social theory that the critics mostly attack without largely seeing the more constructive and worthy arguments of others. The almost hysterical reaction to postmodernism from those largely to be found in the 'Save Modernism Camp' seems to emanate from an evangelical desire to save humanity from slipping back into the primordial sludge from which the Enlightenment lifted them. Second, the critics fall into the trap of mixing their postmoderns or focusing on one aspect (e.g., Scott Lash and culture). This again is partly understandable as many postmodern advocates also blur the distinctions between, for example, social theory and new times. But this is a criticism of them that should not be repeated if a clear picture of the different arguments is to emerge. Eagleton admits that there are different meanings of the postmodern but then fires an indiscriminate grapeshot at them all when a more discerning and selective approach would have appeared less reactionary and more grounded. This raises the point made earlier that many of the critics have more than academic interest at heart. There is an immanent struggle for the future of socialism within the modern/postmodern positions that come down to values and ideology as much as argument and reason. Finally, the critics largely ignore or at best pay lip-service to the positive aspects of the postmodern. In social theory there is a useful thrust of unmasking and deconstructing accepted truths. In new times there are the insights into the evolving nature of capitalism. Unfortunately, the critics tend to want to throw the baby and the bathwater out together. But I am being unfair and portraying the critics as homogenous in the same way that I am accusing them of doing to the postmodernists. There are, of course, gradations of criticism and some, such as Jameson and (to a lesser extent) Eagleton, do try to engage some of the more positive aspects of postmodern theory but only in so far as they see it as an unnecessary distraction and merely a new label on something which is undoubtedly (even if it exists) modern.

So What is the Postmodern?

Throughout this work I have been using the term 'postmodern' but it should be clear from the above that there is a strong body of argument that either questions its existence at all or argues that it is merely part of the modern.

1 DIFFERENCE OR CONTINUITY?

Part of the problem lies in the differing use and definition of the term postmodern. Jones, et al. (1993: 10) point to what they term 'overlapping' usage. For Lash and Urry and Jameson it means a new era of capitalism (Jameson prefers the term 'late' though does use the pre-fix 'post') but within capitalism. For Baudrillard and others it signifies modernity's end and something beyond. For Bauman it is a reflective period, for others it is 'sameness with difference'. The different perspectives on the postmodern depend to a large degree on what you are looking at, the use to which you put it and a plethora of other (often hidden) agendas:

> varied horizons of expectation and significance perpetrated by disciplinary demarcations lead interpreters in different disciplines to interpret ... thinkers in different ways (Jones, et al., 1993: 10).

What is clear is that even with such a caveat, there are significant continuities between the modern and the postmodern in all the fields examined – social theory and new times. The lack of clarity concerning whether the postmodern is 'new' or 'part of' the modern comes down to the cache of the terms and the academic and ideological interests involved. Would a loose collection of views that claimed to be merely a continuation of something gain such prominence?

Turning to the different views expressed earlier in this chapter, it is difficult to conclude anything other than a complex blend of continuity and difference. The technological changes that form the basis of the information society theorists' view of new times can actually be seen to be a continuation of many trends and developments. They provide little more than a feeling of difference:

> Informational capitalism has restructured work and industrial organisation, but in ways mostly consistent with the existing principles of Taylorism and scientific management (not to mention those of capitalist accumulation) (Kumar, 1995: 155).

Technological development is driven in part and is reflective of pressures and trends identified elsewhere under the general sensibility of the postmodern, e.g., individuality, consumption, immediate delivery and ephemeral duration. To claim, therefore, that technology is leading societal change is to miss its relationship to capital and its use as a tool of other motors of change.

Post-Fordist analyses all point to strong continuities and differences. The continuities derive both from the logic of capitalist development (which varies depending on the different emphases) and the resistance and even victory of capitalism (according to Fukuyama). Looking beyond the superficial attraction of the crude post-Fordist analysis, it is clear that the regulation school's interpretation of flexible specialisation and mass production existing side-by-side underlines this continuity view. On the other hand, it is possible to point to changes such as the de-alignment of political voting and parties, the growing feminisation of the workforce alongside non-unionisation and the expansion of temporary work. But differences are merely an symptom of capitalism and not therefore a genuine rupture.

2 NEW OR DIFFERENT TIMES?

Are we living in new times? To answer this question we must first ask what are the manifestations of this? It appears that they are mainly cultural or social, e.g., art, literature, employment characteristics such as part-time working, and many 'feelings' such as insecurity, helplessness, etc. But it is clear from the discussions on post-industrial society in its many interpretations that capitalism is the driving force behind what are broadly termed 'new times.' As such we can point to similarities and continuities as well as radical difference, e.g., the nation–state or poverty. No postmodern social theory adequately theorises this combination of change and similarity mainly because such thinking is precluded by the general dismissal of such grand narratives. What some of the postmodern social theorists have done (particularly Jameson and the early Baudrillard) is add a cultural 'edge' to capitalism arguing that culture has invaded the economy and become a product in its own right.

Culture has ceased to be, if it ever was, a decorative addendum to the 'hard
world' of production and things, the icing on the cake of the material world . . .
Through design, technology and styling, 'aesthetics' has already penetrated the
world of modern production. Through marketing, layout and style, the 'image'
provides the mode of representation of the body on which so much of modern
consumption depends (Hall, 1988: 28).

Capitalism has created a dynamic that has driven massive cultural changes which
undermine and question much established thinking, e.g., Marxism, or even mask
and hide reality behind layers of seemingly significant phenomena. This gives an
illusion of change.

Clearly, there are also some strong parallels and continuities between the
modern and the postmodern that at least raise a question mark over the meaning and
significance of the prefix 'post'. Obviously the emphasis placed on different aspects
plus the uncertainty of forecasting change provide some explanation of this. Another
is provided by Bloch who argues that we can live in several different times at once,
for example, Nazi Germany and the liberal democracy of the US existed side-by-side.
Raymond Williams made the distinction between residual, dominant and emergent
cultures that provide a dynamic and less binary picture of multiple cultures of which
the modern and the postmodern may be part (Best and Kellner, 1991: 279).

But perhaps the best explanation relies more on human psychology for a clue
to the feeling of new times. 'New Labour: New Britain' was the slogan of the *New*
Labour party at the 1997 UK general election. To be new is somehow good and
advancing towards a better destination which is vague enough for everyone to sign
up to. It is tempting and alluring to think we are living in new and different times,
something that marks us out from the past. This feeling itself is not 'new' and has
been around for at least 1000 years. But in the present era the idea of difference
and newness is amplified by a unique nexus of other factors (Allmendinger and
Chapman, 1999). The end of the Cold War and the liberalisation of much of
eastern Europe provides the basis for Fukuyama's 'end of history' thesis and the
feeling of both relief and opportunity (Callinicos, 1991). The neo-liberal ascendancy and dominance of politics in nation-states around the world seems to be
coming to an end, perhaps signalling the breaking of the relationship between the
postmodern emphasis on individualism and the economic and social model of the
new right. There are those who would argue that the alternatives to new right
agendas are really nothing more than 'neo-liberal socialism' but in the UK, mone-
tarist orthodoxy has been combined with a minimum wage, a welfare to work programme and an independent Bank of England. Finally, there is the millennium and
its potent mix of celebration, reflection, boredom and despair. Psychologically
these are powerful influences of 'change'.

The conclusion must be that we are living in different times, just as the 1950s were different to the 1930s.

> Whether 'postmodernism' is the best name for what is going on in this world may be reasonably doubted. That something powerful, deep, and potentially far-reaching is going on seems to me beyond doubt (Lemert, 1997: xi).

The main driving force and consistency is capitalism and its ever-evolving motor of change into new forms of production and consumption and new spheres such as culture. *Different* as opposed to *new* is more than a semantic subtlety. The forms and degrees of consistency effectively mean that planning is facing a capitalist system that has mutated itself. But it is still essentially a capitalist system and planning is still an intervention in that system. It is the mutations of that system that provide the new challenges.

3   POSITIVE OR NEGATIVE SOCIAL THEORY?

There is a disturbing lack of action underpinning much of postmodern social theory that is worrying for a largely action-orientated pursuit such as planning. It is not until the later thinking of, for example, Laclau and Mouffe that theory actually begins to develop principles to guide action (arguably this is not postmodernism at all) but as Eagleton rightly concludes:

> Talk of whether the signifier produces the signified or vice versa, valuable though it doubtless is, is not quite what stormed the Winter Palace or brought down the Heath government (1996: 13).

Some could accuse Eagleton of having his cake and eating it, cherry picking from postmodern social theory for tools or mechanisms, but within a strictly modernist framework. But surely social action requires more than simply revealing or deconstructing 'reality' and waiting for the emergence of change? This is a key difference between the different social theorists that I highlighted at the beginning of the chapter, between the nihilistic thinking of Baudrillard, etc. and the more constructive and critical postmodernisms of Foucault, etc. This is not to say that the tools of postmodern social theory (an artificial label given its rejection by Foucault, Lyotard and others) do not seriously undermine or question modernism, which they clearly do. But given the disaporatic nature of such thinking one is inevitably confronted with choices about what weight to give each, what to do with them and how to proceed. Much of postmodern social theory appears to have close affiliations with a neo-liberal or new-right agenda, particularly concerning its socially atomistic ('no such thing as society') perspective. To follow this 'emergent social structure view' would be to sign up (consciously or not) to a society where intervention and community action were secondary to market principles. Similarly, the emphasis of some postmodern social theory on de-differentiation, in claiming that segregation, stratification and hierarchy are irrelevant and/or dated, is to abandon one form of organisation without offering a replacement. For these reasons I reject the extreme nihilism of some postmodern social theory. What does this leave? Much postmodern theory is good at deconstructing but not so good at rebuilding. The question of how to go about this for planning is covered in Chapters 7 and 8.

If the basis of a new planning is to be predicated upon *action*, *community* and *difference*, then the postmodern social theory that has most use comes in two forms. First, there is the questioning or revealing potential of the different positions per se. This is regardless of whether they are extreme or constructive. Second, there is the constructive basis for a modified modernism. Here the work of Laclau and Mouffe, Haber, and others provides a sound springboard. So postmodern social theory has three uses for rethinking planning: as a critique, as a liberating framework for allowing other kinds of thinking to exist and challenge the status quo, and as a prescriptive basis for planning itself.

MAIN THEMES

From the preceding discussion it is clear that I sign up to a humble postmodern, following in the footsteps of, for example, Bauman and Huyssen. There can never be an answer to the question 'what is the postmodern?' as much as there can be an answer to 'what is France?' or 'what is love?'. Of course, this is infuriating for most people and can be an easy and lazy answer. But as I have tried to show, the postmodern is not something that can be tied down. It is an amorphous, changeable phenomenon precisely because its use of the term 'post' can mean many things. It is used to describe an eclectic and wide-ranging body of different theories and, consequently, it is essentially incomplete and highly personal – one person's postmodern is another's high modern because the term modern is itself equally ambiguous. The modest postmodern is one that rejects the extremes of theorists such as Baudrillard and Lyotard though accepts some of their critiques. It sees the postmodern as more 'late' modern following Jameson but is not founded within the modern. It places some weight on the idea of new times but prefers a more subtle focus on 'different' rather than 'new'. It accepts the thrust of the capitalist dynamic behind these changes but does not reduce current sensibilities to a simple monocausal origin. It rejects the master-narrative and looks for the untold story or the excluded voice but believes that the two exist side by side. It is suspicious of prescriptions but accepts the need for action to arrest the drift to nihilism. It looks backwards as well as forwards and asks 'what can the postmodern tell us about the modern?'. The postmodern

> supplies us a new and external vantage point, from which some aspects of the
> world which came into being in the aftermath of the Enlightenment and the

> Capitalist Revolution (aspects not visible, or allotted secondary importance, when observed from the inside the unfinished process) acquire saliency and can be turned into pivotal issues of discourse ... Postmodernity may be interpreted as fully developed modernity taking a full measure of the anticipated consequences of its historical work ... modernity, conscious of its true nature – *modernity for itself* (Bauman, quoted in Kumar, 1995: 140–1).

So, following from the hundreds of other definitions, here is what I take to be the postmodern. The postmodern can be seen as

- a *cultural logic* which emphasises relativism and diversity
- a set of *theories* that are predicated upon a heterogeneous and dynamic interpretation of structures and meaning and that reflect upon and draw attention to the forms of modernity
- and a manifestation of *economic traits* that lead to the development of cultural, social and economic change (depthlessness, pastiche, insecurity, etc.) that mark it as different from the forms of modernity that preceded it.

Does the postmodern, in all its guises, subtleties, complexities and contradictions provide a basis for understanding and rethinking planning? I believe so, but in a modified form, as I set out in Chapters 7 and 8. The postmodern is an expression of the inherent changes in modernity. Such a crisis is what planning finds itself in at the moment. In the form I have described it, the postmodern is both a tool for analysis and rethinking. Obviously, the radical postmodern theory of Baudrillard is of little use in helping reformulate planning as it points to little other than nihilism. But regardless of the serious criticisms of the postmodern as social theory and new times, much of the postmodern is pushing at an open door. The radical democracy of Laclau and Mouffe for example, fits in with the thinking of much of society in the vacuum of post-socialist alternatives and the open, democratic, pluralist zeitgeist with Citizen Charters, regional parliaments and proportional voting systems (I cover this in Chapter 8). But the postmodern is more than this. It helps to explain the poverty of current planning thought and practice in what are undoubtedly different times. This explanatory role, as Hassan reminds us, is part of the postmodern that it often overlooked. Postmodern theories are part of a culture of 'unmasking' whose key principles include decreation, disintegration, deconstruction, decentrement, displacement, difference, discontinuity, disjunction, disappearance, decomposition, de-definition, demystification, de-totalisation, delegitimation (Best and Kellner, 1991: 256). It can explain and, depending on the emphasis and thinking, help build alternatives as a number of authors have attempted, e.g., Soja (1997) and Lipietz (1997). However, it is in its function of rebuilding that difficulties emerge.

This argument is all built upon a rather large premise. That is that planning itself in some way relates to these debates.

> With a certain exhilaration I write ... of the death of the 'Rational City' – that is,
> of modernist notions of technical rationality providing order, coherence,
> regulation, homogeneity – and celebrate instead the spaces of insurgent
> citizenship, the rise of civil society in the form of organized social movements
> which confront modernist planning with its anti-democratic, race and gender-
> blind, and culturally homogenizing practices (Sandercock, 1998: 4).

The inference is of a mismatch between a modern planning and postmodern new times that can be helped by some form of postmodern social theory. This is not an uncommon view, but is too simplistic, totalising and based (unfortunately, all too commonly) on little appreciation of planning practice rather than some erroneous though neat parallels between different schools of theory. What the next chapter will attempt to do therefore is to explore the influence of the modern and post-modern upon planning.

CHAPTER 4

IS PLANNING A MODERN PROJECT?

INTRODUCTION

The previous chapter tried to map the complex relationship between the modern and the postmodern and concluded that it was difficult if not impossible to separate the two. Nevertheless, I concluded that while we may not be living in new times, we are certainly living in different times and that the label postmodern was as good as any to describe this. The question that arises, therefore, is how does planning relate to these changes? Has it adapted? Does it need to adapt and if so, how? At a broad level, for example, the Thatcher years provide evidence of significant change in many areas of public policy including welfare, housing, policing, etc. and planning was no exception to this. As I go on to argue later in this chapter, at a broad level, the new right can be seen as a political manifestation of the postmodern as new times. By manifestation, I mean that it emerged as a political force out of the political milieu of post-Keynesian politics and sought to reorientate the UK economy towards what was described in Chapter 3 as post-Fordism (flexible, non-unionised, market orientated, etc.). As I argue in Chapter 6, public choice theory can similarly be seen as postmodern with its emphasis on the role of the individual. But Thatcherism also sought to tackle what it perceived as the downside of postmodern times – the vacuous moral framework – by 'strong-state' conservatism. Planning too was subject to this dual approach with an often schizophrenic attitude that sought to deregulate it and at times strengthen it through, for example, green belt or list building control. At one level, then, planning has undergone change that could be characterised as 'postmodernisation'. But the picture is not that simple. While the new right in Britain (and elsewhere in the world) can be characterised as a reaction to and part of the postmodern, it is only so in parts. As I mentioned above, it comprised two distinct parts, a neo-liberal market emphasis and a strong-state authoritarian streak. Planning, as a state activity *was at the same time* both anathema and necessary to the new right, depending on which wing held sway over a particular policy issue. The changes that planning underwent in the 1980s and 1990s remain a mixed bag (Allmendinger and Thomas, 1998, Allmendinger and Tewdwr-Jones, 1997). Brindley, Ryin and Stoker (1996) rightly point out that there were many 'plannings' during this period depending on the locality. Planning changed, but the direction, significance and trajectory of that change is unclear. What is clear (or so I argue) is that planning remains a complex alloy of different traditions and practices that could be labelled either or both as modern/postmodern. Further, that although over-rated in its significance, the trajectory of planning under the new right and latterly under New Labour seeks both a modern and postmodern future. While there is nothing wrong with this per se, it is this future or, more accurately, the emphases within it that is causing the problems, contentions, tensions and dissatisfactions with planning at the moment. Consequently, if we are to rethink planning, then an understanding of its theory and practice in relation to the debates on modernity and postmodernity are necessary.

It has now become common to characterise land use planning per se as 'modern' or at least as part of the project of modernity (see, for example, Healey, 1993, Low, 1991: 234, 128–9, Sandercock: 1998: 2) and to similarly characterise the period within which planning now finds itself and operates as 'postmodern' (e.g. Filion, 1996). The implication is of a potential and real mismatch between planning as a modern project and the needs and demands of postmodern or new times that, according to its proponents, explains the lack of participation and democratic content, failed and unrealised results and expectations, urban decay and a host of other outcomes, intended or not, that characterise 'planning'.

> Evidence of this seemed to be everywhere, from the disaster of high-rise towers for the poor to the dominance of economic criteria justifying road building and the functional categorisation of activity zones, which worked for large industrial companies and those working in them, but not for women (with their necessarily complex life-styles), the elderly, the disabled, and the many ethnic groups forced to discover ways of surviving on the edge of established economic practices (Healey, 1993: 235).

Sandercock provides the most recent work on the relationship between modern planning and postmodern or new times. She argues that utopian thinking about better futures that led to the creation of planning was infused with and colonised by modernist notions of technical and scientific rationality. Such influences limited visionary and progressive thinking by dictating a narrow rationalistic scope for possible alternatives.

> The social sciences have been dominated by a positivist epistemology which privileges scientific and technical knowledge over an array of equally important alternatives – experiential, intuitive, local knowledges; knowledges based on practices of talking, listening, seeing, contemplating, sharing; knowledges expressed in visual and other symbolic, ritual and artistic ways rather than in quantitative or analytical modes based on technical jargons that by definition exclude those without professional training (Sandercock, 1998: 5).

At these levels of generality it is easy to feel a broad consensus emerging that blames various manifestations of urban malaise not on planning per se, but on a limited and rationalistic perspective within planning. Where differences occur in this consensus, it is in the specifics of emphasis, detail and, most importantly, in the various ways forward. This latter point is covered in Chapters 5 and 6. This chapter seeks to explore the relationship between planning, modernity and the postmodern. To do so I follow a similar line to that taken in Chapter 3 by arguing that there are elements of both within planning and that to characterise planning as modern in a postmodern world is abstract, wrong and unhelpful. I use a case study of planning practice to highlight the relationship between planning, modernity and the postmodern that emphasises the rich blend of change, consistency, flexibility and adaption available and inherent within the planning system. I then try to map a more useful historical perspective of planning that draws on recent changes as driving a much more postmodern agenda in parts, though with strong neo-modernist undertones under the guise of the new-right and more recently the Labour government. This, I argue, is where the real danger and challenge to a rethought planning lies.

PLANNING AS A MODERN PROJECT

> Planners claim that their advanced degrees in relevant disciplines and professional fields give them privileged access to scientific knowledge and know-how. They also claim that this knowledge is generally superior to knowledge gained in other ways (from practical experience, for example). In this respect they speak as true heirs of the Enlightenment (Friedmann, 1987: 40).

The broad brush of academic debate on planning paints a familiar picture of modern institutions and processes coming to terms with postmodern or new times. In a review of the North American planning experience Beauregard (1996) concludes that planning strove to:

(i)   bring reason and democracy to bear on capitalist urbanisation,
(ii) guide state decision making with technical rather than political rationality,
(iii) produce a co-ordinated and functional urban form organised around collective goals, and
(iv) use economic growth to create a middle-class society.

Planning evolved in response to some of the less desirable consequences of modernity and capitalism that I outlined in Chapters 1 and 2 as a means of 'cushioning' its less desirable effects while, at the same time, improving the ability of capitalism to develop and maximise profitability (Dear and Scott, 1981, Davidoff and Reiner, 1962). This tension remained unresolved. However, prior to the 1960s, stable economic growth generally meant that both aims were seen as compatible and achievable. The mechanism for planners to achieve this would be 'heroic' master plans undertaken with a belief in progress and the ability of planners to remain aloof from the less noble and more pragmatic intentions of politicians. The tools of their trade during the 1960s and 1970s were two related though distinct areas of theory, the systems and rational approaches, that provided both normative and prescriptive bases for planning. The systems approach was founded on the view of an inter-connected urban form that could be modelled if understood. Given the privileged position enjoyed by the 'hard' over the social sciences, and the growth in computer power, such a model and understanding became based upon quantitative rather than qualitative or design principles. Economics began to replace design and form as the basis of planning and talk of 'flows', 'optimisation' and 'modelling' became common (Taylor, 1998: 64). The rational approach, on the other hand, emphasised process. It was an explicit and logical procedure to be fol- lowed that was supposedly value free. The values were to come from politicians or, more likely, from the 'expert' planners schooled in the new understandings of the systems approach. The rational perspective's most forceful proponent was Andreas Faludi (1973) who found himself pushing at an open door as his ideas fitted in well with the zeitgeist:

> there was a renewed faith in the application of 'science' to policy making – not
> only in applying the findings of scientific research to policy but also in relation to
> the policy making process itself (hence the talk of the 'policy sciences',
> 'scientific management', etc.) (Taylor, 1998: 69).

These high modernist principles were undermined by a number of factors, but Beauregard clearly links the main cause as the relationship between planning and capitalism and in particular the breakdown of the Fordist regime of accumulation. As we saw in Chapter 3, the shift to what has generally been termed post-Fordism broadly began in the 1970s and involved a number of changes in wider society including, for example, the globalisation of capital. Planning consequently began to lose its longer term and progressive nature as the battle to retain and attract foot- loose capital in different localities involved more pragmatic and industry-friendly local political and planning frameworks. More economic development focused forms of planning emerged that had the effect of making planning more overtly political, short-term and pragmatic in nature. Further, the 'command and control' function of planning began to be undermined by these more market-orientated shifts as land use regulation became increasingly embedded in local and national state strategies to attract capital. The result, according to Beauregard, is that plan- ning finds itself suspended between modernity (the original rational and progressive view) and postmodernity (its growing economic development role combined with increasing social diversity) with 'practitioners and theorists having few clues as to how to (re)establish themselves on solid ground' (Beauregard, 1996: 227).

Sandercock (1998) develops Beauregard's arguments further. She argues that the mismatch between modern institutions such as planning and fragmented and pluralistic times are crowding out the possibility and desirability of multi-ethnic, multi-racial diverse societies and cities. Current planning, on the other hand, is anti-democratic, race and gender-blind and culturally homogeneous.

> Modernist architects, planners, engineers – Faustian heroes, all – saw themselves as experts who could utilize the laws of development to provide societal guidance. The hubris of the city-building professions was their faith in the liberating potential of their technical knowledge and their corresponding belief in their ability to transcend the interests of capital, labour, and the state, and to arrive at an objective assessment of the 'public interest' (1998: 4).

Following Friedmann and Kuester (1994) and Beauregard above, Sandercock goes on to identify five pillars of modernist planning wisdom.

1. Planning – meaning city and regional planning – is concerned with making public/political decisions more rational. The focus, therefore, is predominantly on advanced decision making: on developing visions of the future; and on an instrumental rationality that carefully considers and evaluates options and alternatives.

2. Planning is most effective when it is comprehensive. Comprehensiveness is written into planning legislation and refers to multifunctional/multisectoral spatial plans as well as to the intersection of economic, social and environmental and physical planning. The planning function is therefore said to be integrative, co-ordinative, and hierarchical.

3. Planning is both a science and an art, based on experience, but the emphasis is usually placed on the science. Planners' authority derives in large measure from a mastery of theory and methods in the social sciences. Planning knowledge and expertise are thus grounded in positive science, with its propensity for quantitative modelling and analysis.

4. Planning, as part of the modernization project, is a project of state-directed futures, with the state seen as possessing progressive, reformist tendencies, and as being separate from the economy.

5. Planning operates in 'the public interest' and planners' education privileges them in being able to identify what that interest is. Planners present a public image of neutrality, and planning policies, based on positivist science, are gender- and race-neutral (Sandercock, 1998: 27).

According to Sandercock, these pillars need to be 'demolished' , because of the recent processes of change that point to a more diverse composition of the urban, and increasing demand for a more heterogeneous planning approach.

Although few would doubt the sentiments about the 'modern planning in a postmodern world' theses there are a number of problems with the analysis of planning as modern. First, it suffers from what others have seen as the separation of theory from practice. As a piece of academic analysis there is an argument that planning is 'modern' as Friedmann suggests. But, to characterise planning as 'modern' is to accord it a homogenous quality (in the same vein as Lyotard's (1984) 'master-narratives') that is simply not sustainable in practice. Beauregard claims that planning thought depends on controlling and perfecting reality, that planners have a critical distance based on scientific objectivity and knowledge, that they disengage themselves from particular interests and depend themselves on master-narratives such as the superiority of planning to non-planning. Again, few would disagree with these sentiments *as a whole* but few would also disagree that they did not vastly generalise and simplify reality – a reality that is 'messy' and sometimes anything but 'professional' (whatever that means) or rational (All-mendinger, 1996). In a revealing exegesis of planning practice in the Danish town of Aalborg, Bent Flyvbjerg (1998a) points to the duplicity, conflicting objectives, bargaining, abuse of power and post-hoc rationalism that go under the name of planning practice. Instead of the usual theoretical and philosophical justifications for planning (e.g. collaborative: (Habermas), pragmatic: (Dewey), etc. – see Chapters 5 and 6) Flyvbjerg invokes Machiavelli and Nietzsche as being more appropriate. He follows Machiavelli and von Rachau in making a distinction between formal rationality and *realpolitik* and invokes Nietzsche's 'will to power' thesis:

> the Aalborg Project ... is not about producing better arguments, it is about
> strategies and tactics (1998a: 74).

Planners are directly implicated in the misuse of survey information (which in any case had been accused of including leading questions), control of information, deliberate limits on the amount and scope of participation, back-room deals, departmental in-fighting, political trade-offs and the influence of powerful commercial interests. As opposed to the ideal systems and rational approaches, a highly controversial and political decision to build a bus station in the centre of the town is given a techno-rational justification *after* the decision. As opposed to the abstract and general views of planning that form the basis of Beauregard and Sandercock's theses, Flyvbjerg concludes:

> power does not limit itself to defining a specific kind of knowledge, conception,
> or discourse of reality. Rather, power defines physical, economic, ecological, and

> social reality itself. Power is more concerned with defining a specific reality than
> with understanding what reality is. This power seeks change, not knowledge
> (1998a: 36).

Planning, as a system, set of processes and individuals, is deeply embedded in the
power game and is used as a rational barrier behind which political decisions that
favour certain powerful interests are made. The questions of 'what is planning
knowledge?', 'in whose interest does it work?' and 'what aspects of modernity
does it embody?' remain to be answered.

The second problem with the 'planning as modern' analysis regards the
reading of history as a basis for pronouncing planning modern. Dear (1986) identifies modern and postmodern interpretations of planning's history and, although
Goodchild concedes that his classification is 'ideal', there is still a definite demarcation of modern and postmodern. Beauregard similarly identifies 'modern'
characteristics within North American planning history. The problems with this are
twofold. First, knowledge about any period in history has to be produced and the
process of research production necessarily takes place within modern academic
life, i.e., we tend to see what we want to see and it is possible to construct alternative realities, as I argued in Chapter 3. This is an obvious throwback to problems
identified by Nietzsche and Foucault; if the present determines the historian's
themes of interest, there is a danger of the past becoming a more or less inevitable
lead up to the present (Lechte, 1994). As Giddens has put it:

> Getting to know what goes on 'in' history becomes not only an inherent part of
> what 'history' is but is also a means of transforming 'history' (1984: 237).

In other words, it is possible that a 'modern' history for planning has been created
which is now perceived as history itself. Sandercock is particularly guilty of this. For
someone who is concerned with alternative histories and difference she presents a
very homogeneous history/portrayal of planning. An example of possible alternative
histories here could be the distinctly unmodern perspectives of urban critics such
as De Certeau which point to the messy and diverse nature of cities;

> Beneath the discourses of the city the ruses and combinations of powers that
> have no readable identity proliferate; without points where one can take hold of
> them, without rational transparency, they are impossible to administer (quoted in
> Donald, 1992: 435).

Eagleton (1996) also questions the contention that the social sciences were
infused with positivist theory – a point emphasised by Sayer (1993). Discourses,
such as that of modernism, cannot explain everything and placing an 'interpretative
grid' on the situation may produce a pattern or model though may not represent

reality; the *flâneurs* were probably the first to see the possibility of alternative realities to urban modernism while Nietzsche and Weber saw the 'dark side' of modernity as being the antithesis of high rationalism. Modernism was highly diverse and it
is possible, as Mammaas (1996) argues, to see shades of grey rather that black
and white. For example, Rabinow (1984) has described the 'watering down' of
high modernist design principles (such as those of Le Corbusier) through political
and economic expediency and described the result as 'middling modernism'. Such
high 'modern' principles also suffered at the hands of visionaries (such as Howard
and Geddes) in the combination of 'great planning narratives' such as green belts
with the more communitarian values of the welfare state (Donald, 1992). Further,
Beauregard's history projects a global view of planning from a particularly specific
case – what Stuart Hall (1992) has described as the difference between 'the west
and the rest' or what Foucault refers to as 'totalising history' (Philo, 1992). Focusing on a narrow (mainly academic) perspective ignores the diversity and richness
of practice as well as the diversity of space that undermines 'grand narratives' or
histories. The UK planning structure of a national legal framework and guidance
allows wide interpretation by different levels of government and actors. The result
is often that you cannot assume or automatically 'read off' local responses and
actions from policies and procedures operating at a different (often national) level
(Allmendinger and Thomas, 1998).

There is also a fair point to be made regarding the 'straw man' and binary
nature of the debate. Ironically, the diverse world described by Sandercock is
inhabited by a 'them and us' mentality that portrays a frustrated and angry diversity
of peoples that are subjugated by a homogenous racist, sexist and nefarious state
activity called 'planning' who try to keep 'them' (who?) 'out of our communities':

> We make street vending illegal. We close public parks between midnight and 6
> a.m. so that the homeless can't sleep there. We try to pass ordinances
> preventing immigrant day labourers from congregating on street corners waiting
> for opportunities of casual work. We live in fear of gang members encroaching
> into our neighbourhoods (Sandercock, 1998: 21).

According to Sandercock, this conspiracy is based on a fear of the 'other', though
who the 'we' are that she speaks on behalf of is unclear.

The analysis and debates concerning the relationship between modernity and
postmodernity in planning are therefore unsatisfactory and, from my experience of
planning, they present a simplistic and at times grotesque portrayal. There is a
need to move beyond the abstract views of planning as a modern project that are
largely based on a separation of theory and practice. There can be little doubt that
planning has changed (often dramatically) in recent years and one only has to look
at the experience of the UK during the 1980s to see evidence of that. But the legal

framework and policy that forms the basis of the 'planning as modern' theses are not of central importance here because as Planning Policy Guidance Note 1 states 'The town and country planning system has not changed in its essentials since it was established in 1947' (Department of the Environment, 1988: 1). What *have* changed are the local practice and interpretation of guidance within this broad framework. Beneath the centre lies a myriad of local practices because planning practice is a temporal and spatial regime. It is temporal in that it changes over time. As the 1947 Act, for example, contained no aims or objectives for the system, it has depended on what Reade (1987) has termed a 'shifting consensus' of object-ives which, for example, have at different times included (or placed greater emphasis on) redevelopment and rehabilitation, vehicle accessibility and restraint. It is a spatial regime in that it varies between places. This is due to a combination of national general guidance to be interpreted in the light of local conditions, the dis-cretion afforded by the legislative framework and the social, economic, political and cultural differences and traditions between areas. Because of the temporal and spatial nature of planning there can be no *a priori* lists of what to examine in explor-ing the relationship between planning and new times – each area will vary.[1] What we can do is provide a framework as a starting point for analysis derived from what a 'modern' planning regime should look like. The characteristics of planning as a modern enterprise have been identified by Friedmann (1987) and Beauregard (1996: 218–19) as being:

- the control and perfection of reality through the identification and manipula-tion of society's 'internal logic'
- the use of planning to drive society towards 'progress'
- the belief in 'critical distance' between planner and planned
- the use of master narratives and comprehensive solutions as a basis for decision making.

What follows is a case study of planning in practice, or a 'situated analysis' as Mommaas (1996) terms it, that will seek to map the modern/postmodern

[1] Here I am roughly following at a distance what Philo (1992) has interpreted as Foucault's attack on 'total history' and the importance of space, place and geography in history. Foucault argues that 'phenomena, events, processes and structures of history are always fragmented by geo-graphy, by the complicating reality of things always turning out more or less differently in different places' (Philo, 1992, p. 140). Consequently, a postmodern view of history should not present itself as an *a priori* justification of some explanatory framework, e.g., structural explanations, but by juxta-posing events and phenomena in a hypothetical, spatially-dispersed landscape; i.e. a deliberate 'muddling'. As Philo (1992) points out, 'Foucault clearly supposes that there is some order in the dispersion waiting to be discovered, but that this order resides resolutely in the things themselves and not in any order theoretically imposed from without' (p. 149). The approach I have taken does not slavishly follow Foucault's hypothetical landscape (as he himself did not) but instead seeks to avoid imposing *ante hoc* theories or frameworks.

landscape of current practice. The case study is of planning processes in Frome, a small market town which the author was closely involved with from 1991 until 1996 (Figure 1). Three distinct processes have been identified that have a direct influence upon planning processes and procedures. First, the problems of Frome town centre including traffic congestion, the range and availability of shops, accessibility and a declining retail market share particularly since the opening of an out of town superstore. Second, the Local Authority's decision to attempt to tackle these problems through promoting a town centre redevelopment scheme for retail, office and residential use. To enable them to do this, they needed to sell an adjacent shopping centre for enough money to allow them to purchase the adjacent site for redevelopment but at such a price as to allow the purchasers to refurbish it. Finally, the Local Planning Authority's (LPA's) (in fact, the same authority in name but different departments) dealing with the subsequent planning application for this. Running through this process were national and local influences as well as the statutory and non-statutory planning system. This constitutes what Philo (1992) would term a 'hypothetical space or plane across which all the events and phenomena relevant to a substantive study are dispersed' (p. 148) which charts (in a simplified manner) the main influences between these three phenomena.

PLANNING AS A POSTMODERN PROJECT?: THE CASE OF FROME*

Administratively, Frome comes within Mendip District Council's boundaries, an authority that was created in the 1974 local government reorganisation. Formerly, the town had its own Urban District Council though the successor town council retains an important role in the administration of the town, running some devolved services from the district council. Against this general background the three phenomena that have direct bearing upon planning practice in Frome will be examined in a way that will (hopefully) avoid the tendency to impose patterns upon events that totalise history. However, the difficulties of this are not underestimated. For example, it is still easy to see how national policy and trends in shopping and leisure can dictate local policy and process responses to the problems of a town centre. There *is* some order to events and structures *will* appear but the aim is not to presuppose those structures in a deterministic fashion but to reveal them.

*Part of this case study originally appeared as a paper in *International Planning Studies*, Volume 3, No. 2, 1988.

1 FROME TOWN CENTRE

The problems of the town centre have already been alluded to above as that of a declining centre through traffic sclerosis, shopper preference and other factors which had been recognised as far back as the early 1970s (Somerset County Council, 1972). Initial attempts at tackling this had revolved around large scale redevelopment schemes, inner ring roads and demolition of buildings to improve access. As the decade wore on, large scale schemes became increasingly unaffordable and unpopular as Frome's historic heritage became to be seen as an asset not a liability. Nevertheless, this asset was still part of the 'problem' of the town centre. Mendip's proposed solutions began to take shape through its statutory planning framework in the shape of the 1987 Local Plan that sought to replace the 1972 County Plan. Local fears about the district council's intentions for Frome began to emerge and rumours of the council's plan to eject the cattle market located on land it had inherited from the former Urban District Council spread. Mendip had been approached by the Meat and Livestock Commission who had recommended the market should relocate because of its limited space for expansion and the Council saw this as an opportunity to promote a redevelopment scheme that would provide new modern shop units, extra parking, offices and flats. The town council, fearful of the district's intentions, commissioned its own 'local plan' for the town to counter these proposals and provide an alternative strategy for improving the centre without relocating the cattle market. It was this pressure that led to district councillors rejecting the retail allocation on the cattle market site in the local plan (even though the market relocation was now a *fait accompli*) and left the district council without an alternative site when three large supermarkets submitted applications for out of town stores. Because of this lack of alternative in-town site in the local plan and the more relaxed central government guidance on superstores at the time, permission was granted on appeal for two schemes of which one proceeded. This further exacerbated the trade loss from the remaining town centre foodstores, though it did stem some trade loss from the town to neighbouring Trowbridge. With the cattle market now relocated to the edge of Frome, an out of town superstore and a further declining town, local and district councils began to look at a co-ordinated way of planning for the future of the town. Their response relied on three main tenets. First, the district council seconded officers to work on a co-ordinated strategy for the town in conjunction with the town council, local people and the Civic Trust. Second, an officer from the district council was appointed to promote the Catherine Hill shopping area which had the highest concentration of vacancies. Finally, the district and town councils set up the Frome Task Force, a body that had representatives from a variety of local organisations on it to provide a more 'local' voice and encourage support and action from a multiplicity of sources. From this came a

Civic Trust study with a development, environment and conservation strategy and a town centre action plan. But, most important of all came a joint recognition of the need for a redevelopment of the cattle market including the adjacent foundry for a mix of uses. This would provide a large food store to counter the shopping leakage from the out of town supermarket and attract people and shops back into the town.

2 THE CATTLE MARKET

The district council owned the cattle market site and adjacent Westway shopping centre but realised that the parking on the site could not simply be 'lost'; Frome needed the parking and any new use would generate more, not less, traffic. Consequently, more land was needed and this was seen to be possible across the river on land currently used by a foundry. This land would also enable a bridge to be built to allow alternative vehicle access into the town and thereby overcome some of the traffic congestion. Money was therefore needed to purchase this land and refurbish the now rather tired looking Westway centre. The council decided to sell the centre, include its refurbishment as a condition of the deal and use any excess money to purchase the foundry site. This would be supplemented by a grant from the government's Single Regeneration Budget to clear the contamination on the foundry site. A design competition was held for the refurbishment of the Westway centre and the redevelopment of the cattle market that would include parking on the foundry site. Following discussions with the town council and task force a 'preferred' developer was chosen. Terms were agreed for the sale and refurbishment and contracts drawn up subject to planning permission for the refurbishment and redevelopment.

3 THE PLANNING APPLICATION

It was here that the role of local authority as landowner, development partner and promoter came face to face with its role as Local Planning Authority which shaped the processes and objectives to be followed. Following preliminary meetings with the developers and architects an application for the first stage of the redevelopment (the refurbishment of the Westway centre) was submitted in August 1994. It was clear at this point that the proposal had been scaled down from the design which the council had chosen in the competition due, the developers claimed, to the need to retain as much money as possible for Phase II. This need to balance the finances of the two schemes was mirrored in the internal divisions of the local authority between the project team promoting the redevelopment located in the Chief Executive's Directorate (CED) and the team dealing with the application in the Planning Directorate (PD). The planners believed the application – which involved a Georgian/Victorian treatment of a rather functional concrete precinct –

to be a pastiche of styles. This view, summed up in the report on the application to members of the planning committee acknowledged the subjectivity of design,

> but it would not be too controversial to state that the existing design of the centre is not sympathetic to its surroundings. It does, however, have a certain functional integrity that reflects its modernist origins and is part of the evolution of architectural styles within the town. In short, it is honest. What is proposed has no such pedigree. It is a pastiche of styles that confirms the lack of direction (apart from backwards) that dominates architecture at the moment (Mendip District Council, 4th Oct 1994).

On balance, the planning report came down in favour of the proposal because of its wider benefits to Frome. This was not to say that improvements could not be made to the design. District councillors at the planning committee went further and wanted significant changes in some of the proposed extensions to protect trees along the riverbank. The developers claimed these extensions were necessary to make the scheme viable and help subsidise Phase II. Requests to the developers for changes in the treatment of exteriors met with the same response. It is here that the micro-politics of planning practice came into play. Under pressure, district and town councillors succumbed to demands for a scheme that closer resembled that as originally submitted. These demands were made not only to the planners but also to the Chief Executive (CEO) who was closely involved in the redevelopment and project as a whole. Planners and the project officer from the CED felt pressure to get the most from the scheme though not to jeopardise it. As negotiations progressed on design details various forms of brinkmanship on both sides were employed and senior officers including the Chief Executive became more involved. Finally, compromise was reached that involved design changes and the retention of trees and the application was approved. By this time work had already commenced in anticipation (certainty?) of the permission. The Westway refurbishment is now complete but there is still haggling over the work carried out. Phase II is still awaited. As Mommaas (1996) rightly points out, the classification of modernism or postmodernism depends on the time–spatial and conceptual perspectives used. The Frome study is no exception to this. What I have sketched out is the briefest of details to provide a 'picture' of events in a roughly chronological order. Matters such as national or local policy, administrative procedures, political and personal influences are only alluded to mainly because of the pressures of space. What I intend to do now is draw upon more detailed selective aspects of the narrative to explore the questions posed earlier.

1 PROCESSES

The micro-politics of planning practice have been the subject of UK (e.g.,

Underwood, 1980, Tewdwr-Jones, 1996) and US (e.g., Forester, 1989, 1993) study. These works stress the extent of discretion available within the planning system, the importance of language and communication and how situations are 'framed'. Frome corresponds with this analysis. Although certain processes are dictated by central and local government, e.g. the submission of a planning application, its publicity, etc., vast areas of the process are open to debate, interpretation and ad hoc creation. The interplay between different aspects of the local authority (PD and CED) ensured that objectives went beyond a narrow planning-led project and the concerns that would normally frame such discourses. Political input into the creation of these processes and their implementation cannot be over-stressed and neither can the (implicit) presence and interest of the CEO. In other words, the planners involved had little doubt about the outcome towards which they were expected to work. The developers were also aware of these pressures which undoubtedly strengthened their hand in negotiations. 'Rubber stamping' may be too strong a term but the process was secondary to the outcome. The 'modern' interpretation of planning assumes an instrumentally rational process (Healey, 1996a) that concentrates on pseudo-scientific means towards what are seen as given, shared or apolitical ends. In this case the ends were to a degree given in that some sort of redevelopment would take place. But the process departed from the apolitical to the highly political through negotiations with planners, the developers, district and town councillors, civic society representatives and others on detail. This is not an 'unusual' scenario though practice does vary. However, it must be added that 'framing' this political process were statutory procedures and processes concerning consultations and the need to reach a decision. This compromised 'open' negotiations and biased the process in favour of the developer/CED given the (widely-known) knowledge that any negotiations were marginal and the refurbishment would proceed.

2 AIMS/OBJECTIVES AND VALUES

The overall objective from the local authorities point of view was to breathe life into the centre of Frome. This objective could also be seen as representing a general consensus throughout the community. It was against this powerful consensus that the planning application was submitted. Although the planners involved had some reservations about the design of the scheme there was little scope for influencing the proposal beyond some marginal issues of appearance which had public support in any case. If the planners had at any time threatened the whole scheme, there is little doubt that political and CED pressure would have been applied. The irony is that the objections to the proposal were on the basis of it being too postmodern – a pastiche of Georgian and Victorian styles plastered onto a distinctly modern structure. Any values that may have been held by the planners individually or as a Directorate were in this case over-ruled.

3 INCORPORATION OF DIFFERENT VIEWS

Much of the consultations on the idea of a redevelopment and refurbishment was undertaken by the CED prior to any application being submitted using established bodies such as Frome Town Council and others such as the Frome Task Force. By the time the application was submitted there was only the need for statutory procedures to be followed and very few comments (and even fewer objections) were received. Any objections there were related to design issues and the loss of trees. This weakened the hand of the planners in negotiations and set the agenda on what would be discussed; the 'public interest' had been set regardless of any thought or views that the planners may have held. The dangers here were twofold. First, in the exclusion of minority views and second in the presentation of a *fait accompli*. Both these later led to problems in the finished scheme concerning aspects that should have been explored in greater depth such as access and materials. In the rush to create a consensus that would dictate the scope of public interest for the planning process and ensure a momentum for change, the details for the project were left vague.

4 IMAGES AND NARRATIVES

There are a number of images and narratives operating in the Frome study at different levels and held by different actors though, given space limitations, I will focus on five. First, as regards the role of the town centre itself, it was assumed that it must be 'saved' from further decline. This is a common enough idea that emerges from a variety of sources including professional practice, public pressure, sustainable philosophy and conservationary sentiments. This is despite the widely-held preference of the public to live and shop elsewhere. Implicit within this narrative is another: that out-of-town retail is 'damaging' and in-town retail is preferable or 'good'. This is certainly the view of current government advice though again the public support out-of-town retail developments. Third, the assumption behind the approach of the CED was that consensus was 'good' and descensus was 'bad' or potentially disruptive. Disagreement could have scuppered the scheme through delay or outright opposition. Such opposition could also arise in the fourth narrative; that the planning system inhibits development. This idea (harking back to the New Right approach to planning in the 1980s) inspired a definite stance towards the process of redevelopment that effectively marginalised the planning aspect of the process. Finally, the planners themselves had their own ideas on design that they sought to impose (without much success); that modern architecture itself was preferable to the proposed postmodern pastiche. This was contrary to the developer's position and CED view. Obviously, one could identify a number of narratives operating at different levels throughout the planning process but this selection tells us something important about their existence and broadly echoing the work of Alexander and Faludi (1996). First, that they still exist inside and outside the planning system and processes and have significant influences and second, that their existence tells us little about outcomes without focusing on power relations and especially the power to impose narratives upon others.

5 THE ROLE OF PLANNERS AND OTHERS

Planners approached large projects such as the Westway shopping centre with the view that a broad consensus existed that could be agreed on. The methods of achieving this consensus were fixed by statutory processes but these were able to be extended to include ad hoc approaches that went far beyond legislative minima. Normally, planners would lead the consensual building role either prior to an application but more likely following its submission. In the Westway case consultation and public interest identification had been led by the CED and developers. Issues had been identified, problems framed and solutions reached with local interests prior to the application. The planners' role was therefore marginalised. The role of planners and the planning system were characterised by two conflicting demands:

•   to deal with the application in a 'professional' way that would in likelihood have led to major revisions and protracted negotiations
•   to follow the corporate demands for approving the proposal subject to minor changes that would not threaten its viability or future.

Therefore the perceived and actual role of planners was different. In addition, the roles of others in the process was also different from the expectations of planners and others. District councillors, for example, had been involved in the Westway project both as landowners and members of the planning committee. Normally planners would have acted on their behalf and sought legitimacy from them for their actions. Again, agendas and views had already been set. The only minor alteration to this was in relation to the loss of trees because of an extension to the rear of the precinct. The position of planners was therefore isolated and a means towards a specified end. One exception to this can be found in the voices of those left 'unheard' by the pre-application work either because they were never consulted or had other views that did not accord with the 'consensus'. Planning permission was still a necessity and such voices focused on the planning process as a means of being 'heard'. The planners and planning system became a sole channel for any dissension and rather than creating consensus planners, found themselves questioning it, however futile it eventually was.

2 THE ORIGIN OF KNOWLEDGE ABOUT ISSUES

There are a variety of different themes and visions running through the Westway redevelopment (e.g., in-town as opposed to out-of-town retail, pedestrian priority over vehicular, intervention rather than market forces, etc.) but I shall focus on two main ideas. First, the idea that redevelopment of the centre was necessary and preferable to the status quo. Early indications from minutes of the Council's Policy and Finance Committee show that there was pressure for the sake of what could be termed 'civic pride' to take a proactive role in redeveloping and refurbishing the centre of Frome. Concern was expressed about the declining role of the town, its reduced opportunities for shopping, the loss of general business and aesthetic considerations such as boarded up shopfronts, vandalism, litter, etc. At no time was job creation mentioned as a possible reason. Although the impetus for action upon the CEO led to a corporate response and resources for the redevelopment scheme, the idea itself was contained in the Local Plan for the area although the nearby Saxon Vale was seen as the priority. The reasons for this in planning terms were given as increasing accessibility and choice of retail provision for the population. Since then environmental concerns have also been used to justify a town centre scheme including reducing the need to travel and re-using existing brownfield sites. Although important, these planning considerations required demand to be implemented, i.e., they were essentially passive. As there was already an out-of-town store soaking up any excess spending, demand for an in-town site was limited. It was the CEO's more active role involving resources that eventually began to make the town centre more viable through the cheap provision of land, its assembly and clearance. We can see then that it was political pressure that led to the redevelopment of the centre of Frome and the planning system provided little more than a land use justification. The origins of the political justification are less clear than those of planning.

The second idea that shot through the process was that planning inhibited development. Although this would probably never be admitted publicly it provided a backdrop to the scheme. Planners and the planning process were seen as, at best, irritants or obstacles to be overcome and at worst as potentially threatening the whole scheme. Planning's influence was therefore marginalised wherever possible and planners themselves left in no doubt that they were a means towards greater corporate and/or community ends. The justification for this can be traced to two sources. The first relates to the nature of planning in Mendip itself which, as a small rural area, has traditionally been conservative and to some extent negative. Pressure for growth and expansion in the area is an inherent characteristic and the planning system has followed national guidance in resisting this. It has therefore a local reputation of being reactionary and negative. At times this has bred frustration both within and outside the council when 'deserving' cases for development have been thwarted – e.g., the expansion of a local company. The second reason relates to the ideological climate which planners have found themselves in throughout the 1980s. Since the first Thatcher government came to power in 1979 it sought to reduce the range of issue dealt with by planning, streamline the process and orientate it more towards the market. One legacy of this has been a portrayal of planning as holding up development and job creation. Planning knowledge has been less important in the Westway redevelopment than the images of it. It made little difference if planners had developed specialised knowledge about participation or the need for certain aspects of any scheme to be built in or left out if it was marginalised and impotent.

3 HOW DO LOCAL CONCERNS AND PROCESSES INTERACT WITH WIDER NATIONAL AND GLOBAL PROCESSES?

The decline of central Frome could be interpreted as a consequence of national and global economic restructuring as its traditional manufacturing base contracted and consumer preference began to follow car-based access. Equally, the local response to this has been shared with numerous other large and small towns across the country as typified by 'off the shelf' responses such as town centre management, pedestrianisation schemes, reduced parking prices, etc. What these overall approaches mask are the individualities of each case and how such tools will be more or less useful depending on the context. Frome was therefore pushing at an open door in terms of the general direction of policy with strong government backing in the form of Planning Policy Guidance Note 6 (DoE, 1996) on town centres and retail development. The role of planning in the process as we have seen was kept very much at arms length and although this had a certain consistency with national policy during the 1980s in particular, it was more to do with local perceptions of planning as negative and restrictive. National views on planning had started to change in the early 1990s (Allmendinger and Tewdwr-Jones, 1997) and national priorities were seeing a shift back towards a 'plan-led' system. Equally, planning was still a statutory process and the extent to which it could be ignored or marginalised locally was limited. Here at least local concerns for a more limited planning came up against a national concern for more, not less, planning. Any national and local conflict over issues was therefore marginal. A more important issue is what would have been the outcome if a more substantive difference between local and national concerns had emerged.

CONCLUSIONS

So what does this brief study show that other views of planning as a 'modern' project miss? First, it points to a more fluid, contingent and irrational picture.

Although it is obviously brief and much of the rich texture and detailed study has been omitted it resonates with Flyvbjerg's (1998a) broad contention about the misuse of planning (though with less emphasis on the blatant, deliberate and mis-leading role of planning and planners). While Beauregard and Sandercock question the master-narratives of planning techniques such as rationalism, this study questions their own master-narrative of planning as a rational process by pointing to its irrational nature. Nevertheless, there were a number of over-arching themes or doctrines that did structure the whole approach, e.g., the need to regen-erate the town centre, the view that out-of-town shopping was in some way 'bad'. While it is possible to view such doctrines as essentially modern in nature (i.e., homogenising, totalising, etc.) their *raison d'être* were anything but. Among the reasons for wanting to protect and nurture town centres is the need to create diversity, choice and accessibility for residents who may have access to cars or have more eclectic and predictable lifestyles – the very diversity that Jacobs (1961) and Sandercock try to accuse planning of lacking. The very idea of diversity is a master-narrative itself.

Second, it was obvious that planning practice embodied a variety of prac-tices and techniques some of which followed central advice, professional 'good practice' and local tradition. But within this blend there was a good deal of local discretion and fluidity. It was the planners, after all, that provided the interface with the public, arranged meetings, distributed information, challenged designs, etc., often in the face of internal pressure and commercially driven factors. The point here is not that planners act as some kind of arbiter of the public interest (a claim occasionally made by planners) but that (i) there *was* a broad public interest that was not being met (though this was not the planners' fault), and (ii) that it was down to individuals to decide how this should proceed. Discretion works both ways. It can provide additional and much needed involvement or it can be used less progressively to limit involvement, as in Flyvbjerg's Aalborg study. It is through this variety of techniques and discretion that planning derives its rich diversity as well as the option to follow regressive and progressive paths.

Third, the individual planners' roles in the Frome study exhibited many clas-sical modern traits such as a commitment to equality (through attempts to involve criteria other than market-based ones), rationality (even though it was used for essentially irrational means), justice (though under local involvement), etc. The question that Sandercock asks is, for example, 'justice for whom?'. Ideally, the question is relevant and can expose prejudices, assumptions and powerful inter-ests. But in the world of *realpolitik* faced with deadlines, pressures, institutional conflicts and market logic, the question becomes less academic and more prac-tical. Openness, transparency and participation can only be addressed in the context of locally-determined circumstances. Was it the planners (or 'we' as

Sandercock puts it) that pushed through this scheme or did they merely act as an interface, conscience and/or arena for *some* form of wider involvement?

Fourth, in the circumstances described above, what is the 'public good' and is planning right to act in its interests? The postmodern criticism is, of course, that there are many 'public goods' and Marxists would further argue that the good in which planning works is actually that of capitalism. I accept both of these points to a degree. There is no *unified* public good (though as I mentioned above there is a *broad* public good within which dissensus and debate proceed) and we should be wary of either assuming this or working towards it. Given these criticisms (which are particularly relevant for planners who are generally more than happy to hide behind the vagueness of the term) in what ways should planning proceed? In the more specific or easily identifiable interests (e.g. property or commercial) or those more likely to be excluded from decision making (e.g. the poor, ethnic minorities, etc.)? Is it the 'public good' that the town centre is left to decline? In whose interests would that serve other than the out-of-town supermarket, road builders and car lobbies? Then again, the growth of out-of-town stores is based on the market meeting the demand from the population to provide easy, accessible centres. It is too simple to criticise unified and modernist notions of the 'public good' (though this is more than understandable given the arrogance that has historically underpinned the use of the term) without providing some kind of alternative or model upon which to replace it. Deconstructing the assumptions of it are fine in exposing these differences, but in this case there is a danger of atomisation and nihilism. The message from Frome is that a broad consensus (give or take some detailed design issues, loss of trees, conservationary ethics, etc.) *did* exist. The questions that arise are: what weight should be given to dissenting voices, who should be the ultimate arbiters, and what does diversity actually mean in practical terms? (this is a point I will return to in Chapters 5 and 6).

Fifth, echoing Flyvbjerg's point, planning was/is clearly used as a post-hoc rationalistic exercise, a marginal adjustment mechanism to satisfy a growing public demand for a 'say'. Cynical? Maybe. Where did the power lie in Frome? Certainly not with the planners or the planning system though theoretically this was the case (and this clearly echoes the criticism of Marxists which I come to later). The planning system could have theoretically refused the application but how likely was this? Beauregard and Sandercock both paint a picture of the planner as power broker, decision maker, etc. This is a myth that is still perpetuated (for a recent example see Greed, 1996). There are three main problems with this. First, it is actually the CEO in British Local Planning Authorities who signs planning decisions – approvals and refusals. Obviously, in Frome this rather complicates matters of objectivity and impartiality to say the least. Second, and related to the above point, the institutional embeddedness of planning clearly influences its practice.

Issues of individual patronage aside, the planner is caught between acting as an advocate for their employer and having some kind of professional objectiveness. This insidious position is naturally likely to be resolved in favour of the former because different case officers can be assigned to the application if individual ethics should get in the way of a decision. Finally, it is actually the elected members of the council who make the decisions on major applications albeit on advice from planners. Regardless of checks and balances such as advertising departures from development plans, the Secretary of State's call-in powers and the power of information control that planning officers maintain, members of the council are the ultimate arbiters of decisions.

Finally, regardless of the above, I do not want to portray planners as the last great hope for equality and democracy. Clearly they do not have the power to ensure this anyway. But questions arise from the Frome case that point to darker issues. Some of these can be blamed on circumstances – e.g. the position of planning vis-à-vis the CEO – but others highlight a more insidious role. The first is that in some ways the important questions have already been answered by processes that are divorced from the more grassroot issues. For example, residents in the case study where given limited choices of detailed design matters while the more important strategic questions of 'should we?' had already been taken elsewhere through a combination of political decision making and 'accepted' planning doctrine, e.g., out-of-town 'bad'. Second, there remain distinctly modern characteristics that limit and direct individual action both in the processes and institutions of planning but more importantly through the discretion and power available to planners themselves. Finally, there are a number of trends within the planning system that are both pointing towards a more modern and more postmodern perspective which, rather than complementing each other (as we should assume given my rejection of the binary opposition of the modern/postmodern debate in Chapter 3), are providing a tension within planning that is one of the motors of current dissatisfaction and ineffectiveness.

I conclude, then, that:

- planning exhibits aspects of both modernity and postmodernity
- it is a handmaiden to powerful economic and political forces within society embedded in institutional constraints that structure action
- it through its discretionary basis its operation in some ways resembles a lottery (who gets involved, where and how).

The picture is far from clear and is (paradoxically) clearly confused. This then is a snapshot of planning practice. What I want to do now is turn to the wider picture covering the trajectory of planning and how this influences the issues listed above now, and will continue to do so.

PLANNING AS A MODERN PROJECT?: RECENT CHANGES

Certainly planning has its fair share of modern characteristics, including the momentum towards a commodification of control and a dark or sombre side. But as we have seen above, this ignores the changing complexity of practice which, in many ways, can be characterised as postmodern. It also ignores the wider social and political context that undoubtedly structures planning practice. This context has shifted and altered dramatically in recent years, exposing the political context of planning and its modern characteristics in an increasingly postmodern world. I mentioned above that there were both modern and postmodern forces that were at work in structuring planning practice and that, while this pointed towards a blend, their current co-existence is creating tensions that are the basis of dissatisfaction and ineffectiveness in planning. These trends are largely a result of the reaction to the changing economic, social and political contexts that emerged in the 1970s.

By all accounts the 1970s were a period of crisis for planning. As Taylor (1998) points out, the 1960s had seen a growing confidence in both the theory and practice of planning against a backdrop of seemingly endless economic growth. The largely physical design approach of the immediate post-war period had given way to both the systems view (that the objects of planning were linked and any understanding required a holistic approach) and the rational view (that there was a superior form of process that constituted 'good' planning):

> the systems and rational process theories of planning, taken together,
> represented the high water mark of modernist optimism in the post-war era
> (Taylor, 1998: 60).

By 1979, and the dawn of the Thatcher era,

> it was hard to find anyone with a good word to say about planning, and the
> profession was growing increasingly demoralised (Brindley, Rydin and Stoker,
> 1996: 3).

How did such a change come about? There are a number of factors that led to this 'U'-turn, some of which can be laid at planning's door and others which are the result of forces beyond its control. All, however, can be traced back to the general shifts and implications that I identified in Chapter 3 – the broad movement in social, economic and political life to the postmodern in new times.

Of greatest influence was the economic crisis that was initiated by the quad-rupling of oil prices in 1973–4. This exposed the structural weaknesses of the UK economy that had been largely masked by the guaranteed but shrinking markets of the former colonies and the demand created for goods after the war. One of the immediate effects was a contraction in manufacturing employment which fell by

2.9 m between 1971 and 1988 while unemployment generally rose from an average of 3.5 per cent in 1971 to 6.2 per cent in 1977 (Ward, 1994: 190–1). The political fallout from this was at first unclear. The Conservative government under Heath fell in 1974 having been forced to undertake a 'U'-turn in policy towards state support and nationalisation of failing industries. The Labour/Liberal administration initially under Harold Wilson contained the usual tensions between left and right – the reinvigorated left believing they had witnessed the last death throes of capitalism while the right began to search for alternatives to the Keynesian economic orthodoxy. The result was the emergence of both left-leaning and right-wing approaches to public policy and planning that provided no clear direction. Planning theory and practice was still firmly entrenched in the rational-comprehensive ethic that entailed

> [a] challenge . . . to find a way of organising activities which was functionally
> efficient, convenient to all those involved, and aesthetically pleasing as well. The
> objective was to promote and accommodate modern life, as both a project in
> economic progress and an opportunity to provide good living conditions for
> urban populations (Healey, 1997: 18).

This blind faith in the efficacy of planning was reinforced by the call for more 'positive planning' from both main parties as a reaction to the bust and boom property cycles that had plagued the economy in the early 1970s. Although criticised and eventually abolished by the Conservatives, this disenchantment led to the passing of both the 1975 Community Land Act and the 1976 Development Land Tax Act. Both had the effect of allowing Local Planning Authorities to purchase land at existing use value and tax the development value of land granted planning permission. Along with the introduction of the National Enterprise Board these two acts were the last gasps of the rational-comprehensive paradigm. Local Planning Authorities' spending was coming under increasing pressure particularly as the Labour government shifted towards public expenditure constraint as it embraced monetarism. The economic crisis and the end of the long post-war boom also exposed the dependency of planning on growth revealing a largely reactive system. This was particularly highlighted in the increasingly evident inner city problem and the 'rediscovery' of poverty.

The 1970s also saw the maturing of the environmental movement which had started to emerge in the 1960s as a reaction against the slum clearance schemes that had been attempted in many of Britain's cities. Planners were portrayed as being part of this problem and in many ways they were. Although planners were becoming increasingly involved in environmental matters, they remained aloof from the wider debates on environmentalism, insisting on a 'professional detachment' from such political issues. The other problem for planners was that the growth in environmental concerns highlighted and exposed their lack of foundational knowledge, particularly regarding issues such as pollution and ecology. But the integration of environmental concerns went even deeper than that.

> Planners, and the policy system of which they were part, had always seen their role as much more than simply protecting the environment. They had to balance such concerns against the needs for development and growth which were generally seen as essential for national social and economic well-being (Ward, 1994: 203).

The result was that planners were marginalised in the environmental debate, a position from which they have never recovered. As the influence of the European Union began to grow this marginalisation became more acute. The general attitude of both the UK government and planners to this growth in the quantity and significance of EU environmental legislation was one of arrogance and superiority. The Chairman of the planning and transportation committee of the Association of District Councils said in the mid-1970s:

> we in England are already on the right lines ... Europe must learn from us. They copied us in order to have parliaments so perhaps they better adopt our planning system (quoted in Lowe and Ward, 1998: 18).

The overall picture was of an out-of-touch profession with an inadequate theoretical base that had been exposed as pursuing goals of economic efficiency and maximising land values as much as social justice and equity (Brindley, Rydin and Stoker, 1996: 2). Damning as it was, these critiques and developments were not the end of the planners' problems. Three more attacks emerged as the 1970s wore on. The first was a direct response to the tensions and contradictions that were evident from the wider economic changes on-going throughout the 1970s. If planning was a merely reactive mechanism then the possibility was raised that it merely served the interests of capital, and planners were little more than functionaries of the state (Harvey, 1973, Castells, 1977, Scott and Roweiss, 1977). An explanation of how such a view of planning feeds through into daily practice was provided by Pickvance (1977). Planning, he argued, merely follows trends because of its reactionary nature.

> If the planning powers involved in plan preparation and plan implementation (i.e., 'development control') are essentially powers to prevent rather than powers to initiate, then the actual development which does take place depends on the initiators of development or 'developers' ... and not solely on the preventers of development, the physical planners (Pickvance, quoted in Taylor, 1998: 103).

Similarly, procedural planning theory (the 'how to do it'), which largely consisted of the rational-comprehensive paradigm, came under sustained intellectual attack as being contentless and abstract (Scott and Roweiss, 1977) and deterministic and apolitical (Camhis, 1979). The result of such critiques was, in Rydin's words, to increase the self-doubt of planners (1998: 204).

If planners were under intellectual attack for their lack of substantive foundation, then they also came under attack for their perceived slowness and obstructive nature. The Dobry Committee was set up in 1973 to examine development control procedures and proved very critical of the lengthy delays within the system while the House of Commons Expenditure Committee also examined planning in 1976 and largely echoed the findings of Dobry (Rydin, 1998: 40). Finally, the 1970s also witnessed the emergence of studies that sought to evaluate the effectiveness of planning. The most notable being *The Containment of Urban England* (Hall, et al., 1973) which identified three main effects of post-war planning: urban containment, suburbanisation and an inflationary effect on land prices (Taylor, 1998: 99). While urban containment could be described as an intended planning outcome through the effect of green belts, suburbanisation (leap-frogging the green belt) certainly was not. The effect of this latter consequence was to increase commuting while the inflationary effect on land values pushed house prices out of the hands of the poorest in society. The result of these changes was that, by the time the first Thatcher government came to power in 1979, planning was almost universally disliked, without an agreed substantive basis, ineffective at promoting positive change, regressive in its outcomes, divorced from emergent environmental concerns and perceived to be slow and bureaucratic. Obviously, the omens for planning under the radical right anti-planning rhetoric of Margaret Thatcher did not look good anyway, but the malaise of the 1970s provided an even gloomier basis for the changes that would emerge in the 1980s.

As I mentioned at the beginning of this chapter, in economic and social terms the Thatcher years can be seen as a reaction to new times – particularly the economic shifts towards globalisation and post-Fordism and the social and cultural transformations of the postmodern. The amalgam of neo-liberal and strong state authoritarianism neatly mirrored the economic globalisation of markets and the ethical and fragmentary vacuum of postmodern values. The primacy of markets and market mechanisms can clearly be seen as a reaction to the perceived failure of Keynesian orthodoxy as Corporatist and modernist traditions were replaced by footloose capital. Neo-liberalism merely facilitated and exacerbated this. Equally, the strong-state tenet of the new right sought to inject traditional moral values and benchmarks into an increasingly fragmented society with its corresponding feeling of moral vacuity that Conservatives perceived as threatening the fabric of society. There was undoubtedly a symbiotic relationship between the unique fusion of erstwhile disparate philosophical wings of Conservatism that played on the correspondence between post-Fordism and market capitalism, and the atomisation of sensibilities and authoritarianism: the new right found a way, in theory at least, of having their cake and eating it. For example, the attack on union power throughout the 1980s was a clear case of mutual interest for both strands of the new right by strengthening the hand of capital in the form of big business and reducing the loci of power in society thereby concentrating it in the hands of government.

But as I have argued elsewhere, the fusion of these two strands presented problems as well as opportunities (Allmendinger, 1997: Allmendinger and Thomas, 1998). The authoritarians often resented the use of market mechanisms as they rightly saw capitalism as the motor of progressive trends such as greater demands for democracy and the breakdown of traditional family values including increased female participation in the workforce. Liberals, on the other hand, resented the role of the state per se and anything that inhibited market mechanisms. These tensions were routinely evident in the new right's approach to planning throughout the 1980s. While the liberals pushed for deregulation the authoritarians argued for increased centralisation of existing controls away from local authorities and people. The result was often a confused and unworkable amalgam of ideas that achieved neither (Allmendinger, 1997, Allmendinger 1998). While there was no death of planning per se, a strategic overview of planning did die. The result of deregulation, centralisation and confused and often unworkable changes was the project-led approach:

> The debate over planning has splintered as the lines of current economic and
> ideological cleavages have become more sharply delineated. A variety of new
> and old approaches to planning now vie with one another ... it is sometimes
> difficult to see anything other than confusion of competing ideas, each
> promoted by a sectional interest approach (Brindley, Rydin and Stoker,
> 1996: 7).

There is a superficial resemblance in this fragmented approach to the broad shifts of the postmodern – the breakdown of over-arching monolithic doctrines (other than a market emphasis), the emergence of plurality, an emphasis upon contingency and locality, etc. Even with this dual approach planning was beginning to lose its detachment from abstract ideas to local, politically-driven forms within a centrally-directed emphasis on a market supportive role. Strategic planning did not exist, and even a locally-strategic approach through local plans was questioned. Planning became ephemeral, contingent, local, immediate and attuned to matters of detail.

The resurgence and eminence of planning's market supportive role and the shift of planning towards what could be regarded as a more postmodern approach was not without its problems. These stemmed from a number of sources, but the most influential was undoubtedly the attitude of largely Conservative-voting shire residents. Planning was not without support even though its practice was generally criticised. This support related to its function in protecting rural areas from the demands of urban sprawl and in maintaining the high property prices that resulted from the restriction on supply. Such a restriction was obviously anathema to the liberal tenet of the new right and with the property boom that emerged in the mid-1980s, there was a growing demand from the housebuilding industry to release more green-field land for development. Both sides of the debate neatly represented the two different schools of thought in Conservatism and the resolution of the problem, as with other issues such as Europe, threatened to split the party. But the issues concerning planning were small beer compared to other pressures as the third Thatcher government approached what, in hindsight, can be seen as a cusp of change. There was growing dissatisfaction with the 'me first' attitude that underpinned the neo-liberal emphasis of the government, coupled with high profile failures such as the poll tax and the growing importance attached to the environment as witnessed in the popularity of the greens in the 1987 European elections.

When it also became clear even to Mrs Thatcher in the late 1980s that there was no longer parliamentary or general public support for further deregulation of the state, the New Right band-wagon began to falter. As a consequence many changes introduced after 1988 such as water, electricity and rail privatisation seemed to be about giving an impression of progress for a government that now had an increasingly-shrinking mandate. However, the shift to neo-liberalism had become a hegemony as privatisation and deregulation seemed the natural state of affairs even within the rapidly shifting Labour opposition. Given the reducing number of options for further privatisation and growing public disquiet, the Conservatives searched for new ways of introducing, nurturing and perpetuating its project. Its answer was to dump Mrs Thatcher and elect a second generation of leadership under John Major. Major shifted the emphasis away from deregulation and privatisation per se to a focus on empowerment through transparency and accountability in public services. If you couldn't privatise or deregulate, then you could make them work as closely as possible to that model within state control. It is here that we find the shift to a postmodern style of planning being reversed in places.

In planning, the tide of deregulation has already turned in 1989 with the 'U'-turn in policy towards local plans which were now encouraged. But in the place of deregulation came a shift to centralisation. Again, the common interest between the liberal and authoritarian wings was a distrust and dislike of local government. If a market emphasis could not be achieved through deregulation then it could be achieved through centralisation. Consequently, the 'plan-led' approach was introduced. I have argued elsewhere (Allmendinger and Tewdwr-Jones, 1997, and Allmendinger and Tewdwr-Jones, 2000) that the widely perceived renaissance of planning through the 'plan-led' system masks another form of centralisation through the vastly increased output of central guidance that must either be taken into account in the local plan or, if more up-to-date, supersedes it. Centrally-determined priorities and goals are now effectively influencing locally-contingent approaches to a hitherto unexperienced extent. Nevertheless, the 1990s witnessed a shift away from an emerging postmodern planning and towards a fusion of approaches.

Tewdwr-Jones and Harris (1998) make a distinction between the pre-1990 changes to planning as being concerned with *policies*, while the post-1990 changes concerned *procedures*. As I argued with the Frome case, the discretion available within the UK system allows for considerable variation of practice within a broad legislative framework. But this broad legislative framework also allows the government to make significant changes to the procedures of planning through guidance and secondary legislation without recourse to parliament. For example, while the 1980s may be seen as a time of radical change for planning there was actually very little legislation passed to achieve this. But planning also comes under the impact of other legislation concerning, for example, local government. And so it was throughout the 1990s that what Imrie (1999) has termed the market orientation or managerialism of the state emerged to be concerned 'about action rather than reflection' (Clarke and Newman, 1997: 148). The origin of this shift can be traced to the plethora of changes over a long period but the most significant was undoubtedly the introduction of the Citizen's Charter (H. M. Government, 1991).

> The Charter initiative is best viewed as a vehicle for furthering the aims of
> efficiency and quality, which are not exclusive to it, and certainly precede it. The
> use of initiatives such as Citizen's Charter is a much softer approach to
> reorientating development control practice, than we witnessed in the 1980s
> (Tewdwr-Jones and Harris, 1998: 169).

The Major governments' and those of Tony Blair have sought to inject a new impetus into the running of local government and, by association, planning. Imrie terms this impetus 'new managerialism' – the move to make local government more of a business with strict financial targets, centrally-directed objectives which are monitored and the results published, etc. Performance-based criteria are paramount and in planning the criteria are clearly linked to quantitative, efficiency-based indicators such as speed of decision making.

> For local government, since the early 1980s, streamlining procedures and
> cutting waste and bureaucracy have been clarion calls. Targets and
> performance measures have become common place, mission statements have
> proliferated, while ... the using of contracts and monitoring of service provision
> and performance is part of standard procedures (Imrie, 1999: 109).

One result of this is that substantive policy questions relating to the distributional effects of efficiency are seen increasingly as procedural and/or managerial questions that

> [are], therefore, seductive for re-affirming the legitimacy of planning's process based credentials. In this sense, managerialism provides a potential, yet problematic, source of legitimation for the [continuation of the] planning profession (Imrie, 1999: 110).

Thus, rationality can be seen to be back in vogue. But in the hinterland of changes introduced during the 1980s the 'public good' basis for planning has been re-cast in a market supportive form. As demands for greater public involvement in planning grow from grass-root levels, the EU and United Nations (e.g., Local Agenda 21) and academic sources (Healey, 1997, *inter alia*), planning practice is being pushed into procedures increasingly detached from such pressures. But the internal processes and administration of planning are not the only areas where there has been an increased commodification and centralisation. Centralisation and standardisation of local planning has also emerged through the increased scrutiny of local authority decisions and the issue of 'malpractice' (Tewdwr-Jones and Harris, 1998). Malpractice has emerged where local planning authorities have chosen not to follow this increasingly centrally-directed line:

> local authorities [accused of malpractice] have ... shaped and reshaped the planning control process in their localities to meet their own socio-economic and political needs, and the fact that this remains possible after the New Right reorientation of planning in the 1980s is indicative of the resistance of planning control to conform to [strong] top-down control (Tewdwr-Jones and Harris, 1998: 165).

The issue has emerged in part from the encouragement during the 1980s to follow a much more locally-specific and market-orientated line. With the lack of central guidance, a discouragement of local plans and the 'presumption in favour' of development, it is not difficult to understand how and why some localities chose and are still choosing to rely upon local knowledge and priorities as a basis for planning decisions. Even now, the message of the 'plan-led' system is that locally-determined factors should be the basis of decisions. In that light one political leader of a local authority accused of 'malpractice' commented:

> The Secretary of State has gone so far to say that the local communities and local people should decide where and what sort of development take place in their areas. We are guided by the policy guidance note (quoted in Tewdwr-Jones and Harris, 1998: 179).

This does not, of course, excuse the use of the planning system to favour relatives, friends and associates of council members over other local people, which was the basis of one government investigation (DoE, 1993). But it does point towards the emergence of central–local tensions in the interpretation of planning aims and the existence of locally-divergent practices:

> it is possible to conceptualise the planning system as operating in distinct
> socio-political circumstances, according to the political ruling of each local
> authority, the social, economic and cultural circumstances of the spatial area,
> and the ability of external interests to influence the decision making process
> (Tewdwr-Jones and Harris, 1998: 184).

PLANNING AS CONFUSION

Planning is shifting towards accommodating some of the themes of new times though within the limits of largely modern constraints. Both the practice of planning and its development strongly suggest aspects of both modernism and post-modernism. The overall practice of planning, therefore, can be considered to be one of confusion – a confusion that is definitely not solely modern. The amalgam of influences upon local practice including the 'locality effect', the ambiguous and flexible changes introduced during the 1980s, a centralised government system that places the responsibility for implementation and interpretation upon local government, the discretion afforded to planners through their historical profes-sional status and the increased politicisation and fragmentation of local opinion all combine to make the practice of planning an alloy of modern and postmodern. Out of this maelstrom it is difficult to discern a direction. Planning practice, as I argued in Chapter 1, is stuck between the desire of planners to maintain modern vestiges of professionalism and its benefits, the feeling that it needs to adapt and the desire of influential aspects of society to maintain mechanisms that exclude other parts of society. This does not mean that there have not been attempts to chart a new course. What Chapters 5 and 6 set out to do is chart some normative and pre-scriptive attempts to 'make sense' of this situation and provide an alternative way forward. Although there are both modern and postmodern elements to planning practice and the system and processes that influence it, I seek to rethink planning from a more postmodern perspective. This means applying the principles I explored in Chapter 2 in particular, which I do in Chapters 7 and 8.

CHAPTER 5

RESPONSES TO NEW TIMES: different paradigms for a new planning 1

INTRODUCTION

Moore-Milroy rightly concludes that 'the hunt is on for a new foundation for planning theory. Many paths are being pursued' (1991: 182). Out of the collapse of high modernist planning principles has come a variety of ways forward that combine both modern and postmodern concerns. From the plethora of competing and related paradigms I have chosen to focus here on four. These four areas are intended to represent the main areas of thinking as I perceive them at present, and provide a heuristic device with which to analyse current theory and develop it. It should be clear that from the titles I have given them there is a substantial 'backward'-looking character to these fields of planning theory, all of which (if we include the postmodern as part of the modern) draw on established thinking but add a new 'twist' that updates it for new times. The four areas are not mutually exclusive and there is considerable overlap between aspects of each (though there are equally large areas of difference). Further, they are intended to encompass many of the more specific critiques and analyses of planning that have emerged in recent years. For example, feminist perspectives could not be seen as a new paradigm for planning but as a critique of existing theory and practice as well as a potential basis for a more sensitive approach. Consequently, I have included it under the postmodern paradigm (though it could easily be included under our consideration of the collaborative paradigm).[1] The aim of this chapter is to chart this terrain and explore the potential of each for a rethought planning. I do this by setting out the basis of each approach and criticising it from a personal perspective that is informed by the principles of a postmodern planning as set out in Chapters 2, 3 and 4, do these different approaches at a theoretical and practical level meet the principles of a rethought postmodern planning? In particular, how do they address:

- Rationality and power
- Consensus and difference
- Inclusion and exclusion
- Totality and fragmentation?

[1]It is also worth pointing out that the broad groupings of theory are not 'equal' in terms of importance or influence upon planning.

Although I include a postmodern paradigm within my four potential bases for a rethought planning, I do not believe that what comes under the umbrella of this approach could be considered postmodern as I have outlined earlier in the book, and neither could it provide a basis for a new planning. Similarly, I endeavour not to erect 'straw-men' in each broad field of theory only to demolish them as inadequate. As I hope will become clear at the end of this chapter and Chapter 6, while I reject all the theories I do not do so completely. The overlap and differing strengths and weaknesses of each provide the basis for a rethought planning, though some provide more material than others. This is developed more in Chapter 7 where questions of rationality and the theoretical basis for a rethought planning are explored. This chapter deals with the first two paradigms of collaborative and pragmatic planning while Chapter 6 covers postmodern planning and neo-liberalism.

Although I have made a distinction between collaborative planning and neo-pragmatism there is a sense of overlap between the two. Hoch, in responding to criticisms of Feldman (1995) and Lauria and Whelan (1995) concerning the shift to pragmatism, rhetoric, phenomenology and discourse analysis, uses the unifying term 'communication crowd' to describe these positions (p. 14). And, taken at a broad level, there is an argument that both collaborative planning and neo-pragmatism are so dissimilar from political economy approaches and sufficiently similar to each other that this is a fair characterisation. For example, Habermas talks of the usefulness of pragmatic insights rather than basing knowledge upon science. But he is using this as a criticism of instrumental rationality rather than as a general endorsement of the idea and adds his own communicative and consensual edge. As I am concerned with a largely agent-based exploration of new planning, such generalities are too crude. For my purposes there are some important differences between collaborative planning and neo-pragmatism. I am largely using the work of Patsy Healey and Judy Innes as the basis for collaborative planning and while I mention others including John Forester it is only where he has a concern for the more Habermasian focus on ideal speech (the 'critical' in his 'critical pragmatism') rather than Forester's main emphasis on pragmatism. The distinction between the two schools of collaborative planning and neo-pragmatism (in its three main variants) is a fine one but important none the less. The work of Healey has a greater focus on modernist foundational truths in fusing the structuration work of Giddens and the progressive concerns of Habermas. The pragmatists depend more on the non-foundational emphasis of Dewey, Rorty and others (although admitting liberal democracy and scientific method as the bounds of such an approach and an ideal methodology), though they have merged concerns with power to form their neo-pragmatic and more realist alternative. For these reasons this chapter will examine the collaborative and neo-pragmatist school as related though distinct.

1 COLLABORATIVE PLANNING

Communicative or collaborative planning has, without doubt, become the dominant basis of planning theory during the 1990s (Alexander, 1997). This is not that it provides some blinding new insights or has been leapt upon by practitioners eager to approach planning in a radically new way. It has found its historical moment for a number of reasons, including:

•   the shift away from the individualistic attitudes of the 1980s towards the more inclusive social attitudes of the 1990s
•   the echoing of environmental concerns particularly Local Agenda 21's emphasis upon 'bottom up' locally-led processes
•   the need to fill the post-comprehensive-rational vacuum of substantive theory in planning
•   its role in providing planners with the theoretical justification for their continued existence in the shadow of the deregulatory approaches of the 1980s.

As such, collaborative planning is the *theoretical* zeitgeist of the 1990s. I emphasise theoretical here because there has been no rush from planning practice to take on the collaborative approach. The closest examples in the UK seem to be Planning for Real exercises, though there have been many ethnographic studies that emphasise the importance of 'undistorted communication' in daily practice (e.g., Healey, 1992, Healey and Hillier, 1995). This lack of practical application has left collaborative planning largely in the academic realm. Nevertheless, its potential importance in making changes to planning practice, as well as its undoubted usefulness as a tool for examining planning practice, mean that it needs to be included as a potentially new paradigm for planning.

There are a number of influences upon collaborative planning, though the most important is the work of Jurgen Habermas, the German sociologist–philosopher and his influential tome, *The Theory of Communicative Action, Volume 1: Reason and the Rationalization of Society*, published in 1984 (original German in 1981). Within this work Habermas examines the concept of rationality and its relations to problems of social action, intersubjective communication and social–historical change, drawing heavily on the writings of George Herbert Mead, Emile Durkheim and Aristotle (Dryzek, 1990). As I set out in Chapter 3, Habermas' entry onto the stage of the modern/postmodern debate in the early 1980s represented the long overdue left-wing defence of modernism and the attack on what Habermas sees as the destructive anti-modernisms of Lyotard, Foucault and others. His basic argument is that the emancipatory project of modernity must not be abandoned. Instrumental rationality has come to dominate other ways of thinking and knowing and increasingly distanced the 'lifeworld' of everday life from the technical world of 'experts'. In order to counter the invasion of the lifeworld by experts and the instrumentality of the 'system', Habermas develops his communicative rationality. Central to communicative rationality, as in post-structurism, is the role of language and the search for undistorted communication as a basis for consensus and action. In his 'ideal speech situation', 'communication will no longer be distorted by the effects of power, self-interest or ignorance' (Norris, 1985: 149). The foundation for any such approach, as Bertens (1995) has pointed out, is a democratic context in which anyone may question the claims of anyone else,

> so long as each party aims at consensus and agrees to concur with positions
> that he or she cannot refute (Poster, 1989, cited in Bertens, 1995: 117).

'Communicative planning' (Forester, 1989), 'argumentative planning' (Forester, 1993), 'planning through debate' (Healey, 1992), 'inclusionary discourse' (Healey, 1994), and 'collaborative planning' (Healey, 1997, 1998) are terms that have been used extensively in planning theory literature over the last decade or so to describe and transform the concepts of Habermas into planning philosophy. The main components of a communicative rational approach to planning have been advanced by Healey (1992: 154–5). For her, collaborative planning involves:

1. Planning is an interactive and interpretative process;
2. Planning being undertaken among diverse and fluid discourse communities;
3. A respectful interpersonal and intercultural discussion methodology;
4. Focusing on the 'arenas of struggle' (Healey, 1993) where public discussion occurs and where problems, strategies, tactics and values are identified, discussed, evaluated and where conflicts are mediated;
5. Advancing multifarious claims for different forms and types of policy development;
6. Developing a reflective capacity that enables participants to evaluate and re-evaluate;
7. Strategic discourses being opened up to be inclusionary of all interested parties which, in turn, generate new planning discourses;
8. Participants in the discourse gaining knowledge of other participants in addition to learning new relations, values and understandings;
9. Participants being able to collaborate to change the existing conditions, and
10. Participants being encouraged to find ways of practically achieving their planning desires, not simply to agree and list their objectives.

There have been various interpretations of communicative rationality as a basis for planning (e.g. Forester, 1980, 1989, 1993, Healey, 1993, 1996a, 1997, Healey and Hillier, 1995, Hillier, 1993, Innes, 1995, Sager, 1994) and three broad categories emerge from these interpretations. First, there are the micro-political interpretations of planning practice usually based on a combination of Habermasian ideal speech and post-structuralist concern with language (Forester, 1989, 1993, Fischer and Forester, 1993). Following in this tradition are the second category of ethnographic studies comparing this ideal to practice (Healey, 1992, Hillier, 1993, Healey and Hillier, 1995). Finally, there are the prescriptive (though the authors would deny this label) studies aimed at using communicative rationality as a basis for what has now been termed 'collaborative planning' (Healey, 1992, 1996a, 1996b, 1997, 1998). In this latter category we find the most developed accounts of collaborative planning and the critique of instrumental rationality that aim, in Forester's words, 'to work towards a political democratisation of daily communication' (1989: 21).

Running through these more prescriptive studies are graduations of interpretations which demonstrate a change in emphasis, particularly regarding power and normative assumptions. As Richardson (1996) has summarised, communicative planning might be characterised as:

1.   being set within an ideal pluralist political system;
2.   being aimed at redefining rationality in a new communicative way;
3.   attempting to develop a new unified planning theory;
4.   pro-modernist; and
5.   centrally locating the policy analyst/planner.

How could such an approach work in practice? One of the main criticisms of the collaborative approach is that it fails to fully explain how it could make the jump from theory to practice. The basis of any translation is the 'ideal speech' situation of Habermas. This is founded on the assumption that we try to reach agreement on the basis of reciprocal understanding, shared knowledge, mutual trust and accord. Habermas offers four claims that convey the validity of our communication which are necessary if agreement is to be reached and without which we would not claim to be communicating at all:

1.   **Truth** of propositions about our external reality
2.   **Rightness** of our interpersonal relations with the other person
3.   **Truthfulness** about our internal subjective state
4.   **Comprehensibility** of our language.

The employment of these four criteria will, in Forester's view, lead to informed and unmanipulated citizen action (1989: 36). Although we may fail to achieve these claims, communicative action requires us to attempt to achieve them through discourse that is characterised by:

1.   interaction free from domination (the exercise of power)
2.   interaction free from strategising by the actors involved

3.   (self) deception
4.   all actors being equally and fully capable of making and questioning arguments
5.   no restrictions on participation
6.   the only authority being that of a good argument (Dryzek, 1990).

There have been a number of attempts to translate this thinking into practice, but in planning the most comprehensive has been Healey (1997). The basis for any attempt to translate the ideas of collaborative planning into practice must rest on locally contingent and generated processes as there can be no *a priori* imposition or model (268–9). However, Healey suggests that process invention and collaboration can be aided by the use of and reflection upon four 'guides':

1 GETTING STARTED: INITIATORS, STAKEHOLDERS AND ARENAS
Planners do not seem to figure here but 'initiators' can be taken to be a loose equivalent who take the responsibility to launch any process, including who might have a stake and where discussion might take place. Existing political and administrative procedures may be part of the communication problem through their masking of power relations and distorted communication. They can be changed, however, when an 'opportunity' arises and participants start to agitate and organise for a different structure or goals. Once this has commenced then the 'initiators' can begin to decide who to include in the discourse of the new or emerging arena and how to proceed. How this is carried out varies depending on the situation, but there is a lot of discretion left to the 'initiator', particularly in enforcing a form of rules early on in the process before established powers and interests shape it to suit them.

2 ROUTINES AND STYLES OF DISCUSSION
'Opening out' discussions to explore their boundaries as they are perceived by different actors is important, as is questioning 'accepted' assumptions and 'truths' and learning about each others interests, hopes and fears. Healey identifies three particular aspects of this process that require attention. First is the *style* of discussion that ensures everyone has a voice and is heard through sensitivity to cultural differences, room arrangements, who speaks and when. Second is the *language* that each participant uses that gives respect to each other while avoiding ambiguous imagery or misleading statements. Finally is the *representation* which refers to the different ways in which participants are 'called up' to speak and to prevent those 'not present' from being 'absent' from the discussion (1997: 275).

3 MAKING POLICY DISCOURSES
This more 'open' approach will undoubtedly throw up a lot of information, opinions, facts, views, etc., which somehow need to be organised. Normally this is filtered

through the technical planning arena into a planning-biased point which 'smooths out' or blunts the different discourses. This process needs to be less technical and more richly textured to allow for different views to be maintained. This can be achieved through a mutual sifting exercise. But as Healey points out, how can a strategy emerge from such an open process? The answer is not clear but it appears to rely on a collective decision-making process that does not 'close off' options but works through different scenarios and their consequences. From this will emerge a 'preferred' policy discourse which will have been collaboratively chosen.

4 MAINTAINING THE CONSENSUS

Ownership of the strategy should have emerged through the collaborative and open process described above, even though it may disadvantage some. However, as new participants emerge and situations change then the more formalised institutional arrangements become useful in enforcing the consensus. Courts provide an arena for arbitration if required, though their operation and remit will need to be agreed by the participants.

Along with Mark Tewdwr-Jones, I have argued elsewhere that there are three main problems with the collaborative approach that, in my view, precludes it as a basis for a rethought planning (Tewdwr-Jones and Allmendinger, 1998).[2] First, there are its theoretical foundations. As chapters 2 and 3 make clear, postmodern social theory at a broad level questions the desirability/possibility of consensus and shared values. Lyotard (1983) emphasised the empirical and normative argument for challenging totality and consensus on the basis that any attempt would naturally lead to 'terror'. This argument is not only predicated upon a feeling that consensus naturally excludes difference but also that (i) it has been proved to, e.g., the former Soviet Union, and (ii) that grand narratives upon which consensus are based, e.g. Marxism, have and will inevitably break down and be replaced by a multitude of 'small narratives' with an emphasis on micro-politics. The search for consensus will always involve political choices in the 'winning' of arguments — and this winning of arguments for him (and for Foucault) will always mask power and interests behind a facade of agreement. For Foucault, attempting to reinvent the project of modernity carries with it the potential if not inevitable privileging of holistic and teleological views of history that suppress different views of knowledge, reason and 'truth'. The postmodern critique of consensus and reason is a powerful one and the main hiatus between postmodern and neo-modern views of the world lies at a normative level. As Outhwaite rightly points out:

---

[2]Some parts of this section are from a much more comprehensive critique of collaborative planning published in Environment and Planning A (Allmendinger and Tewdwr-Jones, 1998).

> Adoption or rejection of Habermas's theory depends more on holistic
> judgements at the level of social theory than a piecemeal acceptance of
> successive philosophical arguments (1994: 109).

While there is a chasm of understanding between the postmodern and neo-
modern views at the level of social theory, there is a general acceptance by the collaborative school of the postmodern as new times, the associated importance
attached to difference and the post-structuralist concern with the relativity of language. In her rethinking of planning as a collaborative enterprise, Healey accepts
the main tenets of the postmodern critique by emphasising the importance of local
knowledge and that 'There is no privileged, correct "rationality" (1997: 264). But
the acceptance of new times (including the ubiquity of difference) does not feed
through into a prescription for a politics of difference. Just at the point where you
think that the acceptance of postmodern difference will surely undermine or at
least question the modernisms of Habermas and his search for consensus, the
communicative rationalists 'pull back'. Their position could be summarised as 'we
are living in a world of increasing difference with the death of over-arching assumptions and theories which makes it even more important to create a shared basis for
living together'.

These more normative criticisms should not discount the objections to collaborative planning at a more empirical level. Participatory democracy upon which
communicative planning depends is by no means a value held by everyone, nor is it
problem free. Even proponents of participatory democracy feel that it has its limits
given the emphasis/preference on local rather than national concerns (Pateman,
1970). What happens when the two meet? This is one of the perpetual issues of
planning practice that I discuss in Chapter 6. Increased demands for involvement
go hand-in-hand with an expectation of a participatory approach, i.e., that when or
if a local community makes a decision then that decision is absolute and not 'taken
into account' by planners or others who have authority. Participatory democracy
therefore includes a shift in the loci of power that is unlikely to occur or undesirable
given the increased prevalence of 'Nimby' type attitudes. The assumption that
involvement in democratic processes breeds more involvement is also open to
question (Held, 1987). Collaborative planning cannot therefore overcome tensions
that currently exist at different institutional levels simply by shifting the loci of
decision-making power nearer to individuals.

A basic (if not *the*) assumption of communicative rationality is that consensus
can be reached. Although Habermas accepts that this might not always be the
case there are two aspects of concern here. The first aspect is what to do, and
how to mediate, when such consensus is not reached. Most collaborative planning
theorists are silent on this possibility. The use of 'courts' as adjudicators as

suggested by some accepts a dominatory and representative approach to politics absent from communicative rationality and involves using the same mechanisms rejected by Habermas and his followers. More fundamentally, attempts to mediate disagreement involve an acceptance of ontological difference but also a desire to unify it. Reaching agreement through open discourse is then dependent upon a threat of imposition: hardly 'uncoerced'. This remains a glaring problem for the collaborative approach. As Healey puts it:

> consensus on problems, policies and how to follow them through is not something to be uncovered through collaborative dialogue. It has to be *actively created* across the fractures of the social relations of relevant stakeholders (1997: 264, emphasis added).

Second, practical problems have dogged any attempt to translate communicative rationality into realistic projects and have overtly focused on process as opposed to outcome. Communicative rationality places too much emphasis on the plan as a vehicle for embodying 'ideal speech' while either failing to recognise or choosing to ignore the practical workings of planning practice. Such workings involve a large amount of incremental decision making (even where a plan is in place) that is constituted in a power-laden political arena of local and national concerns, some of which (such as the pressure to make quick decisions) preclude anything but the most superficial nod at undistorted communication. Again, the study of Aalborg provides an excellent example of this (Flyvbjerg, 1998). The stakeholders present within the arena of discourse will possess different aims and values and professional agendas. There is also a difficulty in questioning how far values are held in common, and what assumptions can be made about this. The collaborative planning approach assumes that all those who do present themselves into the discourse arena would share the same desire to make sense together. This assumption does not relate to the nature of the human psyche; why should consensus among all those attending be regarded as a positive attribute, when clearly different agendas and different objectives form the very essence of the planning argumentation process? Little is also forthcoming about how different sections of the community can be included in the 'big tent' of collaborative planning. Problems of who to include, how to identify them, where the different 'limits' of interest lie present practical and ethical problems not only in theory but also in allocating the responsibility – who decides?

Both Forester (1989) and Healey (1997) recognise the political, value-laden nature of planning practice and its ability to express values and carry power. However, they argue that the power component of planning practice can be transformed through a transfiguration of social processes and relations within particular places. As Healey (1997: 86) argues:

Aspatial and environmental planning practices are embedded in specific
contexts, through the institutional histories of particular places and the
understandings that are brought forward by the various participating groupings,
and the processes through which issues are discussed. Through this double
activity of *embedded framing*, spatial and environmental planning practices thus
both reflect the context of *power relations* and *carry power* themselves.

So the power dimension is viewed as a matter that can be transformed through a
restructuring of power relations and social contexts, with individuals recognising
and identifying the distribution of power between those actors participating within
the collaborative exercise. Power is therefore compartmentalised by Healey (1997)
into a process to be *recognised* by stakeholders, rather than as a process to be
removed, although she does call for 'a vigorous pluralistic politics' (p. 213) to
counteract these tendencies. The key issue is for communicative action to transform the machinery of formal government and politics, to enable more checks and
balances to develop against the bureaucratic and administrative elites that,
together, form governance.

The distribution of power between individual stakeholders is recognised, but
communicative rationalists suggest that by building up trust and confidence across
these fissures in interpersonal relations, 'new relations of collaboration and trust . . .
[will] shift power bases' (Healey, 1997: 263). To say that this is optimistic would
be an understatement. The theorists are advocating a redesigning of institutions to
foster collaborative social learning processes; that is, they are arguing for the
replacement of existing power structures with inclusionary argumentative governance, and this is the theory's weakness. Habermas and his planning interpreters
argue for communicative rationality to foster an alternative to existing power structures. By simply changing the institutional framework of governance, it is argued
that a more open discursive style of governance can develop. This, however, dis-
plays little regard for individual perception and motivation. It only tackles the institutional aspect of power structures, and denies the existence of power inherent
within the individual.

Communicative planning is founded on the rationale that individuals will
decide 'morally', and that negotiative processes within collaborative discourse
arenas are founded on truth, openness, honesty, legitimacy and integrity. It fails to
include the possibility that individuals can deliberately obfuscate the facts and
judgements for their own benefit, and for the benefit of their own arguments.
Forester (1989) systematically addresses this issue, but little has been said by
Habermas or his interpreters in planning concerning how communicative planning
should take account of this. They believe that individuals will simply alter their
persona once a more collaborative process is agreed to. This expectation is simply

too optimistic for practice to incorporate. What is needed is a more realistic model of the potential impact of individual stakeholders employing 'strategic behaviour' within collaborative planning, and how the 'self' question could be mitigated at the micro-political level other than through the even more optimistic and generalised call for the redesign of institutions. The style of language utilised and the type of knowledge shared can also never be constant, or universal. In such a heavily-politicised arena as planning, consensus is completely utopian – there will always be winners and losers – and it will never be possible for all individuals to abandon their political positions and act neutrally. The assertion that individuals put across their own principles in an open and honest manner, and are then subjected to 'mutual mind changing' as other individuals' principles conflict, fails to show any regard for the benefits of argumentation. If everyone is to agree, or achieve consensus, what would be the purpose of individuals with differing opinions initially participating in the discourse arena, only if there is a slight possibility that their views will find favour with the majority? Would not communicative planning solely benefit the 'moral majority', however defined, and possibly exclude minority interests – in some case, the very sections of society it is seeking to support? Forester (1996) and Healey (1997) claim that the rituals associated with communicative practices require a minimum degree of commitment and trust on the part of the parties to enable them to proceed.

> 'Successful' strategy-making efforts produce strategies and policies which convince stakeholders of the value of a new direction and its implications, through the creation of a new discourse or story about a set of issues (Healey, 1997: 267).

Agreement between stakeholders of the benefit of a particular strategy is only successful for that particular strategy; it does not mean that the same stakeholders will readily agree to new forms of practices or working for strategy-making in the future. 'Success' in spatial strategy-making is therefore dependent on the degree of persuasion individual stakeholders can impose on the other members of the discourse arena. The debating arena might well produce new relations and forms of practice that all stakeholders concur with; this would be successful for that particular day, but there is no guarantee that successive meetings would witness a same degree of mutual mind-changing. Similarly, a 'successful' practice might only exist for one particular issue within a discourse arena – individuals come together as a 'temporary aberration' but drift apart again into retrenched positions for the remainder of the exercise. Individual actors will only feel a desire to co-operate or agree on the basis of whether they trust the stakeholders advocating a particular position (that is, on examining – consciously or sub-consciously – the origins of the perspective) and on the length of time they are prepared to give listening to the subject and the viewpoint; the power associated with acceptance or non-acceptance of interpersonal relations is therefore carried within the individual stakeholder's psyche as a consensual-determining force.

Collaborative or communicative planning would not replace the self-conscious autonomous individual from either expressing a divergent view or from disagreeing with a consensual view. Nor is it realistic to expect that even, after discourse, an individual possessing a divergent opinion from the consensus would then abandon all claims to the separate view and not lobby by other means to achieve their preferred outcome. The key issue is, what could be regarded as legitimate means of lobbying? Making sense together could well be a positive feature of participatory democracy, and prove useful as a debating arena and method through which people express different opinions on development issues and community desires. But it would be wrong to think that the only purpose of such a system would be to enact the processes of participatory democracy, without any discussion of the outcome from the process. An evaluation of the outcome from collaborative planning action does not seem to be an important question for the theorists to address, on the basis that the outcome will only be appropriate (and of interest) for individual localities and their debating arenas. As Healey (1997: 264) makes clear, 'Consensus on problems, policies and how to follow them through is not something to be uncovered through collaborative dialogue'. But if individuals (as stakeholders) within the discourse arena are to be persuaded to be involved in the exercise, and are to be persuaded to openly discuss their preferred options and strategies, they will want to know how the process will lead to policy outcomes or decisions. If the sole benefit of communicative planning is to establish the arena for discourse among competing, multi-stakeholders, the whole process will be castigated as nothing more than a talking shop.

Earlier translations of Habermas into communicative planning theory suggested that all those involved in the discourse arena should challenge the hierarchical traditions within which planning is set, through questioning the role and opinions of central government, for example, and establishing an opposing 'bottom-up' view formulated through collective decision making that would have to be accepted (Healey, 1992). Later interpretations recognise that to achieve any meaning to consensus, and for individuals to begin to consider how those desires could be transposed into practical planning solutions, necessitates wider institutional, legal and political restructuring before transposition can take place (Healey, 1996a, 1997):

> The collaborative approach to strategic place-making ... is ... unlikely to flourish without some changes in political culture and institutional design (Healey, 1996a: 19).

This reflects the disappointment that might arise in translating agreed discourses into practical outcomes. Recent work in South Africa has indicated that the establishment of a collaborative technique involving all relevant stakeholders within a community, and their quest for an agreed discourse, floundered because more emphasis was placed on the process of collaborative planning than on considering how the discourses could be translated into practical realities (Oranje, 1996). Similar research in the UK on a local planning authority's attempts at innovative participatory democracy found that it had been successful in involving a high proportion of stakeholders in the community, and of generating discourse among a range of different interest groups, but less successful in translating the agreed discourse into the nuances of the land use planning policy process (Tewdwr-Jones and Thomas, 1997). While this brings into play matters relating to communities' (and planners') frustrations with existing institutional parameters within planning, it serves to raise community and stakeholders' expectations of delivering concrete results. Habermas and the communicative planning theorists have argued that there may be times of disappointment, when collaborative action techniques fail, but imply that the 'failure' is one of implementation alone, and relates to the institutional processes evident in localities immediately following the collaborative planning exercise that can mitigate against shared discourses, thus neatly avoiding the attachment of any fault to the theory itself. Within the UK local planning authority's exercise covered in Chapter 4 stakeholders felt aggrieved by the authority's failure through political and legal constraints to transpose desires into the planning system, and believed that the more innovative, progressive democratic pluralism advanced had been a waste of time, since little attention had been focused on outcome. It is somewhat ironic to note that, in the mind of the planners within this local planning authority, the exercise had been 'truly successful', since a democratic process had been created; the fact that the process had failed to deliver what the community expected was not regarded by the proponents of innovative participation as a problem.

It is necessary for collaborative planning theorists to explain how individuals should explain to stakeholders the usefulness of such a strategy when there is little or no possibility of delivering results or outcomes, and how community expectations should not be raised by the development of more innovative processes. This begs the question, what is collaborative planning seeking to achieve? Is it the arena within which the development plan is debated that is more important, or the usefulness of the strategy or plan (as an outcome) once developed? If the focus is exclusively on the process rather than the outcome, it raises the issue of scale: if each tier of the planning hierarchy has to be subject to stakeholder consensus, how could collaborative planning work?

Finally, and related in some ways to the normative arguments earlier, it is the case that those who pursue collaborative planning as a theoretical exercise seek to speak on behalf of others that do not hold similar views. This point is related to the imposition of values but is more focused on local level perceptions rather than theoretical concerns. In particular, it reflects recent evidence that demonstrates that these values are not widely held by planners and politicians which itself undermines the general social democratic view of planners and planning.

A main theme of collaborative planning is the denial of a central co-ordinating role for the planner who is (crudely) perceived as the 'abuser' of power and the 'distorter' of communication. Planners need to 'go native' and engage with local stakeholders more in an unbarred search for local consensus. The assumption is that planners will act democratically and collaboratively. Two questions arise: Why should this be the case? And are planners guilty of the crimes of which they have been accused?

Collaborative planning theorists want a levelling down of planners' roles to that of any other stakeholder. The logic of this would seem to be a call for de-professionalisation though, like the acceptance of new times, this is a point from which collaborative theorists pull back. The other alternative would be to follow Davidoff's advocacy line which would seem more appropriate in some respects, though this implicitly accepts that there are distinct and identifiable interests with society where planners work on behalf of interests within the existing representative system. But what is stopping planners and others from acting more collaboratively in the first place? As we saw in the Frome study, there is nothing to stop planners as individuals working in a more inclusive way (though within the more exclusive system). Are planners therefore guilty of being exclusive? Yes and no. The discretion afforded them works in both ways allowing individuals and local authorities to be more or less inclusive. We may all be democrats now (Held, 1987) but acting democratically is an assumption that underlies the possible implementation of collaborative planning. It also assumes that unspecified individuals (other than planners) will act as facilitators within the discourse arena between the competing stakeholders, without the recognition of what roles planners would perform, or how the facilitator and/or planner mediates between a representative democratic viewpoint and a participatory democratic viewpoint. The person facilitating the discourse arena is also in a potentially powerful position. How can the neutrality and independence of the facilitator be agreed and checked? Planners themselves can equally be stakeholders eager to implement either their employers' political or planning desires (normatively-regulated action), or personal planning ideologies developed over years of planning education and training (teleological action). Assuming that planners would act neutrally in this respect, in the face of competing (even opposing) interests, is a naive assumption. This issue goes to the very heart of the position of the planner: can stakeholders trust the planner to translate agreed discourses into practical realities? Would 'interdependence' be achievable?

Within the UK, the planner is not under any obligation to facilitate the process of learning, nor is the planner grounded in an ethic of inclusion. And convincing planners that they should operate in this manner is, currently, ambitious. Recent research in Britain has suggested that planners are suspicious of questions of social justice (Campbell and Marshall, 1996), and do not believe that the planning system could, or indeed, should address these matters. There is even some evidence to suggest that planners have very little regard for public consultation and participation, since it potentially undermines their professional autonomy and 'threatens' their independent professional judgement (Allmendinger, 1996, Kaufman and Escuin, 1996, Tewdwr-Jones, 1996, Campbell and Marshall, 1998). The professional element can also be diverse. Not every planner in the innovative public participation scheme might accept an agreed public involvement approach. Indeed, some planners are extremely reluctant to develop a greater, innovative participatory role for communities for fear of losing (or at least dissolving) their professional positions.

Collaborative planning assumes that individuals, by acting openly and honestly, will be prepared to see their values subjected to scrutiny, criticised by stakeholders, and would then admit 'defeat' in the face of competing arguments. Individuals are far more 'behaviourist', and to treat the re-evaluation process as a scientific concept in this way is to do nothing more than to attempt to separate the human senses from the body, to split behaviour from action, and to divorce emotion from fact. They do not address the inherent bias ('bias' being used not in a pejorative way) that William James and others in the pragmatic school identified and argued for. Arguing against the positivist hegemony of the nineteenth century, that investigations in particular and humans in general should distance themselves from any form of subjectivity when approaching questions and truths, James contended that people naturally form opinions and 'frames' that guide research. Not to do so would make any research which had to first discount all possible alternatives before settling on a favoured option take forever: 'one develops, as it were, a nose for what is plausible' (Mounce, 1997: 90). Bias is therefore part of human nature. Would not some stakeholders feel aggrieved by this process? Would not some stakeholders feel a desire to act further, rather than rationally and scientifically by saying, 'OK, I agree with you. I may have really strong views and values about this issue, but in the light of other views expressed at this meeting, I'm prepared to go along with them'? Imagine representatives of a large, powerful property company being prepared to 'back down' in the face of residents' concerns within this forum, without first attempting to enact political and planning lobbying (such as quasi-legal argumentation) to secure their multi-million pound property deal.

Finally, little has been said until recently about 'rights of appeal' in a collaborative exercise. As outlined earlier in the paper, the acceptance of an arbitration process (that is, through courts or appeals mechanisms) to solve unresolved disputes promotes the dominatory principle Habermas has been attempting to argue against in his theory of communicative action, since the discourse arena will be continually threatened by the imposition of a way or process of action if the open discourse arena fails to reach agreement. The assumption must be that individual stakeholders, feeling aggrieved by decisions taken against their own (even minority) desires, would be afforded an opportunity to challenge the consensus – or at least to be heard – at a later date. But to enact any 'right of appeal' is to suggest that the agreed view developed from the discourse arena could be overturned in favour of other, more pertinent considerations expressed by stakeholders either later in the process or by stakeholders who decided not to participate in the original collaborative exercise. Would the consensus become an 'informal blueprint', or would it be more flexible? Healey (1997) recognises the need for an appeals arbitration process within a collaborative technique, as a form of 'backstop formal arrangement' (p. 310) when breakdowns in agreement occur. This not only undermines the development and continued commitment of stakeholders to participating in a collaborative planning technique (that is, it would surely encourage the powerful development interests to employ those quasi-legal political and lobbying argumentation methods to secure their teleological action, rather than through discursive arenas), it also undermines high Habermasian communicative rationality.

So, what is the future for collaborative planning and how does it relate to the need for a rethought planning in tune with new times? First, it is not enough to equate innovative participatory techniques with collaborative planning. The problems with collaborative planning, not least of which is the reluctance of its proponents to tackle deeply-embedded institutional mechanisms by focusing merely upon processes, precludes any realistic prospect for it as a basis for planning practice. There are few, if any, champions for collaborative planning practice. Even if practitioners actually knew about collaborative planning (which they evidently do not) it is doubtful that they would be willing or able to embrace it. Those who I have spoken to tend to accept that a more participatory approach may be useful in theory but point to the difficulties in pursuing it added with a general reluctance which basically echoes the criticisms above. This is not a devastating point as planners and others are unwilling to challenge the status quo anyway. Any change to planning will either need to be:

1.   Generally agreed upon by planners and powerful interests, in which case it is highly probable that it will be unlikely to make a radical impact, or
2.   Forced upon the system and its actors, in which case it would appear to make little difference if it has champions or not.

The problem with condition 2 above is that in reality it *does* make a substantial difference. One of the main reasons why many of the more radical new right proposals were thwarted in the 1980s was precisely due to the 'top-down' approach to implementation taken by the government. The lesson was that the discretion afforded local officials meant that in some circumstances they could delay or even ignore some changes. The point is that in either scenario planners and others need to be persuaded about the need for, and direction of, change. In the case of collaborative planning there is little in the way of an incentive for this.

But regardless of these points there remain many practical and normative issues that collaborative theorists seem either unwilling or unable to engage. I address its relation to the themes of the postmodern at the beginning of Chapter 7. Here, I want to focus briefly on a number of other points. The assumptions upon which collaborative planning is based are at the very least questionable. Many of the issues I mentioned earlier can be traced back to the neo-modern origins of collaborative planning, and in particular Habermas' project to defend it against the postmodern critique. How it addresses the criticisms of Lyotard, Foucault, et al. is not clear as, like many modernist-inspired works, it regards it with a degree of contempt and consequently it does not directly engage them. As such it fails to answer important questions that remain to pick apart its modern basis. On a final note when I was a planner practitioner I wanted to help those who I felt needed it – those normally excluded from planning or those in most need, e.g., the homeless or unemployed. The collaborative approach would not allow you to 'fight' on anyone's behalf. I find it depressing and difficult to get across to planning students (many of whom find it difficult to be motivated by planning anyway) who are wanting to be enthused with a sense of purpose for their chosen career that they cannot 'fight' on anyone's behalf. I conclude therefore that the collaborative approach is a last ditch attempt to provide a 'progressive' basis for planning practice that ignores the darker side of modernity (the anti-democratic, messy, power laden aspects) as well as the changing nature of society. Simply, if it seeks to be a basis for planning in new times, it does not understand them or go far enough.

2 PRAGMATISM AND NEO-PRAGMATISM

Pragmatism has a long lineage that can be traced back to the American philosopher Charles Peirce. However, what is now commonly referred to as Pragmatism seems to have little in common with his philosophy:

> In the modern world, pragmatism is viewed as a variant of empiricism, and even

as a hard headed empiricism; its connections with religion are forgotten (Flower and Murphy, 1977: xvii).

This development has left the earlier Pragmatism with its emphasis on Realism far behind:

> The development of Pragmatism from Peirce to Rorty exhibits a moment between two sets of ideas which are directly opposed to each other . . . The two have nothing in common except that they are called the same (Mounce, 1997: 229).

This has led to confusion about the terms of its use:

> it is not clear to me what it takes to be a pragmatist. It is not clear in what ways the philosophers who have been called pragmatists are nearer in outlook to one another than to philosophers who are not so called. I suspect the term 'pragmatism' is one that we could do without. It draws a pragmatic blank (Quince, quoted in Festenstein, 1997: 2).

The current use of the word in planning appears to follow the pragmatism of Dewey and Rorty rather than Peirce and James, though both Dewey and Rorty (the neo-Pragmatists), build upon the earlier work of Peirce and James. Hoch focuses on the work of Dewey in particular for two reasons:

> first, Dewey placed concern for the understanding of public problems at the center of his philosophical work; second, he was by far the most prolific writer, making his ideas available to a wide-ranging audience (1984: 336).

Regardless of these difficulties Festenstein (1997) (among others) identifies common themes among these 'two pragmatisms' as Mounce terms them.

First, there is a rejection of realism about ethical and political values. Traditional empiricist philosophy assumes there is a separation between reality and experience that is interpreted by the mind (I cover this in more detail when discussing critical realism in Chapter 7). Alternatively, rationalists from Plato onwards have agreed that the senses cannot grasp absolute truth that can only be understood intellectually. The task of the philosopher in either school is to uncover truths as a basis for politics or science. The Pragmatist view is that such a dualism between reality and experience is false. James, for example, agreed that the world consists of experience but argued that the mental and the physical are merely different ways of interpreting it. Objects or reality do not exist independently of our senses – our interpretation *is* the object. The result, according to Rorty, is that there is no philosophical 'problem' about knowledge and that the history of philosophy from Descartes onwards has been about supplying solutions to problems of its own making. Rorty is not saying that either the rationalist or empiricist view of the world is not true, merely that it cannot ever 'work' for useful or practical purposes and as such we should 'give up' on the idea of truth as correspondence to the world. Philosophy has for too long claimed a privileged position in the search for such truths as a basis for deciding what we should or should not believe. We do not need such a world in order to decide what or what not to believe. Instead, we decide what to believe not because it corresponds to the reality of the world, but because they make sense to us and help us act. We change our beliefs not because we have been given a new or privileged view of the world, but because new beliefs make more sense of it or resolve inconsistencies. What does vary and where we should focus our attention is the language we use to describe experiences. I cover this aspect of Pragmatism in more detail below.

Rather than philosophising about problems, Dewey and Rorty argue instead for an intellectually practical approach. 'Doing and making' as an activity both alter the problem as perceived and provide a solution. Knowledge, argued Dewey, is only one aspect of experience, he also

> emphasises praxis and the application of critical intelligence to concrete
> problems, rather than a priori theorising (Festenstien, 1997: 24).

On this basis we have an incremental and pragmatic view of the world devoid of a priori theorising. But, Pragmatists do not discount the atavistic and cultural inheritance that influences our reasoning. This becomes evident in the second of the themes of Pragmatism. There is a refusal to embrace scepticism or subjectivism and its consequence that no judgement can ultimately be considered either right or wrong:

> Pragmatism rejects the conception of a cognizable structure of things
> independent of human interpretation (Festenstein, 1997: 5).

There are two aspects to the second Pragmatic theme that are worth highlighting. First, there is the rejection of scepticism. The logical positivist view that belief should be withheld until sufficient evidence is collected is discarded as unrealistic and unhelpful by James. We need to take decisions and act in life on the basis of intuition. We develop instincts and a 'nose for the possible'. We also do not encounter the world without belief and use what James terms 'apperceptive mass', or the 'assumptions, beliefs and tendencies one has acquired in the course of one's life' (Mounce, 1997: 76). Such a mass is difficult to alter even in the face of evidence that undermines it – we tend to believe things regardless of other views that dispel or ridicule it, e.g., religion. This is because such beliefs are not simply a matter of weighing up evidence. Pragmatists argue that we cannot be expected to give reasons for such belief or answer every conceivable doubt, only those that we have ourselves. But, while we know that we must be sceptical about the future, as we cannot guarantee it, we need to act and do so on the basis of our instincts – we are pragmatic in the everyday sense of the word. If there is a conflict between rationalism and intuition, then intuition is likely to convince you.

This leads us to the second aspect of the Pragmatic rejection of scepticism and the relativistic view of right and wrong. If we have an apperceptive mass of beliefs and values then the consequence is evidence of an attitude or bias. Pragmatists do not use the term 'bias' pejoratively, but as an inherent part of Positivism that has previously been ignored (what is scepticism, an inherent part of positivism, if not bias?). The implication of this bias is developed by Rorty who follows the approach of Quine and Sellars in arguing that, as we cannot get outside our own beliefs and language, then certain views will be incommensurable and conflict therefore inevitable. There can be no recourse to an outside 'truth' with which to resolve differences. The only way around such difference is through discourse. As Rorty puts it:

> Disagreements between disciplines and discourses are compromised or transcended in the case of conversation (quoted in Mounce, 1997: 194).

This may begin to sound rather like Habermas' communicative rationality through ideal speech though, importantly, Pragmatists follow a far more postmodern eschewal of absolutes, consensus or transcendental truth other than a commitment to democracy and liberalism. Further, the philosopher (or planner?) is given a privileged position in this process in making new and innovative suggestions that may overcome an impasse to help reach a 'normal' discourse situation, i.e. one where there is broad agreement or truth. For 'truth' is whatever we come to agree on at any time. There are a number of implications of this including the breakdown between theory and practice, as theory becomes a provisional truth (agreed upon, but for how long?) while practice is often suffused with non-theoretical elements, e.g., James' apperceptive mass.

> Since believing is something we do, and what we do is premised on what we believe, it is odd to imagine that we can hold these two categories apart (Festenstein, 1997: 6).

Pragmatism signs up to the Kuhnian criticism of logical empiricism that questions the empirical basis for knowledge. Instead of such an empirical basis, it posits a more discursive and contingent picture of knowledge ('paradigms' in Kuhn's phrase) that emphasises our inability to test any sort of theory on the basis of empirical experience. This provides the basis for understanding theories as incommensurable. Theories become little more than expressions of beliefs – a pick and mix collection of thinking that resembles what we already believe to be the case.

Festenstein is at pains to point out that this refusal to embrace scepticism and the view of a contingent nature of truth does not entail a relativism of ethical or political values. Rather than the absolutist claim that differences can be resolved through recourse to some agreed rationality or agreed reference point (i.e., a point outside all discourses), pragmatists argue that knowledge is open to revision and critical examination which, through conversation and open discourse, will expose misunderstandings, etc.:

> there is a basic continuity between theoretical and practical reason, that is,
> between reasoning about what to believe and about what to do (Festenstein,
> 1997: 6).

Rorty believes that it is possible and desirable to provide an 'ethnocentric' basis to political morality including liberal democracy. But, providing discourse is open and the actors reflective ('ironic', in Rorty's terms) then conflicts can be overcome and agreement reachable. Thus, Pragmatists are not rejecting reasoned evaluation, simply foundationalism. Such reasoned evaluation is the basis of the third characteristic of Pragmatism.

Following from the need for open and reflective discourses to develop and challenge established beliefs and morals, Dewey and Rorty explore the role of liberal democracy as a means to achieve this. It is here that the biggest difference to the early pragmatics of Peirce and James is evident, with Peirce in particular rejecting the empiricism of science due to its treatment of knowledge and belief as a mechanical effect of outside forces (Mounce, 1997: 128). With Dewey, however, pragmatics becomes what he considers empiricism should be, i.e. an open-ended, contingent search for knowledge or truth. To achieve this he introduces two foundational truths of his own. First, that liberalism in its purest form, i.e. concerned with the individual and freedom, is the best basis for a pragmatic society. Second, that a scientific approach or methodology to this liberalism is the best method of ensuring that it remains relevant and is the most appropriate means of providing an open ended and contingent search. It was this latter aspect that most alienated Peirce with his inherent dislike of the foundational claims of science to knowledge. The two aspects of Dewey's pragmatism are obviously related: liberalism providing the political and societal framework best suited to pragmatism while scientific method with its emphasis on continual criticism and reflection allows democracy and liberalism to evolve to meet changing needs and desires. There are also obvious problems. Dewey has been criticised for providing the basis for 'technocracy' as scientific method invades the political and social realm. This is particularly so as Dewey's conception of liberalism involves an active rather than passive society. Rejecting negative conceptions of liberalism, he argues that to be fully reflexive people have to be given the means to participate fully in society. Avoiding *a priori* ideas of how this might be achieved he instead argues from first principles that if liberalism is taken as the liberation of human capacities to achieve their full development then this may involve, for example, the redistribution of wealth to overcome the biggest obstacle to full participation through lack of resources. Such detailed policy prescriptions cannot be foundational within pragmatism – they need to be considered in the light of specific situations, which has led to the criticism of incremental conservatism as well as the view that his interventionist society is basically another justification for socialism. He is aware of this latter charge and claims instead that he is aiming for a 'planning' rather than 'planned' society. Here, again, we encounter some connections with the collaborative approach and its eschewal of *a priori* limits upon processes other than the ideal speech concerns of Habermas. And, like the communicative and collaborative school, there is little detailed prescription with which to assess how such a society would work or what it may look like. The pragmatic contingent approach through the use of scientific method would mean continually evolving state structures and policies which would undermine sclerotic bureaucratic machinery that has a tendency to develop interests of its own (Festenstein, 1997: 85). Consistent with the pragmatic emphasis on discourse and communication, Dewey argues that the combination of liberalism and scientific method would foster both open communication and a transformative attitude towards one's own values and those of others. Again, the parallels with the communicative approach are clear, particularly when Dewey goes on to talk about the need for individual commitment to participate and when he introduces his own 'ideal speech' approach.

Rorty does not follow Dewey's commitment to science but does share his belief in liberalism and communication as the basis of a pragmatic approach: 'nothing is more important than the preservation of . . . liberal institutions' (quoted in Festenstein, 1997: 113). In place of science as the methodology for pragmatic progress he posits a dual system depending upon the circumstances. Under 'normal' discourse where people share principles or criteria and arrive at common values, then an epistemological approach of obtaining knowledge from common principles is relevant. However, in situations of 'abnormal' discourse or deeply embedded cultural or value differences, discourses cannot be ameliorated through epistemological considerations and consequently a hermeneutic approach is more appropriate. As mentioned above, this allows philosophy to find a new role as a mediator, provoking new views or different ways of describing the situation in an attempt to 'feel' a way around the impasse. Again, Rorty focuses his attention on conversation as the method of progress

Any conversation must be 'kept going' or at least have the potential for this if a temporary and contingent agreement is reached (and here there is a clear difference with collaborative planning and its aims for consensus). But following his focus on contingent truths and the rejection of recourse to foundational principles, he also argues that discourses should focus on local rather than general points. As Festenstein points out, Rorty rejects the view that his 'ethnocentric' approach comes down to a form of relativism. The claim that incommensurable discourses cannot be judged by each others' standards is rejected as part of a binary understanding of absolutism and relativism. We are not precluded from evaluating the beliefs of others and frequently do, but neither does incommensurability stop us from understanding the contingency of different views: 'We cannot justify our beliefs ... to everybody, but only to those whose beliefs overlap ours to some degree' (Rorty, quoted in Festenstein, 1997: 123). Where this leaves us is not entirely clear as it rejects relativism but does not seek to replace it, but merely to understand it from within a normal discourse position.

Like Dewey, Rorty also seeks a continual evolution of liberalism and democratic institutions but he focuses on the role of individuals *vis-à-vis* the state and public. He introduces the concept of the 'ironic individual' who is someone who

- has radical and continuing doubts about the final vocabulary s/he uses and is impressed by other vocabularies.
- understands that she cannot resolve these doubts
- accepts that her philosophy is no closer to reality than any other (Mounce, 1997: 206).

In public, the ironist will partake in normal discourse and be in tune with liberal philosophy. In private, however, there is the potential to redescribe situations in the secure knowledge that it is private and s/he is protected by a public liberal ethic. But the ironist will be in the minority. The majority of people will fall into another category of common-sense non-metaphysicians who will not worry or reflect on how they live because they are secure in their non-foundationalist way that they are right. It will be the minority ironist who will worry and understand the need to be reflective and invent new ideas that challenge existing beliefs.

These then are the three main aspects of pragmatism. It should immediately become clear that there are significant overlaps and equally significant differences with both the postmodern and communicative approaches, as I mentioned at the beginning of the chapter. But the main difference is that pragmatism provides a commitment to liberal principles with a rejection of foundational knowledge and a relativistic view of theory and opinion. The Pragmatist, in William James' view,

> turns his back resolutely and once and for all upon a lot of inveterate habits
> dear to professional philosophers. He turns away from abstraction and
> insufficiency, from verbal solutions, from bad *a priori* reasons, from fixed

principles, closed systems, and pretended absolutes and origins. He turns
towards concreteness and adequacy, towards facts, action and towards power.
This means the empiricist temper regnant and the rationalist temper sincerely
given up. It means the open air and possibilities of nature, as against dogma,
artificiality, and the pretence of finality in truth. At the same time it does not
stand for any special results. It is a method only (quoted in Muller, 1998: 296).

But it should also be clear that there is not *one* pragmatism. James' conception of
Pragmatism and that of Dewey and Rorty obviously differ in important respects, not
least of which is James sole emphasis on method against Rorty's (and to a lesser
extent Dewey's) championing of liberalism.

So much for the theories of pragmatism, but what does this mean for planning? Charles Hoch (1984, 1995, 1997), the leading exponent of this approach
for planning directly addresses this question and takes Dewey as his model of
pragmatism. At the heart of his interpretation are three core themes of Dewey's
work. First is the role of experience in providing truth and as the motor of progress.
Experience provides the only real test of truth and practicality. Second, following
the idea of contingent truth, he focuses on the search for practical answers to real
problems. This experimental approach is based on experience as the arbiter of
progress:

> When we test plans of action, we try to determine which plan will work best, that
> is, which plan is right for us. For Dewey, this sort of thinking constitutes the
> appropriate form of understanding ... truth emerges when an idea (alternative
> hypothesis or plan) proves successful in solving a problem (Hoch, 1984: 336).

Truth is a consequence of what 'works best' in solving a problem or 'making sense'
of an issue. Finally, Hoch argues for Dewey's emphasis on practical activity or
inquiry through socially shared and agreed means achieved through democratic
association. A pluralistic competition of ideas following an experimental method
serves freedom best. Like the collaboratists, he also feels that conflict will be overcome through intelligent and reflective discourse.

Having identified these three themes Hoch goes on to analyse and draw parallels with a selection of mainstream American planning theories including Meyer-
son's 'middle range planning', Lindblom's 'incrementalism', Davidoff's 'advocacy
planning', Friedmann's 'transactive planning' and Grabow and Heskin's 'radical
planning', 'Clearly there are many differences among these authors, but I think their
reliance on pragmatic concepts outweighs those differences' (Hoch, 1984: 340). It
is difficult to share Hoch's enthusiasm because of the superficial analysis of both
pragmatism and the mainstream of American theory – especially as in the mean-
time Rorty has substantially developed the former while the latter has gone on to

include variants of both pragmatic Habermasian thinking (e.g. John Forester) and collaborative planning (e.g. Judy Innes).

While Hoch's analysis of the pragmatic foundations of American planning theory provide an unconvincing account, of more use is his criticism of both pragmatism and the basis of pragmatic planning theory. This can be summarised into three broad themes. First, Hoch considers that the pragmatic dependence on experience treats it as homogeneous and inadequate in the identification of problems. There is an inherent historicist and progressive assumption underlying Dewey's assumptions regarding the efficacy of social action and consequently the role of planners to tackle problems. This assumption, according to Hoch, provides no analysis of the problem beyond the boundaries imposed by the incremental and necessarily short-sighted limits of incremental action.

> Davidoff does not evaluate the specific injustices that require advocacy,
> Friedmann gives no agenda to guide transactive dialogue, and Lindblom
> provides neither size nor direction for any increment in particular (Hoch, 1984:
> 341).

Second, Hoch questions the assumption that the problems pragmatic inquiry seeks to tackle are founded in the obstruction of social learning and reflection. They assume that we share a natural predisposition to solve problems through instrumental inquiry and that this predisposition is both a value and a tool of human progress. Hoch considers that we cannot simply assume the significance of such learning which may expose deep divisions within society based, for example, on gender, class or race. In other words, we cannot assume a single direction as an outcome of social learning nor should we expect common responses – irrationality or more deeply-held desires may distort the interpretation and process of social learning through the use and misuse of power. Hoch's point seems to be more directed at some planning theories here rather than pragmatism itself particularly in the light of the more relativistic basis of truth that was also a mainstay of Dewey and latterly Rorty's thought. However, his general point is that pragmatism is power blind and that there is a danger of it perpetuating rather than tackling social problems. This is a fair criticism until you realise that the whole liberal *Weltanshauung* of pragmatism in Dewey's work accepts inequality of outcome but argues instead for equality of opportunity. As such it is not power blind so much as power accepting. Hoch seems to be arguing for a different conception of pragmatism than the Dewey/Rorty variety that is more radical in its potential for change and would not really be pragmatism at all.

Finally, he criticises Dewey's reliance on the role of professionals in initiating and championing greater public participation in order to challenge moribund and inhibiting social structures that stand in the way of individual freedom and

development. He feels that Dewey's confidence in the ability of voluntary associ-
ations between different interests ignores the socio-historical influences upon the
role and opportunities for professions to initiate change. Most professionals work
for state bureaucracies which limits their role. Further, given the centralisation of
power and the vested interest of professionals, Hoch feels that it is unrealistic to
expect this to occur especially as

> The practical development of plans, the implementation of regulations and the
> allocation of resources, while they require the use of problem-solving ability, are
> still guided more by the force of politics than by the force of argument (Hoch,
> 1984: 342).

The result is that understanding pragmatism is more of a useful theoretical insight
as opposed to a worthy normative position for Hoch mainly due to the issue of
power. The criticism of power blindness in pragmatic thinking has spurred Rorty to
rethink his approach in response to accusations by feminists that maintaining a
strict distinction between the private and public spheres will perpetuate rather than
challenge existing power imbalances. As Harrison (1998) points out, Rorty tackles
this through the introduction of a notion of *prophecy*:

> Prophecy is about thinking what is still unthinkable. By inventing new
> metaphors, languages and ways of thinking, the prophet entices society in a
> particular direction and makes possible what might not otherwise be (Harrison,
> 1998: 10–11).

Like the ironist, the prophet is charged with imaging better futures and then acting
to achieve them. This therefore adds to the normative commitment of liberal democracy by including and making explicit moral choices and, in planning terms, is
beginning to resemble Davidoff's advocacy approach. Relativism is addressed
under this revised pragmatism through the bounding of normative values and
prophetic irony within a liberal consensus:

> the liberal societies of our century have produced more and more people who
> are able to recognise the contingency of the vocabulary in which they state their
> highest hopes – the contingency of their own consciences – and yet they have
> remained faithful to these consciences (Rorty, quoted in Harrison, 1998: 12).

In the light of Rorty's revisionist thinking concerning power there have been three
broad responses in planning theory that merge pragmatism with other aspects of
thinking to form what some theorists term 'neo-pragmatism' to distinguish it from
the earlier 'crude' form. First, Charles Hoch's later work (1996) seeks to tackle the
question of power through fusing Dewey and Rorty's notion of pragmatism with
Foucault's critique of power relations. He takes a far more sympathetic line than his

earlier work that has spurred a reaction from critical realists and political economists (Feldman, 1995, 1997).

Second, John Forester has combined pragmatism and Habermasian notions of ideal speech to form what he terms 'critical pragmatism' (1998). This approach seems to follow the grain of US planning with its emphasis on negotiation which stems from its general lack of strong formal powers and its reliance of a plethora of different mechanisms (Teitz, 1996a, 1996b). This plurality of styles and negotiative attitude appears to be characteristic of Rorty's liberalism and it is not surprising, therefore, that much of the work on communicative and collaborative approaches to planning championed by Forester and others has originated in this fertile ground. For Forester (1989) planning practice is essentially pragmatic, though structured by different forms of power relations. His concern is to explore

> the ways planners can anticipate obstacles and respond practically, effectively,
> in ways that nurture rather than neglect – but hardly guarantee – a substantially
> democratic planning process (1989: 5).

Planning is essentially a communicative exercise and planners the gatekeepers who selectively organise 'attention to real possibilities of action' (1989: 14). Though Forester rejects Lindblom's incrementalism he embeds his practice of planning firmly within an incremental liberal–democratic framework that lacks an overall direction (capitalism is a powerful structuring force but it cannot be questioned *en masse*). Planners are too busy

> putting out brushfires, dealing with 'random' telephone calls, debating with other
> staff, juggling priorities, bargaining here and organizing there, trying to
> understand what in the world someone else (or some document) means (1989:
> 15).

Planners, like pragmatists, work in the real world and employ bias in the formulation, presentation and choosing of future options – they focus citizen's attention 'selectively' (1989: 19). Forester has no problem with this per se. But what he seeks is a more open and creative form of pragmatism that recognises 'distortion' and seeks to eliminate the 'needless' aspects of it by 'politicising' the planning process:

> 'Politicizing' here means more democratically structured, publicly aired political
> argument, not more covert wheeling and dealing (1989: 40).

Forester follows the pragmatic emphasis on communication in resolving conflicts but uses Habermas' ideal speech approach. And like Rorty's ironist and prophet the hope for a future planning lies in the hands of Forester's mythical 'progressive planner' who recognises these constraints and seeks to challenge them in order to 'make sense together' (1989: 10). Planners should seek to challenge such need-less distortions in order to enable full citizen action, for it is only with consent that planning can justify its existence.

The actions that planners need to employ to eradicate needless distortions are essentially pragmatic and dependent upon the situation encountered. Like the pragmatic theorists above, Forester eschews *a priori* theorising and prescription about what planners should do when they encounter unnecessary distortion. Simi-larly, he also rejects relativism as a possible outcome from an open approach to action:

> To say that all claims express interests does not mean that all claims are equally
> sincere or warranted or respectable. There is simply no reason to accept as
> equally deserving of public consideration a claim by the owner of a small
> business seeking a zoning variance and a claim by an avowed bigot seeking to
> send people of one race to another country, people of one gender to the
> kitchen, or people of one religion to the jails (1989: 59).

Planners must learn to anticipate and recognise distortion and act, like Rorty's prophets to invent new ways to approach issues and new questions to ask of inter-ested parties.

Forester presents planning as a potential non-zero-sum game – if unneces-sary distortions are removed then he implies that everyone will be a winner as open communication will inevitably lead to agreement. I have covered criticism of this view in the collaborative part of this chapter and will therefore not repeat it here. A further issue, however, is that there is an uneasy relationship between Forester's liberal convictions and the pragmatic rejection of foundational thought on the one hand, and the *a priori* Kantian ethical agenda and the critical understanding of power distortion in the other. For one thing, he wants to have his cake and eat it – a postmodern/pragmatist concern with recognising difference and a modern desire for consensus, a pragmatic suspicion of prescriptive thinking and the grounded though vague ethical framework that rejects some claims (bigots) over others (small-business owners). Now, as I set out in Chapter 7, this fusion of foundational and non-foundational thought is the common position of most postmodern thinking if it is seriously concerned with acting in the real world. However, the fusion detracts from his excellent exegesis of the undoubted communicative role of plan-ners by advancing short sighted and (ironically) uncritical claims. At the core of the problem is the question of 'what foundations?'. For example, 'distortion' is of central concern to Forester, but distortion from what? Whose standards? Rorty side-steps this issue to a degree by setting out his stall as being unashamedly western/North American liberal-democratic. By fusing pragmatism with critical theory Forester opens himself up to critical analysis that Rorty avoids. On whose behalf is Forester speaking? Why should planners give up power? Forester's analysis presents us with a pragmatic approach to a largely pragmatic activity called planning – but in fusing his critical theory however unsatisfactorily, he exposes some of the shortcomings of pragmatism itself.

Finally, another recent development of the pragmatist approach has been advanced by Harper and Stein (1995) who seek a greater integration of pragmatism with some postmodern concerns. This is achieved through concentrating on pragmatism but adding postmodern themes such as difference and an acceptance of new times. However, they reject the postmodern social theory as a basis for a new planning. Postmodernism for them, poses

> a clear threat to the very possibility of a normative planning theory which can legitimize liberal planning practice (Harper and Stein, 1995: 235).

They continue:

> The *last* thing we need is a postmodernist *theory* which needlessly exacerbates this alienation (Harper and Stein, 1995: 241).

Like the collaborative approach, the neo-Pragmatists find the new times thesis irresistible but take a different point of departure. Many of the claims and bases of this neo-pragmatism appear to shadow a more postmodern perspective including a concern with non-foundational truth and its naturalistic and anti-essentialistic elements. Harper and Stein reject what they see as the relativisms of the postmodern and the absolutisms of the modern in favour of an incremental and pragmatic pursual of change founded upon reason and 'the now' – theory is eschewed in favour of praxis or the fusion of theory and practice ('if it works, carry on'). This approach is firmly embedded within liberal-democracy (p. 239) which the relativisms of postmodernity seek to undermine.

The problem is that this is not some middle way but a highly conservative and modernist approach parading as 'postmodern lite'. The argument that Harper and Stein (1995) advance concerning the need to maintain a distinction between rationality and power is undermined by the work of Flyvbjerg (1998) on the inseparability of the two. What advantages are there in maintaining a distinction between power and rationality? 'Persuasion through rational argument is the only alternative to power' (Harper and Stein, 1995: 241). This demonstrates how wedded they are to the binary notions of modernism and the lack of sensitivity to the works of many postmodernists including Foucault who seek to expose the misuse of rationality. They reject the notion that all language is coercive on the basis that if it were then we could not identify the really coercive instances. Why not? Flyvbjerg (1997) demonstrates clearly that it is possible to make those distinctions, and we should not reject the notion of power behind rationality simply because to do so would make life difficult for the social analyst. Harper and Stein admit to incredulity that planners should wish to follow the nihilism of Foucault rather than the progressive route of Habermas. But this again exposes their normative and modernist notions of planning as well as their limited and stereotypical/extreme views of the postmodern. Because Foucault and other postmodernists do not advance any alternative theory is not a reason to fall back on the modernism of Habermas – it is instead a challenge to either think of a non- or modified-modern way forward, or to develop the less atomistic theories of, among others, Laclau and Mouffe for example. While I agree that fragmentation and pluralism need not necessarily be a block to consensual planning, Harper and Stein rely too heavily on the neo-modernisms of the collaborative planning and neo-pragmatism while ignoring or turning a blind eye to the (C)conservative implications of an incremental approach combined with a collaborative search for commensurable bases of action. It is not enough to simply use the postmodern as a tool for exposing the nefarious uses of power and rejecting it as a basis for a more pluralistic planning without first exploring the limits of that alternative.

Their alternative is firmly founded in pragmatic and modernist conceptions of emancipation, accountability and hope for the future while they use postmodernism as a tool for exposing some of the less desirable aspects of such ends. The problem they do not address is what happens when a less monolithic approach generates ends that differ from theirs? If a greater emphasis on multiple voices and empowerment is pursued, there is the possibility that the assumed benefits of Enlightenment ideals will be challenged. They accept that they may not always agree with the views that a postmodern emancipation could release and end up falling back on the hope that more open communication will lead people back to their liberal–democracy.

Pragmatic concerns have been raised in the study of practice by theorists referred to by some as the 'practice movement' (Watson, 1998). Hillier's (1995) survey of postgraduate planning practitioners elicited the response that their practical deliberations were based on 'common sense', or 'raw pragmatism' as she terms it, as opposed to technical or epistemic knowledge. In doing so practitioners demonstrate a clear pragmatic approach in rejecting traditional scoping exercises that seek to evaluate all possible methods and outcomes in favour of an intuitive sense – much like the apperceptive mass. It is in this intuitive flavour that the differences to the work of Forester and others emerges and in particular the 'practice movement's' eschewal of any form of theory beyond the pragmatic test of 'does it work?' or 'is it good?'. Rather than the Habermasian-inspired ideal speech methodology, Hillier recommends a hermeneutics while Colman (1993) believes that more planning education should go on at the 'coal face' of practice. This emphasis on 'learning on the job' is, in part, being driven by employers who want planning graduates with broad rather than specialist skills that allow them to be flexible and adaptive in response to the varied demands of practice (Gunder and Fookes, 1997).

The upshot of the emphasis upon neo-pragmatism in its three main forms is that a pragmatic planning has five characteristics (Harrison, 1998). First, pragmatism can provide planners with an ironic perspective on themselves and their actions. In line with the Kuhnian paradigmatic understanding, planning is a contingent and evolving activity that serves varying purposes over time. Second, planning does not seek to uncover reality but to serve a practical purpose in our understanding of it. This is a never-ending engagement where different vocabularies emerge and then are superseded depending on their practical use. Theories of planning become competing discourses which should be judged along the lines of 'how does this set of ideas help our capacity to deal with the world around us?'. Like postmodern thinking, there is an emphasis on the pick and mix approach to theory. Rejection of foundational thinking allows the fusion of eclectic ideas that provide a temporary and contingent understanding *within liberal boundaries*. Third, the renewed interest in the practice of planning in theory underpins a broader shift towards a pragmatic understanding. Forester and Hoch have both focused on the micro-politics of planning practice and the incremental and communicative basis of knowledge and action. Practical situations do not lend themselves to abstract theorising and require instead understanding and action based on specific situations. Fourth, the pragmatic focus on choice and contingency rather than abstract foundationalism emphasises ethical deliberation. The lack of objective criteria against which to act requires critical reflection on choices through a political process. Finally, Harrison identifies the emphasis on human action as opposed to the abstract thinking as found in idealism, realism, Marxism, etc. The pragmatic approach allows one to examine the practicality of such thinking thereby sidestepping structuralist thinking and emphasising a more agency-centred model.

According to Hoch (1996) critical pragmatism is based on shared inquiry and common purposes. But how far this can be taken in the messy world of planning is open to question. Do the developer and the conservationist share a common purpose and if purposes are not common can they have a shared inquiry? Part of the problem, it seems to me, is that Hoch's defence of pragmatism against the political economists' onslaught side-steps their critique by saying 'of course pragmatism can incorporate it – it's merely one theory among many'. Is pragmatism becoming all things to everyone, losing its substance and becoming meaningless? Hoch rejects Feldman's claim that pragmatism is 'theory laden' and therefore not simply empiricist. But I do not think there is anything to be gained here in sticking to a 'pragmatism as empiricism' claim (though Hoch seems to argue that pragmatism is not theoretical and not empiricist). If Feldman means that pragmatism is a theory in the sense that it incorporates normative values then yes, pragmatism does in the form of its preference for liberal democracy. In its more sophisticated and developed forms, as found in Forester or Harper and Stein, it is even more so because they add further normative dimensions. But the other aspect it seems to me is to be found in the naive assumption that means and ends can be evaluated under a pragmatic approach without a concern with the means to do this.

> Pragmatism does not tell us what ends to pursue, but offers a kind of inquiry that compares the value of different courses of action alternately weighing means and ends – facts and values. It binds together what dualistic thinking keeps apart – knowledge and action (or perhaps a bit more precisely) theoretical reflection and common sense (Hoch, 1997: 24).

The problem with common sense, as Rorty implicitly admits in his shift towards prophecy and power-conscious pragmatism, is that it can mask relations of power. Hoch's response is to concede that power relations may well come into play, but it is up to the pragmatist to promote more 'thoughtful, critical deliberation in the face of cynical masquerade, sincere ignorance, fundamentalist dogmatism and so on' (Hoch, 1997: 26). Here we come back to the weight placed on factors such as openness, truth, etc. embedded in Forester's critical pragmatism. However much pragmatists try to incorporate power into an open approach to theory and values, they come back to having to formulate it in terms of more fundamentalist principles. Is this a problem? Not really. The answer to it could be to take a pragmatic approach and side step the confines of pragmatism. If pragmatism is having to move away from its eschewal of any particular theoretical viewpoint to incorporate issues such as power, then it could simply apply its own more practical avoidance of largely irrelevant questions, as Rorty and others did with their attitude towards the rationalist versus empiricist debate. By saying that the answer to that particular dualism was irrelevant to day-to-day thinking then surely the same trick can be used to similar effect on the question of incorporating other aspects of thinking to pragmatism – what difference does it make? If this is so, then the force of Feldman's argument against the pragmatists becomes much duller – the response could be a pragmatic shrug of the shoulders. But, it is a long way to jump if we accept that pragmatism is theory laden to then accept a political economy approach as argued for by Feldman (1997). Besides, pragmatism *is* foundational in its embrace of concepts such as liberal democracy, so adding other foundational aspects is hardly diminishing something that is pure. Just as the postmodern ironical theoretical position is a rejection or grave suspicion of theory or meta-narratives, so pragmatism's theoretical position is a similar suspicion of foundational theory in the singular, but a practical embrace of theories in the plural. This is why Feldman and Hoch are arguing past each other from different paradigms, each unable to comprehend the position or arguments of the other and each having no more or less claim on truth: Hoch from neo-pragmatism and Feldman from critical realism (Feldman, 1997).

The real problem for me is not that pragmatism needs to 'tack on' other aspects of understanding and to avoid accusations and the consequences of power blindness (though pragmatists would argue that it does not 'tack them on' but incorporates them into one of a multiple of views). It is instead more to do with its modernist foundations in liberal democracy, and the particular routes chosen to tackle such issues of power blindness through, for example, Habermas' ideal speech approach. Pragmatism is essentially conservative in that it starts from a given position and moves from it only in short steps within a given boundary. Like the collaborative school, there is a 'threat' of limits (you can work within liberal–democracy, but not outside it) that will naturally structure the outcome and limit the options. This is not a problem for the *methodology* of pragmatism, but its *values*. And like the postmodernisms of Lyotard, the pragmatists 'pull back' from the potentially nasty or unacceptable consequences of their logic. In Lyotard's case this is his desire not to grant parity with values such as Nazism and democracy. The pragmatist's equivalent and similar response to the potential consequences of relativism is to embed it within liberal–democracy.

In another clear link with the collaborative approach, the refined approach of Forester and Hoch also seeks to create a universal or comprehensive planning:

> The critical pragmatist does not speak to a well defined universal audience, but shows how we might foster this universality in different ways (Hoch, 1997: 33).

Monolithic rationalism may have been rejected in favour of more pluralist routes, but the possibility of different or diverse planning outcomes is thwarted by the necessity of single outcomes. This is why Lauria's (1997) criticism of Hoch's relativism misses its mark, as Hoch argues for relativistic means not ends. Relativism is also a problem for Feldman (1997). He argued that the 'nothing is right or wrong' approach of pragmatism masks the liberal–democratic bias of Hoch and others who in reality would ignore inconvenient claims that contradicted or threatened the basis of pragmatism. This is perhaps unfair to the individuals involved but it is certainly a fair criticism of the pragmatic approach per se, and an elaboration of the inherent 'threat' argument above.

The issues of realpolitik shadow the pragmatic approach in a similar vein to the collaborative paradigm. Feldman (1997), for example, explores the likely impacts of following a collaborative approach including the impact of unequal power as well as the institutional limits to a discursive approach. This whole field of deliberative democracy is one where largely sympathetic writers are exploring the potentials and, more importantly, the limits of open discourse (see, for example, Elster, 1998, Bohman, 1996, and Nino, 1996) and has led to a variety of research which, as

Elster points out, is turning to the view that 'deliberation essentially makes no difference – for neither good or bad' (1998: 2). The reasons for this seem to be based
around the complex relationship between the three methods of collective decision
making: arguing, bargaining and voting. While collaborative planning and neo-
pragmatism are essentially grounded in a normative preference for arguing, there
will inevitably also be forms of bargaining (using power relations and compromise)
as well as voting when consensus does not emerge (Elster, 1998: 5). Due to issues
such as time constraints, modern democracies tend to use all three methods. But
the assumption that deliberation per se is both desirable and that shifting the
balance between the three modes towards deliberation is desirable is naïve. First,
deliberation is based on arguing and that must include the 'argument for argument'
as Elster puts it (1998: 9). Simply assuming that deliberation is inherently superior
or more desirable is inadequate. This is highlighted by the practical problems of
deliberation – the sort of issues that pragmatism is supposed to concentrate on.
Take for example deeply-held beliefs. 'Normal' and 'abnormal' discourses as Rorty
terms them. They may not be as exclusive as he portrays them and could easily
occur within what he terms 'normal' discourse or liberal democracy. Religious
beliefs such as those found in Northern Ireland provide a clear example. In bringing
together the different communities in order to encourage a peaceful settlement
there is the possibility that allowing the different participants to speak may actually
inflame the situation rather than lead to an inevitable settlement. This may then justify
less not more open discussion. Without a clear idea of what an emphasis upon
deliberation will achieve and a realistic appreciation of its limits then pragmatic planning, even with its acknowledgement of power and other structuring forces, falls
down some of the same holes as the collaborative approach.

Having said this, I would agree to a point with Hoch that

> pragmatism provides an antidote to the quest for certainty by exploring how we
> can democratically anticipate and prepare for different contingencies using
> practical and scientific knowledge to inform our purposes and plans (1997: 26).

For me, its value lies in three characteristics. First, its non-foundational basis
echoes many of the concerns of postmodern social theory and the trajectory of
new times without falling into the issues of relativism inherent within the extreme
postmodernisms of Baudrillard, et al. Second, because of this, it does provide a
methodology or direction which provides a basis for the future. Third, because it is
more of an attitude than a theory (a meta-narrative in the postmodern sense) it can
and does lend itself to adaptation as Forester, Hoch and others have found. This is
an important point as it allows for some of the criticisms that I have briefly outlined
above to be addressed as well as allowing it to be used as a basis for a (modified)
new planning.

CHAPTER 6

THE POSTMODERN AND PLANNING

Following a burst of activity during the late 1980s the interface between the post-modern and planning has largely gone quiet (Soja, 1997 and Sandercock, 1998 notwithstanding). However, it is perhaps not surprising that like the postmodern, postmodern planning is gloriously eclectic and vague. One looks in vain for a 'post-modern planning' after wading through countless critiques that purport to reflect upon the postmodern (as new times and social theory) and planning. Again, this is hardly surprising as the very essence of the postmodern is its penchant for dif-ference and its distrust of imposition. Soja (1997) claims that part of the reason for this lack of engagement between planning and the postmodern is also because of planning's essentially practical nature that calls for *praxis* as well as theoretical pondering. This practical nature has focused theorists' minds on the day-to-day work of planners in the 'real world' rather than giving them time to reflect as much as, say, geographers. There is undoubtedly something in this but I would contend that planning theorists have also been reticent in transforming ideas into practice because practice exposes the redundancy and impractical nature of their thinking. A far more important reason for this hiatus is that the *force majeure* of current plan-ning theoretical debate has taken on board the libertarian aspects of postmodern new times thinking but shied away from the consequences of a postmodern altern-ative which is seen as likely to involve either no planning or a less progressive, conservative approach. For example,

> the uncritical adoption of postmodernist assumptions would bring us to the brink
> of an abyss of indeterminacy, impairing our ability to maintain social continuity
> through change, to treat each other in a just and fully human way, and to justify
> public planning (Harper and Stein, 1995: 233).

Though how Harper and Stein can make such a judgement on the postmodern when a few lines earlier they state that no one exactly agrees as to what postmod-ern means is not clear. While planning theorists largely accept the 'postmodern as new times' critique they tend to focus their energies on the collaborative approach which provides a superficially progressive and emancipatory alternative that embraces the postmodern critique of modernist planning though provides a differ-ent neo-modernist and less nihilistic alternative.

Postmodern works on planning consequently fit into two broad camps (there is an irony in categorising them naturally): those that take a postmodern perspective in critiquing planning and call for greater diversity and tolerance, and those that actually try and explore the implications of this. None of the latter category provide anything more than a skirmish with the 'enemy' of modernist planning. The reason for including the postmodern and planning in the current group of four paradigms lies more with its unfulfilled potential rather than any clear alternative to the status quo (though as I note in Chapter 4, planning practice is adapting to the postmodern challenge, a fact ignored by postmodern planning writers who tend to present it as monolithically modern). I shall therefore examine both critics and those who suggest a more prescriptive postmodern way forward for planning.

POSTMODERN CRITIQUES OF PLANNING

Some of the literature on this has already been covered in Chapter 4 (e.g. the work of Beauregard and Sandercock) though more disparate work draws on other work, e.g., feminist-inspired critiques, that could be labelled postmodern through their use of social theorists such as Foucault and their emphasis on postmodern themes such as difference and plurality. For example, Moore-Milroy's (1989) Derridian analysis of planning texts and Boyer's (1983) Foucauldian analysis of planning history. Another strand has emphasised a postmodern analysis of planning that has focused on its 'darker' side following Nietzsche, Weber and the Frankfurt School (e.g. Yiftachel, 1994, 1998, Flyvbjerg, 1998, *inter alia*). Others could also be included because of the interface between postmodern analyses and the collaborative approach. For example, Forester's focus on language and power in planning practice has postmodern and post-structuralist elements. Most of these analyses have emanated from the US where the plurality of politics, society and planning practice provide a different context to the study of planning. Planning has also continued its magpie-like 'pick and mix' of social theory as regards the postmodern and drawn on other areas of thinking, including geography and cultural studies that provide non-specific thinking on space as opposed to process and politics.

As mentioned above, an important recent turn in the postmodern critiques has examined planning's 'dark side' building on Nietzschean and the Frankfurt School's analysis of the 'double-edged sword of modernity'. Yiftachel (1994, 1998) has been foremost in this approach, though he builds on the identification of a less progressive tradition in planning following Little (1994), Sandercock (1995), Wilson (1991), Thomas and Krishnaraynan (1994) and older Marxist-inspired think (e.g., Dear and Scott, 1981, Harvey, 1973, 1989). In a similar fashion to the 'is planning modern?' debate in Chapter 4, he argues that planning evolved with distinctive progressive ideals:

> a discernible consensus underlaid the development of planning thought and the emergence of the planning profession: planning should, first and foremost, act to improve people's (mainly physical) living conditions (Yiftachel, 1994: 217).

He argues that because this broad consensus is so widely accepted, most studies of planning focus on evaluating it. From his experience in Israel he argues that planning may well have a progressive potential, but that it can equally be used for regressive purposes. In what he terms 'pluralistic societies' (such as the United States, Australia and the UK) difference and threats to multicultural change are accommodated more subtly through, for example, market mechanisms. Whereas, in deeply-divided societies mechanisms such as planning can and are used to resist change and reinforce divisions. Yiftachel identifies four dimensions that anti-progressive planning control can take.

1 TERRITORIAL

Plans and policies determine land use which can be used to control weaker groups and minorities in such deeply-divided societies. This can be achieved through containment of minority settlements and allowing members of the majority group to settle there thereby altering the cultural homogeneity of the area. Further, territorial segregation according to class, race and/or ethnicity can be achieved through land-use policies that maintain distinctions and reinforce the status quo.

2 PROCEDURES

As Forester (1993) has demonstrated, planning can directly affect power relations through its communicative nature. But processes also affect the amount and level of participation and negotiation and thereby can be used for exclusion of groups or minorities and thereby reinforce or extend existing exclusion or repression.

3 SOCIO-ECONOMIC DIMENSION

This is a longer term impact of the 'darker side' of planning which results in both positive and negative distributional changes. Yiftachel has in mind here the mainly monetary impacts of planning such as land price rises due to the granting of permission to develop or the development of a road thereby improving accessibility. Planning can therefore be used as a form of 'socio-economic control and domination by helping to maintain and even widen socioeconomic gaps through the location of development costs and benefits in accordance with the interests of dominant groups' (1998: 11).

4 CULTURE

Yiftachel claims that a core culture within a city or nation-state is usually favoured over minority cultures, thereby forming another method of social and ethnic control.

Planning can and does have an impact on this minimisation of peripheral cultures 'by creating settlement patterns, dispersing or concentrating certain populations, placing communal, religious or ethnic facilities, housing and services in particular places, and governing the character and norms of urban public places' (1998: 11).

The significance of each of these four dimensions varies between different states and systems. In established liberal democracies it is likely that the socio-economic control will dominate while in 'homeland ethnic states' including Israel, the cultural and territorial dimensions are likely to dominate.

Yiftachel's concern therefore has been to 'broaden our understanding of planning by exploring as a double-edged activity with a potential to act regressively, using similar principles and tools' (1998: 12). Planning has the potential to oppress subordinate groups and is structurally devised to exert control and oppression. His argument depends on his assumption that planning was and is largely progressive in nature. While there are plenty of writers who sign up to that, there are equally many more, particularly of the Marxist school, who would argue that planning was never anything but an extension of the arm of the state. This market-supportive role has received particular prominence in recent years in the UK under the new right when planning was reorientated towards a clearly defined set of criteria that charged it with little more than maintaining property prices by restricting development in the exclusive Conservative-voting shire counties. In areas such as inner cities, where potential development did not harm elite interests, planning was largely removed (Allmendinger and Thomas, 1998). The market supportive and property value role of planning has long been recognised but simply came into sharper focus during the 1980s and 1990s. The answer to Yiftachel's 'revelation' that planning can be used for ends other than progressive social ones must surely be 'what did you expect?'. This is not to say that his typology of the different mechanisms by which this is achieved is not useful. It provides a non-Marxist analysis of the mechanisms by which planning can and is used in both neo-liberal and deeply-divided societies to the benefit of the state and elites. That planning has been used in more repressive regimes for more nefarious and less subtle ends again is not surprising. But the planning that Yiftachel describes in Israel, Masselos (1995) discusses in India and Mabin (1995) in South Africa can be said to resemble planning in less-divided countries in name only. Planning was used in South Africa to maintain segregation and prop up apartheid (Mabin, 1995). But where did that use originate from? Planning orthodoxy? Planning and its aims were a tool of the state which has little to say about planning other than it is a vacuum which is filled by ends and means that emanate elsewhere. Why should planning, if a modern project, be any different from other aspects of modernity which have 'dark sides'. If planning is modern then it becomes a tautology to say that it has 'dark sides' – all aspects of modernity do. We should be surprised if it didn't.

Yiftachel's real concern, along with Sandercock and the collaborative school, is that the market dominates planning and planning largely exists in modern societies to aid the market. 'It should have social aims!', they cry, like reducing inequality, increasing participation and saving the environment. The kind of use that a form of land-use control has been put in Israel and South Africa is likely to be abhorred by most and quite rightly. A further criticism can be directed at the *level* of Yiftachel's analysis. While he demonstrates that planning has undoubtedly been used to maintain and develop divisions within society, it does so at a broad, macro level. It tells us little about mechanisms, motivations or potential counter hegemonic practices at a local level that work either in favour of or against such broad uses of planning. To be fair, Yiftachel never claimed that his analysis aimed to do this, but a more holistic analysis might have drawn on the more micro-level political motivations of actors as Forester does to balance any claim that planning was repressive. Yiftachel's analysis of planning fits in loosely with a postmodern approach in that it questions its modern foundations. However, this is not for any postmodern alternative, but a better, more progressive modern basis for planning

POSTMODERN PRESCRIPTIONS FOR PLANNING.

My earlier point regarding the paucity of thinking on postmodern planning needs some qualification here. Because of the persistence of a theory-practice gap in planning, and its dependence upon thinking in other less practical orientated fields such as geography, sociology and cultural studies, there has been a degree of work on the interface between postmodern social theory, new times and planning at a theoretical level (e.g., Mommaas, 1996, Dear, 1986, Filion, 1996, Innes, 1995, Beauregard, 1996, Moore-Milroy, 1991, among others). Within these works one can find hints rather than route maps for a postmodern planning.

Some works have sought to be more prescriptive on the possibility of a postmodern planning. There is not a clear distinction between the analytical and more prescriptive approaches as the two often blur together. Most analytical interpretations include a nod in the direction of prescription. Beauregard's analysis, for example, includes the following as a basis for a postmodern planning:

> The texts of a postmodern planner, in fact, should be consciously fragmented
> and contingent, nonlinear, without aspiration to comprehensiveness, singularity
> or even compelling authority (1996: 192).

Ed Soja (1997) provides a thoughtful exploration of postmodern planning theory that builds on his earlier work (Soja, 1989) and its concern to map the postmodern landscape of geography. In a familiar build-up, Soja argues that planning finds itself in an 'increasingly postmodern world' that includes social restructuring

and reality and that planning theory still has a long way to go to adapt to these conditions.

> Such adaptation requires a much deeper and more disruptive critique than has
> yet occurred, especially if planning is to maintain the progressive project and
> emancipatory potential that have always been central to its purpose and
> development. For planning and planners to take advantage of the new
> possibilities and opportunities of postmodernity and to avoid its very powerful
> anti-progressive tendencies and enticing diversions into whimsy, planning theory
> and planning practice must engage in far-reaching deconstruction and
> reconstruction, perhaps a more far-reaching and wrenching conceptual
> restructuring than has ever occurred before (Soja, 1997: 238).

Soja follows the thinking of Eagleton (1996) and others that warn against the
conservative and anti-progressive character of theory in postmodern times *and* the
hijacking and abuse of postmodern theory to justify neo-liberal and right-wing policies including the 'end of history' theses and 'capitalism triumphant' claims of
Fukuyama (1989) among others. This pro-market/postmodern alliance is behind
the shift of planning towards a more market-orientated approach that rejects the
progressive aspects of planning as antiquated and part of the terrors of the *ancien
regime* of modernity. But there are possibilities for a more 'left-leaning' postmodern
planning that retains its progressive potential:

> Today, rather than responding by reasserting old epistemological truths,
> planning theorists must attempt to meet the opposition head on, on its own
> grounds, by creating a critical and progressive postmodernism of resistance
> and reconstruction, by opening up the possibility for a planning process and
> a planning theory that are radically in and for postmodernity rather than
> outside and against it – or else perilously suspended between (Soja, 1997:
> 245).

Soja advances three broad principles that should underpin such a project. First,
any new postmodern planning theory must build upon epistemological openness
and flexibility that are 'suspicious of any attempt to formalise a single totalising way
of knowing, no matter how progressive it may appear to be' (p. 245). Second, such
an openness should be used as a basis for understanding *and encouraging* social
reality including fragmentation, multiplicity and difference. Here Soja appears to
move towards verging on the cusp of endorsing a form of incrementalism and political fragmentation in practice (though it is difficult to gauge because the point is
not developed sufficiently). Finally, the basis for Soja's approach is the critical
writing of a host of postmodern theorists who provide a number of directions that
postmodern planning theory might take, including an interest in the politics of the

body, non-oppressive built environments and a new cultural politics of location, positionality, place, site and context (p. 247).

Soja's contribution should be welcomed for its attempt to provide some pointers towards a postmodern planning theory (and, by consequence, he assumes for planning practice as well). He takes a distinctly modern/postmodern approach that argues for a postmodern planning that works towards largely modernists aims – a typical postmodern 'pick and mix' approach – and thereby walks on the safer and less nihilistic side of the postmodern street. In this way he is similar in approach to the less radical postmodernists such as Fredric Jameson, for example. Nevertheless, while I would agree with much of Soja's analysis and parts of his approach, there remain serious questions over this attempt at a postmodern planning.

First, is it enough to focus on theory? Soja signs up to Beauregard's and Harper and Stein's 'planning theory at the edge of the abyss' thesis and like Beauregard, puts far too much emphasis on the basis, origin and importance of planning theory in implicitly portraying it as having an exogenous and exclusive cause and effect impact on practice that originates from a uni-directional 'top-down' source in the form of academic reflection. Is planning theory at an abyss? Simply, no. Much of what passes for planning theory as used in practice derives from a complex blend of personal, local and national concerns that largely follow an incremental route dictated by powerful discourses that derive from central government advice (e.g., Planning Policy Guidance Notes in England and Wales) and what Alexander and Faludi (1996) have termed 'planning doctrine' that includes, for example, the idea of green belts. Would it matter if planning theory were at an abyss? Not one jot. Because of the complex accretion of thinking behind planning practice and the role of planning as a state activity as much concerned with promoting economic growth as participation and environmental protection, it is unlikely that planning practitioners would notice if planning theorising disappeared overnight. 'Planning theory' as portrayed by Soja is of little consequence to planning practice.

Second, Soja falls into Lyotard's trap of attempting to force and ensure diversity which he sees as the essence of the postmodern. Diversity may be a *leit motif* of the postmodern but the postmodern must also include the right to homogeneity and modernity if it is to mean anything. It also surely includes the right to choose rather than be coerced into a straightjacket of diversity. Further, Soja also sets out some *a priori* concerns for a postmodern planning including race and gender. While it is difficult to criticise him for this from a practical or personal point of view these themes do present an issue that emerged in Chapter 3 and will do so again in Chapters 7 and 8, that is, should any attempt to build a postmodern planning include any *a priori* themes or thinking and if so, which? Does their inclusion add up to the replacement of modernist meta-narratives with postmodern ones? (in which case, is the postmodern merely fragmented modernism?). I argue in Chapters 7 and 8 that there do need to be some foundational rules for a postmodern planning but for different reasons.

Finally, the principles upon which Soja seeks to build his postmodern planning theory are both so abstract as to mean virtually anything to anyone, and are themselves based on a narrow concept of the postmodern. At the level of generality that Soja employs terms such as 'fragmentation, multiplicity and difference' (p. 246), neo-liberals could rightly argue (as I point out further on in this chapter) that market mechanisms could and do provide the basis for such concerns. Similarly, 'non-oppressive built environments' are an aim that virtually anyone could sign up to (as Held, 1987 says, 'we are all democrats now') though he accuses the political right of portraying the postmodern as a theoretical justification for such vague concepts as the 'end of ideology'. The implications of this vagueness for planning theory and practice are obvious. The detailed thinking on means and concrete ends, however worthy in aim, could come up with a very divergent and potentially oppressive planning that was arguably 'non-oppressive' to some depending on what 'non-oppressive' was taken to mean. The point is that without a more specific approach (which would itself be very 'un-postmodern' and falling even further into the Lyotard trap mentioned earlier) it is difficult to imagine a postmodern planning based on Soja's ideas. I return to this problem at the end of this chapter.

Leonie Sandercock's work has already been referred to earlier in the book because of her analysis of planning and modernity. However, her main aim in *Towards Cosmopolis* (1998) is the exploration of a 'postmodern utopia' in the form of

> A large city inhabited by people from many different countries (1998: 163).

Her concern therefore is squarely with a postmodern of difference and how planning (which is still assumed to exist though not in its current form(s)) can work with this. This stems directly from her analysis of current planning forms as being socially exclusive, gender biased, racially intolerant and unifying the diverse voices of minorities. Planning is out of step with changing social realities including migration, the rise of post-colonial and indigenous peoples and emergence of so-called minorities which all push for a more inclusive and sensitive planning that works with the changing faces of cities and regions. As opposed to Soja's account, Sandercock grounds her account of postmodern planning in the practical rather than the theoretical sphere. To provide such a postmodern city, Sandercock identifies five broad themes or principles that are

> The minimum foundations necessary to create a new order of urban civility out
> of the current new world disorder, and link these to debates about urban
> governance and planning (1998: 183).

(I) SOCIAL JUSTICE

The problem of current conceptions of social justice is that they are equated with market outcomes. Although some planning theorists have tried to address this bias, Sandercock argues that a broader definition of injustice and/or inequality is required that is not limited to the material, economic realm. Gender studies and feminist critiques have provided an alternative approach that links injustice with oppression and domination. Oppression is particularly relevant in the forms of cultural imperialism and violence against increasing diversity in the 'new world disorder'.

(II) THE POLITICS OF DIFFERENCE

Having identified the problem, the answer Sandercock proposes lies in an improved politics of difference based on an inclusionary commitment through discussion. Such a discursive commitment would emphasise the positive aspects of difference. Concerns over group unity and the focus of such on a proposal or immediate or local issues in such an 'identity politics' is raised and addressed by Sandercock. These groups, she claims, now participate in broader coalition politics to achieve more macro level aims such as social justice. And the homogeneity question is not an issue according to Sandercock as in *realpolitik* such demarcation does not exist. A politics of difference requires 'big tent' politics that includes such groups rather than excludes them.

(III) CITIZENSHIP

Building on the inclusionary ethic the next principle of a postmodern city concerns the question of citizenship. The *auslander* status of many citizens in increasingly fragmented societies requires a more fluid conception of citizenship that constantly reinterprets and refines what is meant by the term. Rejecting homogenising approaches that set out *a priori* what it is to be a citizen. Sandercock follows James Holston (1995) in his thinking on insurgent citizenship that push at the accepted boundaries of inclusion.

(IV) THE IDEA/L OF COMMUNITY

Building on the individually-orientated concept of citizenship, Sandercock goes on to argue for a reformed conception of community. Communities have traditionally been associated with either territorial exclusion ('we're in so you're out') or have been so vague as to be almost meaningless. Instead, like in formulation of citizenship, there are communities of resistance that refuse homogeneity and argue instead for multiple communities biased on the multiple interface of 'I'.

(V) FROM PUBLIC INTEREST TO A CIVIC CULTURE

Modernist planning is based on the vague and unified notion of the 'public interest' – how does this relate to a postmodern planning concerned with difference?

Implicit in the notion of the public interest is a planner and planned split – the technical expert working towards what are assumed to be commonly-agreed goals. This assumes a high degree of uniformity and sameness within society all of which has come unstuck with postmodern critiques. Consequently, Sandercock's unified public interest becomes a heterogeneous pubic interest. Avoiding the natural response to this that it would consequently lead to nihilism and inaction Sandercock instead argues that it is not the fragmentation of politics that would pit groups or individuals against each other, but power and domination. Here she begins to raise the spectre of the collaborative approach by arguing for a more inclusionary and pluralistic politics ('decision makers' are retained, though a veto power remains for 'important' aspects). The struggle is therefore *against* representation (though what it is *for* is not clear). The assumption is that allowing 'hidden' voices to speak will change existing processes and outcomes to appeal to some overall concept of justice (p. 198). So, the demonised 'public interest' becomes a more pluralistic and open 'civic culture'. Then, reluctantly, Sandercock turns to the *realpolitik* that precludes 'togetherness in difference' (p. 199) because of the economic rationality that divides society (though the link between the two is left for the reader to assume).

So what do these principles mean for a postmodern planning? What Sandercock is aiming for is a 'broader and more politicised definition of planning's domains and practices' (1998: 204). This new form of planning involves an eclectic approach including 'mobilisation, protests, strikes, acts of civil disobedience, community organisation, professional advocacy and research, publicity as well as the proposing and drafting of laws and new programmes of social intervention' (p. 200). Overall, Sandercock's planning is more active in the face of injustice and oppression. A new form of rationality is required to complement technical rationality, one that focuses on goals and is 'communicative' in nature[1] relying more on practical wisdom. Planning no longer needs to be comprehensive and can instead concern itself with being negotiative, political and focused. Planning should 'open up' its knowledge base and move on from a positivist basis to embrace different ways of knowing (e.g hermeneutics). In particular, local knowledge, founded in experiential, intuitive and contextual knowledges are not to be founded in traditional planning thought. There is a call for planners to become involved in community empowerment using their skills and a commitment to social and environmental justice to help communities and individuals to help themselves. But, stepping back from the implications of relativism, she perceives in a postmodern approach there is a wariness of community-led planning.

---

[1]Sandercock does not make clear whether this is the same as the basis for collaborative planning but I am assuming it is.

> Victories at community level almost always need to be consolidated in some
> way through the state, through legislation and/or through the allocation of
> resources (1998: 206).

Sandercock's *Cosmopolis*, it seems, applies to the micro-level processes, but not
to the structures and processes at 'higher levels' which are there to place a check
on the consequences of local planning.

Finally, there is the normative commitment to working in a *specific* rather than
the *public* interest on the basis that because it has never been value neutral, it
might as well own up and work in the interest of the most vulnerable. Overall,

> The emerging planning defined ... as an insurgent planning, is dedicated to a
> social project in which difference can flourish (1998: 206).

There are undoubtedly aspects of Sandercock's critique that echo with aspects of
the postmodern. The emphasis on difference, diversity, pluralism, etc., all provide
links with such thinking. Similarly, her analysis (already touched upon earlier in the
book) picks up many of the points I have raised. This work comes closest to a
postmodern planning. But coming 'close' needs to be clarified. First, it is *not* postmodern but a *blend* of modern and postmodern concerns and picks up aspects of
both in an eclectic mix that lies neither here nor there and consequently nowhere.
To be fair, Sandercock does not claim that it is postmodern planning perhaps
because the term is itself largely used pejoratively in the social sciences and planning theory. Nevertheless, it will be clear from my outline of her proposals that it
derives some if not most of its inspiration from postmodern concerns. But it is a
begrudging postmodern – one that wants to take the concerns with difference and
fuse them with traditional 'modern' thinking and processes: 'we will allow you to be
different but only to a degree because we still know best'. The second main
problem concerns the vagueness of the whole project. This in itself has two components. The first is the vagueness of theoretical basis of the book. It is now a
truism to say that the postmodern is a 'pick and mix' approach but Sandercock
takes this to an extreme by avoiding any theoretical principles upon which to
ground her project. It is a pinch of participatory democracy here and a bit of (even
vaguer) feminist-inspired critique there. Consequently, her *Cosmopolis* becomes
little more than an abstract collage of ideas and prejudices that do not equal the
sum of their parts. In another critique of the book, Sorensen and Auster have
attacked what they perceive as the lack of clarity in her thinking:

> the book frustratingly does not explain the nature of postmodern planning in
> which we presume that theory is either conspicuously absent or becomes
> intensely personal and wide ranging – reflecting each person's Weltanshauung
> (1998: 4).

They go on to criticise the multiplicity of normative thinking as well as the promotion of planning as both the cause and potential solution to many social ills such as injustice, inequality, prejudice and exclusion. The focus on a socially just and tolerant society does not engage with other aspects of a liberal society such as political stability, freedom of association, minimal government control, etc. Similarly, the book assumes that planning can address the social ills that Sandercock identifies. Income inequality and ethnic intolerance, argue Sorensen and Auster, are best tackled through other more related mechanisms such as adjustments to tax regimes, public education and anti-discrimination laws. But their biggest problem with Sandercock's analysis emerges from their own neo-liberal position concerning her preferred role for planning in social justice rather than market support. Such 'overtly' political concerns as this take planning outside a technical and professional arena and are 'incurably romantic' (1998: 9):

> Perhaps insurgent planning is not urban land-use planning at all, but akin to
> political activism or social work (1998: 10).

The attack on Sandercock's normative agenda and its lack of engagement with other aspects of liberal society is not really fair, as Sorensen and Auster clearly though implicitly pursue a economic liberal normative agenda of their own. But their criticism of the view of planning as both the origin and potential saviour of social justice is more apt. As they rightly point out:

> There have of course always been those ... who have wanted planning to be
> less about bricks and mortar and more about social justice (1998: 9).

There is nothing wrong with this and I find their criticism that the book is based on personal emotional ideology difficult to follow – what books are not? What is more relevant, however, is their focus on more achievable objectives for planning, the possibility if not inevitability of dashed expectations when planning cannot deliver the high objectives Sandercock sets it and the lack of any engagement with planning practice.

The case study of planning in Frome outlined in Chapter 4 demonstrated that planning practice was not stuck in the classic modernist past that Sandercock assumes. It attempted to work in the interests of others, particularly those who have been excluded by one means or another but it was also realistic about what could and could not be achieved through planning and where the real power in society lay. Sandercock, like postmodern social theorists and collaborative planners, assumes that by exposing power it will go away. But part of that power for her lies in the role of planning which, through unsubstantiated generalisations, works against issues such as social justice:

> In the past, policy issues have typically been defined on the assumptions and priorities of the privileged (Sandercock, 1998: 198).

Masselos (1995) demonstrates clearly how planning regulation is sometimes not instrumental in the structure and growth of inequality and how 'living together but differently' is, on occasions, a wishful dream in the face of deeply-embedded cultural differences. In the case of Bombay which he describes, it was not planning control that led to the growth and decline of different areas or the exclusion and inclusion of certain groups, but a complex blend of cultural differences and archaic rent controls. Order and regulation over what is developed where has emerged to replace the paucity of planning controls through informal channels enforced through deeply unequal mechanisms of money and extortion. This 'postmodern response' (the localised emergence of informal rules and regulations) masks coercion, exploitation and the maintenance of the status quo for hundreds of thousands of Bombay's poor. In another examination of inequality Marcuse (1995) identifies the perpetual existence of inequality within cities and its origin in the capitalist motor that almost defines the word 'city'. Spatial inequality is a product of economic inequality. For him it is not a two-way process, i.e., the spatial will not affect the economic. Consequently, it is difficult to envisage how planning can be expected to address inequality that is basically economic in origin.

It is not as though Sandercock's 'postmodern' planning is based on any higher form of morality. Difference is a relative term, particularly as it seems to apply solely to a narrow conception. Sandercock's difference is in reality little more than a rant about white, male, middle-class attitudes. Her so-called Utopia excludes communities such as Seaside or Celebration because of their white, middle-class dominance and their throw-back to less tolerant times. Confusing architectural style with social attitudes, Sandercock attacks these settlements for being 'highly unequal, feudal, patriarchal and . . . imperialist' (p. 194). But postmodernism, like liberalism, must learn to come to terms with attitudes that it may not agree with. If you are going to argue that one size no longer fits all then you have to live with the consequences. For all the talk of diversity, bottom-up processes, multiple communities and rejection of patriarchal, homogenised and biased systems, Sandercock accepts the need for some form of imposition. Locally-determined solutions, it seems, are not the answer as they can encourage myopic, selfish and anti-progressive and democratic attitudes.

> Sometimes it is only at the level of the city, or region, or even nation, that some encompassing conceptions of rights can be found, *and imposed* (1998: 196, emphasis added).

Sandercock, at the very least, appears both inconsistent and intolerant. The similarities between her and Lyotard become obvious – both feel a need to embrace diversity and relativism but both withdraw from its conclusions.

So what do I conclude from the postmodern critique of planning and the pre-scription for a postmodern planning? As I have mentioned throughout the post-modern analysis above, all of the approaches come from a distinctly left-leaning, socially progressive and market suspicious view of planning. Sorensen and Auster's neo-liberal critique of Sandercock's *Cosmopolis* highlights this well. As a consequence, they wrap their modern progressive planning in a postmodern shell while not addressing issues such as power that are at the heart of problems that they identify rather than questions of social justice. Both Soja and Sandercock are more concerned with planning in postmodern times rather than postmodern plan-ning. Although Soja does seem more concerned to explore a postmodern planning he does not get beyond broad principles and maintains a safe distance from the realm of practice. Neither truly gets to grips with how a postmodern planning could really work. Harper and Stein provide a highly partial view of postmodernity in their argument for a pragmatic alternative (Chapter 5). Although their characterisation of the postmodern relies on the extreme work of Derrida and others, they rightly point out that 'taken to its extreme, full-blown postmodernism would inevitably reduce planning to the impotent state feared by Beauregard. It would leave us with no basis for legitimate action' (1995: 240).

The central drawback of all the postmodern planning approaches to date is that they have focused on *themes* rather than *processes* or *structures*. Writers have set out general postmodern themes such as diversity and then over-optimistically expected them to filter down to processes, structures and everyday practice. The problems with this view is that, if the aim is to encourage postmodern planning practice, then the intervening processes and structures 'cushion' broad principles or changes introduced at higher levels, often leaving practice immune and free to carry on regardless. This was most evident during the Thatcher years when, despite fiery rhetoric about planners 'locking jobs in filing cabinets' and legislative and other changes to deregulate it, very little actually filtered down to the practice of planning (Allmendinger and Thomas, 1998). This is not surprising given the UK administrative tradition which emphasises a large degree of discretion at the local government level, giving professionals such as planners wide scope for interpreting the necessarily vague legislative and policy changes introduced centrally.

Soja falls into Lyotard's trap of enforcing diversity as a basis for postmodern planning. Enforcing diversity is not postmodern in the *strictest* sense as a number of his critics have pointed out (if the postmodern is to remain at a largely theo-retical or analytical level) but is perhaps a necessity if it is to move into the realms of praxis necessary for a discipline such as planning. If we take it as a necessity, then enforcing themes rather than processes or structures provides an unsatisfac-tory basis for a postmodern planning. This is because it represents a new master-narrative to replace older ones found in more modern approaches. It would also fail however because it is both too vague and does not address the 'meat' of planning where such a concern would need to be located – in the processes and structures as well as in themes and attitudes (planning doctrine). If a practical postmodern planning is to tackle these issues, and if we are to bite the bullet and admit their necessity (and they would naturally need to be much more specific), then an emphasis on process and structure needs to accompany an emphasis on themes. This would allow issues such as diversity to be 'built in' to the system but not enforced and thereby allow the possibility of other concerns emerging, including locally-determined priorities and thinking. The day-to-day practice of planning driven by doctrine (Alexander and Faludi, 1996) would then reinforce this and be working with, not against, postmodern structures. Surely a planning that was concerned with, but did not enforce issues such as plurality, social diversity, etc., and allowed them to be dismissed as well as fine-tuned to local circumstances would be more postmodern?

NEO-LIBERALISM

It is fair to say that the neo-liberal approach to planning is less a coherent theory and more a hegemonic force that has driven UK and other planning regimes in the past 20 to 30 years (Allmendinger and Thomas, 1998). While the collaborative approach may be a cause without a rebel, neo-liberal thinking has had plenty of rebels or champions both at an individual and organisational level that have been highly influential in government. As the UK planning system is highly centralised, such influence had been the driving force behind planning in the closing years of the twentieth century and, as I go on to argue at the end of this chapter, looks likely to continue well into the new millennium. But, like the other three schools of theory considered in this book, there is no one neo-liberal planning theory, but a diaspora of views, theories, prejudices and thoughts that come under the umbrella of 'anti' or 'less' planning. Of the four theories, it is the only one that comes out for a reduced role for state intervention in land use matters, and of the four it is and has been the most influential in directing planning thought. As such, neo-liberalism must be an important practical contender for planning in new times (as it has and will continue to have significant influence) as well as being a highly significant force on any rethought planning and the antithesis of theories such as collaborative planning. Ironically, there is an overlap between the radical atomisation of the postmodern perspective and the public choice individualism of neo-liberal economic theory – both could, from wildly different perspectives and ends of the political spectrum, argue for less or no planning at all.

WHAT IS NEO-LIBERALISM?

It is worth pointing out here what I mean by the term neo-liberal. As will become clear from the neo-liberal approach to land use regulation described below, it is a complex mix of liberal economics, public choice theory and normative beliefs concerning the role of the state and the primacy of markets. The broad umbrella of 'neo-liberal' can be seen to be a synonym for the new right in politics and as Low (1991) points out, a good starting point in any theoretical exploration of that can be found in the seminal work of F. A. von Hayek called *The Road to Serfdom* published in 1944. Hayek's work was a counter to the growing hegemony of interventionist thinking that was becoming popular in the west following the example of the Soviet Union. But he also linked the growth of the planned economy not only to a left-wing response but also to the right-wing variants in the guise of the growth of Fascism in Germany, Spain and Italy. Opposed to this is the 'liberal' age which Hayek defines as freedom in economic affairs and the accompanying personal and political freedom that was closely associated with it.

> Political freedom of the individual is thus seen to depend upon economic
> freedom, which in turn depends upon and is supported by the philosophy of
> individualism (Low, 1991: 165).

Hayek is not against all state planning, but the centrally-directed 'blue-print' variety reminiscent of the Soviet Union or the UK land use system after the Second World War. He accepts some role for planning, providing it is directed at identifiable externalities of urban living and orientated towards a market supportive role. However, such a planning must not be based on the whim of government:

> There must be no *ad hoc* action by governments. Laws must be universal,
> consistent and non-retrospective (Hayek, quoted in Low, 1991: 170).

Where government intervention is necessary, such as in the control of the money supply, then neo-liberal theory argues that it should be based on the concept of a 'rule of law' rather than administrative discretion. Such a rule of law would set out a framework for decision making that would be agreed beforehand and within which subsequent decisions would be made (Thornley, 1993). This minimal state based on the rule of law is a central theme of the neo-liberal approach. Other very strong themes running through the neo-liberal approach are the many variations of public choice theory. As Udehn (1996) concludes, in the last three decades there has been such a spread of economic thinking in the social sciences that it is now no exaggeration to speak of 'economic imperialism'. The public choice school is varied but a broad definition would be those

> who, influenced by classical economics, treat the individual not only as the
> empirical but also – in the model of the rational, self-interested, calculating, and

> utility-maximizing man – as the theoretical unit of analysis ... the so called
> 'economic' approach sees politics as a set of rules or strategies by which
> individuals order their relationships (Eulau, quoted in Udehn, 1996: 6).

Contrasted with the largely behavioural collaborative or pragmatic approaches, public choice theory views humans as *homo economicus* rather than *homo socio-logicus*.

There are five broad schools within the school of public choice theory (Udehn, 1996). First, there are the early and highly influential works of Downs (1957), Black (1958) and Buchanan and Tullock (1962) that reassessed the behavioural orthodoxy of political science by arguing that people act to maximise their own ends. This is true of politicians who seek to win the popular mandate as it is of the electors themselves. Politicians therefore promise policies that attract a vote on purely selfish grounds, while voters choose leaders who will improve their situation. Downs' theory regarding the convergence of political parties towards the centre as they compete for the floating voter was given a new twist by the ideological father of the new right Keith Joseph, when he talked of the 'ratchet effect' of socialism. Every new government made more promises concerning universal social welfare, pensions, full employment, etc., which attracted the support of voters who then demanded more at the next election. Second, there are the analyses of political business cycles (Wagner, 1977, MacRae, 1977). This manifestation incorporates pressure groups and bureaucrats into the analysis of self-serving behaviour, but argues that vote maximisation by politicians is skewed to the period immediately before elections. Politicians also do not treat all voters or groups of voters (interest groups) equally. They select for preference those interests that are more likely to benefit them. Third, like the refinements above, another school of public choice theory has examined the role of bureaucracies in politics (Tullock, 1965, Downs, 1967, Niskanen, 1971). This route views bureaucrats, contra Weber, as any other self-interested individual who will look to maximise their own interests first and those of wider society second. The influences upon bureaucratic decision making are varied and include:

> salary, perquisites of the office, public reputation, power, patronage, output of the
> bureau, ease of making changes, and ease of managing (Niskanen, 1971: 38).

Bureaucrats reflect the outlook of the population as a whole in that they are a mixture of self-interested and public-spirited individuals but the emphasis is on the former. Fourth, interest groups are also included within the remit of public choice theory (Olson, 1965, Stigler, 1975, Becker, 1983). The basic premise of the interest group field of public choice theory is that government regulation does not, as widely perceived, benefit the public at large, but is primarily, for the benefit of industries and occupations and, secondarily, for the benefit of politicians: representatives and their parties (Udehn, 1996: 27).

According to Stigler, regulation amounts to a redistribution of wealth from some groups in society to others. Consequently, the detail of that distribution will vary according to the interplay between the different groups in the political process and ultimately who can influence politicians most. Interest groups therefore lobby for special privilege that might include, for example, deregulation, a contract, tax exemptions or for a group to be recognised as a profession. Finally, public finance has also been included under the remit of public choice theory (Buchanan, 1979, Buchanan and Wagner, 1977). Public debt or deficit financing by national governments is seen as the bogeyman of public choice theorists as it encourages politicians to promise more than the country can afford. People will sign up to this system because they do not directly perceive the costs, particularly if they are the beneficiaries of such a route. There is a relationship or 'unholy alliance' between the self-interest of bureaucrats and that of the wider public in the bidding for such deficit budgeting:

> Without doubt, some considerable part of the observed growth in the public sector, at all levels, is directly traceable to the demands of the citizenry, genuine demands for more services accompanied by an increasing demand for more services accompanied by an increasing willingness to shoulder the tax burdens required for financing. But, once this is acknowledged, there can be little doubt but that a significant and remaining part of the observed growth in the public sector can be explained only by looking at the motivations of those who secure direct personal gains from the government expansion, gains that are unrelated to the benefits filtered down to the ordinary citizen (Buchanan, 1977: 6).

The public choice input into neo-liberalism provides little in the way of necessary public action. But, as Bosanquet (1983) and Gamble (1988) have argued, neo-liberalism is not simply a shift towards less government. The post-war welfare state has created a dependency culture which requires a change in attitude through encouraging the idea that inequality is an inherent and natural part of life. The potential problem of a state based on high inequality is that it can create tensions:

> In so far as unimpeded market forces tend to generate inequality, poverty, resentment and hostility, government must pay closer attention to the problem of political stability (Eccleshall, 1984: 109).

This requires a strong state as well as a deregulated one under neo-liberalism, as opposed to the more traditional 'one-nation' Conservatism that embraced redistributive policies and the welfare state. Thus the state has an added function. Not only is it to police the market but also provide stability through minimising dissent.

Gamble (1988: 8) has summed up the neo-liberal approach as 'free economy, strong state' and at a broad level it is difficult to disagree that there are elements of both inherent within it. However, it is equally the case that these two elements potentially contradict each other. Before I explore how in reality this has undermined the neo-liberal approach, I will first turn to how these broad arguments have been interpreted as applying to planning. The debate over the effectiveness and impact of planning from a neo-liberal perspective has a long history and is diffuse. I have focused mainly on UK critiques, though the neo-liberal school of theory has a powerful US component (see Evans, 1985, Harrison, 1977 and Stephen, 1988 for more international overviews). Although eclectic, it is possible to identify three broad categories of neo-liberal attitudes towards planning: the relationship between planning and the role of the market, the concern with the economic costs of land use regulation ('cost') and the ability of planning to take account of a multitude of market interactions ('perfect knowledge').

PLANNING, THE ROLE OF THE STATE AND MARKET

This criticism of planning develops the 'crisis of the state' themes popular during the 1970s in particular, and the questioning of social democracy and the post-war welfare consensus generally. Following Hayek, the issue of freedom is central to this critique (the freedom of the market being incrementally eroded by the impact of planning and other regulations). Such an evolution of land use control in the post-war period has not involved any fundamental assessment of the impact, objectives or direction of planning regulation. Far from tackling the problems it sought to eradicate, intervention has perversely created further problems that have led to further intervention (Walters, 1974: 6). Although it is conceded by the neo-liberal critics of planning that the externalities of 'communal urban existence' require amelioration, they argue that this should be through market mechanisms (third party insurance, compensation, the purchase of planning permissions, etc.). The problem of bureaucratic intervention is that it inhibits the ability of the market to function properly and leads to reduced individual choice (Pennance, 1974). The main difference between market-based intervention and that of bureaucracy is the concept of 'public good' and 'community interest':

> In Britain, we are in danger of lifting the community above the individual. Powers are given to ministers and officials to act in the name of the community with an arbitrariness which disregards the rule of law and property rights of citizens (Denman, 1980: 3–4).

Because the operation of planning is essentially a political rather than technical activity, it is open to the competing claims of powerful interest groups and the murky world of political bargaining (Butler, 1987a). This encourages a NIMBY-type attitude where objectors to a proposal, often in undeveloped land on the edge of existing settlements, have significant influence on the outcomes of decisions because such decisions are taken locally, by politicians wanting re-election. On the other hand, those who would benefit from any development through increased jobs or easier access to facilities, for example, are not *directly* related to a specific proposal because their interest is not recognised until after development. Thus, the pro-development lobby is naturally diffuse, and

> The prospects of a rational policy are inevitably dimmed when such powerful partisan forces are at work against the vast but unmustered interests of the general public (Butler, 1987a: 2).

There is, according to Peter Hall, an unholy alliance of left councils in London wanting to keep development in their areas and right-wing councils in the shires who are essentially 'anti-development' (Bennett, 1987: 21). This political domination of planning permeates the national and local levels. Some MPs, for example, have blamed the loss of their seats on the changing socio-economic background of their constituencies through the development of upper-class housing (Irvine, 1987: 26) and it would be naïve to expect that this did not influence government or local policy. Bennett (1987: 26) accuses some local politicians of schizophrenia, wanting both the benefits of growth (increased local spending, jobs, increased political majorities, etc.) while arguing against it on conservation grounds. A public choice approach, like that adopted by Pennington (1996), explicitly blames bureaucrats and politicians of replacing individual and transparent self interest with collective and opaque advantage:

> Government failure is a product of perverse incentives in the political process which are largely to the benefit of politicians, interest groups and bureaucrats (Pennington, 1996: 15).

This highly political dimension to planning leads to the growth of what could be termed 'planning doctrine' (Alexander and Faludi, 1996) where certain ideas and concepts become hegemonic and dominate decisions and outlooks. One such doctrine, according to Butler (1987: 2), concerns green belts which are presented as being 'a touching image of rolling downs and charming farmsteads' while the reality is that a large proportion is not green, but brown. Gravel extraction, rubbish pits, mining slag, disused factories, warehouses and quarries all exist in the 'green' belts, though the rustic image perpetuates and is the basis of a virtual ban on any new development. Corkindale (1998: 41) further argues that the political basis of planning is not conducive to the adoption of clear policy goals for it – a situation that inhibits the efficient use of land.

The overall impact of land use intervention is to create uncertainty in the development process and discourage development and/or redevelopment that would otherwise take place in an unfettered market.

PERFECT KNOWLEDGE

Perfect knowledge concerns the inability to understand and cope with the complexity that makes up life. Hayek contended that central planning required foresight which will then be used to direct human endeavors. This direction, or plan, runs contrary to the development of successful human societies. As planners (and everyone else for that matter) are unable to replicate this complexity they are forced into meaningless simplifications when they 'plan' (Jones, 1982). Because of the discretion available to planners through their professional status and the highly centralised UK administrative structure which grants wide interpretive powers to individuals, planners are less likely to indulge the views of others. This compounds the problem of a small number of decision makers trying to second-guess the multiple interactions of many players. Without the power to coerce, planners have no more predictive ability than any other individual:

> Because the collection, collation and dissemination of information is impossibly lengthy virtually all statutory planning is years behind the times in outlook (West, 1974: 31).

However, the view that planners do somehow possess such a superior knowledge is accepted by the public at large because they fear the effect on their property prices. So planning proceeds as a myth of technical knowledge, perpetuated by professional groups such as the RTPI and planners themselves who benefit from the view of 'planning as control'. Butler argues that planners and government should be more honest about the ability of planners to look into the future:

> We must also accept our inevitable ignorance of what the future holds, and recognise the shortcomings of all our attempts to plan for it (Butler, 1987: 8).

He goes on to list some of the consequences of this ignorance, including the unexpected and unplanned for increase in demand for retailing space in the mid to late 1980s. Plans approved in 1979 severely underestimated the amount of retail floor provision that would be needed in the coming ten years – the number of hypermarkets in the UK doubled between 1979 and 1985. This led to incremental decision making in retail proposals which often damaged rather than complemented town centre retail provision. Similarly, many plans continued to allocate land for light industrial purposes long after the recession of the early 1980s decimated manufacturing industry. Service industries experienced a massive growth in the same period but were largely ignored in approved plans, prompting the government to allow changes of use from industry to offices without the need for planning permission. Overall,

> Policy is merely recognising established market forces, neither anticipating nor effectively controlling them (Waters, 1987: 14).

Because of the complex nature of the market, planning necessarily abstracts from reality in order to plan. The result can often be counter-productive according to Waters (1987) as was demonstrated with the changes to the Use Classes Order in 1987. This order defines categories of use for buildings and land and permits changes of use within categories which do not require planning permission. In the mid-1980s, the Conservative government decided to 'simplify' it by reducing the number of categories in order to attempt to promote development. However, they were forced into creating sub-divisions within categories after lobbying from concerned parties, including conservation groups and professional bodies, that the proposals went too far and would lead to damaging development. The result, according to Waters, is that the new system is now more complex and less understood than the one it replaced. Connected to the market intervention and cost arguments is the natural outcome of the complexity arguments: planning needlessly distorts competition and market mechanisms. As Bennet (1987: 23) puts it:

> If government wishes to pursue a demand led economy, then they have to bite the bullet and recognise where the market wishes to go: the South East.

The complexity of planning is a result of trying (and failing) to intervene in another complex system – but planning remains simply because its complexity suits the status quo, i.e., the preservation of greenfield land for affluent and influential residents. This has an obvious cost, according to the neo-liberal critics of planning.

COST

The arguments concerning cost fall into two camps. First, there is the administration of the system that causes delays and development opportunities and hence jobs and prosperity. The second concerns the wider implications of the economic impact of planning regulations based on the assumption that there is unlimited demand for land and development that is only constrained by supply-side constraints including planning regulations.

On the former of these two points, Pennance (1974) considers the cost of planning in terms of innovation and initiative is 'probably very high'. He considers six months a conservative estimate of the time taken to secure planning permission, while Jones (1982) points to some authorities that deal with only 14 per cent of planning applications within the statutory eight-week period. This leads to what Morris terms the substantial unseen costs of the planning system:

> namely the very great delay that can occur between deciding to make some
> alteration to one's property and the eventual granting of permission (1998: 8).

Corkindale (1998: 15) estimates the cost of running the planning system to be around £1 billion per annum (though he does not take into account the fee income generated which would substantially reduce this figure). Criticism, it seems, is not confined to right-wing politicians. Walters quotes the former Labour minister Richard Crossman as concluding there were two things wrong with planning, 'the delay it causes, and the quality of its results' (1987: 13).

On the second point, Walters (1974) and Bramley and Watkins (1996) believe that planning increases land prices through scarcity and thereby discourages redevelopment. Denman (1980) lays the blame for the large increases in land and house prices during the 1970s squarely at the door of land use policy and claims that such delays in dealing with applications directly accelerate and inflate house prices. Where development does take place, Walters argues, the planning system extracts extra costs that are passed on to the consumer in the form of high property prices (1987). But it also creates a form of economic segregation.

> While those who are fortunate enough to get their neighbourhood restricted
> against outsiders enjoy an economic rent, people in other localities have to pay
> its price (Butler, 1987: 4).

This increase in land prices restricts the movement of labour as those wishing to relocate to the South East from the North find it increasingly difficult to do so without a significant increase in salary to pay for higher housing costs. This in turn has a spillover affect on wage inflation and competitiveness. The Confederation of British Industry has collected evidence of this effect:

> [There is)] Almost no opportunity to successfully recruit people living north of
> Peterborough in low cost housing areas, purely because of price differentials.
>
> On several occasions we have endeavoured to recruit more skilled staff from
> other areas of the country, particularly the North East; and on each occasion,
> after an initial trial period in the area, they have moved back with the main
> comment that it would be impossible for them to adapt to the living cost in the
> Cambridge area ... Skilled engineers and welders, particularly, are available in
> other parts of the country but are unable to move to the South East (quoted in
> Bennett, 1987: 19).

Bennett (1987) believes the consequences will be increasing polarisation between rich and the poor in the South East. But there is also a qualitative or quality of life

aspect that is a theme that is taken up by Evans (1987) who charts the intensifica-
tion of developments in the South East as a consequence of these restrictive planning policies. The number of bungalows built in the South East in 1969 was 26 per
cent of the total housing stock, while the proportion of flats was 3 per cent. By
1985, the proportion of bungalows had fallen to 12 per cent and flats had risen to
13 per cent.

> There is a shift towards land intensive uses with respect to housing. People are
> in a sense being forced, by economic pressures, to avoid land-intensive sites
> (Evans, 1987: 31).

Reading University has calculated the personal economic cost of restrictive planning policies. They estimate that the people of Reading are about 10 per cent
worse off because of the planning system, due to various costs such as land
prices, extra travelling to work or shops, etc. (Evans, 1987: 32). This equates to
between £640 per household per annum at the urban periphery and £775 per
household per annum of household income at the urban core (Corkindale, 1998:
15). The relaxation of planning controls would not result in a desert of tarmac,
according to the same study, but an increase in Reading's area of around 30 per
cent. The result is that preservation of one hectare of land in that part of the south
east costs society around £1 million (at 1987 prices).

    Pennington (1996) examines the impact of this cost upon rural business devel-
opment and argues that the ever-growing list of regulations leads to a presumption in
favour of existing inefficient and mainly agricultural land uses. Designations such as
green belts increased from 1.7 m to 4.5 m acres between 1979 and 1990. Farmers
have been replaced by conservationists such as the Campaign for the Protection of
Rural England and the National Trust as the dominant interest group of the countryside,
leading to the gradual shift in countryside and planning policy towards conservation.

> Local authority planning committees are filled with politicians, so afraid of
> raising the ire of Nimby (Not in My Back Yard) and Banana (Build Absolutely
> Nothing Anywhere Near Anybody) . . . that it is virtually impossible to achieve a
> planning permission for any non-agricultural, small business development
> (Pennington, 1996: 44).

Given these costs and drawbacks, the question that Evans (1987) asks is, 'is it
worth it?'.

THE ALTERNATIVES TO CURRENT ARRANGEMENTS
The answer to the above question would seem to be 'not in its present form'. Apart
from the wide-ranging criticisms of the principles and practices of post-war planning, most critics do not follow Siegan's laissez-faire line that

better zoning is no more the answer to no zoning than better censorship is to no censorship (quoted in West, 1974: xii).

Instead, they come forward with proposals for a modified form of land use intervention that takes account of the externalities of modern living. The underlying theme is of neo-liberal deregulation that reorientates planning in a market supportive rather than restrictive role. The overall position of the critics can best be summed up by Jones:

> Planning policy in Britain is ill-conceived and poorly administered. The aims of it
> are obscure and there is little evidence that they are achieved even where they
> can be discerned (1982: 25).

Following Jane Jacob's work (1961), a common criticism is that planning discourages diversity and competition between uses particularly in urban areas. Such diversity is a natural outcome of the market and encourages efficient uses of land. Rather than trying to control land use per se, the negative externalities that spring from such diversity should be the focus of planning (Pearce et al., 1978). Pennance (1974) calls for planning to concentrate on identifying these externalities, how they call for planning intervention and how they might be handled. Like the problem of immediate and diffuse interests concerning individual applications, Jones considers the main impediment to the shift towards an externality-focused planning are the images of unregulated urban form:

> Defenders of planning are apt to conjure up visions of the hideous and garish
> free-for-all which would result if it were removed. It is quite possible, though,
> that the resultant order might be more popular to tastes and convenience than
> the environment imposed by the planning class (Jones, 1982: 21).

From the plethora of alternatives there are three broad schemes put forward for a re-thought planning: wholesale structural reform with a market emphasis, partial reform with differing 'levels' of control and, finally, a system that remains similar to the current approach but with power and decision making centralised, decisions reorientated towards a market emphasis and a strengthened strategic dimension.

The first form of alternative has been advanced by the likes of Steen (1981), Jones (1982) and Evans (1987) among others (Steen and Jones were MPs during the 1980s and had significant influence upon land use policy development of the Conservative governments during that decade). Jones (1982) proposes a five-point plan. First, a major structural reform would place the entire planning system with land use tribunals. These would decide on cases of noise and pollution and between uses and what should be done. Second, private covenants would replace conditional planning permission and conditions that would be drawn up on an

individual or area basis. Third, there would be direct ministerial control over politically sensitive proposals such as green belts, Areas of Outstanding Natural Beauty
and conservation areas. Fourth, third-party insurance would be required for all
private buildings to cover claims against externalities such as loss of light caused
by adjacent development. Fifth, there would still be the need for public inquiries for
large proposals such as power stations. Over and above this system, Jones argues
that conservation and listed buildings should remain and be separated from planning controls as the two have 'nothing to do with each other'. Jones believes that a
shift to a more deregulated system would naturally encourage the market to fill
some of the gaps vacated by planning. Mortgages for certain areas currently
subject to planning blight because of uncertainty about their future would become
available, but at different rates to reduce the risk to the lender. Insurance companies would emerge as a major player in the regulation market, and private
covenants, which were widely used before comprehensive planning legislation
appeared and are still very popular in the US, would once again fill the role currently
the remit of planning regulations. Whatever the system, the overall sentiment is that
'planning policy will have to be mediated through the market' (Evans, 1987: 29).

A refinement of this approach has been put forward by Corkindale (1998)
who argues that as the state cannot be relied on to make economically-efficient
decisions about development proposals or satisfactory judgements about the
appropriate balance between economic and environmental gains and losses, then
the only answer is to privatise land use development rights. This would involve a
form of the 'User Pays' principle which would involve government setting out in
advance what constitutes acceptable and unacceptable externalities. Should the
developer breach these standards, they could be challenged in the courts who
could grant compensation to the community (Corkindale, 1998: 43). Planning permissions could be 'sold' by a community at a price calculated to compensate them
for any noxious externality.

> Landowners owning development rights can either exercise those rights in
> development zones or sell them to others (Corkindale, 1998: 53).

Thus the planning system would concentrate on identifiable externalities rather
than uses.

The second form of alternative follows the approach proffered by the Adam
Smith Institute (Adam Smith Institute, 1983) and Waters (1987) and is based on
the spatial differentiation of regulation into three zones. The first type of zone, the
'restricted' zone, would still have controls as now although procedures would be
simplified and administration would be by a central government body. The second
type of zone would be for industrial areas and inner cities where the only regulation
would be on the grounds of safety, public health, pollution and noise control. The

third type of zone, a general zone, would cover the rest of the country and include residential areas and, according to Thornley (1993), would occupy a middle ground between strict conservation and planning-free 'industrial' zones. Whether there are eventually three zones or another number is less relevant than the idea that

> there should be a clearer spectrum of different planning regimes applied
> appropriately in different ways (Walters, 1987: 26).

Finally, and more recently, there has been a shift towards a more centralised, market-orientated and strategic role for planning. This approach accepts the overall thrust of a planning system, but seeks significant reorientation of policy:

> In deciding land use, we need a strategy which is flexible enough to
> accommodate new and unexpected opportunities while preserving what is best;
> a policy which takes national costs and benefits into consideration when local
> planning decisions are made; a policy which is quick and predictable in its
> operation (Butler, 1987: 8).

Butler's main idea is to correct what he terms the 'cost–benefit imbalance' (1987: 9) of local decision making that favours NIMBY style attitudes over strategic questions. To achieve this, he proposes three possible changes. First, he would take decision making away from the local political arena to a development commission or planning body which would balance local and national interests and thereby de-politicise difficult decisions. Such decisions would be made quickly on the basis of explicit guidelines that form the second plank of Butler's proposals. In the area of green belts, for example, national guidelines would make clear which areas of green belt were worthy of protection and which could be developed. They would also make clear what kinds of development would be permitted and prioritise uses, e.g., environmentally sensitive, and what proportion of land would need to be reclaimed. Finally, another approach could be to follow the example of the French government who determine how many developments would be permitted of a certain use over a period of time. For example, it could be that there is the demand for six regional shopping centres across the UK in the next ten years. A cost-–benefit analysis approach would then be used to determine the areas and then there would be a moratorium on any further developments. Butler's proposals have clear implications for locally-led planning and, in Water's opinion,

> It is significant that it is not just the regulations but also the 'democratic'
> procedures of the planning system which have to be relaxed at the laissez-faire
> end of the spectrum (1987: 14).

But the problems in attempting this should not be underestimated:

to impose a more rational structure over the heads of local representatives has always been thought a prickly political problem (Butler, 1987: 7).

This gives a flavour of the neo-liberal approach to planning. As I mentioned above, the main difference between the neo-liberal and other approaches lies in its use as a basis for planning in the UK throughout the 1980s and beyond. It is the experience of that jump from theory to practice that I now turn.

THE EXPERIENCE OF THE 1980S

Reflecting the rather eclectic basis of neo-liberal theory, the approach to planning throughout the 1980s was similarly varied. Various initiatives were introduced throughout this decade that, to greater or lesser degrees, sought to reorientate planning, though not abolish it altogether. The *scope* of planning control was limited to land use matters only through government circulars such as 22/80 and 23/81. The *purpose* of planning was shifted to a market supportive one with the introduction of circular 1/85 while alterations to the Use Classes Order and the General Development Order lifted planning controls from some business and householder developments. But the most high profile of changes introduced during this period was undoubtedly Urban Development Corporations, Enterprise Zones and Simplified Planning Zones. Urban Development Corporations, for example, took planning controls from local authorities and posited them with an elected board. But, regardless of the ideological foundations to these changes the Conservatives never seriously challenged the planning system systematically. As one of the most libertarian of planning ministers commented at the time:

> There will be those that say we are intent on weakening the planning system.
> Nothing could be further from the truth. A strong and effective planning system
> is the best way to encourage sensible development and protect the countryside
> where it is necessary (Nicholas Ridley, quoted in Thornley, 1993: 123).

Instead they pursued a 'middle way' that emphasised pragmatic shifts over whole-sale reform. The problem was that the Conservatives were as much wedded to planning as any other party mainly because of the need to appease conservation-ary interests within the largely Conservative-voting rural areas and the patrician authoritarian conservative faction within the parliamentary party. But the experience of the Conservative governments' attempts to embrace elements of the neo-liberal agenda during the 1980s and 1990s highlights some important aspects of the limits of this approach (Allmendinger, 1997, Allmendinger and Thomas, 1998). First, many of the more radical proposals that the Conservatives originated when in opposition such as their Freeport concept were eventually severely watered down when finally implemented. Originally, the Tory flagship of Enterprise Zones were to be akin to Peter Hall's 'Essay in non-plan' where

> Small selected areas of inner cities would simply be thrown open to all kinds of initiative, with minimal control. In other words we would create the Hong Kong of the 1950s and 1960s inside inner Liverpool and Inner Glasgow (Hall, 1977: 417).

Far from being a radical deregulatory solution to the problems of inner cities that initially included exemption from trade union recognition, health and safety legislation and taxes, there was a

> definite change of emphasis ... in the package. Originally in Howe's [the government minister in charge] proposals the problem was one of planning blight or decay, the 'mortmain' or dead hand for which the remedy was deplanning. As a negotiated package emerged, however, the planning freedom was increasingly qualified and the advantages of the zones were to be seen as primarily fiscal (Botham and Lloyd, 1983: 36).

The dilution of the deregulatory aspects of Enterprise Zones came from government departments and the objections of other government bodies and local authorities that were concerned with the impact of it. Regardless of the merits of such arguments, the point is that a radical neo-liberal government concerned with removing supply-side constraints such as planning regulation could not implement their proposals in the face of concerted pressure.

Second, where deregulation was introduced, it did not have the impact the Conservative government envisaged. While the attraction and success of Enterprise Zones was essentially fiscal, simplified planning zones, on the other hand, were mainly areas of deregulation. In a zone, planning permission was granted in advance for a variety of uses subject to certain conditions, such as a maximum height restriction. The government considered that such an approach would promote development by creating 'certainty and flexibility in the development process' (Department of the Environment, 1988). Although they could be any size and be designated in just about any area of the country by a local authority or any other body (including developers and landowners) they were not attractive to private or public bodies and only 13 were ever adopted. The reason was that developers and businesses did not consider regulations such as planning to be inhibitive of development. Of far more concern to them was the state of the economy generally, or more local matters such as taxes (Allmendinger, 1997).

Third, there was actually significant support for existing regulation from businesses and voters. On the whole businesses did not like the 'open' deregulated approach where 'anything goes'. They were investing large amounts of money and wanted some certainty that their investment would not be undermined by a new adjacent development that, for a variety of reasons, might devalue their own. The planning system provided that level of certainty by allowing landowners to comment or object to proposals on an ad hoc basis. As the Conservatives found in the late 1980s, voters also liked the existing planning system for similar reasons. A rash of proposals had emerged for new settlements around London that would have meant large areas of greenfield land being developed. Local residents in these areas tried to use the planning system to fight these proposals but found that the planning framework had been weakened throughout the 1980s leaving a strategic vacuum. All the proposals were eventually thrown out by central government who feared alienating the largely Conservative-voting protesters. One outcome was a 'U'-turn on planning policy by government that reintroduced a locally-led strategic approach to planning. This, however, did not equal the end of a neo-liberal approach.

CURRENT ANTI-PLANNING SENTIMENTS

Although the 1980s can be seen as the confrontational high-water mark of deregulation and neo-liberalism in UK, planning in the 1990s has witnessed a less blatant reorientation that can be seen as more strategic and subtle in its approach. It is more strategic in that it does not seek to deregulate planning controls for purely ideological reasons. It is far more practical and linked to economic growth. Change is also emanating from outside the traditional land use government machinery, and important policy statements on the future of planning are coming from other departments, particularly the Department of Trade and Industry and the Treasury. It is subtler in that there is an eclectic mixture of centralisation, decentralisation, regulation and deregulation at work. Nevertheless, there is a clear underlying push to rethink planning and to question the shibboleths of doctrine that have remained largely unchanged in the past 50 years.

This re-emphasis has taken two forms. First, there has been the more subtle doubled-edged shifts found in *Modernising Planning* (DETR, 1998a) that have seen both deregulatory and regulatory proposals. For example, the commitment to a more influential European context for planning, as well as strengthened and expanded national planning policy statements, imply a shift towards more, not less, regulation. Similarly, the implication of devolution to the Scottish Parliament, the Welsh Assembly and an elected Mayor for London, as well as the possibility of English regional government may be welcome shifts in terms of democratic accountability but they do not add up to a deregulated regime. However, there has been a parallel emphasis on speed and deregulation through the proposal to increase the use of expedited procedures for major applications (for example, road and rail links, airports, mineral extraction, etc.). There are many parallels with the 1980s' emphasis in this shift and particularly in the mechanisms such as Special Development Orders.

Second, there is a groundswell of government and other reports and thinking that point towards an even more radical reorientation of planning. The government has always placed a high emphasis on the traditional Labour concerns of employment and made it clear even before the election that regulations, including planning, would not stand in the way of employment. The then Shadow Minister for Planning and Regeneration, Keith Vaz, talked about the 'cancer of delay' in planning (Vaz, 1996) while current planning Minister Richard Caborn has commented:

> I think the planning process has locked in for far too long, with its
> procrastination and delays, a considerable amount of potential investment that
> was available (Planning, 1st May, 1998: 18).

This attitude has been growing with the publication of a number of government policy documents. The Chancellor's Statement on the Economic and Fiscal Strategy Report in June 1998 made it clear that the Government were committed to a wholesale review of government regulation:

> where government is unnecessary or restrictive we should not act at all and the
> results of the spending review will mean reform or modernisation (Brown,
> 1998).

The Pre-Budget Report in November of that year committed the government even further by setting out a strategy that included ensuring that regulation promotes economic growth and, in particular,

> [to] work on the effects of the planning system on the competitiveness of
> businesses, particularly in growth industries (H. M. Treasury, 1998: Chapter 3).

But the most recent development has been the publication of a report on UK competitiveness by the McKinsey Global Institute (1998) and the government's response in its White Paper on Competitiveness (DTI, 1998). The McKinsey report examined the reasons why some areas of the UK economy were performing better than others, and one of its main conclusions was that planning regulations were playing an important part in the poor performance of companies and holding back those sectors of the economy that were performing well. Food retailing was seen as a successful area of economic activity by world standards, though there were still a high number of small stores which had low productivity and the larger, more productive stores with higher productivity were not reaching their full potential. The primary reason, the report concludes,

> is that land use and planning regulations make it difficult for large-format
> operators to develop new sites or expand existing ones. This limits their ability to
> compete with, and ultimately displace, less productive operators (McKinsey,
> 1998: 14).

Similarly, the hotel sector was identified as being less productive in international comparisons because of the extra 40 per cent owners have to pay to redevelop or refurbish hotels due to the cost of planning regulations, building codes and listed building status. Software, one of the fastest growing and most productive aspects of the UK economy, was also being held back from being more productive due to the role of planning. There was a great benefit to productivity from creating clusters of like companies:

> But the development of such clusters around Oxford, Cambridge and other
> natural communities has been slowed or even prevented by local planning
> restrictions (McKinsey, 1998: 16).

The report called for a comprehensive reform of land use regulations and claimed that piecemeal reform would prove inadequate.

Urban Regeneration is another of the government's main concerns and this too has been linked to the role of planning. In a fusion between the language of the 1980s and the concerns of the 1990s, Robinson et al. (1998) argue that statutory rules and regulations can inhibit the progress in economic and social regeneration of communities. What is needed is

> an environment where rules and regulations can be made more flexible to
> ensure these activities (community development and enterprise) are properly
> supported (Robinson, et al., 1998: 1).

As will be obvious from the description of the plethora of anti-regulation reports on planning above, the McKinsey report is not the first examination of the UK economy that has found planning regulations wanting. But what made the McKinsey report different was the public weight given to it by Ministers immediately after its publication, and the direct link to the Competitive White Paper published only a month later (DTI, 1998). The competitive and productive focus of McKinsey was picked up in the Department of Trade and Industrys approach which addressed the particular issue of reviewing the planning system to promote the needs of hi-tech clusters.

It is too early to come to any firm conclusions regarding the implications of these shifts or the weight that is given to such statements in the outcome of any assessment of planning. But what is clear is that the future direction of land use control is being influenced by government departments other than the DETR who occupy highly-influential positions and who are headed by influential ministers.

CONCLUSIONS

The over-riding basis of public choice theory is of self interest or 'utility maximisation' in the economic jargon. There have been ample studies of the predictions and
foundations of the various strands of public choice theory to enable us to conclude
what might appear obvious, namely, that 'Political man is not the selfish creature
suggested by public choice' (Udehn, 1996: 60). Tufte (1978) and Hee-Soh
(1986) have highlighted the important role of ideology in economic policy making
and downplayed the limited evidence for the existence of business cycles in
national politics. But, while it is appealing to reinforce the generally cynical view of
politicians as being ready to manipulate economies for their own benefit, this still
does not necessarily imply self-interest, merely a desire to win elections. This can
be for reasons other than self-interest, e.g., public interest. Similarly, the public
choice view of bureaucrats as being concerned primarily with maximising budgets
to benefit from increased salaries, reputation, power, patronage, etc., is also highly
questionable. Dunleavy (1985) criticises this view on three grounds. First, the view
of bureaucracies as homogenous is mistaken – they are varied in aims and constitution. Rather than assuming that bureaucrats in such heterogeneous circumstances are all concerned with maximising their own benefits through budget
maximisation, there are other ways of achieving personal benefits – managers
might, for example, be concerned with minimising budgets and costs in order to
please political masters. Second, there are many ways for a bureaucrat to act in
their own interest that do not involve budget maximisation. While self-interest may
be a motive, this cannot be automatically assumed from any method employed by a
bureaucrat. Finally, and related to the above point, bureaucrats can also be motivated by a conception of the common good.

The view that voters seek to maximise their utility is, in Udehn's (1996) view,
the most problematic of the public choice assumptions. In their study of local politics, Wilson and Banfield stated:

> We have shown both that a considerable proportion of voters, especially in the
> upper income groups, vote against their self interest narrowly conceived and
> that a marked ethnic influence appears in the vote (1964: 885).

Other studies have demonstrated that voters reflect on national economic conditions and vote in a *sociotropic* way, i.e. reflecting their assessment of

> inflation, unemployment and business climate; their estimation of the economic
> performance of the incumbent party and their belief about the competence of
> parties to run the national economy (Udehn, 1996: 79).

However, of more relevance to an analysis of public choice theory is not 'how' but
'why' people vote. The expected benefits of voting are so small, given the tiny

impact an individual vote will have on the outcome that public choice theory would imply, it would not be rational to vote. If public choice theory accurately reflects the economic basis of decision making, why do people vote? This is a question that public choice theorists have had difficulty in answering. The point is that voting is 'irrational' from a utilitarian perspective and can only be explained using a more sociological perspective, e.g., duty.

The neo-liberal attack on planning has been accompanied by a left-wing critique of equal ferocity. But regardless of these critiques, planning has survived because of its market supportive role – precisely the characteristic that critics accuse it of. There is little doubt in my mind that planning in the UK is slow and does inhibit development. But this is merely a tautology. Understood in a slightly different way one could say, 'A public mechanism for inhibiting development inhibits development'. The more sophisticated neo-liberal debate concerns the balance and mechanisms involved. As different approaches in a unified state struc-ture like the UK's are seldom attempted, it is difficult to point to evidence either for or against the various proposals put forward. Ironically, given their fundamentally different perspective on questions such as equality and power, a postmodern framework or attitude combined with a more federal structure could allow such comparisons to be made. There is evidence that the UK is shifting more towards such a system and I propose something along those lines in Chapter 8.

Although *Modernising Planning* (DETR, 1998) talked of consideration being given to 'instruments and other modern policy tools to help meet the objectives of modern planning' (para. 3) there is no hint that the neo-liberal approach is remotely what the government has in mind. Any changes that are considered will be to sup-plement rather than replace the traditional discretionary regime. Any embrace of the kinds of instruments proposed by Corkindale, Jones and others would

> result in a wholly different planning system with quite different objectives (Grant, 1998: 70).

While Grant is right that there are many problems with the current system (as I argue in Chapter 1), including its slowness and over-attention to detail, there is no point in rejecting it outright. What many of the neo-liberal critiques come down to is a normative preference for public choice over welfare economics. Pennington is right to claim that the larger developers and landowners such as the House Builders Federation (HBF) do not favour a totally deregulated system because

> Planning regulations allow the larger developers to restrict entry into the market because they are the only ones able to afford the cost of planning inquiries. Likewise, restrictive planning laws artificially inflate the value of their land banks (Pennington, 1996: 48).

CHAPTER 7

THE SCOPE FOR A NEW POSTMODERN PLANNING: theory

INTRODUCTION

> For those who have been marginalised by the reign of reason – a reign which
> has ruled at least since Plato – postmodern critique can be liberating. It lays
> bare the artifice of all grand narratives and so frees us to create our individual
> and collective lives, to articulate our own voices, to diffuse the 'Other' into just
> one more other.
> Or does it? (Haber, 1994: 113).

> Once upon a time a valiant fellow had the idea that men were drowned in
> water only because they were possessed with the idea of gravity. If they were to
> knock this notion out of their heads, say by stating it to be superstition, a
> religious concept, they would be sublimely proof against any danger from water.
> His whole life long he fought against the illusion of gravity, of whose harmful
> results all statistic bought him new and manifold evidence. This valiant fellow is
> the type of the new revolutionary philosophers in Germany (Marx and Engels,
> quoted in Sayer, 1993: 320).

I have now explored various aspects of both postmodern social theory and a variety
of alternatives for a rethought planning. It will be clear from the comments I made
throughout Chapters 4, 5 and 6 that none of the alternatives that I explored fit what
I would regard as an adequate basis for a rethought or postmodern planning – and
this includes the postmodern itself. What I intend to address in this chapter is how
the principles of postmodern social theory can be translated into a framework for a
rethought planning. There should be no surprise that postmodern social theory per
se is not an adequate basis. What I do in the course of this chapter is argue that
there needs to be a broader basis to a postmodern planning that addresses issues
that would preclude a more extreme postmodern approach, such as the need for
action, the implications of relativity and the lack of methodology, for example. But
this is not enough and tackles what I argue are the inadequacies of attempts to
explore postmodern planning that equate it with a narrow liberalism. What is also
required and what is deficient from these attempts, though central to the idea of
the postmodern, is a postmodern attitude or framework that is flexible enough to
allow diversity to flourish even if the results themselves are less progressive. This is
a distinction between means and ends. While Sandercock and Soja focus on a

postmodern that highlights its penchant for challenging the status quo, they assume that any alternative will automatically be more democratic, progressive and inclusive than what went before. My point of departure, however, is that the postmodern is both a form of planning (à la Sandercock's approach) and a framework for freedom of local expression. Under such a framework, there will be a diversity of plannings. A postmodern approach as envisaged by Sandercock may be one of them (though, as I argued in Chapter 6 and also below, there are problems with this). But, equally, there may be other thoughts and approaches – that is the true postmodern.

Before addressing the limits of postmodern social theory as a basis for planning, I first want to briefly discuss the suitability of the four areas of current planning theory for a rethought planning.

THE ADVANTAGES AND DRAWBACKS OF CURRENT THEORY

At the beginning of Chapter 5, I set out four criteria against which I was going to assess the four different paradigms of theory:

- Rationality and power
- Consensus and difference
- Inclusion and exclusion
- Totality and fragmentation.

My argument, set out briefly there, was that none of these four were appropriate as a basis for a postmodern planning even though one of the four was a review of postmodern attempts at planning. I reviewed and criticised them in Chapters 5 and 6, and what I intend to do briefly here is discuss their relationship to the above points and consequently where they do or do not overlap with postmodern social theory.

Collaborative planning in many ways is the antithesis of a postmodern approach. Although its proponents touch upon many postmodern concerns such as difference, rationality, power and domination, they pay neo-modern lip-service only. It is as though a highlighter pen has been used to flash up a concern with public feeling and a sympathetic ear leant to the reaction against high modern planning: 'Yes, we agree that those terrible high rise blocks are awful, but, you see, it was the wrong kind of planning ... '. Their cause is an old-fashioned, left-leaning paternalism convinced of its own self-righteous conviction that planning is not to blame. What else can one conclude from a school of thought that *actively* seeks to stultify difference and then maintain that, through whatever mechanism is appropriate. Greater openness and involvement are seen as crucial to any 'collaborative' approach, but exactly the mechanisms by which more people are to be involved are unclear, as are strategies for dealing with the mediation of many voices into the single: there can only be one plan after all. Other problematic issues include dealing with power: the only strategy to deal with powerful interests and voices is to expose them to the force of 'better argument' (better for whom?) and then hope that they will back down. One can only conclude from this that they cannot be serious in their endeavours or (and this is more likely) they are con-strained by a modernist straightjacket that compels a 'progressive' planning. By progressive I mean a view that planning is a 'good thing' and that the debate is not 'why' planning, but 'how' planning. This is why there is a concentration upon ques-tions of process in the collaborative approach and a lack of engagement with questions of planners' values. Consequently, the collaborative approach may offer fine words on such matters as difference and inclusion, it may even offer other forms of rationality based on open communication, but ultimately it seeks to change little. The Frome study demonstrated that a commitment to openness and communication will fail miserably if there is a lack of engagement with the real sources of power, and people will be willing to become involved only if there is a genuine chance that what they feel will have an impact. If not, disillusionment is likely.

The great problem with evaluating pragmatism against postmodern thinking is deciding which pragmatism to use. As I set out in Chapter 5, there are various forms, some of which are closer to postmodern thinking than others. Mainstream pragmatists and their planning interpreters (Hoch and Forester) firmly follow the Rorty approach of embedding pragmatism within liberal democracy. There are significant overlaps between postmodern thought and that of pragmatism and, in particular, the joint suspicion of foundational thinking and positivism. However, while they overlap on questions of rationality they diverge on totality and consen-sus. The pragmatism of Forester is clearly concerned with achieving consensus and maintaining it as a basis of progress. Like the collaborative school, pragmatists recognise and celebrate difference but seem to want to smother it through working towards consensus and all of the potentially dominatory dangers that go with it. Distortion may be linked to the postmodern concern with power but there is little other than the status quo that is presented as a foundation from which pragmatists seek to move. This is an overlap with some of the postmodern social theorists who are more concerned with exposing rather than changing per se (the assumption being that the former will lead to the latter). But, the main difference is that Rorty, Forester, Hoch, et al. have their foundation in liberal democracy and for postmod-ernists (excluding Laclau and Mouffe) there is no such foundation. Pragmatism is still wedded to modernist notions of progress and consensus stressing a 'common purpose' of planning. This common purpose is discussed but never defined, other than within the limits of liberal democracy. This is very different from the postmodern which eschews any such boundaries (though I inevitably come up against *inherited* boundaries myself in exploring a postmodern planning. While inherited and practically limiting, they are not *ideal* boundaries though). This comes down to a question of relativity: pragmatists take a subjectivist line in theory and opinion, but 'pull back' from the implications this has for alternatives to liberal democracy. Without such boundaries and foundational thought there is the possibility that an alternative planning might be less progressive – and it is that potential that postmodernists would balk at in teleographic assumptions of pragmatism. However, this is not to deny that there are many common concerns and possible areas of interest. For example, I discuss methodology further on in this chapter and how both postmodern and pragmatic thinking overlap in this area.

I have mentioned earlier in this book that there are some overlaps between neo-liberalism and postmodern social theory. Both, for example, emphasise individuality and have a suspicion of meta-narratives such as communism, and it must not be forgotten that many of the manifestations of new times are derived from the dynamics of capitalism. But, equally, there are significant differences. While neo-liberalism focuses on equality of process, postmodernism is more concerned with equality of process and outcome. Power to neo-liberals is an inherent within capitalism. It is assumed that there is a pluralist framework of power relations that act much in the same way as utility maximises. 'Hidden' power does not exist in the form of societal disciplining as noted by Foucault, for example. As with pragmatism, neo-liberalism is not so much power blind as power accepting.

Postmodern planning perspectives have been noticeable by their absence. However, where they have been explored, there is a emphasis on the postmodern as another form of progressive planning through the focus on individual liberty, empowerment and the exposé and challenge to power. While these are all important aspects of postmodern social theory, they also correspond with some original modern concerns and seem to have been picked upon because they correspond with individual agendas of empowerment and freedom. This selective *à la carte* approach ignores what these individuals see as the less desirable aspects of postmodern thinking and of liberalism generally: that releasing freedom can sometimes lead to less progressive forces and alternatives emerging. A postmodern planning framework (as opposed to a postmodern planning method) that sought to challenge the status quo and provide for a more locally-led and sensitive form of land use planning could just as easily end up with a market-orientated neo-liberal approach as a collaborative one, or no planning at all. This is why the emphasis on postmodern concerns such as a lack of prescription, local sensitivity and a distrust of over-arching thinking must also live with the consequences if it is not merely to be another form of liberal–modernism.

Thus, as I argued at the beginning of this chapter, there needs to be a distinction between a postmodern planning and a postmodern framework for planning. The latter may well encompass the former, but there can be no guarantee of that. This forms the basis for my approach to planning in postmodern times that I outline in this and Chapter 8. What I now go on to address are the theoretical principles of both a postmodern planning and a postmodern planning framework.

THE PRINCIPLES OF A POSTMODERN PLANNING

On the face of it, we could easily reject any basis for a postmodern planning. Abstracting from the extreme postmodernists, Antonio and Kellner (1991) argue that the three assumptions that form the basis of any modernist enterprise – its core metatheoretical foundations – are undermined by the postmodern thrust. First, Baudrillard attacks the assumption that theory represents social reality. The poststructuralist shift that separates signs from signifiers, seeing the former as floating, has been added to by Baudrillard's argument that all we experience are a procession of simulacra or simulations. Such an argument relativises truth and meaning and instead posits a discursive basis to reality:

> Thus, different social theories should be viewed merely as conflicting narratives
> or as incommensurable perspectives rather than as portrayals of external social
> realities that can be judged and evaluated on the basis of research and
> discussion employing inter-subjective standards and procedures for determining
> valid knowledge (Antonio and Kellner, 1991: 129).

Second, the fragmentation and social disintegration of society and the 'death of the subject' reject the idea of a coherent social structures and processes. There is no continuity, but sharp, discontinuous breaks without inherent meaning beyond the moment. There is no longer anything such as social structure (e.g. class, race, gender) that can be planned or comprehended. Equally, there are no longer patterned social phenomena making classical social theories obsolete. Finally, extreme postmodernists also undermine the idea of the rational subject who is self and socially aware and able to improve his/her condition according to rational self-interest and thinking. Nietzsche and Foucault questioned this conception with their exploration of the structured subject through the 'will to power' inherent within disciplinary societal control.

But beyond this more aberrant postmodern, there are some ideas that could form the basis of a postmodern planning. Lyotard's *Pagan Politics* sought to replace a politics of reason with one of opinion. His infamous solution to the question of an ethical vacuum – the law of difference – tried to ensure that the very forces that a radical pluralism unleashed would not destroy it. This had the effect of labelling consensus as the least desirable of political outcomes *between* 'language games'. Each 'language game' would create its own rules of legitimacy with the proviso that no position could challenge any other as inferior, ironically subjugating a law of difference to meta-narrative. For 'language games' we could substitute planning systems or processes. But imagining Lyotard's approach as it relates to planning brings us right up against its drawbacks. Much like the collaborative approach, in a situation where conflict is endemic, how would actions or decisions come about if there was no way of judging? It is fine for Lyotard to implore us to celebrate difference rather than suppress it, but the practical implications of this can only be a strategy where multiple positions can be taken without affecting the others – art criticism for example. In planning, there has to be an ultimate decision – to build or not to build, to allocate or not.

Foucault's alternatives fair a little better as a basis for a rethought planning, but mainly because he remains at a largely abstract level and refuses to be committed to any particular concrete strategy. Although Foucault was more concerned with analysis than resistance, his two main approaches to a non-modern alternative could be summed up as being to free political action from all unitary and totalising paranoia and to act through the principles of proliferation, juxtaposition and disjunction, not sub-division and hierarchy. I find the idea of proliferation to be superficially attractive as a basis for any form of postmodern project. It reflects a very postmodern theme in the potential for multiplicity, a competition of ideas and variety of alternatives. Similarly, Foucault's principle of freedom from unitary and totalising paranoia can be seen to imply proliferation. But he is much more concerned with exposing and analysing the effects of power and modernity than he is in proposing or exploring alternatives. Consequently, his work fails to adequately engage with thinking beyond this.

Of even more abstraction is the work of Baudrillard who developed his own concept of resistance based on politics of difference. Unlike Foucault and Lyotard, Baudrillard saw his alternative as actually against something – in this case the values and practices of capitalism. He was seeking to perpetuate the class struggle in the absence of class. But Baudrillard's symbolic exchange which transcended use or exchange value focused on what he saw as the practicalities of everyday life, and was a tool that was already being used by groups such as gays and blacks who were pursuing their own needs above those dictated by capitalist culture. This was a highly-cultural reaction against what Baudrillard saw as the current and developing manifestation of capitalism. Although Baudrillard concentrated on the main themes of difference and resistance found in the postmodern, there is little threat to capitalism in an approach that seeks to by-pass at such an oblique level rather than challenge its basis. While Baudrillard did offer his symbolic exchange as a form of alternative to capitalism, his later work shows little interest in developing this or any other postmodern resistance and seems more concerned with the nihilistic, cynical and apolitical implications of semiotics. Jameson has a similar Marxist interpretation of the postmodern though, in place of Baudrillard's semiotics, he emphasises disorientation and fragmentation as a consequence of the postmodern condition for his left-leaning interpretation. Such a condition undermines collective action and hence any realistic response or reaction to capitalism. Consequently, Jameson seeks to address this through a 'New Politics' that encourages individuals to perceive or 'map' their position within this maelstrom and seek out alternatives. Jameson's response is more hopeful than Baudrillard's though he seems to parallel Baudrillard and narrow down his interpretation and consequently his reaction to the cultural sphere. Presumably, prior to the condition of postmodernity, class-consciousness was a potential, though unfulfilled, condition. If little was achieved in an era when that was possible, then it is not clear how trying to re-invest conditions for its potential would achieve much in an era when there are more impediments.

Laclau and Mouffe provide the most practical and realistic engagement with the postmodern. Like the extreme postmodern social theorists, they are concerned with issues of collective action in the face of diversity. But unlike, say Baudrillard, they are explicit in their objectives, which include equality and participation. To reach this end they encourage a rethinking of politics towards a radical pluralist and democratic basis that employs postmodern and post-structuralist analysis and seeks a fusion of postmodernity and a rethought modernity. This builds on new social movements that have developed through the invasion of the public and private spheres by the extension of capitalism. As society is discursively constituted and identities not closed, then there are 'nodal points' at which temporary identities and meanings coalesce to form the basis of action. The achievement of a political struggle from the temporary nodal convergence of interests is to be realised through 'radical democracy'. Such a democracy has achieved a rapprochement with capitalism as the basis for the diversity that they now celebrate. Laclau and Mouffe have provided a combination of postmodern analysis and mechanisms with a concern for typically modern commitments to the market and concepts such as freedom and democracy. But, although a significant improvement on the previous attempts at postmodern political theory, Best and Kellner (1991) criticise Laclau and Mouffe for their lack of specificity concerning how to go about a radical politics, and what aspects would have priority over others. Nevertheless, their unique use of postmodern social theory as both analysis and tool, while keeping hold of some modern themes with which to direct their project, provides the most fruitful attempt at postmodern political theory to date, as well as the best potential basis for a postmodern rethought planning. As many feminist-inspired critiques of postmodern theory have argued, many of the extreme approaches fail to tackle the practical problems of politics as well as ignoring modern emancipatory themes such as liberty and fraternity that are necessary to challenge the mainstays of repression. Best and Kellner go further, and argue:

> Postmodern theory in its more extreme form tends to be exactly what it accuses modern theory of being: one sided, reductionist, essentializing, excessively prohibitive, and politically disabling (1991: 214).

The less extreme interpretations attempt to overcome some of these traps through engaging with aspects of modernity with the practical aspects of politics. A composite and thoughtful third way that seeks to combine certain aspects of extreme and practical postmodern theory with sympathetic aspects of critical modern theory is provided by Best and Kellner (1991) and Antonio and Kellner (1994). Their overall criticism of postmodern social theory is that it tends to map the fragments while ignoring the more systematic features and relations of social structures. In addition, the extreme theorists are too quick to abandon too much focus on dubious modern manifestations as well as the more progressive modern heritage of the Enlightenment, democracy and social theory. Some modern social theory does not fit into the simplistic hole that the postmodernists seek to shoe-horn it, and there are theorists within the modern tradition who anticipate and mirror postmodern concerns while avoiding the rejection of modernity *in toto*. Baudrillard, for example, is typical in his approach when denying that social reality cannot even be represented by social theory as it has exploded into a sea of signs. In such a situation, facts and reasons which are the very stuff of modern social theory no longer exist. Differing social theories should merely be viewed as competing narratives or as incommensurable perspectives rather than reflections of social reality that can be judged and evaluated through objective standards. But even the subject of modern social theory has fragmented to such a degree that social structures such as class and gender, as well as social processes including exploitation and differentiation, no longer exist (Antonio and Kellner, 1994). Best and Kellner (1991) and Antonio and Kellner (1994) argue from two positions against this extreme postmodernism: first, that modern social theory has been largely misunderstood by this postmodern onslaught and second, that while some of it was dogmatic and based on positivist foundations, this should not taint the more open forms of thinking.

> Although there are overly totalizing and positivist currents in almost all modern theory, there are also critiques of positivism, scientism and reductionism within modern theory itself (Best and Kellner, 1991: 257).

The more dogmatic thinking that was based on Cartesian views of omnipotent and impartial scientific interpretations continued as an important current in twentieth-century social science. Classical social theorists such as orthodox Marxists overemphasised the structuring features of society and underplayed the active agent and the capacity for resistance. But this was only one theme in social thought. Dewey, for example, criticised the myth of objective knowledge as we saw in Chapter 6, and heralded many of the antifoundationalist themes of the postmodern. Weber further analysed the increasing cultural fragmentation, irreconcilable value conflicts, historical specificity as well as a defence of theoretical and social pluralism. He commented that

> Culture's every step forward seems condemned to lead to ever more devastating senselessness. The advancement of cultural values, however, seems to become a senseless hustle in the service of worthless, moreover self-contradictory, and mutually antagonistic ends (quoted in Antonio and Kellner, 1994: 134).

The difference between the extreme postmodern analyses and those of, say, Weber, was that the latter argued to retain systematic inquiry and theory to maintain integrity in the face of entropy, while the former claim that such attempts are futile as social reality is unmappable and indeterminate.

Best and Kellner admit to the postmodern concern that, under the direction of capitalism, society is becoming more complicated and the forces of capitalist structure are invading and influencing greater areas of life. But for them, this does not imply the *end* of attempts to understand it, *à la* postmodernity, but the need for more sophisticated maps or theory. To do so will involve shifts in classical social theory in order to take account of the more sophisticated dimensions of theory that could involve postmodern approaches. The aim should not be an ironic shrug of the shoulders but an attempt to understand contemporary society.

> Consequently, we reject the postmodern renunciation of macrotheory while attending to some of its proposals for the reconstruction of theory (Best and Kellner, 1991: 259).

Postmodern social theory, for Best and Kellner, is a tool and a reflection upon modernist or classical social theory. They convincingly if dogmatically argue that there is still a strong need for maps of society in order that people can ' ... intelligently analyze, discuss, and intervene in social processes' (1991: 260). Such maps provide the 'big picture' to see how the economy, polity, social institutions, discourses, practices and culture interact to produce a social system. Such an aim also recognises that any attempt to produce an overall and exhaustive knowledge is important given constantly-changing social processes.

For land use planning, their argument is convincing. Few of the postmodern theorists that we have examined has provided anywhere near an adequate proposal for a rethought planning, never mind a half-way reasonable analysis of factors such as the role of state, actors such as planners and the potential and possibility for collective action. I also agree that postmodernism on the whole lacks concrete social analysis, is reductionist, relativistic, places aesthetics above political action and is implicitly neo-liberal in its treatment of individuals and community. Sure, postmodern analyses have been enlightening and productive in exposing the rigid and power-laden aspects of a modern institution such as town planning. But to move that institution on and address the criticisms that the postmodernists have levelled requires more than a critique. It also requires alternatives and directions. Consequently, while postmodern social theory has provided a tool for deconstructing the malaise of planning, as well as some insights into the micro-political world of power and contingent identities, it is inadequate in its attempts to rectify them other than at the level of abstracted key principles. One way around this is to look at other alternatives to postmodern social theory as identifiers of these issues and possible pointers to their resolution.

ALTERNATIVE PARADIGMS FOR A POST-POSTMODERN SOCIAL THEORY

It is clear from the above that postmodern social theory is diffuse and does not engage with alternatives to modernism but focuses on exposure instead. This book is about the possibility of a postmodern planning and is primarily based on postmodern social theory. But two other fields of social theory in particular help both expose some of the limits to postmodern social theory as it needs to be interpreted for planning, and point to possible ways forward to overcome these issues.

1 CRITICAL SOCIAL THEORY

Best and Kellner attempt a reconstituted critical social theory in response to their perceived shortcomings of both classical and postmodern social theory. The key aspects of postmodernity that they consider to be the major contributions to what they term a multidimensional and multiperspectival critical theory are:

- Detailed historical genealogies of the institutions and discourses of modernity and the ways in which these normalise and discipline subjects;
- Microanalyses of the colonisation of desire in capitalism and the production of potentially fascist subjects;
- Theorisation of the mass media, information systems and technology as new forms of control that radically change the nature of politics, subjectivity and everyday life;

- Emphasis on the importance of micro-politics, new social movements and new strategies of social transformation;
- Critiques of flawed philosophical components of modernity;
- New syntheses of feminist and postmodern theories (1991: 262–3).

However, it would be a mistake to believe that Best and Kellner are sympathetic to postmodernism:

> extreme postmodern theorists have abandoned politics for an avant-garde posturing that is bloated with cynicism and opportunism (1991: 285).

> Much postmodern discourse is thoroughly apolitical and deconstructs every opposition except the boundary separating its own isolation within the academy and the outside world (1991: 286).

They combine normative modern concerns including democracy and collectivist issues such as welfare with the recent experiences of new times which they claim undermine rather than underpin many of the concerns of postmodernity. The recent changes in eastern Europe, for example, are seen as emphasising the desire for over-arching ideals such as democracy against the suspicion of such concepts as found in the postmodern oeuvre. In a broadside against the postmodern fetish with micro-structures, Best and Kellner question its one-dimensional focus and ignorance of competing theoretical and political frameworks. One such dimension is, of course, capitalism, and Best and Kellner posit this as *the* structuring force in society that is ignored by the cultural emphasis of the postmodern. Another important question left unresolved by postmodernists is the question of relativism. How are the different dimensions in any analysis to be weighted? Best and Kellner compare the 'real life' analysis of an issue that would highlight different perspectives depending on the issue. For example, if one were to examine gender issues, then a research methodology that privileges issues such as feminist studies and political economy may be employed. The problem with shallow and ahistorical postmodernism is that no particular view would be privileged other than a fragmented and cultural approach. The loss would be one of different and potentially rich perspectives, and its replacement with a reductionist optic that argues all views are of equal worth. This is not the direction for progressive social science:

> the task of social theory is not simply to multiply perspectives but to provide original and illuminating perspectives that call attention to new phenomena, that disclose relationships hitherto obscured, or that even provide new ways of seeing (1991: 270).

According to Best and Kellner, postmodernism is merely an intellectual shop front for neo-liberalism which emphasises an atomistic basis to society and precludes issues such as community or a common response to common issues or problems. And although neo-liberalism points to the market as a reconciling force between conflicting voices postmodernity provides little or no other alternative and so, by default, falls back on this.

What they propose instead is a new theoretical constellation to which post-modern theories would contribute. Such a constellation is a combination of micro- and macro-theory with the micro element being based on the postmodern concerns with analysis and deconstruction as outlined above. Macro-theories, on the other hand, are based on the recognition of capital accumulation as the driving logic in society, but with further recognition of the need for theories to help understand and cut across divisions of sex, race and class:

> Without such macrotheories that attempt to cognitively map the new forms of social development and the relationship between spheres like the economy, culture, education, and politics, we are condemned to live among the fragments without clear indications of what impact new technologies and social developments are having on various domains of our social life (Best and Kellner, 1991: 301).

Such an approach is dialectical and non-reductive. It is dialectical in that it empha-sises the interconnections and mediations between different levels or domains of social reality, e.g., economics, cultural, political and social. It is non-reductive in that it refuses to reduce any social phenomenon to any one dimension. The example they give is of advertising. Any study of advertising must theorise its emergence in the capitalist economy, its economic functions and effects. It must also examine how advertising appropriates certain cultural forms and, in turn, how it influences cultural production. This stresses the dialectical relationship between the level of influence (e.g. the economy) and the social phenomenon (e.g. advertising). Such an approach rejects the ahistorical character of postmodernity by emphasising historical influences though takes a more postmodern view of facts as interpreta-tions. Thus it recognises the contingency of its analysis, but seeks to open up new theoretical discourses or perspectives in an almost postmodern eclectic play of views. In doing so it preserves particularity (i.e. the contingency of situations) by illuminating specific events and artefacts but seeks to link them to broader forces at work. The result is that it can expose fundamental relations of domination and exploitation at both micro and macro levels of society, as opposed to the micro emphasis of the postmodern approach. But it does embrace a more postmodern view of facts as interpretations as well as the recognition that there is no one true or absolute perspective in which one could ground social theory. This 'open systems' approach is again quite postmodern in its eclecticism and lack of founda-tional claim to any one approach. Where it differs is that such a view may favour a foundational theory itself, e.g., political economy. There is no suspicion of any particular theory or approach and, in a pragmatic way, if it 'makes sense', it should be used.

While Best and Kellner make some fair points regarding the drawbacks of postmodern social theory as a basis for social theory per se, they can be accused both of lacking any detail to their prescription and of selectively interpreting wider societal shifts and their significance *vis-à-vis* postmodern thinking. For example, it is true as they claim that the fall of many former Eastern Bloc countries signified a desire for modern concerns such as freedom and democracy, but they equally represented a reaction against highly modern regimes that were built on common principles, centralised state control and the belief that individuals had to subsume difference for the common good. Further, there were no violent uprisings against the erstwhile regimes but a largely peaceful transition based on the will of individuals which mirrors the 'micro-politics of resistance' approach typical of postmodernism. Best and Kellner's approach would account for this transition through a combination of micro and macro analyses, e.g., Foucault's analysis of disciplinary power tightly controlled from the centre and a more structural analysis of the causes of its breakdown that might include relative economic decline with their western neighbours. This methodological vacuum is both critical theory's strong and weak point. It is a robust and exploratory framework but it lacks a direction or epistemology – why should one approach be favoured over another? If some approaches are more appropriate than others and truth is relative to the position from which it is viewed, the only real advantage of critical theory seems to be that it adds a macro-theoretical layer to postmodern micro concerns. This entails a limited view of postmodern social theory that rejects its assumptions regarding the suspicion of over-arching theories and is simply prepared to use aspects of postmodern thinking such as Foucault's genealogy as tools.

It is this emphasis on structuring forces that highlights the potential difficulties in translating postmodern social theory into a rethought planning. Planning is undoubtedly structured by, for example, concrete processes (the need to submit a planning application), established power centres (planners, councillors, etc.), institutional functions (central and local government) and powerful economic forces (developers and landowners). Postmodern social theory does not take account of such structures adequately and, consequently, cannot be regarded as adequate in understanding or addressing such issues. The counter argument would be that a truly postmodern planning would not resemble the highly-structured approach outlined above. However, in a world of existing structures, there needs to be rapprochement between the ideal and reality. Even in an ideal world of micro-politics, it is impossible to envisage a planning (if such a planning existed) that did not involve or necessitate some form of structure. This would need to set the 'frame' for any planning – how decisions were made, who adjudicates, etc. A truly postmodern planning would approach such questions along postmodern lines that emphasised, for example, difference and plurality. But nevertheless, there would still be structures of sorts. So, for our purposes, I find postmodern social theory to be structure blind – which, by definition, it is – and in need of modification in this respect if it is to be used as a basis for a rethought planning.

Another issue is the distrust and even hatred of consensus, and the lack of reconciling mechanisms within postmodern social theory. There is an assumption within postmodern social theory that exposing and revealing remove the contentious aspects of life (in a similar way to Habermas' communicative approach). But there is also an absence of thinking concerning the question of collective action: consensus is parallel with terror in Lyotard's view. Like the issue of structure above, there needs to be a recognition of the practical necessity of planning action as opposed to analysis. In a structured world such as planning, there will inevitably be both disagreement and the need to reconcile any disagreement as a basis for action. Even in a highly pluralistic and transparent planning, there has to be a *final* decision on whether something happens or not or where something should go. Such a decision is unlikely to be uncontentious particularly in a small, crowded island such as the UK, with competing demands on the use of land. Consequently, there will be winners and losers. Postmodern social theory does not address this. Nor does it consider the possibility of consensus on some issues emerging, and theorise a response to that other than one of antagonism. A postmodern concern with avoiding a forced consensus should not preclude one emerging where genuine interests coincide. I therefore find postmodern social theory inadequate to contend with the need for reconciling competing claims within planning (indeed, by definition, it eschews any attempt at reconciliation). Critical social theory therefore provides a useful, though incomplete analysis and alternative to extreme postmodern social theory. It highlights the structural inadequacy of the postmodern, its inability to deal with agreement and consensus and the attraction of values such as justice and integrity. Another area of social theory that provides both critiques and possible alternatives is critical realism.

2 REALISM

The postmodern is highly critical of meta-theories and the positivist search of the sciences for truth or foundational knowledge. As such it rejects an ontological realism, that is, that what we experience or observe is a representation of some ultimate reality. No such reality exists and what we are left with is a myriad of 'language games', personal opinion and ultimately incommensurable ideology. This leads to another question that the postmodern must address:

> Given that we have scientific theories, and that on the whole they seem to work
> remarkably well as an explanation of the world, what must the world be like in
> order for science to be possible? (Outhwaite, 1987: 18).

In other words, if we cannot hope to grasp reality, how come science 'works'? The
world is not a construct of man at an ontological level, but

> is structured and differentiated ... [This] can be established by philosophical
> arguments; though the particular structures it contains and the ways in which it
> is differentiated are matters for substantive scientific investigation (Bhaskar,
> 1978: 9).

The central issue that this raises is one of ontology and it is one that critical realism
has sought to confront in a way that raises further significant questions for the
postmodern. There are important similarities between critical realism and postmodern thinking as I discuss in more detail further on in this chapter, but the main difference can be found in the realist concept of epistemic fallacy which raises two
related issues that the postmodern must contend with. Archer identifies a tripartite
relationship between three levels of understanding in the social and natural worlds:

> Social Ontology → Explanatory Methodology → Practical Social Theories
> (1998: 194).

This formula encompasses the idea of *intransitive* elements of social theory, i.e.,
permanent structures. Society is one such structure that is central to critical
realism, along with the idea that society constrains our actions. It is important to
emphasise that structures such as society are not immutable. They are, in fact,
changeable but only over a relatively long and enduring period of time that allows
them to be studied: ' ... society is both the ever-present condition and the continually reproduced *outcome* of human agency' (Bhaskar, 1979: 43). This position is
distinguished from other attempts to overcome the dualism of structure and
agency through its greater emphasis on structures as enduring entities of society
that are separable from the influence of agency. This is not to take an extreme
structuralist position which treats actors as automatons, but it is to emphasise the
enduring nature and real influence of society upon individual action.

> Society does not consist of individuals ... but expresses the sum of the relations
> within which individuals ... stand (Bhaskar, 1998: 207).

The implications of this are twofold. First, *contra* postmodern social theory, critical
realists argue that there are structures that influence individual action and, second,
that actors or individuals are not passive dupes as postmodern social theory portrays them, but active and reflective and able to determine their future over time.

According to this view positivism and postmodernism have collapsed ontological questions in epistemological ones (i.e. confused what *is* with our *interpretation* of it, or confusing transitive with intransitive elements). Now, the critical realist position is clearly a metaphysical one for, if we can never approach the real, it can never be proven to exist.

> Explanation of social matters requires the generic assertion that there is a state of matter which is what it is, regardless of how we do with it, choose to view it or are somehow manipulated into viewing it (Archer, 1998: 195).

But, looking at the practice of planning as argued above, there are clearly structures that inhibit individual action. And, as critical realism argues, actors are reflective and can, through time, alter the structures that constrain them, as I argued in the critique of collaborative planning earlier in the book. Because both postmodern social theory and critical realism appeal to metaphysical notions to underpin their positions, I do not want to engage in a debate about the appropriateness of either. However, the issues of intransitive but morphological structures (semi-permanent but changeable over time) and of active individuals and agents is one that is difficult to deny. As Bhaskar has famously put it, all individual action presupposes a social context:

> A tribesman implies a tribe, the cashing of a cheque, a banking system. Explanation, whether by subsumption under general laws, advertion to motives and rules, or rediscription (identification), always involves irreducibly social predicates (1998: 209).

How can postmodern social theory and a postmodern planning handle such a concept? It would appear that it cannot without becoming something else. But, this is not absolutely so as we do not follow the prescriptions of an extreme postmodern planning. As Best and Kellner point out 'Extreme postmodern theory . . . announces the end of the political project in the end of history and society' (1991: 283). This precludes any conception of progress and attacks social institutions, norms and practices as oppressive. Obviously this posits a not insignificant problem for a practice such as planning.

Critical realism adds a further set of problems for postmodern social theory as well as another perspective with which it can be fused and combined to provide a more practically useful alternative basis for planning. Both critical social theory and critical realism provide foundations from which other problems of postmodern social theory can be addressed. There are three main problems for the postmodern as I identify them: the rejection of macro-politics and structures, the detestation of consensus and the lack of methodology or reason by which progress can be made. I discuss each of these in turn below.

DIFFERENCE OR CONSENSUS

The basis for any form of rethought planning for new times is the question of difference. This is both ontological and normative – difference exists and is increasing and we should be concerned with difference as a political goal. However, there is a danger in worshipping difference for its own sake and, in doing so, slipping into the individualism that characterises neo-liberalism. Two issues related to difference arise from using postmodern social theory as a basis for a rethought planning. First, is the need to integrate an adequate macro understanding of difference that was addressed above. The second concerns the need to balance questions of difference with that of consensus or the need to act. As Haber puts it, the question is

> whether empowerment is possible in a postmodern world built upon the
> precepts of post-structuralism which insists everywhere on difference and the
> illegitimacy of the subjective position (1994: 113).

This then raises the need to consider both the advantages and the dangers of postmodern social theory. By dangers I mean the tendency to consider that difference and empowerment are mutually exclusive. The extreme postmodern social theorists such as Lyotard and Baudrillard either fragment experience into incommensurable parts or draw back from what they see as the unacceptable consequences of a relativity of values. The positive and potentially emancipatory aspects of the postmodern critique of structure (including the claim that any structure is open to redescription, which undermines any claims to sovereignty and hierarchy as well as encouraging marginalised voices to participate and redescribe such structures) is lost because the mechanisms for such resistance lie in a new form of structure which is being castigated.

> When read as a universal principle, the law of difference forecloses on the
> possibility of revitalizing the discourses of otherness, and so forecloses on the
> possibility of voicing marginalized concerns (Haber, 1994: 117).

The result is a form of purgatory – suspended between the unifying concerns of modernity and the nihilistic extremes of the postmodern. But there are very real implications for this 'in-between' position. Existing structures such as planning processes and systems embody certain assumptions that include some and exclude others. A political theory that unmasks this but then cannot address it simply perpetuates this situation. However, like most dualisms, this is a false opposition. It is based on the equation by postmodern social theorists that unity equals terror, a position most closely associated with Lyotard. And as unity is required for resistance, action and identity formation, this assumption destroys the basis for a planning that is built upon a celebration of difference. Haber (1994) argues that the postmodern 'law of difference' should not be equated with the demand to universalise difference. A *universalisation* of difference precludes the possibility of resistance or action as there can be no community or even individual. A *law* of difference is concerned with breaking down monolithic descriptions and structures to release any embedded diversity. However, accepting that structures are or can be repressive and functions of power, does not detract from the need for such structures in any attempt to reconstruct and rethink the status quo. What is important is the *recognition* that structures are temporary, partial and potentially open to abuse, not the rejection of any form of structure altogether because of these characteristics. Such an approach acknowledges the importance of ontological and normative difference, while pragmatically accepting the need for some form of structure to advance that claim. This is not to say that structure (in whatever form) is not in conflict with difference:

> any structure ... comes into conflict with the law of difference because
> structure, traditionally understood, presumes to provide closure and coherence,
> unity or totality. Difference is repressed by structure. The question is whether or
> not this repression is terroristic (Haber, 1994: 115).

Haber proposes, and I agree, that it is not in itself terroristic. Lyotard and Foucault disagree and give in on structure. But the alternative approach offered by Haber is to use difference to rethink our idea of structure. Such an approach accepts the postmodern and post-structuralist critique that argues for a fluid and temporary idea of structure that is open to redescription and de/reconstruction. However, it is based on the idea that structure is not necessarily unjust or terroristic: 'Difference can accommodate unity (structure) so long as unity recognizes its subservience to difference' (Haber, 1994: 117). What Haber is attempting to do is embed unity within a foundational claim to difference – her *law* of difference. This actually brings her far closer to Lyotard than she cares to admit. He too subjugated difference within his own universal 'law of difference' while Haber is seeking to prioritise difference within her recognition of unity. The difference is that her 'law of difference' is less of a law and more of a theme that is ever present. Such a law is based on three principles:

- The possible narrative constructions or stories we can tell about ourselves, the world, and others, are always open to redescription;
- The self is never a culmination of a single, or even necessarily coherent narrative;
- The tools of narrative are not the property of an individual, but the product of history, culture, and community, which are themselves not monolithic entities (1994: 119).

This distinguishes her law of difference from the postmodern universalisation of difference. This distinction can also be understood as the difference between 'unity' (or the requirement that an idea or action be coherent enough to be identifiable and described) and 'unicity' (the demand that we speak with one voice) – we can have the latter without the former. Central to the idea of unity is community. A community (like structure) can also be subject to the law of difference and it is also necessary for the identification and articulation of difference. For there to be an appreciation of difference and otherness, it is necessary to appreciate that we are all members of many communities simultaneously – gender, age, social, cultural, economic, political, etc. As Chantal Mouffe puts it, because women are oppressed by men and capitalism 'there exist[s] objective points of contact between the struggle against women's subordination and the anti-capitalist struggle' (1984: 142). Once this is realised then we can identify ourselves with marginalised communities and then 'find the tools, i.e., the images and vocabularies, with which we can imagine a world other than one suited to the interests of bourgeois liberalism' (1998: 121). This potentially releases the individual within a community to rethink and challenge the basis of that community. For example, planning practice is justified as being in the 'public interest' – a broad and amorphous community. But this community contains many competing and conflicting interests – the developer and the conservationist for example. The challenge to the public interest has been a theme of criticisms of planning for some time, and it has been deconstructed from a number of different perspectives. The current challenge now is not only to deconstruct it but also to help those who are excluded from it – 'the environmental movement is arguing for my needs as a lone parent', 'I want to protect the environment but I'm unemployed and the new development may lead to a job'. This is a further deconstruction of 'the public interest' that potentially allows for its redescription, challenging both the accepted homogenous public interest and an empathy with those who have been silenced by it. This deconstruction

> gives us the basis upon which an oppositional politics can be built – a politics
> where difference rather than hierarchy, heteronomy rather than homogeneity
> and protean rather than disciplinary and normalising discourse, is the goal
> (Haber, 1994: 122–3).

The key is the sub-division of existing communities or interests by redescription or analysis through the law of difference – any community can be further redescribed or deconstructed. This is Haber's oppositional politics. Environmentalism, for example, can be further deconstructed into gender, race or economic sub-communities, all of which provide different perspectives and force an appreciation of difference.

Haber's interpretation of postmodern and post-structuralist social theory as a basis for an oppositional and rethought politics is deeply attractive. The main benefit to her argument is a rejection of closure to any structure. In planning, this could be interpreted as process, system, decision, etc. This promotes a fluid attitude towards such matters and, consequently, directly challenges the homogenous and closed modern status. However, Haber also argues that closure is not necessarily bad or terroristic. Indeed, it is actually necessary for a more diverse and plural structure to exist because 'There is no politics without sameness and unity, even if that unity always has a remainder' (1994: 128). All we need to do is to be aware of the contingency of closure or structure while working with it.

However attractive Haber's interpretation of postmodern social theory is for planning, it does not go far enough. Although her reinterpretation of postmodern social thought rightly rejects the 'unity equals terror' position, and pragmatically considers community and structure to be a (suspicious) necessity of any political action, there are four main areas that she does not address which would undermine her project. First, simply being aware that there is no closure to structure or to classification, naming or collective action is not enough. There will be a danger that this will be forgotten. How do we 'remember' this, resist the tendency for any new structure to become the status quo, and maintain a fluid attitude? Second, even if we treat all structures or closures as temporary, this does not mean that their effect will be as such. There is a possibility of an *appearance* of fluid or protean structures and of non-closure. But what guarantee is there that what people experience on the ground will be any different? Third, the assumption behind Haber's approach is that simply redescribing a community or deconstructing it will force an appreciation of the differences involved in amorphous concepts such as 'the public interest' and thereby lead to an inclusion of erstwhile ignored perspectives. She claims that 'the law of difference forces politics to give up on its exclusivity; it must construct itself with the voices of "otherness" ' (1994: 129). Why *must* it? The problem with this assumption is that merely exposing otherness and encouraging people to recognise the plurality of 'I' is not enough. Haber's approach is power blind. A developer or conservationist may begin to appreciate the multiple communities of which they belong, but it does not automatically follow that they will act accordingly. The developer is still driven by the need for profit, the conservationist by a deeply-held belief in the righteousness of their feelings. Finally, another potential difficulty is the possibility that releasing a highly plural environment may actually lead to *in*action through disagreement. This question is partially addressed by Haber, and she follows Lyotard and Foucault and the law of difference in arguing that we must encourage difference no matter what the consequences. However, this is unsatisfactory because it does not fully answer the question of how we can act in a deeply pluralistic environment or the issue of who should decide. The danger of imposing a voice from the theorists' view is that you will be replacing the terror of the *ancien regime* with that of a new order.

Naturally, Haber's approach is not the only non-extreme postmodern basis for politics. I will now turn to another approach that attempts to address some of these issues from a slightly different direction.

> Our central problem is to identify the discursive conditions for the emergence of
> a collective action, directed towards struggling against inequalities and changing
> relations of subordination (Laclau and Mouffe, 1985: 153).

Radical democracy splits the difference between modern and postmodern bases for politics and as such provides an attempt at a politics of difference but with foundation though changeable bases such as emancipation, freedom of the individual, etc. Such concerns are discursively created and are therefore open to challenge and alteration. The framework for such an approach in a post-socialist world is, as Mouffe (1996) argues, firmly and realistically embedded within liberal democracy. Socialism is dead, but its traditional aims including the struggle *against* subordination and *for* individual freedom can be achieved:

> liberal political institutions should be a necessary component of any process of
> democratization and that socialist goals can only be acceptably achieved within
> the liberal democratic framework (1996: 20).

But such goals for socialism must also need to take on board the cultural manifestations of modern capitalism, as well as the non-economic nature of subordination and alienation in society such as racism, sexism, etc. This is not to say that they take current liberalism as an uncritical starting point. Part of the problem with working within the liberal framework is that, in recent times, it has come to be more of an *economic* rather than a *political* liberalism – i.e., concerned with the free play of private interests rather than a more active, 'rights' and morally-laden liberalism. This is not a form of pluralism as it also rejects a single or homogenous outcome of any political process that seeks to act in the 'public good'. Pluralism, as defined as the free interplay of equal power, can only be part of radical democracy if 'it precludes any dream of final reconciliation' (Mouffe, 1996: 25). Radical democracy needs to discard

> the dangerous dream of a perfect consensus, of a homogenous collective will,
> and [attempt] the permanence of conflict and antagonism (Mouffe, 1996: 20).

Instead, Laclau and Mouffe argue for a new normative dimension to politics that shifts away from the atomised model of economic liberalism to a constant search for new and better forms of liberty and equality. Within this constant search there will be nodal points of temporary stabilisations of meaning and agreement that can form the basis of collective action. From these nodal points comes the ability of radical politics to judge between different positions and values. But such a politics is also based on the basis of conflict being good and even necessary to avoid the emergence of potentially dominatory discourses. Thus, a tension emerges between the temporary nature of nodal points as a basis for collective action and the avoidance of relativity and the need to avoid 'closed systems'. The ways of achieving this are not explored in any real depth and, consequently, it is difficult to envisage how this could happen in practice. Two suggestions are made, however, and involve the need to persuade people of their common identity as radical democratic citizens and the need for public institutions to seek to guarantee citizen's rights.

In terms of planning one can envisage both how such an approach might work and the pitfalls of it. The guaranteeing of citizen's rights (or 'subjects' in the UK) could be achieved through setting out prescribed rights for participation, third-party involvement and appeals within a less discretionary and more prescriptive planning regime. Also, there could be far more specific reference to the aims and objectives of planning at both local and national levels. The role of planners would shift from their ambiguous role as arbiters of the 'public good' to a more proactive stance in working towards specific aims related to equity and liberty. However, the main issue in the radical democratic approach seems to be decision making and the need to both reach collective decisions and keep such discourses open. There is little if any advice on how this can be achieved and it is difficult to envisage a practical way of achieving this.

While Laclau and Mouffe attempt to balance the issue of retaining 'openness', while hanging on to some foundational issues within a liberal democratic framework, is a more sophisticated attempt to tackle a politics of difference, it still leaves the question of collective action under-theorised or explored. This is perhaps not surprising as, in tackling this, we are really trying to fit a square peg in a round hole: the postmodern is fundamentally against such conceptions of unity. However much philosophers try to reconcile the two, they are forced back upon the need to make both foundational claims and tackle collective social action. This poses a significant problem for a postmodern planning; a problem for which, as I set out in the next chapter, I can only offer a similar watered down modernism rather than a full-blown postmodernism. Another implication and issue for a postmodern planning to address concerns *how to go about things* – a methodology. How to approach an issue to tackle problems of exclusion or traffic congestion requires an approach. It is to the question of methodology that I now turn.

METHODOLOGY FOR ACTION

The fear of many social scientists is that

> the abandonment of the simple certainties of empiricism leaves the philosophy
> of science on a slippery slope towards a position where the choice between
> alternative theories appears to be a matter of taste or an arbitrary leap of faith
> (Outhwaite, 1987: 20).

This is equally a concern with postmodern social theory that eschews empiricism
and favours (though with a heavy heart in the case of Lyotard) relativism. This is a
significant problem for a postmodern methodology for, as Sayer characterises it,
the postmodern

- refuses all talk of truth and falsity;
- denies any relationship between thought and the world;
- rejects the possibility of empirical testing;
- asserts that we do not 'discover' things empirically but constitute them
  socially and theoretically;
- prioritises local knowledges over foundational meta-theories;
- relativises cultural differences (1993).

Is this undermining of a methodology a problem? Given its practical and socially-
embedded nature planning needs to *act*, and to act requires a form of rationality
(as the word 'planning' suggests). Consequently, to provide a basis for understanding and action we need a methodology concerning how to approach certain
issues. If a locally-perceived issue revolves around the lack of availability of affordable houses for local people, for example, then the problem must be analysed,
understood and then addressed through an agreed method. This is not necessarily
an instrumentally rational method, as it could just as well be based on hermeneutics and is therefore not *prima facie* contrary to the concerns of the postmodern.
However, the worry for some is that, in postmodern social theory 'knowledge is
only discussed in terms of speaking and writing, never doing' (Sayer, 1993: 328).
Consequently there are few hints relating to how to go about a method concerned
with doing or action under postmodern thinking. I will therefore briefly explore three
possibilities: pragmatism, critical theory and hermeneutics, and an extreme form of
methodology in the natural sciences championed by Paul Feyerabend.

1 PRAGMATISM

As Harrison (1998) rightly points out, pragmatists could recognise and adopt many
of the potential contributions of postmodernism to planning whilst avoiding or
actively rejecting those elements of postmodernism that leave planners less able to

act effectively. For example, in criticising Feldman's (1997) assertion that pragmatists do not care about causal knowledge, Charles Hoch claims that they do:

> but [they] just don't like to use the adjectives 'grand', 'total' or 'basic' to describe
> how they propose we think about them (1997: 24).

This seems to follow quite clearly the postmodern rejection of meta-narrative à la
Lyotard. Similarly, Harper and Stein claim that neo-pragmatism is postmodernist in
its non-foundational and post-positivistic preferences (1995: 240). Mouffe (1996a)
also considers that both pragmatism and postmodernism deny the existence of an
Archimedian point from which issues such as reason can be judged objectively.
Both are also committed to the defence of the political side of the Enlightenment,
that is, a desire for democratic institutions that are based on universal franchise, an
independent judiciary and a separation of church and state.

While there are significant overlaps between pragmatic thinking and postmodernism, as well as a lot of sympathy for aspects of the postmodern from pragmatists, there are also significant differences as I argued earlier on in this chapter.
In particular, the extreme postmodern concern with fragmentation questions the
basis for collective action as I have detailed above while the ethical relativism
(which resembles that of vulgar pragmatism) excludes the pragmatic foundation of
liberalism:

> For the pragmatist, it would be irresponsible to adopt a theoretical position that
> leads to nihilism, intellectual anarchy or the death of meaning (Harrison, 1998: 16).

Like postmodernists, pragmatists also reject (or more accurately, side-step) the
idea that the mind is a mirror of nature as well as the objective subject. But, unlike
postmodernists, pragmatists are willing to develop their own social theory in the
light of this – a position that would be ridiculed by extreme postmodern social theorists. And, unlike the more extreme versions of postmodern social theory, pragmatists do provide a foundational basis for their deliberations. Dewey and Rorty firmly
place liberal democracy as the means to achieve open and reflective discourses
much as radical democracy does. Following in their footsteps, pragmatist-based
planning theory also seeks to embed method within liberal democracy (e.g., Hoch,
Forester, and Harper and Stein). There is no politically neutral ground, argues Rorty
in his attack on the Kantian, inspired thinking of Habermas, and neither should we
look for one.

> Pragmatism does not tell us what ends to pursue, but offers a kind of inquiry
> that compares the value of different courses of action alternately weighing
> means and ends – facts and values. It binds together what dualistic thinking
> keeps apart – knowledge and action (or perhaps a bit more precisely)
> theoretical reflection and common sense (Hoch, 1997: 24).

Three forms of methodology emerge as possibilities for a pragmatic approach. First, there is Rorty's ironist and his later development the prophet. As I set out in Chapter 5, Rorty considers there to be a constructive role for the philosopher (or planner) in situations of 'abnormal discourse' (discourses where there is no common agreement or understanding). Here, the planner should act as a mediator, providing new views and ways of describing situations in order to stimulate an open-ended discussion and 'feel' for a reconciliation or route around an impasse. Rorty's 'ironic' individual is another approach that provides a more solid basis for the role of a social actor such as a planner. In public the ironist should take part and uphold liberal democratic principles while in private they should have continuous doubts and explore ways to resolve them, thereby inventing potentially new frontiers of liberal democracy. Finally, Rorty also introduces the role of prophet as a response to the accusation of power blindness in his ironist proposal. The prophet has a similar role to the ironist in thinking the unthinkable. Rorty's model provides a framework for planners in a rethought planning that can be seen to fit with the broad thrust of creating a more open and democratic system. Forester's critical pragmatism, for example, emphasises the 'deepening of democracy' and the central role of his mythical 'progressive planner' who, like Rorty's prophet, seeks to push forward the boundaries of understanding. But in practical terms, there are serious implications of this approach for the traditional role of the planner which I explore more in the next chapter.

Second, there is phenomenology and hermeneutics as a pragmatic methodology. Both have a long history in the social sciences and share many broad assumptions with pragmatism and idealism. It is not surprising, therefore, that they should be used as a methodology for pragmatism and, given the overlap, for the postmodern too. The basis of phenomenology, like the postmodern, is that all human knowledge is subjective. It's primary objective is:

> the direct investigation and description of phenomena as consciously
> experienced, without theories about their causal explanations and as free as
> possible from unexamined preconceptions and presuppositions (Spiegelberg,
> quoted in Johnston, 1992: 62).

Although there are a variety of methods, phenomenology has a common set of these including:

- The belief that people should be studied free of any preconceived theories or suppositions about how they act. This involves suspending the observer's view of the world so as not to contaminate interpretation.
- The search for understanding of the act is the goal of social science, rather than explanation.

- The belief that, for people, the world exists only as a mental construction, created in acts of intentionality (Johnston, 1992: 62–3).

The methodological approaches of phenomenology include techniques such as participant observation and detailed ethnographic studies, where the researcher becomes part of the world of the subject being studied. Hermeneutics is related in its assumptions but focuses on looking for the meaning behind actions – looking for an appreciation of why certain action takes place rather than trying to explain it. Neither approach seeks universal truth but a contextualised understanding.

Rorty recommends hermeneutics for his abnormal discourse situations. In relation to planning, Hillier recommends a hermeneutic approach and admits to being suspicious of broad, systematic generalisations and prefers instead the particular (1995: 294). She argues for what she terms 'phronesis', that is based on Aristotle's ideas on practical wisdom or common sense. It is 'learning by doing' or a formal link between action and knowledge that is concerned with pragmatics as opposed to universal theory. Within such a conception the role of planning is to 'clarify values and interests and to debate possible actions in a context sensitive manner' (1995: 294). Calling on empirical usefulness planners, can make useful inputs into ongoing practices of dialogue through conversational skills, sensitivity and insight 'in order to identify and interpret the particularities of the various perspectives involved' (1995: 294). The basis for a pragmatic planning is the recognition of

> difference, flexibility and contingency, and that no one theory or conceptual
> framework can suffice. We need to ask pragmatic questions concerning
> appropriate strategies which may help satisfy people's contingent needs and
> desires and ethical questions about the issue of developing plans for the public
> good in the light of socioculturally conditioned self-interpretations and
> knowledge (Hillier, 1995: 295).

Finally, Dewey advances a vague notion of pragmatism as empiricism with scientific method as the basis of any approach. Scientific method is the best means of achieving and maintaining the values of liberalism and the goal of ensuring an open-ended search for knowledge and truth. Scientific method has a constant reflective mode that allows liberalism and democracy to evolve and meet changing needs and desires.

The common thread between the three methodological options of pragmatism is a commitment to liberal democracy – a feature that it shares with radical democracy. Liberal democracy provides the framework within which pragmatism in its many methodological forms fits.

2 CRITICAL REALISM

Critical realism is similar enough in some ways to provide a methodology for the postmodern through its insistence on the ubiquity of open systems and social construction of knowledge. As Sayer concluded, the postmodern and realist emphasis on difference is one overlap leading both schools to be

> critical of the totalising pretensions of marxism, regarding them as a cover for reductionism (1993: 321).

There is also a common distrust of ideas concerning absolute truth and foundational knowledge with a shared appreciation of the social construction of such knowledge. However, realism's attraction to difference does not come from any distrust of meta-theory per se, but its belief in open systems. Similarly, it also insists on elements of structure and realism, that a rejection of objectivism need not entail relativism and that there is still the potential for progressive science with Enlightenment ideals. The big difference between the two approaches, and where critical realism provides a way out of the dead-end of relativist indecision, is by adding its realist ontology. Theories are attempts to describe and understand *real* entities. The postmodern denies that such entities exist. So, in an attempt to describe such entities, theory can be better or worse if it explains reality in a more or less useful way (a better theory, for example, would explain something the previous theory had done plus an added aspect previously left unexplained). Realism is what Sayer (1993) refers to as the 'third way' between the totalising concerns of modernity and the relativising binary opposite of postmodernism. As such, realism has the potential to maintain some of the concerns of the postmodern while providing a methodology for action.

However, that potential is not straightforward to realise. Yeung (1997: 70) rightly claims that 'critical realism is still largely a philosophy in search of a method', while Pratt echoes the comments of many writers by pointing out that 'critical realism has remained problematic both as a research approach and as a practical methodology' (1995: 63). Such problems as they are stem from the philosophical focus on critical realism and the separation (*contra* postmodern social theory) of the ontological and epistemological spheres. Consequently, critical realism is more of a philosophical argument about the nature of reality and not simply another epistemological prescription leading to the claim that realism is ontologically bold and epistemologically cautious (Outhwaite, 1987: 34). Regardless of these views there have been numerous investigations of methodology in critical theory as well as actual research that embodies it.

The first point to make is that, because of its ontological emphasis, critical realism does not license approaches but provides a framework in which alternative social ontologies can be rationally compared and discussed (Outhwaite, 1987: 57).

Methodological explorations under the umbrella of critical realism therefore start from first principles that include the search for causal powers and generative mechanisms. In doing so they appreciate that any such search is a fruitless endeavour. This is because we can only focus on the actual and the empirical levels of reality rather than reality itself. Thus we observe the *transitive* aspects of reality, not the *intransitive* which may or may not produce events to observe. Such transitive characteristics may lead us to postulate models or theories but these exist in an open system where truth, as with postmodern social theory, is relative and contingent, not absolute. Consequently, while there is a reality, our knowledge of it changes. However, critical realists such as Bhaskar have to perform some definitional gymnastics to include society under the concept of intransitive and consequently argue that natural realist ontology is also applicable to the social. This is achieved through the argument that societies pre- and post-exist individuals and accepts that societies are intransitive and transitive but are intransitive enough to be studied.

A further central methodological feature of critical realism is the possibility of naturalism – that it is possible to use common methods in both the natural and social sciences but that there are significant differences between the two in terms of detailed approaches that reflects their ontological difference. Unlike earlier attempts under the guise of positivism, this is more of a recognition of the social construction of knowledge in both fields and the constant search for models and theories to understand and shift closer to ontological reality. But this should not detract from the significant differences between the two. Bhaskar identifies three limitations on such a naturalism:

- social structures, unlike natural sciences, do not exist independently of the activities they govern;
- social structures, unlike natural structures, do not exist independently of the agents' conceptions of what they are doing in their activity;
- social structures, unlike natural structures, may be only relatively enduring (so that the tendencies they ground may not be universal in the sense of space–time variant) (quoted in Outhwaite, 1987: 53).

The upshot of this is that there is a very broad church of methods that are compatible with a critical realist approach. However, there are caveats to this ecumenism. Archer (1998) argues that, because of the ontological emphasis upon intransitive elements, realism in practice leans towards structural interpretations in social theory. Given these practical limits Yeung (1997) identifies some indications of how a critical realist would approach issues such as studying society. The key is an *a posteriori* abstraction of causal mechanisms and the constant reflection and critique upon them. This leads Yeung to identify three broad avenues that can be employed in critical research.

ITERATIVE ABSTRACTION

This combines the twin critical realist concerns of abstraction and reflection in an attempt to mirror social structures by focusing on those characteristics which have a significant impact on the phenomena and the deeper causal structures that generate them. 'A realist thus starts an empirical problem and proceeds to abstract the necessary relation between the concrete phenomenon and deeper causal structures to form generative mechanisms' (1997: 58). The iterative aspect comes in when empirical evidence is collected that leads to revisions in the original abstraction and this continues until no further contradictory evidence is obtained.

GROUNDED THEORY

This is a variant on iterative abstraction that emphasises a more qualitative methodology and the use of systematic procedures for generating and testing theory. In some ways it is linked to hermeneutics as the researcher is expected to embed themselves in the subject area prior to developing broad categories that are meant to stimulate theorising and modelling. Evidence is gathered to saturate the models until they are robust enough to gain the researcher's confidence and then they are compared against other existing theories.

TRIANGULATION

This is a more multimethod approach that aims to break down barriers between qualitative and quantitative methods. Triangulation can be used in respect of time, place and level, multiple observers of the same phenomenon, different theoretical perspectives and methodologies. The aim is to improve the validity and reliability of data collection in revealing different facets of the social world.

   None of these approaches are problem free, and some such as triangulation have been employed in empirical approaches pointing to ontological neutrality. However, they all stress the importance of openness in method and broadly align themselves with an approach that is sympathetic to the concerns of postmodern social theory *apart from the search for explanatory or generative mechanisms*. This ultimate goal of these methods can be modified to leave a more open understanding with a competing set of ideas or frameworks within which understanding can be aided. Consequently, as a tool, critical realist methodologies can be used for a postmodern planning.

3 FEYERABEND'S 'ANYTHING GOES'?

Finally, a more mainstream postmodern methodology can be found in the work of Paul Feyerabend who, like Thomas Kuhn, starts from the premise that knowledge is a social construct and that science does not progress on the basis of shared understanding but of paradigmatic revolutions where our understandings are

turned upside down. Unlike Kuhn, however, Feyerabend uses the incommensurability of different 'world pictures' as a basis for both attacking the privileged position of science and for arguing that no knowledge should be regarded as superior
to any other. If we want to believe that astrology is superior to physics as a basis
for knowing, then there is no way for either belief to be evaluated by the other *from
within* that world view, nor is there any foundational point against which to evaluate
them objectively. Because our world view defines the world in which we live *it
becomes the world* and directs the causal relations between things, thereby
making comprehension of different world views impossible. For example, if your
world view is religious, then God created the earth and scientific argument is not
going to dispel that belief. However, you will also not be able to comprehend the
methods and logic behind the thinking that is challenging your view.

Consequently, science should have no special place in our lives because it is
merely one world view. This includes areas such as education, the law and medicine – if parents want their children to learn voodoo rather than chemistry then this
should be allowed. The implications for a postmodern methodology are clearly
extreme, impractical and potentially dangerous. Feyerabend's ontological relativism
can be seen as paralleling and echoing the social construction of knowledge
underpinning postmodern social theory. But Feyerabend goes further than Lyotard
in following the logic of this, while providing no guarantee against the relativism
and potential growth of extremism against a backdrop of indecision and inaction.
However, critics of Feyerabend's approach argue that it is not true to claim that different world views are incommensurate and lack understanding of the frames of
others. There is enough common understanding between world views to allow an
appreciation and understanding while there may be disagreement. A developer and
a conservationist can understand the needs and arguments of each other but continue to disagree. Although there is disagreement between these two groups, there
will be agreement on other matters such as the need to settle their differences
through democratic mechanisms and respect the outcomes. This is a disagreement *within* a world view as well as between sub-sets of it. There is also an evolutionary aspect to knowledge and understanding within world views that can lead to
different emphases over time. The growth in environmental understanding in the
past 20 years, for example, has altered our understanding and world view. The
binary world view that Feyerabend conjures up seems to be too simplistic to
account for the complex, temporal and overlapping nature of theory as well as
arguing for more, not less, agreement. While it is undoubtedly a postmodern
perspective, it is too relativistic for use in planning.

Overall, these three broad areas of methodology all interface in some way
with postmodern social theory and provide potential routes for action. While there
can be no privileged approach to postmodern thinking, it is clear that there are

various approaches that, to greater or lesser degrees, fall within the postmodern genre.

AN INTERPRETATION OF POWER

Any rethought planning needs an understanding of power relations in order to achieve its potential more successfully. A more plural and transparent approach to planning is unlikely to achieve much if it aims to tackle monolithic institutions through an understanding based on economic determinism if the root of power lies elsewhere. Neither will individuals be empowered if the challenge to their current constraints is misdirected. So, as Foucault asks himself and us, 'how is it exercised; by what means?' and 'what are the effects of the exercise of power?' Currently, there are a plethora of understandings that have been used to dissect planning as a professional activity, a function of the state, etc. Postmodern social theory rejects such thinking. Foucault is the only postmodern social theorist who provides more than a superficial analysis of power. Prior to Foucault's analysis, there were broadly two schools – the juridical-liberal concept that treated power as a commodity to be possessed, and the Marxist school that focused on relations of production and domination. Foucault's groundbreaking analyses demonstrated a far more complex and less reductionist reality that provided a positive role as well as a disciplinary function as I outlined in Chapter 2. To reveal relations of power as constituted in the social body Foucault puts forward a five-point methodology:

- Analysis should not address centralised or juridical forms of power but that which has become embodied within local discourses and institutions.
- It should not concern itself with centres of power in the form of positions (e.g., councillor) but with the practice of power and how it is wielded. Thus traditional plural concerns with interest groups, classes and individuals is replaced with a varied analysis of power relations wherever they may be present.
- Power should not be seen as related to any particular individual or class but as a network of connections in which we are nodes. Consequently, we are both a victim of power and a body through which it is articulated.
- Any appreciation and study of power should proceed from a bottom-up or micro-institutional level, rather than a top-down perspective that will reveal the historical make-up of power has been embedded and how it links to more macro-level manifestations. This tracing of power may lead to an analysis that reveals how it has been appropriated in a way that benefits a particular class or group.

- Finally, an analysis should also be aware of the role of knowledge in power, in that the latter inevitably influences the former. Certain assumptions and 'common' knowledge will involve power relations that will favour some individuals over others.

This multi-centred view of power emphasises a capillary characteristic that is not secondary to other interpretations and perspectives such as class, whose existence is only a temporary concentration or manifestation of the constant flow of power relations.

> I don't want to say that the state isn't important; what I want to say is that relations of power, and hence the analysis that must be made of them, necessarily extend beyond the limits of the state ... because the state, for all the omnipotence of its apparatuses, is far from being able to occupy the whole field of actual power relations, and further the State can only operate on the basis of other, already existing power relations (Foucault, quoted in Smart, 1985: 124).

Thus, like the individual, the state is itself constituted of power relations as well as being a source of power itself.

There have been a number of criticisms of Foucault's approach on the basis of this conception of the role of the state that accuses him of severely underestimating its function and power in modern societies. Poulantzas (1978) offers a modification of Foucault's work that employs it as a tool of analysis but within a class-based framework that has a single basis in the form of class division and struggle. This structural embedding of power allows Poulantzas to address the issue of resistance because, under Foucault's flows and networks of ubiquitous power there is no reason to resist. Poulantzas argues that it is to be found in class struggle as epitomised by the state. Far from undermining Foucault's work, Poulantzas has actually improved its foundations. Modern forms of state apparatus including prisons, the judiciary, central and local government are substantial and real concentrations of power. While Foucault acknowledges this, his analysis claims this is a temporary phenomenon and that resistance to it comes from a micro or individual level. Three issues arise from this. First, the concentration of power in state apparatus is largely consensual, i.e., people agree to it. They recognise the need for some form of state intervention in their lives and have the right to change that through periodic voting. Second, if this is the case, resistance to a concentration of power comes not in overturning or radically altering it but in modifying it within agreed boundaries, often in an incremental or pragmatic way. Finally, the concentration of power under these conditions is unlikely to be temporary but permanent as far as the lives of people are concerned. Consequently, a more sophisticated understanding of the role of the state is required that does not detract from Foucault's analysis concerning disciplinary power, etc.

Thus a rethought planning along postmodern lines can address relations of power through the genealogical approach of Foucault that might (and probably will) expose the large degree of discretion that is available to planners and those who Lipsky (1978) terms 'street-level bureaucrats'. It is at this level that concentrations of power can be most easily exposed and challenged because their legitimacy is shallow and fragile (professional opinion, etc.). But whilst current procedures and practices within planning allow a reasonably wide interpretation of central government guidance by planners, there are limits upon the extent of this discretion within central constraints, including the impact of policy guidance and the Secretary of State's reserve call-in power. Here, there is a qualitatively different issue of power that is more legitimised through its electoral accountability and more juridical in its role of determining a final outcome. Foucault's analysis is of less help here in the short-term because of the state's endurance and support. Consequently, a rethought planning needs to consider a more structural analysis of power. This does not necessarily imply a materialist analysis such as that offered by Poulantzas, but it needs to understand about how structures such as the state affect the individual, are formed or transformed by him or her, and are perpetuated. One such understanding is provided by Roy Bhaskar. I touched upon aspects of how Bhaskar (1998) emphasises the prior existence of social forms above – they exist prior to any one individual (e.g., state structures or language) and will continue after them. I cannot communicate except by using existing media for example, thus the social cannot be reduced to the product or aggregate of the individual. This is not to say that individuals are mere dupes, but that

> society must be regarded as a ensemble of structures, practices and
> conventions which individuals reproduce or transform, but which would not exist
> unless they did so (Bhaskar, 1998: 216).

If we take the themes of the postmodern to include issues such as diversity, difference and openness, then questions of power are central. The postmodern analysis of Foucault is a crucial tool but not in isolation from other understandings of power. A rethought planning needs to be aware of and constituted in such a way as to resist concentrations of power or, more accurately, dominatory centres of power. A combination of the above approaches provides a basis for that awareness, but it is in the institutional and procedural designs that the real guarantee of transparent and accountable power lies. This is covered in the next chapter. Overall, *a rethought planning should start from an analysis of unaccountable and dominatory centres of power and aim to create a more transparent and accountable system.*

CAN WE ESCAPE FROM RELATIVISM?

One of the accusations most often thrown at postmodern social theory regards the question of relativism that I briefly touched upon under methodology above. And, overall, it is a fair accusation to make as Lyotard admitted when he imposed his own law of difference. How can we judge between competing positions without any criteria? Is there a right and wrong under postmodern thinking? And, critically, as planning implies some form of foresight in human affairs and collective choice, can there be a planning under postmodern thinking? The case for the prosecution has been put by Sayer who has summarised the postmodern perspective on agreement as being totally undermined by the view that knowledge is split into numerous self-contained, incommensurable, local discourses between which communication is impossible (1993: 323). As there is no appeal to any reality there can be no judgement either *a priori* or *a posteriori*. But we do in fact have commensurable theories and incommensurable ones simultaneously and, as Bhaskar has pointed out, to argue that there are two theories that clash and cannot be reconciled is to ignore what the theories are referring to. In other words, the postmodern focuses on the epistemological rather than the ontological question of truth. Now, this is a normative position and argument that basically comes down to a difference between ontological realism and a non-foundational epistemology. But the realists have a reasonable logical argument. As I have pointed out throughout this book, the claim that there is no foundational knowledge is a foundational claim itself. Truth has no correspondence to reality but is merely a matter of convention in postmodern eyes (Sayer, 1993: 324). However, like the foundational claim to non-foundation above, there is a binary opposite at work here in the extremes of realism and idealism. Looking beyond this semantic and normative ontological impasse, what are the practical implications of the postmodern penchant for relativism? The first point to make is that accepting that knowledge is provisional, socially constructed and fallible does not consequently entail leaping onto the postmodern relativist bandwagon. Neither does the opposite hold either. We do not have to sign up to the ideal of absolute truth or Platonic *forms* simply because we reject the idea of subjectivism. The extreme postmodern position points clearly towards an incommensurability of values, foundational principles and languages. But as a number of commentators have pointed out, the rejection of foundationalism does not automatically imply relativism – there are other less nihilistic alternatives. The postmodern can hold onto its fallible truths without relativism but it needs to accept that in the world in which we live anything does not go.

> If truth were purely a matter of convention, we would be able to live by any
> convention we cared to invent: we don't because we can't (Sayer, 1993: 326).

Although Sayer is overstating the postmodern case somewhat, his point concerns the question of structures and their impact on truth, individuals and action. As I pointed out earlier, planning is highly structured and the outcomes of the planning system are a complex accretion of individual and structural influences. This does not mean that there is one option, only that there needs to be one solution, e.g., to build or not to build. You cannot half build a house. So relativism (or the need to choose) in planning is possible only in discreet points of the process – examining options, weighing them, negotiating, bargaining, etc. And this ignores the question of *who* decides which I discussed earlier. A postmodern planning must reconcile its penchant for incommensurability with the imperative to choose.

How could it go about this? The answer must lie in the basis of incommensurability and the practical aspects touched upon above. Clearly life is structured and constrained and people need to make choices to get by. This does not detract from the normative principle (which postmodernists see as absolute truth) that individual 'truth' is preferable to collective 'truths' – the basis of relativism. But, in society and planning we are dealing with individuals *and* aggregates of individuals or a wider good or interest. It is this higher 'level' of interest that the postmodern denies and which has to be incorporated for a rethought planning. I attempt to address this by modifying some of the key aspects of postmodern thought. First, while knowledge is socially constructed, it is also constructed in other ways including practically. So, while texts, situations, etc., can be constantly redescribed in an open and fluid system, there are practical limits to this including structural influences and the common agreement or practical implications of holding a particular view.

> We can't get outside discourse to see how it compares with real objects, but it is
> evident from observation and action within a particular world-view or discourse
> that some conventions about what is the case hold and others don't (Sayer,
> 1993: 330).

I could argue in court, for example, that the 'rules' of society that stop me from speeding in my car are arbitrary and conflict with my own standards but that would not stop me from being fined. Consequently, there *are* conventions, and planning is a prime example of this. The point at which postmodern thinking can be applied is how these conventions or rules are reached.

When a community is faced with a number of competing arguments regarding the future of their town involving, for example, whether to allow an out-of-town supermarket to be built or not, there are likely to be at least two opposing views that encompass a variety of arguments. The pro-development lobby, for example, will be aware of the issues concerning loss of greenfield land, impact on the town centre, increased road traffic, etc., but will have balanced that with the gain in local

employment and increased choice and accessibility. The theories behind the arguments on either side are socially constructed in that they have no call on 'reality' to
resolve them and are largely determined by factors such as profit, social position
(whether I already have a job/car or not) and normative positions on questions
such as nature conservation, market competition, etc. They are, in the classic postmodern sense, incommensurable in *empirical* terms – at the level of the individual
or aggregate of individuals. This is so even though empirically certain aspects of
the argument can be partially judged or tested such as 'do out-of-town supermarkets lead to an increase in CO_2 emissions'? The assumption is that an increase in
emissions is bad because of the effect on greenhouse gasses and the impact on
global warming – this assumption itself is another structuring factor. The nature of
the open system which planners are dealing with in addressing this and other
questions means that they are ultimately unresolvable. Assumptions, focus, and all
the other subjective elements in empirical research have meant that two completely
different views can and do emerge in trying to answer this question. But these
positions are not incommensurable in practical and political terms. Some positions
are more embedded or structured than others. On the whole, there has been a sea
change in opinion concerning out-of-town supermarkets at a national and local
level in the UK in the past 20 years or so. So while it may be ultimately unresolvable whether out of town supermarkets lead to a rise in CO_2 emissions, there is
what pragmatists would call an apperceptive mass of opinion which would feel that
they do. Should we be making decisions on such a basis? The fact is that
decisions are made on a complex mix of factors. Theory-laden positions do not
automatically preclude evaluation – but what the postmodern argues is such evaluation should not take place. Clearly some form of evaluation needs to. Given that
these arguments are *empirically* incommensurable though not *normatively* so, as
postmodernists argue, I would suggest the following: the way forward is to consider how to encourage an open practical choice that agrees upon the criteria for
evaluation while encouraging and recognising the development of socially-
constructed and incommensurable views or theories on a issue. This follows what
Lent (1994) has termed the 'democratic imperative'. This asserts that the closure
of an argument through a conclusion or the need to act is not necessarily anti-
postmodern providing that 'any alternative conclusion is free to exist and free to
exercise challenges to one's own and other conclusions' (1994: 229).

    The important approach in achieving this principle appears to me to lie at
what point incommensurability of ideas or theories occur in the planning process. It
seems that planners' roles in the gathering of data, the choosing of options and
alternatives, the presentation of information and recommendations to elected councillors have the key role in both currently limiting or closing off competing theories
or ideas, as Forester has argued elsewhere (1989, 1993). It is at this point that

'closing off' of different views should be reversed to an 'opening out' and encouragement of perspectives. The practical reconciliation occurs largely at the political level – deciding in the interest of communities between the competing ideas and theories that have emerged around an issue. It is here, too, that the criteria for judging at the level of community are best decided on the grounds of practical effects.

THEMES FOR A POSTMODERN PLANNING

This chapter has explored some of the theoretical and practical difficulties in translating postmodern social theory into a rethought planning. A number of alternatives have been touched upon that modify postmodern thinking in ways that make it feasible to be used as such. I asked the question at the beginning of the chapter, 'are we now dealing with something that is not postmodernism anymore?'. The answer I believe is yes and no. Yes, because if we fuse aspects of, say, critical theory with postmodern theory, then the outcome clearly ceases to maintain aspects of postmodern thinking. In that example, there is the difficulty of combining ontological realism with a more transitive epistemological focus. But the answer must also be no, in that an extreme postmodern position that precludes any recourse to practicality (and by this I am referring to aspects such as consensus) must remain in the theoretical sphere only. What I am attempting to do, much in the same way as Best and Kellner and the critical realists, is to use postmodern social theory as a tool – but one among many others that may or may not be postmodern.

What are the principles upon which a postmodern planning can be built? Below I list the broad themes that I will use to develop a practical approach in Chapter 8.

1. Narrative constructions are always open to redescription – are historical and cultural constructs. However, not all structures or power relationships are constructed discursively (e.g., the practical element of knowledge) and in some circumstances, such as in considering the structuring impact of society, it is not useful to consider them as narrative constructs. This latter point adds an important temporal dimension in that, as critical realists rightly point out, change to society occurs over a long period.

2. A rethought planning should be based on an underlying assumption that all processes and procedures are not closed until necessary. Any decisions that are made are done so on the understanding that it is a temporary alignment of interests only.

3. To maintain openness throughout any process, all options and views need to be maintained up until the point of decision or closure.

4.   To avoid merely the appearance of openness, procedural and systematic checks have to be in place that ensure constant reflection.

5.   Procedures need to be open to change. A fluid framework of rules (which are themselves open to challenge and change) should ensure that processes and procedures are modified or altered as regularly as necessary.

6.   A suite of explicit rights that encourage a radical and challenging attitude on behalf of citizens will be required to engender an attitude to challenge and allow procedures and processes to be legally and legitimately challenged.

7.   Part of the aim of mechanisms to create a radical form of democracy must include a stronger link between voter and representative.

8.   Existing relations of power need to be both exposed and challenged. This can be achieved by maintaining constant reflective mechanisms and making decision makers and other actors more accountable and processes more transparent.

9.   Planners should take a more active and creative role in the sustenance and encouragement of fluid structures and processes. This would be similar to Rorty's prophet.

CHAPTER 8

THE SCOPE FOR A NEW POSTMODERN PLANNING: practice

> The very object of having local representation is in order that those who have
> any interest in common which they do not share with the general body of their
> countrymen may manage that joint interest by themselves (J. S. Mill, quoted in
> Harvey and Bathe, 1982: 396).

INTRODUCTION

As I argued earlier in this book, there have been numerous attempts to discuss the
implications of the postmodern for planning. However, all of them have remained
abstract and failed to tackle the crucial question of how they engage with the detail
of planning practice. I think there are possibly two reasons for this. First, postmodern thinking has shied away from prescription because of the natural suspicions
regarding imposition and totalising thinking. Second, it is undoubtedly a difficult
task. This is not only because postmodern social theory at worst precludes planning or at best cannot be easily interpreted as a basis for planning, but also
because there are a plethora of different approaches that could be 'postmodern'. It
is a tautology that the postmodern is very postmodern just as a postmodern planning is or will be eclectic. This is both an advantage and a disadvantage in trying to
explore a postmodern planning. Just as there can be no right or wrong answer
under postmodern thinking, so there can be no one postmodern planning. In fact,
there should be many postmodern plannings. So I cannot prescribe an approach
but simply paint a mosaic of possibilities. Having said this, the approach I take is to
present one example of how postmodern planning could work.

Another problem with attempting to explore a postmodern planning is where
to start and what to assume. Unlike some of the work on postmodernism and planning, it is important to recognise that we are not beginning with a blank sheet. There
are inherited structures, land use patterns and processes, as well as influences
beyond planning such as European legislation and the government's wider commitment to questions such as social inclusion that bind any new approach. Questions
of practicality also emerge that inevitably shape any approach, as do my own values
which steer me away from a more extreme interpretation towards one that could be
described as more a form of social democracy. This is particularly the case with the
context of planning, i.e., local governance. This then provides limits on thinking that

in principle should be unlimited – a lack of 'closure'. I am not the first to come up against the problems of trying to shoe-horn what are essentially theoretical ideas into a predominantly pragmatic and practical world. It is for this reason that many of the accusations against postmodern thinking as impractical and abstract have validity. Perryman (1994), for example, puts together a volume of work on postmodern politics that in broad aims is similar to this book, though related more to politics than land use regulation. However, the outcome is more a shuffling of the cards as opposed to any realistic alternative. Similarly, Trend (1996) attempts something similar with regards to postmodern democracy and ends up with a re-hash of postmodern social theory that has little in the way of practical use.

What I attempt to do in this chapter is provide a number of ideas that could form the basis of a postmodern planning within the UK. I follow the themes set out at the end of the last chapter and explore what they could imply for a rethought planning. To do this, I start from first principles in Part 1 and discuss the context of land use regulation within wider questions of local governance and how planning could relate to it. I then turn to the question of whether there should there be a planning system at all. In Part 2 I move on to the finer grain of what the answer to these questions imply for the role of planners and the daily practice of planning. Here, I engage the implications for a postmodern planning through an illustration of how it might work and what the implications could be for a locality in pursuing a postmodern planning framework and a postmodern planning.

One question that has been difficult to resolve in writing this chapter is 'where to start?'. The approach I outline below necessarily needs to embed any rethought planning into a wider context of local governance. Postmodern planning points towards decentralised, plural, community-led, fluid and reflective thinking which has a number of significant implications not only on planning but also on such issues as voting, community identification, freedom of information and, fundamentally, whether we need a planning system at all. However, while it is not beyond the limits of possibility that a planning approach similar to the one that I outline below could emerge and work, it should been seen in isolation from other services that are currently administered locally. For example, creating a framework for people to (i) decide what their community is and (ii) in what form (if at all) they want land use regulation could be the basis for a rethought planning. For example, recent devolutionary changes in the UK as well as voluntary arrangements on structure planning point towards such an approach as I discuss in Chapter 9. But at the level of healthcare or education, for example, more foundational questions, on areas such as inequality, bear down on the liberal conscience. Decentralisation of such issues will inevitably lead to inequality of provision and while that is currently a reality, it is not an ideal for non-regulatory services. Consequently, I confine myself to land use regulation in this chapter.

PART 1: THE CONTEXT OF LAND USE INTERVENTION

Land use regulation does not exist in isolation from other forms of governance and regulation. Currently the UK system is implemented through different levels of government (central, regional and local) and a number of different government bodies (e.g., the Department of Environment, Transport and Regions, County Councils, District Councils, Unitary Councils, the Appeals Inspectorate) and a variety of quangos (e.g., the Countryside Commission and the National Rivers Authority). Consequently, I cannot simply begin to explore a postmodern planning without first addressing some questions of relationship to these different levels of government and other bodies. Other factors also arise that impinge on a postmodern planning, such as a system of collective agreement (voting) and at what level should planning operate? It is these more fundamental questions that Part 1 engages with.

SHOULD THERE BE A PLANNING SYSTEM AND WHAT FORM SHOULD IT TAKE?

An extreme postmodern approach would preclude any form of planning as we cannot draw conclusions or forecast from a fragmented society, possibly think about patterns of urban form or hope to agree upon a desired trajectory for regulatory outcomes. It should not automatically be assumed, therefore, that we need a planning system per se or in a form that we might recognise. The general thrust of the themes of a postmodern planning set out at the end of Chapter 7 call for a fluid and open approach, and this must also apply at a spatial level. Different areas need to be able to decide for themselves what form of planning, if any, they want for their area. But I think we need to go even further than this and impose the first foundational rule – there should be an assumption against planning unless any community decides it desires some form of land use regulation. This presumption against land use regulation helps meet the principles concerned with constant reflection upon the system and processes of planning, as well as helping to challenge existing embedded power relations. If this foundational rule is maintained and planning is required to justify itself periodically, then this would help ensure that not only are the systems and processes fluid but that they are less likely to slip into becoming 'established' and potentially dominatory. This constant reflection and justification needs to be balanced against the issue of uncertainty – having a particular form of planning one year and possibly having it change or disappear the next. I think this potential problem is less likely to happen for three reasons. The first is that, as critical realists point out, the structural elements of society change over a relatively long period. It is unlikely that change would occur over night and safeguards could be put in place to avoid this. The second reason that instability is unlikely to occur is to do with the nature of agreement or consensus. In particular I am referring here to voting, and this is a point that I explore in more detail below. Suffice to say here that I feel a postmodern form of planning and government generally needs a much stronger link with any community, and this can be achieved through the introduction of a form of proportional representation (PR) in voting. PR regimes are far more stable than the current 'first past the post' approaches and are less likely to lead to sudden swings in opinion and policy. Finally, I believe that all communities, including the business community, will want some form of land use intervention. As a recent DETR report put it:

> business, along with the general public, developers and other parties, broadly accept the need for a land use planning system. They recognise that England is a crowded country, in fact with the Netherlands the most densely populated in the European Union. England must accommodate nearly 50 million population in only 4% of the EU land area, hence it is unexceptional that development is subject to restriction. To reinforce the case for land use planning ... in England around half the total land is effectively precluded from development, being either subject to an array of protected areas like national parks and green belts, or already built up. For these reasons there are few objections to a system of land use regulation, such as that which has been operating in the UK now for 50 years. Businesses are, on the whole, more concerned with the efficiency of the present system, and to its perceived cost than with abolishing it, or substituting an alternative (DETR, 1998:1).

Consequently, I feel that there would still be a planning system or, more accurately, planning systems because of the generally recognised need for some form of land use intervention. The question that immediately arises is at what scale should different systems operate? The basis of any agreement on intervention must be at the level of community. Obviously, communities are not simply identifiable at a spatial level as there are identifiable communities of interest too that are spatial. What the postmodern argues is that such communities at a level above the individual do not exist at all. We are all members of infinite numbers of overlapping communities. This implies as many planning systems as there are individuals and falls foul of the relativistic criticisms of the postmodern. Avoiding relativity is necessary in planning, as I argued in the last chapter, as at the end of the process there needs to be a decision – to build or not to build, where to allocate, etc. The postmodern penchant for incommensurability can be accommodated at certain points within any process so the question of identifying a community is both a question of process and a definite outcome too. We cannot have two competing forms of land use planning working in the same area. So, community can be decided as a process with postmodern concerns of identity but in the end there needs to an identifiable area which needs to decide on what it should do. This is not to say that any community needs to be fixed in stone and, like the need to justify planning and 'reinvent' it periodically, it can be identified on a fluid or temporary basis.

An example of community identity will be familiar to anyone who was involved in the (tortuous) process of local government reorganisation in the early to mid-1990s in the UK. Basically, local authority boundaries were open to change and many local authorities, including my own at the time, attempted to justify their exist-ence by pointing to various indicators of community affinity within their local author-ity. The general assumption behind all of this work was that a sense of community or belonging made for an effective basis in local governance, i.e., local authority boundaries should be coterminous with perceptions of community. Many councils commissioned public opinion surveys of people's identities and feelings of 'belong-ing', where they felt an affinity. Other data on travel to work areas, shopping habits, etc., were also collected to provide proof of a community identity commensurate with the administrative boundaries of the local authority. Not surprisingly, the evid-ence demonstrated nothing of the sort. There were multiple and overlapping communities depending on the criteria used in determining what constituted a community. For example, leisure use crossed administrative boundaries and included large cities, depending on the facility while shopping again paid little attention to local authority area. Research undertaken by the Joseph Rowntree Foundation (1996) found a similar lack of 'community identity' above an immediate neighbourhood or village. The general conclusions from this and other work must be that there has been an attitude towards local governance that ignores people's attachment to place. Unfortunately, as the Rowntree report points out, the objec-tive definition of community (travel to work areas, etc.) and the perceived definition (a sense of community) differ, and neither has corresponded with actual local authority areas. In addition, patterns of objective community increasingly go beyond nation–state borders to include European and even international links in work, leisure and administration. Williams (1996) identifies the six regions of Europe that have been used in drawing up the Europe 2000 report on strategic planning. These divide the UK into three areas and link northern England with Denmark and northern Germany while southern England is linked with France, Belgium and parts of Holland and southern Germany. Both objective and subjective definitions of place ignore the third dimension of community – that of interest. Communities of interest do not necessarily have a spatial dimension. As such, interest communities cannot be the basis for a form of planning (which requires a spatial dimension) but are integral to the process and outcome of planning, i.e., the desire or will of a community.

Why should there be an assumption that place or sense of community should coincide with administrative boundaries? The simple answer is commitment, empathy and understanding. If the aim of any form of local governance is to create and underpin community involvement then that is far more likely to happen if the community feel that it 'belongs' or has a stake in governance there. While there are obviously many communities, the principle of heterogeneity needs to be resolved to provide an identifiable area upon which intervention can be based. There are a number of possible ways of defining communities and I offer this as one example. Taking the existing regional administrative boundaries used in the UK, of which there are nine in England (including London) and one each for Wales and Scotland, would provide a regional form of community. Within this regional level (which is a combination of objective and subjective levels) other systems and approaches can be formulated at the more subjective level. The more bottom-up or subjective identification of community, through the kind of exercise undertaken during local government reorganisation in England, would then provide a local level of community as a basis for land use regulation. The Local Government Commission's recommendations following local government reorganisation were controversial as the identification of community is a highly-emotive issue, given, for example, the reaction of residents of Yorkshire and other traditional areas when they were reorganised into new areas such as Humberside in 1975. However, they did weigh the varying evidence which, for example, in stage three of their deliberations (covering 21 district councils and 12 county councils) amounted to 44,000 individual letters and public surveys of 10,000 people. This may not be the ideal way of helping to identify a 'natural' community but it is a start. Once a community is identified it will be up to that community to decide how they want to form collective decisions, and what form any communal local governance might take. This is covered in Part 2 below. What I intend to turn to now is the form of local land use regulation.

Planning cannot exist by right. It must be up to individual communities to decide (i) if they desire a planning system and (ii) what form it should take. But as I mentioned above, to avoid a planning system and associated processes slipping into becoming a dominant and permanent feature, there should be a foundational rule which requires any community to regularly justify the existence of their approach to land use regulation. The onus should clearly be on the community to show

- why it needs land use regulation;
- what the objectives of any system are; and
- what benefits accrue.

To help in any deliberations I would propose five principles to be considered as a basis for any approach to ensure its link with a more postmodern planning:[1]

[1] I have taken these five criteria from those recommended by the Government's Better Regulation Task Force which published its report in September 1998 (HSMO: London).

- *Transparency.* The reason regulation was introduced has too often been lost, and planners and others simply 'go through the motions' without reflecting upon why they are doing so. To meet more postmodern concerns of openness and clarity, any form of land use regulation needs to justify its existence to those who will be affected. Such a justification should include an assessment of who is likely to gain and lose from any system, the alternatives to the approach chosen, and why this particular system was selected.

- *Accountability.* Central to any concept of regulation in a more open and transparent system is accountability. Concepts of accountability have usually related solely to public bodies such as local authorities. However, a more postmodern approach would also be concerned with the accountability of self-regulatory bodies such as the Royal Town Planning Institute, particularly as planners can and often do hide behind the decisions of elected officials. The role of planners is covered further on in this chapter, but where a community decides to allow representatives to makes decisions on their behalf, there needs to be mechanisms that make clear how local people can challenge such decisions. Again, the relationship between representatives and the represented in local decision making is covered in more detail further on.

- *Targeting.* Any form of land use regulation needs to be specifically targeted at the issue a community feels it is necessary to address. Widespread and vague powers need to be avoided if reflection and accountability are to be maintained. The aims and objectives of any regulatory framework must be clearly spelt out so that those involved in local governance do not perpetuate their position through the use of inappropriate regulation, and that the performance of regulation can be evaluated.

- *Consistency.* Although it is important that regulatory regimes are applied consistently over the area in question, there should be no need to assume that they will be so between different areas. There is a potential drawback of confusion here between different regimes operating across the UK. However, the flip-side of this is that different systems better reflect the wishes of an area (e.g., a large city may wish to have a more deregulated approach in order to encourage new development) and also competing systems offer what in broad terms could be seen as a 'competition of ideas'. This should be a competition of ideas between different areas that encourages innovation in systems and processes which allows reflection upon the different approaches.

- *Proportionality.* The balance between regulation and the freedom of citizens to act must be decided locally. However, as I have set out above, the presumption must always be that there should be no intervention unless it can be justified. Implementing any form of regulation effectively so that it can achieve its objectives requires the support of the public. Any such support is far more likely to be forthcoming if any regulation is felt to be fair and appropriate, which is related to proportionality.

These five criteria provide guidance to ensure any form of land use regulation remains the minimum required through reflection upon it and comparison with other approaches. One further way that such reflection and involvement can be achieved is through representation and in particular, the voting system used in local governance.

LINKING VOTING WITH ACTION

As anyone who has studied different voting systems will tell you, there is no perfect system. The UK tradition has been to follow the First Past the Post (FPTP) approach at both the national and local levels though, as I go on to discuss later, this is beginning to change. As a basis for electing representatives of a particular locality to represent it, FPTP is easy to understand and effective. However, it

- Favours a two-party system and makes it difficult for any third or fourth parties to receive a fairer proportion of seats;
- tends to mean that one party gets an overall majority of seats even though they did not receive an overall majority of votes;
- is inefficient at distributing seats according to a party's share of the vote at a national level;
- 'wastes' a large number of votes because they are not represented in a preferred candidate which leads to lower voter turnout as people become disenchanted;
- leads to lower voter choice as smaller parties are highly unlikely to be successful.

The above points can be demonstrated with reference to Table 8.1 below. Here it can be seen how the Labour party had a disproportionate number of seats in the 1997 election (43.2 per cent of the vote and 63.4 per cent of seats) while smaller parties such as the Liberal Democrats received 16.8 per cent of the vote and only 6.9 per cent of seats.

It should not be assumed that a more proportional system would automatically modify the distribution of seats shown in Table 8.1. In studying the outcome of the 1997 election under different forms of PR, Dunleavy (1998) found that using an Alternative Vote or Supplementary Vote would have given Labour an even larger majority. A Single Transferable Vote system would have led to a Labour majority of 44 and the Alternative Member System would have denied them a straightforward majority.

Table 8.1 Voting at the 1997 UK General Election

Party	Number of votes	Vote %	Number of seats	Seats %
Labour	13,516,632	43.2	418	63.4
Conservative	9,602,857	30.7	165	29.4
Liberal Democrat	5,242,894	16.8	46	6.9
Referendum	811,827	2.6	0	0
Scottish Nationalists	621,540	2.0	6	2.0
Ulster Unionists	258,349	0.8	3	0.5
SDLP	190,814	0.6	3	0.5
Plaid Cymru	161,030	0.5	4	0.6

A postmodern planning would require a more proportional and representative approach as FPTP restricts plurality and choice, discourages participation and limits the extent to which existing power relations can be both exposed and challenged. Here, I am arguing for an alternative to FPTP at a sub-national level as it is here that the focus of a postmodern planning should be located. A national level alternative has already been examined in the UK by the Jenkins Commission and there is a commitment from the government to hold a referendum on an alternative before the next general election. There are two aspects to a reformed system of voter representation that I wish to briefly explore. The first is obviously an alternative to FPTP and how this could relate to planning, and the second is the use of referendums.

I do not want to get into the intricacies of different forms of voting system. The guiding principle under which a postmodern planning should be based is that of representation of opinion – even where that opinion is in a minority – it should be represented and given the opportunity to be heard. This corresponds with Laclau and Mouffe's thinking on closure and their argument that closure per se could be justified providing it did not silence the voice of others. The main debate between the FPTP advocates and those committed to an alternative proportional system, as McLean has noted (1993), is centred on a difference between process and outcome. The postmodern concern is with process, but any realistic alternative must also have an eye on outcome, as too much emphasis on process can sometimes preclude an outcome. Oranje (1996) gives an excellent example of this in relation to the emerging democratic processes in South Africa. He argues that as institutions and individuals 'feel their way' democratically, too much emphasis has (understandably) been given to inclusion, to the extent that very few decisions and outcomes have emerged. This has led to disenchantment with the new form of post-Apartheid government. In 1991 the Labour Party's Commission on Electoral Reform also focused on the balance between process and outcome and concluded that any balance between them was political rather than technical (Labour Party, 1991). There are at least half a dozen different forms of proportional system that place a far greater emphasis on process as opposed to outcome (as I touched upon above). Although the UK has used the FPTP system it has also dabbled with forms of proportional representation (PR). In 1973 a form of PR was used in Northern Ireland and again in 1979 for elections to the European Parliament. More recently PR has also been used for the elections to the Scottish Parliament and Welsh Assemblies and is proposed to be used for the European elections in future.

What would a form of PR mean for planning, and how might it work? First, representation of a community through councillors or whoever could be through a form of PR. The implications of this would be to immediately 'open up' local governance to a wider variety of interests and groups beyond the traditional party groupings that currently dominate. The downside of the current party political dominance is that voting on issues can and tends to be along party lines, whereas many of the issues that local government deals with require a more sensitive, less confrontational approach. Locality, specific interest groups would also be more likely to gain representation increasing the plurality of representation.

One potential problem with the PR route as a basis for local representation does arise, however. All forms of PR are more likely to produce coalitions. Coalition rule encourages a more co-operative style of representation and tends to be more stable than FPTP forms of governance. Obviously, more co-operation and greater inclusion are postmodern principles. However, coalitions and stability, though more inclusive of minority voices, have the potential to become stultifying and thereby work against a more plural and open governance. The answer to this is not easy and it is a danger with any form of PR. Nevertheless, the advantages of the approach far outweigh the potential disadvantages. It is important to break the stranglehold that FPTP has given single parties in certain 'rotten boroughs' in recent years. There has also been a strong correlation between these single party authorities and various 'scandals' over the planning system. Notwithstanding high-profile cases such as North Cornwall and Bassetlaw there have also been others such as Doncaster, Sutton, Eden, Hull, Peterborough and Canvey Island to name a few. Because planning involves potentially large financial gains there is always the possibility (and, in recent years, this has been an actuality) of corruption or for the system to be reorientated towards other ends by both elected members and planning officers. I cover the renewed role for planners under a more postmodern approach further on, but the point I am making here is that while no form of voting system is perfect, the more proportional system required by a rethought planning has distinct advantages over the current FPTP approach and fits in with a postmodern direction.

IMPROVING AND ENHANCING LOCAL INVOLVEMENT

Greater participation in issues of community concern has been a growing characteristic of local government for the past 30 years or so. As will be clear from
Chapter 7, it is also a central theme of a postmodern planning. A recent survey of
public involvement in local government found that only 3 per cent of people were
interested in politics and over three quarters said that they had little or no interest.
Two thirds of residents considered that they would object or take action if the local
authority did something that they disapproved of (DETR, 1998b). Why have these
cynical and reactive characteristics come about? The DETR report identifies four
obvious reasons for this:

- negative views of the council including its services, officers and members;
- a lack of awareness about the opportunities for participation that were available;
- a feeling that it would be pointless because the council would not do anything;
- a strong sense among many that participation was for others – the educated
  middle-class and middle-aged.

Under the historical and current system, local government works on the basis of an
arms length implementer of central government policies. Any involvement local
people may have is usually based on consultation. During the 1980s, the centralis-
ing Thatcher Governments' ... seriously eroded the scope for choice and variety in
local government policy making and implementation', with the result that 'The
scope for local authorities to exercise their preferred political choices now
depends very significantly on whether these are compatible with the direction of
government policy' (Joseph Rowntree Foundation, 1995: 1). It is hardly surprising
therefore, that local people should feel alienated and cynical about involvement. As
I argued at the beginning of this chapter, no one approach will achieve a more
postmodern planning, and simply allowing people more say will have little if any
impact on the 40 per cent or lower typical turnout at local elections. The changes
that I have already outlined, including the introduction of a form of PR in voting and
some of the other changes I discuss further on, all work together in strengthening
the link between citizen and community. A genuinely participative approach is
crucial to a postmodern planning in that it helps challenge and expose existing
concentrations of power, encourages plurality and difference and gives voice to
those previously excluded. To achieve these aims, two main changes are required
in addition to the others detailed in this chapter. First, there needs to be an active
approach to encouraging radical citizenry. Second, local communities need to be
given more than simply an implementation role in the form of a genuine degree of
independence and competence.

The Neill Commission was set to examine party funding and proposed an Electoral Commission which would have responsibility to oversee elections and monitor party political spending. But the Commission could have a much wider remit that could include acting like a proselytising body that encourages a more active role for citizens while avoiding a party political affiliation. Their aim could be to promote greater participation in local and national elections (which should be far easier with a more representative voting system when voters can see that their choice is better reflected). However, the encouragement of a radical citizenry is not simply a case of a more proactive approach to involving people. There has to be a genuine recognition that to encourage people to participate more and continually challenge the status quo requires changes to the political environment that directly relate an action (e.g. voting or expressing a view) to an outcome (e.g. a change in policy). I have already discussed some of the changes necessary above, including a more proportional voting system. But one further change in the nature of local government is required that will make it more representative and accountable and thereby encourage people to partake more. The UK is one of the few countries in Europe that does not have a doctrine of general competence for its local government. As was demonstrated in the 1980s, central government can and has abolished local councils at its whim, as the lack of a written constitution guarantees no right of existence. Local government in the UK exists under the doctrine of *ultra vires*, i.e., it can do (with a few exceptions) only what parliament permits it to. This has made local government an outpost of central government in many people's eyes. Implementing central policies naturally shifts attention of political power to the centre and away from the local. Giving local government power of general competence would counter act that. Under such an approach local government would be responsible for core services as now. But there would be two main differences. First, local government would need to raise more of its revenue from local sources, would have the power to increase this independently of central government, and spend it on other services in their area. Any such change should aim to restore the link between local spending and taxation as the effectiveness of a general competence, relies on having control over the amount of resources available. Second, because of their general competence they could go beyond the statutory minimum service requirements and meet the needs and desires of the people in their area. If a particular locality wants to increase or even decrease the level of services in an area, this would be permitted within a law of general competence without interference from central government.

Another tool that could be used that fits in well with the concerns of openness and accountability are referendums. To date these have been held on the Scottish Parliament, Welsh Assembly and Mayor for London. There are referendums proposed on a new voting system and the UK's entry into the European

Single Currency, and for local people to decide if they want a directly elected mayor for their area. Referendums help in deepening participation by putting spend and tax choice directly to local people. However, to avoid referendums becoming a rubber stamping exercise for local decisions, their scope needs to be widened to include a role in consultation that would encompass a range of choices. They also need to be used beyond a merely financial remit to other policy questions that could include development plan strategies or housing allocations for example. The initiation of a referendum also needs to allow for citizens to demand a direct vote on issues if a proportion of them required it.

Other mechanisms to help develop a more profound involvement include the use of citizen's juries. Juries are normally comprised of between 6 and 12 members chosen to be representative of the people in the area who then consider an in-depth issue over a number of days. The jury hears evidence from expert witnesses and can question them. Then, with the aid of a facilitator, makes a non-binding recommendation to the council. There have been a variety of situations where citizen's juries have been used, including planning. Horsham District Council used a jury to examine housing allocation in the district. The emergence of a more radical citizenry also requires the ability of local people to have access to the kind of information that will help them make informed choices.

A RIGHT TO KNOW

A lack of openness and transparency has characterised UK government at both central and local levels. This has been brought to the public's attention by two high-level examples in recent years. The Scott Report on arms sales was one. In the view of one body, a

> theme of secrecy runs throughout the Scott Report. It links the refusal to reveal to Parliament the change in the guidelines on the export of military equipment; the insistence that public interest immunity should be sought for policy advice documents regardless of their actual contents; and Scott's criticism of the way in which decisions on arms export license are taken ... we believe that an effective Freedom of Information Act would make a significant contribution to the problems identified in the Report. Above all it would signify a substantial change of culture (Campaign for Freedom of Information evidence to the Public Service Committee, House of Commons (1995–6) 313–II: 97).

Another example of government secrecy afflicting people regards BSE:

> With a problem as important as this (the relationship between BSE and Creutzfeldt-Jakob disease), the lesson that screams through my own mind about this issue, ... is that it is always a good due process to get a variety of

opinions about complicated databases which may have implications for public
health ... My criticism is the culture of secrecy that seemed to pertain at the
time, such that very few groups could have access – if any, none as I am aware
– to the information to carry out independent analysis. That would be the lesson
that remains in my mind most strongly (Professor Roy Anderson, University of
Oxford, to the BSE Inquiry, 16 March 1998).

A more postmodern approach to planning requires openness, the opportunity to
challenge and expose the status quo and existing power relations, and the need for
constant reflection. To achieve this, citizens need to be able to have access to
information. This works at broadly two levels. The first is the citizen who feels
aggrieved by a decision and wants to find out more about the circumstances. In
planning this could be a refusal of planning permission, enforcement proceedings
or why a piece of land was allocated for one purpose over another. Although planning documents are public in that they can be inspected, many of the decisions
and procedures of planning are taken outside of the formal planning arena such as
negotiations, internal meetings, letters, legal agreements, etc. The second level is
what I would term the more macro level of information. This relates less to a personal or site-specific situation and more to broader issues such as government
policy on economic matters, for example. Access to information for local planning
regimes is more likely to involve the first level. What postmodern planning requires,
therefore, is a Freedom of Information Act (FOIA) that would aim to

*   make it easier for members of the public to find out what information govern-
    ment holds about them;
*   make it easier for politicians, journalists and members of the public to hold
    the government to account by making government cover-ups more difficult;
*   make it easier for members of the public to participate in an informed way in
    the discussion of policy issues, and improve the quality of government
    decision making because those drafting policy advice know that they must be
    able, ultimately, to defend their reasoning before public opinion (H. M.
    Government, 1998, chapter 1, para 3).

How could such an approach benefit planning? Planning is part of the wider
process of local governance and an FOIA would impinge upon its functions as they
relate to other areas of governance such as voting by representatives, representation on committees, background documents on council policy and personal
information. In terms of planning per se, a FOIA would make pre-application discussions open to scrutiny, including negotiating positions and their development.
Planning agreements and their background would be more open as would meetings between members and officers on policy development. Although such documents would be available after the event they would help create a new, more

honest and open form of government and planning that made it explicit who would get what and what elected officials and officers considered to be the public interest. Mistakes would also be laid open, encouraging a more conscientious approach to land use regulation. All of this would be with a series of exemptions based on a 'substantial harm' test and a number of over-riding interests including defence, law enforcement, commercially-sensitive information (trade secrets, etc.), personnel files of public sector employees, legal professional privilege, and personal privacy. However, though exclusions such as the need to protect commercially-sensitive information are broad, they should not encompass issues such as the details of a public–private venture and who is being paid what. Confidence in public financial affairs is low and while certain commercial interests and public bodies may prefer to keep such information private, the benefits of public disclosure and the increased confidence that may bring far outweigh such concerns. In fact, the greater disclosure of information is actually likely to help developers and public bodies through a greater access to relevant and up to date information on property deals for calculation of yields, etc. As the Royal Institute of Chartered Surveyors put it in their submission on the Government's proposed FOIA:

> Many areas of market information are beyond the public domain or have restrictions on their availability and use. Where information is available it is often inconsistent, fragmented and disorganised. This inhibits the development of an effective property market ... It is hoped that the Freedom of Information Act will have the effect of promoting a simpler and more transparent property market, and improving decision making in the management of land, construction and the environment (RICS, submissions to White Paper on Freedom of Information Act, February, 1998: 2).

Postmodern concerns with openness, inclusion and transparency and the more active encouragement of challenges to existing concentrations of power and its relations requires a more open approach to governance which will be achieved by a Freedom of Information Act.

Part 1 has set out a number of themes for a postmodern planning that contextualise planning practice. These themes can be summarised as involving:

- a locality-determined approach and spatial organisation to planning;
- a presumption against any form of land use regulation with clear criteria to help reflect upon any system;
- the introduction of a more proportional form of voting system;
- active encouragement of greater local involvement;
- greater openness about the mechanisms and processes of planning through a Freedom of Information Act.

These are five principles that many western democracies have embedded within their constitutions. However, like many principles they mean little without an attempt to translate them into practicalities and reflect upon what they mean. This is the subject of Part 2 below. However, before I embark on exploring the implications of these more general prerequisites for postmodern planning practice I will first briefly explore some themes of postmodern planning practice. This is not an exhaustive list by any means and merely provides a number of possible pointers within the current broad thrust of current UK planning that may help shift planning towards a more postmodern approach.

1 ROLE OF THE CENTRE

The UK administrative tradition is one of central control despite recent moves towards devolution and decentralisation. Notwithstanding the discretion of individual officers and local planning authorities, the minor differences between England, Scotland and Wales and a small number of mechanisms described further on, the planning system largely follows a centralised approach. This has some advantages including the possibility of national consistency, regional planning and merging land use regulation with other national policy areas such as economic growth. However, the tight reins that central government maintain over planning mask significant regional diversity and attitude. This is becoming apparent in the diverging approaches to planning in England and Scotland where the former is pursuing a deregulatory approach while the latter are increasingly concerned with re-imposing a form of regional government. With the Welsh Assembly and the potential of regional assemblies in England, there is a shift towards a more regionally-diverse form of planning, though each area will still be under the jurisdiction of a national planning system and nationally determined planning guidelines.

Local control is more than local administration. It involves accountability and, therefore, a link to local needs. Part of the reason why there is low local involvement in planning is because of its lack of reflection of local needs. A more postmodern planning should devolve both the planning system and processes away from the centre and be more locally accountable and reflective. Within an increasingly globalised world and with the influence of supra-national bodies such as the European Commission, the nation–state is becoming obsolete as a body to ensure consistency. Whether at the regional level or otherwise, a postmodern planning needs to be more accountable and reflective of sub-national concerns. One way that this can be achieved is through maintaining the current trajectory of change. But there are currently methods and mechanisms that can be employed as I describe below.

2 FLEXIBLE MECHANISMS

Rather than a prescriptive approach, local communities should have at their dis-
posal a 'kit bag' of tools and mechanisms that they can use or adapt to their
particular circumstances. In some ways this is not far from the same mechanisms
available under current procedures and is closely related to proposals that were
explored in the 1980s. For example, the General Permitted Development Order
(GPDO) is a mechanism that automatically grants planning permission for certain
categories of development. In the early 1980s, the Royal Town Planning Institute
proposed that local authorities should have the power to grant localised GPDOs to
suit the local circumstances of an area. A form of localised control over development is currently available though two mechanisms: Article 4 Directions and Simplified Planning Zones. Article 4 Directions allow local planning authorities to
withdraw the provisions of the GPDO making it necessary to once again apply for
planning permission. Simplified Planning Zones (SPZs) achieve the opposite. By
adopting a zone, a local planning authority grants planning permission in advance
for a range of developments in an area. A zone may be of any size and cover virtually any uses.

These examples of flexibility in planning regime run from the relatively minor
(Article 4 Directions) to the potentially dramatic (SPZs). Although the actual impact
they have made on planning practice is minimal, what they do show is that there is
a tradition for localised land use regulation regimes that deviate from an otherwise
centralised approach. A more postmodern planning could build on this and extend
the principle of a flexible and localised form of land use control.

3 ROLE OF PLANNERS

The current professional/technical role of planners is not conducive to a more postmodern planning. As Davidoff rightly pointed out, planners cannot escape ethical
and moral choices by turning them into technical and rational ones. Planners see
themselves as being concerned with means, not ends, while in reality the two are
conflated.

> Our contention rests on the thesis that goals are value statements, that value
> statements are not objectively verifiable, and, therefore, that the planner, by
> himself, cannot reasonably accept or reject goals for the public (Davidoff and
> Reiner, 1962: 22).

This is a parallel of the postmodern concern with avoiding prescription and its
emphasis on the subjective and normative basis of values and theory. Planners,
through their professional status, must strive to perpetuate the idea and practice of
over-arching technical and value-free activity. However, a postmodern approach
needs to question the role of planners and consequently their attachment to the

current idea of a profession. Davidoff argued for planners to become advocates on behalf of communities with whom they shared values emphasising their political role. Advocacy is similar in some ways to Rorty's prophet and Forester's progressive planner who seek to challenge the tenets of planning and improve understanding through an open-ended dialogue.

A postmodern planner's role needs to be more than representing a vague public interest with hidden though influential values. There needs to be a commitment to openness and a requirement to reflect upon practices and outcomes. While remaining a profession, planners cannot achieve this new role because of the requirement to provide an expert technical view. The other obvious impediment to planners questioning and reflecting upon their role and existing processes is their employment status. While employed as an expert advocate for a local authority, it is unlikely that planners will engage in any activity that will question the position of their employers. This has been a major factor in inhibiting the growth of Davidoff's advocacy planning in the UK – while planners may like to work on behalf of a cause with which they agree or have sympathy, local communities are unlikely to be able to employ a planner. But local authorities can help by changing the ethos of a local authority to allow planners to become community advocates and can also impose ethical or moral codes of their own that challenge and supersede those of the professional ethic.

4 CONFLICT RESOLUTION

The current UK planning system allows no third-party right of appeal and consequently the focus for any proposal is squarely on two main parties – the applicant and the local authority representing the public interest. While public consultation and involvement provides an avenue for third parties to become involved, they are essentially tangential to the applicant-local authority axis. A postmodern planning should seek to diffuse that axis and provide many different routes that empower and thereby encourage greater involvement. One way to achieve this is through third-party appeals.

Third-party appeals are found in other planning systems that resemble the UK's, such as the Republic of Ireland and New Zealand. In Ireland they are closely tied in with statutory time limits to avoid the system becoming too delayed, and experience there has shown that they have not become a charter for NIMBY attitudes to halt or delay development. In the UK there was support for a limited form of third-party appeal from the Labour party prior to the 1997 election, following their consultation exercise on planning entitled *Planning for Prosperity: A Review of Planning Issues* (Labour Party, 1996). Commenting on the proposals, the then Shadow Environment Minister Keith Vaz commented:

> third parties should have the right [to appeal] when a local authority grants
> planning permission for itself. But I would not like to see a situation where third
> parties intervene in the planning system willy-nilly (Planning Week, 26th
> September, 1996: 11).

After a hostile response from property interests, the idea has been dropped
and there is undoubtedly a variety of positions on the concept, both for
and against. However, a more inclusive system prior to the determination of a
proposal or during the preparation of a plan may well mean that third parties do
not feel the need to resort to challenging the decision of the authority. Further,
different forms of representation and planning systems may well obviate the desire
to challenge decisions, though the existence of such a route or mechanism
would have two influences. First, it would encourage a more inclusive form of planning as both developer and the council will be aware that if they did not include
many interests, there might be a challenge that delays or even overturns the proposal. Second, it could alter the attitude of third parties and the public generally
towards planning. If the strength of the applicant–local planning authority axis is
weakened and the option of challenge is there then it is likely that the public will
feel the planning system is more about a community interest rather than a narrower
one.

After offering these thoughts on some themes for a postmodern planning,
Part 2 will now focus on planning itself and how it might be interpreted within more
postmodern thinking and the context set out above.

PART 2: THE PRACTICE OF POSTMODERN PLANNING

How can I explore a form of postmodern planning when it could be constituted of
an infinity of forms? What I have chosen to do is present an example that I hope
will highlight some of themes and principles that have been discussed throughout
the book. This involves treading a line between a system that is recognisable to
those who know local government and planning in the UK, but also attempts to
shift away from elements of that familiarity towards a more postmodern approach.
Here, I develop a postmodern *framework* for planning as well as a postmodern
form of planning. I have had to make a few assumptions and take some liberties
which naturally involve a number of problems which I address later. The example
centres on the mythical Nowhere District Council (NDC) and its neighbour Elsewhere District Council (EDC) who, in the wake of enabling legislation from the
centre (London, Edinburgh or Cardiff), embarked on a programme of bring planning 'closer to the people'. This is an account of their experiences.

Previously, NDC had been a progressive authority and although they had been based on A Town (population 100,000) they had moved towards a series of area committees and offices. Nevertheless, the council was still centralised and A Town dominated the two other main centres in the district, B Town (population 80,000) and C Town (population 20,000). A Town is the dominant town and a regional financial centre. It has relatively low unemployment with a high proportion of jobs in the town being linked to services. Although B Town is nearly as big as A Town, it has suffered from decline and high unemployment given its former dependence on manufacturing employment. The town's population is static and although there have been a number of measures to tackle employment decline none have succeeded. This has bred suspicion that A Town has been attracting more than its fair share of new employment further fuelling the traditional rivalry between the two. C Town is the antithesis of the other two NDC centres. It is much smaller and a historic market town, internationally recognised for the quality of its medieval buildings and urban form. Employment in the town is mainly related to tourism which has led to increased pressures for development that have traditionally been resisted. Finally, in the areas around the towns there are a large number of small villages and hamlets that provide commuter housing and workers for rural industries such as farming and forestry. Although these rural areas vary in character and outlook, they are united in their resentment of the towns which took over their previously autonomous governance status in 1974. In planning terms, the issues that NDC and its constituent parts have to deal with are typical. Growth and regeneration, conservation and development, jobs and the environment are the tensions that many local authorities have to deal with.

In common with other areas of the country, NDC holds a referendum on the future of land use regulation. Prior to this, however, they set up an 'Inquiry into the Future of Planning in Nowhere District Council' in order to formulate the questions and alternatives that will be put to local people. There is a presumption that land use regulation will be decentralised in line with government thinking. The inquiry aims to evaluate the desirability and practicalities of such a move. The inquiry panel is comprised of residents representative of the area as a whole and will report back to the full council. While the inquiry is doing its work, elections are held for the full council under the newly introduced STV system (Table 8.2).

The new authority, which is a coalition of Labour, Independents and Liberal Democrats undertake a number of initiatives to help 'deepen' democratic involvement prior to the report of the inquiry.

The inquiry into the future of land use regulation reaches a number of conclusions after questioning expert witnesses, local representatives, evaluating different alternatives and weighing costs and benefits, and comes up with the following conclusions:

Table 8.2 Election Results for Nowhere District Council

Party	Seats
Labour	12
Conservative	6
Independent Conservative	2
Anti-European Socialist	1
Liberal Democrat	3
Liberal	1
Green Party	2
Anti-Ring Road Coalition	4
A Town for Growth	2
Conservation of C Town Alliance	3
Independent	9

- The current form of land use regulation is too inflexible to the needs of different areas within the district. In particular, it does not account for the diversity of situations within the towns and seeks to impose a uniform set of objectives that are at variance with the needs of different communities.
- New forms of land use regulation that are flexible to the needs of different areas are required.

It recommends that the referendum allows local people to opt out of the current arrangements and, in line with government guidance, formulate their own system, processes and objectives for land use regulation. The inquiry has identified four main areas within the district that it perceives are different enough to warrant a distinctive approach, based on the three main towns and the remaining rural area.

A Town wants to consolidate its role as a regional service centre which, it argues, requires an emphasis on a high-quality environment including housing provision. Their objection to the current system is that it is too restrictive on new housing and retail growth in the green belt and that there was too much of an emphasis on industrial employment. The system was too 'open' to external influences such as environmental groups who lobbied for policies that ran counter to the long-term interests of the town. What was required was an approach that emphasised growth and was more flexible to the needs of commercial interests in the town. The planning framework was also not restrictive enough in that it also promoted development of a variety of housing types thereby reducing land for other uses that would help achieve the town's objectives.

B Town felt that the current planning framework was part of the reason for its continued high unemployment. This was despite the planning system providing a generally supportive approach to employment uses. The issue, B Town respondents felt, was that planning was too 'negative' and the very presence of a planning system inhibited development and created uncertainty in the development process. Planners themselves wanted to put barriers in the way of business through their insistence on committee procedures while large areas of land lay undeveloped. 'Do we really need such a complex and costly system?', they asked. They wanted to reduce 'red tape', streamline the approach and 'lift the burdens off business'.

The view in C Town was the opposite from that in its neighbour B Town. Here, development pressure and the need to maintain and enhance the urban environment led to local people wanting a strengthened system with some of the current exclusions from planning control abolished. Negotiation and a strong planning framework were considered the hallmarks of any system in C Town as were the introduction of policies relating to the loss of retail facilities in the town centre. C Town needed to enhance its environment to protect the town and ensure its role as a tourist centre. The current planning system did not help in this regard.

In the remaining rural areas there was a general feeling that new housing encroachment from A Town in particular was threatening the character of existing communities and raising house prices beyond the means of local people. Equally, the more restrictive policies on development were having a harmful impact on rural industries such as farming and forestry and the feeling was that any planning system should seek to encourage rather than restrict this. The pressure in rural areas was for a planning regime to help local people and industries. Within these broad parameters, the feeling in rural areas was that the actual mechanisms of a planning system should be as inclusionary as possible. The role of parish councils in a very large area was felt to be crucial in harnessing local feeling.

NDC considered the inquiry's conclusions and a referendum was held in each area. In the three main towns the proposal to run their own form of land use regulation was passed. Each of the towns had their own town council which entered into a legal agreement with NDC to develop their own form of land use regulation on the council's behalf. The rural areas decided that their administrative centre would remain in A Town. Work in the four areas was then undertaken to develop a locally-orientated system and set of processes in conjunction with residents and other representatives. Each council used a variety of methods to garner information on what approach to take. Their approaches fell into distinct categories depending on the area.

A Town and B Town saw the exercise more as an exchange of information. They held traditional consultation exercises based on documents that they published, exhibitions, public meetings and question and answer sessions. C Town and the rural area undertook the exercise on the basis of learning and exchange. Their methods included citizen's panels, advisory referendums, focus groups, visioning exercises and public forums.

The result of these exercises was four different approaches to land use regulation (Table 8.3).

Table 8.3 Overview of different approaches to land use regulation in NDC

	A Town	B Town	C Town	Rural Area
Overall approach	Plan and project-led – presumption in favour of plan but plan's loose framework allows considerable discretion.	Project-led – presumption in favour of development.	Plan-led – presumption in favour of preservation and sustainable development.	Plan-led – presumption in favour of indigenous industry and housing.
Basis of local involvement	Consultative	Notification	Participative	Consultative
Typical tools	Promotion of services in town centre. Environmental improvements. Relaxation on out-of-town retail development and restrictions to office use.	Widespread zoning with combination of plan and permission. Wide exemptions from development control.	Extension of restrictions on exemptions from development control.	Strict and clear criteria plus the widespread use of legal agreements and other financially-related tools to direct and control development.
Decision systems	Elite cabinet of members in conjunction with Chief Officers delegated to negotiate on individual proposals. Very pro-business.	Widespread use of delegated powers to officers and Committee Chair.	Use of referendums. Third-party rights of appeal. Consultative committees and panels report to main committee.	Traditional committee system.

Once the direction of each planning regime was decided locally, the different systems were implemented. Each town immediately noticed a change in culture of planning control. In B Town there was a far more pro-active attitude towards development from planners and other regulatory bodies. It decided not to adopt a development plan for the area but a broad proposals map akin to a zoning regime. In some areas zoned for industrial purposes planning schemes are adopted that grant permission for a broad range of uses. If the proposal conforms to the criteria in the zoning ordnance then no planning application is required. Similarly, erstwhile tools such as the General Development Order and Use Classes Order that exempted certain proposals from the need to obtain planning permission are extended and consolidated into Permitted Development Ordnance. This covers wider aspects of control, including almost any change of use outside residential areas. In other areas, a 'default' system is adopted where applicants submit brief proposals and if the B Town Development Board do not require a more detailed proposal within 21 days, then the proposal is deemed to have been approved. There is considerable delegation to planning officers and full-time paid representatives making the need to hold planning committee meetings rare.

C Town also experiences a radical change in approach, though in a different direction than B Town. Here, the emphasis is much more on regulation rather than speed and development. Although C Town experiences a wide range of development proposals, the limited number of sites and the high quality of the urban environment mean that it need not accept any proposal but negotiate for high-quality design. In negotiations for major proposals a panel is set up comprising architects, planners, councillors and local people to judge the scheme. Wider involvement of local people is also actively encouraged to help maintain grassroots support for a restrictive land use regulation approach. The new planning regime has also altered the definition of development to include works such as external painting and window replacement normally considered as maintenance and exempt from control. The council also decided to explore other areas of control outside of land use regulation including the licensing of entertainment, pubs and restaurants in an attempt to capture the right 'aura' for C Town.

A Town has taken a more composite approach to land use regulation than B or C Town. It is commercially minded but does not suffer from the same levels of unemployment and deprivation as B Town. And while it has historic areas worthy of retention, the emphasis is more on conservation rather than preservation. The overall aims for A Town are to continue its growth as an important regional financial services centre. It seeks to achieve this through providing high quality sites for development; the 'right' environment for companies and individuals to feel attracted to the town and an atmosphere of certainty *and* flexibility in which investors can feel secure. Land use regulation plays an important role in achieving these objectives. A development plan has been prepared for the area that enshrines the pro-development philosophy. Public involvement is more along the lines of consultation, and information as an ethic emerges of elitist decision making. Changes in the direction of policy reflect a greater emphasis and freedom regarding service development to support the commercial focus of the settlement. This includes a 24 Hour Town initiative that encourages food retail development in the centre, a relaxation on out-of-town retail and housing development to provide a attractive environment for in-coming and existing businesses.

Finally, the remaining rural areas around the three towns have taken a pro-local economic development initiative that encourages small-scale industrial development and farm growth and diversity. Tight restrictions remain on new

development in the open countryside and the change of use of shop units in villages into housing is resisted. Because of the expansion of A Town, the area
around it is designated green belt and the Nowhere Rural Development Board alter
their regulations to require permission for any house to be used as a second home.
Any residential development that does proceed is also restricted by covenants to
those 'currently resident in the area' which severely limits the attraction of house
building outside of A Town and reduces land prices thereby helping make any new
housing more affordable. However, another consequence is that existing housing is
becoming more desirable and therefore expensive. Not surprisingly, this has
caused a great deal of friction with the residents and planning approach of A Town
as it undermines their strategy of releasing out-of-centre land for high quality residential development. A Town has, however, negotiated with the planning board of
the adjacent Elsewhere District Council who are happy to see further development
occur in rural villages in order to help local services such as schools and shops.
One consequence of this is that there is a large increase in commuting over longer
distances into A Town and considerable congestion along the main road at peak
times.

The four planning regimes and their representatives cannot come to any
agreement on strategic guidance to help overcome some of these issues even
though there is support for an overall framework in parts of the council as a whole.
Even a Citizen's Jury set up to examine alternatives cannot agree.

After two years the review of the different planning regimes is initiated again
with a public inquiry. The inquiry found that the division of planning into different
approaches has had both advantages and disadvantages. The advantages include:

- A more representative and accountable land use regulation system that more
  accurately mirrors the wishes of local people.
- A greater involvement of local people in planning processes and a greater
  consensus on the aims of the system.
- Those involved both professionally and otherwise have found the changes to
  be stimulating for the community as a whole, leading to increased turnouts at
  elections.
- That the different regimes have more or less achieved what they set out to.

The inquiry also identified a number of disadvantages, including:

- The lack of strategic overview and mechanisms for conflict resolution
  between planning regimes.
- Although the rural area had adopted its own planning regime it was administered by planners in A Town who had to implement two different schemes
  that conflicted with each others' objectives.

- Although different planning regimes had overall public support there had inevitably been confusion in the minds of people and investors as to the objectives and mechanisms of different schemes.
- Some of the boundaries chosen at the time of the previous referendum had been selected more for aspirational reasons than practicality. Rural wards immediately adjacent to B Town, for example, did not want to be governed by a more laissez-faire scheme, though their close proximity 'made sense' in terms of planning for the town as a whole.
- Although there had been moves towards greater public involvement in some areas, which had been helped by the shift to a form of proportional representation in local elections, the freedom to determine the choice of planning regime had in some cases also involved less participation – particularly in A Town and B Town.

Following on from these conclusions the inquiry also made a number of recommendations:

- That, as previously agreed, referendums were be held to reaffirm existing planning regimes following reviews in each area.
- That a strategic planning board be set up for the district as a whole to resolve disputes and provide overall guidance.
- That public involvement become more formalised in each of the areas.

Although generally welcomed, the last recommendation in particular was controversial and was portrayed as a 'big brother' intrusion upon the autonomy of the different areas. However, local council elections had returned a higher proportion of Green candidates who began to lobby for greater environmental concern in all four areas. Their case was strengthened when information was gathered under the Freedom of Information Act that local representatives in B Town had known that an Environmental Impact Statement submitted with a proposal for a large new abattoir had failed to mention the potential impact upon the water table from polluted run-off water. The approach of B Town was labelled inadequate in the legal challenge the Green Party mounted against the town's planning regime and the High Court decided it did not sufficiently take into account national planning priorities concerning environmental protection. Revisions were therefore made to the town's planning regime that ensured environmental issues were openly discussed where necessary. This required a dilution of the delegated decision scheme at the introduction of committee meetings.

C Town were also concerned about the length of time it was taking to adopt a development plan for the town given the open and inclusive nature of the process they had created. Voting for different options in the plan was undertaken on a proportional basis with each issue requiring discussion and voting. The problem was not only one of time but also of outcome. Different interests began to emerge and coalesce into groupings that lobbied for or against particular proposals. Voting consequently became less an aggregate of varied interests and more a reflection of powerful interests. There was also a strong reaction against the tough regime from local businesses. Expansion of existing premises and shops was increasingly difficult and even where proposals were permitted, the time taken following widespread consultation was considered inordinate. The local elections saw C Town with a higher proportion of pro-business interests returned who immediately began to lobby for a relaxation of the planning regime.

B Town's troubles were also not over. Their deregulated planning regime had been seen as a crucial element in attracting footloose industries and allowing existing businesses to expand. And while some development had taken place it had tended to be the kind of use that would have not normally have been granted permission in the town, such as the abattoir. The introduction of some 'bad neighbour' developments had led to employment growth but had also put off other developers and companies from coming to the area. Developers wanted more certainty that if they set up in B Town then they would not find themselves next to a glue factory in six months. This led B Town to introduce more conditions on the permissions granted by their zoning schemes and a level of public participation to allow neighbouring users to comment on development proposals.

A Town had also come up against what seemed to be a problem caused by the fragmentation of planning jurisdictions. Their strategy of creating a high quality environment to encourage growth was paying off with firms either moving in or willing to do so. A Citizen's Jury panel had accepted the evidence of planners and others that 2500 new houses would be needed over the next five years to meet the demand from such growth, and that the most appropriate place for them given existing congestion to the west was greenfield land to the east. However, the rural areas remained determined to resist further encroachment into open countryside or existing villages. The conflict that arose could not be easily resolved within the fragmented framework.

Each town also witnessed a clear change in planners' roles. Planners in C Town are now being slowly replaced by urban designers and architects, though some planners have retained a role (which they have had to adapt to quickly) of community participation and negotiation. In B Town the emphasis, even after the changes to include a greater environmental say, is still very much on non-plan. Those more involved in the economic of land, such as surveyors, were finding an increased role particularly after B Town decided to out-source what remained of its development control function to a national planning and surveying company. In A Town the elite approach to land use regulation gives the planners a privileged position *vis-à-vis* the public and developers as most of the important decisions are taken out of the public gaze. This is still the case even though voting through the formal committee processes and the introduction of initiatives to encourage greater public involvement have given the appearance of increased local involvement.

LESSONS FROM NOWHERE

So what can be learnt from the experiences of Nowhere District Council's attempts at a more postmodern planning? Well, as it is a fictional case then it is obviously contrived to illustrate some of the points I would like to make. However, I feel that it does highlight relevant issues in the shift of any form of land use regulation to a more open, devolved and participative approach. The first point to make is that the *forms* of planning I describe above are not necessarily postmodern but they do encompass elements of the themes I identified in Chapter 7. What is distinctly postmodern is the *framework* for planning. It was a more open, less centralised, more participative, less dominatory, more locally sensitive and less centrally directed form of planning. Huw Thomas pointed out in his comments on a draft of this chapter that these kind of issues can be discussed and debated within a modernist framework (i.e., modernism can also lead to difference, etc.). This may be true in some cases but the dynamic and principles of modernism do not guarantee it. Although there are a multitude of different systems that could have fitted that mould, and while the examples were contrived to create a straw man, the points I highlight reflect what I would argue are relevant for any form of planning that seeks to move along the postmodern path. But what flows from this and what would be a realistic scenario in the absence of more foundational rules is that a postmodern framework does not necessarily imply a postmodern form of planning. There are both a variety of plannings under the more postmodern framework and a blend of different forms of planning. A Town could arguably be perceived as a new right and pragmatic approach while C Town was a combination of collaborative with an underlying theme of restriction and the rural areas more postmodern though exclusionary. Although obviously contrived, would not a more locally-led planning be likely to follow a similar route of pick and mix from different theories and concerns (Grant, 1994, 1994a)? The rather binary nature of the theories as traditionally presented in planning perhaps need to be modified to a less digital and more analogue model. Jill Grant's work on the use of different theories in Halifax, Canada illustrates this point. She found different planning theories used for a variety of different tasks. Rather than a dominant paradigm, she found an eclectic mix of theories being employed side-by-side and often in conflict with each other. As she put it 'People promote theories that fit their normative perspectives' (1994a: 74).

Other issues that need to be addressed both in a postmodern planning form and a postmodern planning framework are those of common themes. While the postmodern rejects any idea of commonality, there are undoubtedly issues that will arise that have common currency. Questions of where housing should go, for example, have a significance beyond the individual. There are issues of strategy in a fragmented world, how can 'meta' thinking such as sustainability be implemented if a locality such as B Town decides to move away from a planned approach. Similarly, can there be a resolution of conflicts between different planning regimes or are they incommensurable in a postmodern world? There clearly can be a resolution providing this is enforced, but this is moving away from the postmodern ideal and back towards the erstwhile modernist approach. The tension that arises in these questions, as it has done throughout the attempt to explore the practical implications of the postmodern, is that of the danger of slipping into relativism. Lyotard's fears regarding the postmodern licensing Nazism is as relevant to planning as it is in any other field. The tension that arises is that a postmodern approach unleashes local freedom that may then turn around and bite the hand that freed it. If such freedom is to be curtailed in order to ensure consistency, then this is moving away from the principle of the postmodern. It appears that the liberal concern with modern concepts such as equality is the main enemy of the postmodern. Of course, one could follow an extreme postmodern line and say that we should live with its implications whether we agree with them or not. This is to argue that the postmodern emphasis on difference should be followed regardless of the consequences and that concepts such as equality are merely fronts for modern unifying concerns that mask dominatory power relations. But, what I hope is that one lesson from the example above and the argument throughout the book is that it does not have to be a choice between the two extremes.

Chapter 4 highlighted the extent to which planning practice is already pushing at a more postmodern form of planning. In terms of the methodology or approach used by planners in Frome, it is clear that a more pragmatic basis was initiated. Similarly, they seemed willing to challenge the notion of set solutions. I termed this the 'postmodernisation' of planning practice because of the emphasis on challenging some of the doctrines of practice. The problem with the Frome approach was that, although it attempted to challenge powerful interests, it clearly did not succeed. However, if there is to be a *practical* translation of postmodern thinking for planning then both the Frome example and the scenario I set out above provide pointers as to how it might be achieved. Within this practical world realpolitik pervades, conflicting interests have to be resolved, selfish motives can underpin decisions and powerful economic and political forces are played out. As such, there can only be a partial move towards postmodern planning as envisaged by some theorists. But this does not necessarily mean that there cannot be a postmodern planning per se, only that it is a certain kind of postmodern planning. This is if one takes the postmodern as

- a *cultural logic* which emphasises relativism and diversity;
- a set of *theories* that are predicated upon a heterogeneous and dynamic interpretation of structures and meaning and that reflect upon and draw attention to the forms of modernity;
- and a manifestation of *economic traits* that lead to the development of cultural, social and economic change (depthlessness, pastiche, insecurity, etc.) that mark it as different from the forms of modernity that preceded it.

The planning I set out in Nowhere conforms to these broad concerns. The question then becomes not *'can we have a postmodern planning?'*, but *'do we want one?'*.

CONCLUSIONS

I have touched upon a number of issues that I feel would arise from the adoption of a postmodern planning framework and postmodern planning form. The issues I have highlighted are by no means the only ones but are perhaps the main ones. A different approach, perhaps one that included more foundational principles, would lead to different issues arising. A more extreme postmodern planning would certainly lead to others. It is worth pointing out my own position here. I am not arguing for a postmodern form of planning, i.e., one that pursues abstract ideas of difference. I would argue that there can be no practical postmodern planning that does not also involve the need to employ foundational principles and other aspects of thinking and theory. But, more fundamentally, there needs to be a realistic normative assessment of the desirability of such a planning. It has been conflated with a broadly liberal (individual) emphasis on tolerance and rights while I would argue that it can preclude as well as empower. If the postmodern means anything, for me, it is about choice. And choice means the right to choose a form of planning that is not as liberal – as was the case in NDC. Consequently, a postmodern planning framework provides this. Within such a framework which conforms to the broad thrust of the postmodern as I defined it, a community may wish to follow a more diverse and inclusive approach. But equally, they may wish not to.

CHAPTER 9

CONCLUSIONS

Can we have a postmodern planning? No (an answer that is itself not postmodern). Can we have a planning that is more open, sensitive to the needs of the many, radically challenges existing notions and actively seeks to encourage wider participation from those previously excluded in an continuously open discourse? Yes. Whether this is postmodern planning or not depends on semantics and particularly on the extent to which the postmodern can overlap with foundational thinking, and the extent to which what passes as postmodern thinking could equally be argued to be part of a pragmatic planning and/or draw on elements of critical pragmatism. Also, as I argued in the previous chapter, there are two aspects of postmodern planning that are related though imply different outcomes: a postmodern form and a postmodern framework. The outcome of a postmodern planning and the answers to the question above will vary depending on the approach taken. The approach I took was a conservative one and the outcome was structured by that. But regardless of my approach, I maintain that a postmodern planning does not necessarily imply postmodern tenets. If taken as a framework that releases difference and seeks to challenge totality and closed systems, then it may well lead to a postmodern form of planning but it may equally release a less than progressive or liberal form of planning. The rules and foundational principles that I introduced into my postmodern framework in Chapter 8 sought to allow different forms of planning to develop, but also precluded them from becoming dominatory themselves. The form of planning that mostly resembled a postmodern approach, that of the rural areas, had inherent problems and difficulties including a strategic overview and conflict resolution procedures with neighbouring communities. However, the postmodern planning framework did not necessarily imply that form of planning. It could easily have led to a perfectly workable form. The point is that the framework does not determine the form.

I could quite easily be accused of creating a more social democratic form of planning that builds on current trends and consequently becomes a self-fulfilling prophecy. And it is true that many of the changes that are currently being experienced in the UK fall within the ambit of what I have defined a possible postmodern planning. Devolution is providing a more federal approach to local governance, the government's proposals on Beacon Councils will allow them to develop different powers and increasingly diverge. But, as experience in Italy and New Zealand has shown, constitutional change is a process not an event. Powers are changed leading to demands for more change and reflection on what has happened. It is a constantly shifting process where equilibrium is achieved only to be unbalanced again. The main source of instability is in the relationship between the different centres – in the UK's case between Edinburgh and London for example.

The form devolution in the UK is taking is leading to an asymmetrical development of different regions. Many of the problems that I touched upon in the development of an asymmetrical planning system are also being encountered as the UK begins to diversify. For example, tensions between different areas in asymmetrical governance are inevitable. As I set out in the Nowhere District Council example in Chapter 8, cross-border disputes are a likely source of conflict. In the UK this could include situations where a devolved power such as the environment is effected by a reserved power such as foreign affairs. Westminster will still be responsible for entering into international agreements on the environment which could conflict with the policy direction taken by Edinburgh. This would mean the London government maintaining an interest in those policy areas where there has been devolution and the possible need for vetoes on some proposals. Similarly, environmental concerns tend not to respect either national or administrative demarcations. Ultimately, following the splitting up of UK-wide bodies such as the Nature Conservancy Council into national bodies, the devolution of control over environmental matters and the right of member states to determine their own environmental standards under the subsidiarity following the Single European Act in 1987, it is not improbable that England and Scotland could evolve different standards on a number of environmental matters.

Against this general trend of devolution and its emphasis on difference and inequality are also definite shifts in local thinking concerning involvement. Recent research has found that local authorities in the UK were embracing initiatives to 'deepen democracy'. They found that:

- 47 per cent of local authorities had focus groups;
- 26 per cent visioning exercises;
- 23 per cent some form of user management services;
- 18 per cent citizens' panels and;
- 5 per cent citizens' juries (DETR 1998d).

The government have also introduced proposals under the Beacon Councils initiative that will allow local authorities, who can demonstrate their ability, to take on extra functions from central government. There are also proposals for regional government in England, London now has an elected Mayor and others areas may follow. On the whole, there has been and will be an extraordinary decentralisation of power and control from the centre in the closing years of the twentieth century.

As regards a shift to a more proportional voting system in local government, the Jenkins Report published in October 1998 recommended a mixed system, which it described as either an Additional Member System (AMS) or Alternative Vote (AV) Top-up. Approximately 80–85 per cent of the Commons would continue to be made up by constituency members, though they would be elected by AV. But AV alone was considered unacceptable as it could lead to disproportionality (a straight AV system would have led to an even larger Labour majority in the 1997 general election). To overcome this Jenkins recommended that between 15 and 20 per cent of MPs be elected through lists in city or county top-up areas. The major political parties would submit one or two names (though other candidates could be submitted by anyone) and voters would then have two votes – one for the constituency and one for the top-up.

The Jenkins approach, if implemented after a referendum, would shift the UK's voting system to one similar to much of Europe, and there is little doubt that it would be broadly more proportional than the current FPTP approach. Such an alternative or any one of the more proportional systems could also be easily used at a more local level with the advantages I outlined in Chapter 8. Indeed, it appears that there is a momentum towards a more proportional system of voting of which Jenkins is only a part. With the Scottish Parliament, Welsh Assembly, European elections and the London Mayor and Assembly already being decided by forms of PR (AMS for the Scottish Parliament, Welsh Assembly and London Assembly, SV for the London Mayor) it seems this change is pushing at an open door. All of the major parties have groups advocating different forms of PR as well as a number of influential outside bodies including the Electoral Reform Society and Charter 88 all lobbying for change. However, it should not be forgotten that different forms of PR lead to different outcomes and any voting system is imperfect. The outcome of the shift to another form of PR called a Mixed Member System (MMS) in New Zealand in 1992, which was used as a basis for the 1996 election, was mixed. Half of the 120 seats in parliament are elected using the old First Past the Post approach while the other half are returned under MMS. The outcome of the election was a hung parliament led by Winston Peters' National Party who formed a coalition with the right-wing New Zealand First Party. The shift to the right in New Zealand politics as a result with the New Zealand First Party's anti-immigration policies have to be balanced against the undoubted greater proportionality of the election result. One outcome has been the disintegration of the New Zealand First Party because of splits over its relationship to the National Party, the collapse of the coalition and the call for another voting reform.

It is not automatically the case that the outcome in New Zealand would be replicated in the UK. The main reason for this is that the Jenkins' proposals take into account some of the lessons learnt, and the terms of the reference referred to the requirement for broad proportionality, *the need for stable government*, an extension of voter choice and the maintenance of a link between honourable Members and geographical constituencies (Jack Straw, 1st January 1997, Hansard 302, col. 57–8, emphasis added).

Commitment to increased participation is also a feature of the Labour government's plans for local government. In its consultative paper, *Modernising Local Government* (DETR, 1998a) it comments that:

The Government has a clear vision of successfully modernised local government. It will be characterised by councils which once again engage directly with their local communities. Such councils will actively promote public participation (DETR, 1998a: 6).

And in the government's White Paper, *Modern Local Government. In Touch with the People* (DETR, 1998b), they commented that:

The Government wishes to see consultation and participation embedded into the culture of all councils ... and undertaken across a wide range of each council's responsibilities (DETR, 1998b: 14).

While the government's initiative on *Best Value in Local Government* emphasises the need to consult local people about the quality and cost of services, and the reviewing and setting of performance targets (DETR, 1998c), other recent government initiatives emphasise participation. Initiatives include:

- The Crime and Disorder Bill requires the responsible authorities to obtain the views of persons or bodies in their area about the level and pattern of crime and, more generally, argues for widespread consultation about strategies for reducing crime and disorder.
- The Health White Paper and proposals for Health Action Zones place emphasis on improving general health as well as providing better health services. Achieving these objectives requires a capacity to involve the public.
- Proposals for new tax-raising powers at the local level (e.g. congestion charges) and, more broadly, plans to enhance local financial accountability, suggest the need for a local authority to have capacity to consult with and gain the support of particular groups of taxpayers to persuade them that what their money is being spent on is acceptable (DETR, 1998d).

Local communities coming to agreements on what they consider to be appropriate regions for planning was encouraged during local government reorganisation from 1995 onwards. 'Voluntary arrangements' were entered into and have been refined since. In 1999 various local authorities in the south-east of England discussed a

new planning 'super-region' stretching from Norfolk to Kent in an attempt to maintain a coherent planning strategy for London and its hinterland. Such a group overlaps a number of existing regional planning areas as well as the Regional
Development Agency boundaries. Cross administrative border co-operation is also
a feature of environmental policy following the break up of the Nature Conservancy
Council in 1990 and formal mechanisms are being put in place to ensure greater
co-operation on wider government matters following devolution in the form of con-
cordats.

The tension between freedom of information and individual privacy raised in
the last chapter is currently being addressed through the proposed Human Rights
Bill which gives fuller effect in UK domestic law to the European Convention on
Human Rights, the Freedom of Information Bill which will allow people a legal right
to official information and the Data Protection Bill which seeks to uphold the confi-
dentiality of personal information held by private and public bodies. The tensions
between these are obvious:

> On the one hand, there is a risk that by taking a liberal approach to Freedom of
> Information the UK may find itself in breach of Article 8 of the European
> Convention on Human Rights. On the other, there is a risk that over-scrupulous
> concern for privacy may prevent the disclosure of information of legitimate
> concern to the public (H. M. Government, 1998, Chapter 4, para 14).

Primacy appears to be given to privacy as the Data Protection Bill seeks to 'protect
the fundamental rights and freedoms of natural persons, and in particular their right
to privacy with respect to processing of private data' (Article 1 of Directive
95/46/EC). As the Data Protection Bill is derived from European law, it will take
precedence of UK law including a Freedom of Information Act. This has obvious
implications for any rethought planning approach and does not seem to help in
deciding upon principles of freedom of information versus rights to privacy for
practical circumstances. This should not, however, be used as an excuse to limit
change, as a poll by the Joseph Rowntree Reform Trust and Mori in 1995 revealed
that 81 per cent of people wanted access to information collected by public
authorities. In terms of planning there are some aspects of a generally free access
to information that need to be resolved. A number of public bodies have expressed
concern at the possible burden imposed by having to provide such information and
that it may detract from their core functions.

There is also a potential danger that the openness of decision making may
work against reflection of different options during policy formulation. This is particularly so if debate over a policy issue is evenly split. Collective responsibility would
require planners or others to abide by any final decision though if the minutes of
any meeting showed dissension this could be used to undermine a collective front.

This is an important point though any freedom of information act need not limit policy-making processes. It is more likely to encourage a more open form of discussion that recognises that any aspects may be open to future scrutiny. Planners should be encouraged to hold a professional opinion that may or may not be different from any collective view. Consequently, I am unconvinced that this may prove to be a major problem.

Other potential drawbacks of the shift towards a more postmodern planning include questions of delay, inflexibility and NIMBY thinking. These are standard responses aimed at proposals such as third-party appeals, and they can have validity. The recent experience of shifting from 'predict and provide' to 'managed change' in the identification of housing projections has led to a distinctive NIMBY-type approach at the county and regional level. Without powers of imposition from a central level this is an issue that will undoubtedly plague any form of postmodern localised planning that does not have mechanisms to balance local and national concerns.

I could rightly be accused of providing a theory-heavy justification for what are sensible changes to planning that are already part of the landscape of practice or are soon likely to be so. The trajectory of change initiated by the Labour government is not postmodern. It does, however, have a number of postmodern themes, but blended with distinctly centralised thinking. The extreme NIMBYism that would undoubtedly be a feature of the NDC approach and a devolved postmodern planning is far less likely to be an issue in the UK's evolving system. However, such an accusation of trend-following also misses the point of this book. I have endeavoured to provide an exploration of postmodern social theory and its relationship to planning and what a postmodern planning may look like. I could have followed a far more extreme version of postmodern thinking for planning or interpreted it in a variety of different ways. What my approach also does is provide some theoretical underpinnings for a direction in government policy that seems to be 'feeling its way' rather than working towards an agreed end.

Would Foucault, Baudrillard, Jameson, et al., accept this form of planning as postmodern? The answer must be a resolute no. It is too conservative and pragmatic for their liking. But it is equally far more workable and, unlike much of the thinking put forward by postmodern social theorists, attempts to reconcile the need for unity with a desire for difference.

BIBLIOGRAPHY

Adam Smith Institute (1983) *Omega Report: Local Government Policy*, Adam Smith Institute: London.

Adorno, T. and Horkheimer, M. (1979) *Dialectic of Enlightenment*, Verso: London.

Aglietta, M. (1979) A Theory of Capitalist Regulation: The US Experience, Verso: London.

Aglietta, M. (1982) 'World Capitalism in the Eighties', *New Left Review*, 136, 5–41.

Alexander, E. R. (1997) 'A Mile or a Millimeter? Measuring the "planning theory-practice gap" ', *Environment and Planning B, Planning and Design*, 24, 3–6.

Alexander, E. R. and Faludi, A. (1996) 'Planning Doctrine: Its Uses and Implications', *Planning Theory Newsletter*, 16, 11.

Allmendinger, P. (1996), 'Development Control and the Legitimacy of Planning Decisions. A Comment', *Town Planning Review*, 67: 2.

Allmendinger, P. (1997) *Thatcherism and Planning: The Case of Simplified Planning Zones*, Avebury: Aldershot.

Allmendinger, P. (1998) 'Simplified Planning Zones', in Allmendinger, P. and Thomas, H. (eds) *Urban Planning and the British New Right*, Routledge: London.

Allmendinger, P. and Chapman, M. (1999) *Planning in the Millennium*, John Wiley: Chichester.

Allmendinger, P. and Tewdwr-Jones, M. (1997) 'Post-Thatcherite Urban Planning and Conflicts', *International Journal of Urban and Regional Research* 21(1).

Allmendinger, P. and Tewdwr-Jones, M. (1998) *Deconstructing Communicative Rationality: A Critique of Habermasian Collaborative Planning, Environment and Planning A*, 30, 1975–89.

Allmendinger, P. and Tewdwr-Jones, M. (2000) 'New Labour, New Planning? The Trajectory of Planning in Post-New Right Britain', *Urban Studies*, 37, 8: 1379–402.

Allmendinger, P. and Thomas, H. (1998) (eds) *Urban Planning and the British New Right*, Routledge: London.

Amin, A. (ed.) (1994) *Post-Fordism. A Reader*, Blackwell: London.

Antonio, R. and Kellner, D. (1991) 'Modernity and Critical Social Theory: The Limits of the Postmodern Critique', in Dickens, D. and Fontana, A. (eds) *Postmodern Social Theory*, University of Chicago Press: Chicago.

Antonio, R. and Kellner, D. (1994) 'The Future of Social Theory and the Limits of the Postmodern Critique', in Dickens, D. and Fontana, A. (eds) *Postmodernism and Social Inquiry*, UCL Press: London.

Archer, M. (1998) 'Introduction. Realism in the Social Sciences', in Archer, M., Bhaskar, R., Collier, A., Lawson, T. and Norrie, A. *Critical Realism. Essential Readings*, Routledge: London.

Banham, R., Barker, P., Hall, P. and Price, C. (1969) ' "Non-plan": an experiment in freedom',
    New Society, Mar 20th.

Barraclough, G. (1964) *An Introduction to Contemporary History*, Penguin: Baltimore.

Baudrillard, J. (1968) *Le Système des objects*, Gallimard: Paris.

Baudrillard, J. (1970) *La Société de consommation*, Gallimard: Paris.

Baudrillard, J. (1975) *The Mirror of Production*, Telos: St Louis.

Baudrillard, J. (1976) *L'échange symbolique et la mort*, Gallimard: Paris.

Baudrillard, J. (1979) *De la Séduction*, Denoël Gonthier: Paris.

Baudrillard, J. (1987) *Forget Foucault*, Semiotext(e): New York.

Baudrillard, J. (1983) *Simulations*, Semiotext(e): New York.

Bauman, Z. (1989) *Modernity and the Holocaust*, Polity Press: Oxford.

Becker, G. (1983) 'A Theory of Competition Among Pressure Groups for Political Influence',
    The Quarterly Journal of Economics, 48, 371–400.

Bell, D. (1973) *The Coming of Post-Industrial Society*, Basic Books: New York.

Bell, D. (1980) 'The Social Framework of the Information Society', in Forester (1980).

Benko, G. (1997) 'Introduction: Modernity, Postmodernity and the Social Sciences', in
    Benko, G. and Strohmayer, U. (eds) (1997).

Benko, G. and Strohmayer, U. (eds) (1997) Space and Social Theory, in *Interpreting Moder-
    nity and Postmodernity*, Blackwell: Oxford.

Bennett, A. (1987) Housing and the Labour Mobility Crisis, in *An Environment for Growth*,
    Adam Smith Institute: London.

Berg, L. (1993) 'Between Modernism and Postmodernism', *Progress in Human Geography*,
    17, 4, 490–507.

Berger, A. A. (ed.) (1998) *The Postmodern Presence*, Sage: London.

Berger, A. A. (1998) *The Postmodern Presence. Readings on Postmodernism in American
    Culture and Society*, Altamira Press: Walnut Creek.

Berger, A. A. (1998) *The Postmodern Presence. Readings on Postmodernism in American
    Culture and Society*, Altamira Press: Walnut Creek.

Berman, M. (1982) *All That is Solid Melts into Air*, Verso: London.

Bernstein, R. (ed.) (1985) *Habermas and Modernity*, MIT Press: Cambridge, Mass.

Bertens, H. (1995) *The Idea of the Postmodern. A History*, Routledge: London.

Best, S. and Kellner, D. (1991) *Postmodern Theory*, Macmillan: London.

Bhaskar, R. (1978) *A Realist Theory of Science* (2nd Edition), Harvester: Brighton.

Bhaskar, R. (1979) *The Possibility of Naturalism*, Harvester: Hemel Hempstead.

Bhaskar, R. (1998) 'Societies', in Archer, M., Bhaskar, R., Collier, A., Lawson, T. and Norrie, A.,
    Critical Realism. Essential Readings, Routledge: London.

Black, D. (1958) *The Theory of Committees and Elections*, Cambridge University Press:
    Cambridge.

Bohman, J. (1996) *Public Deliberation*, MIT Press: Cambridge, Mass.

Bosanquet, N. (1983) *After the New Right*, Heinemann: London.

Botham, R. and Lloyd, M. G. (1983) 'The Political Economy of Enterprise Zones', *National Westminster Bank Quarterly Review*, May.

Boyer, C. (1983) *Dreaming the Rational City*, MIT Press: Boston.

Boyer, R. (1990) *The Regulation School: A Critical Introduction*, Columbia University Press, New York.

Bramley, G. and Watkins, C. (1996) *Steering the Housing Market: New Building and the Changing Planning System*, Policy Press: London.

Breton, A. (1974) *The Economic Theory of Representative Government*, Macmillan: London.

Brindley, T., Rydin, Y. and Stoker, G. (1996) *Remaking Planning: The Politics of Urban Change in the Thatcher Years* (2nd Edition), Unwin Hyman: London.

British Property Federation (1986) *The Planning System – A Fresh Approach*, British Property Federation, London.

Brown, G. (1998) 'The Chancellor's Statement on the Economic and Fiscal Strategy Report', Bramley, G. and Watkins, S. (1996) *Steering the Housing Market: New Building and the Changing Planning System*, Policy Press: London.

Brown, G. (1998) 'The Chancellor's Statement on the Economic and Fiscal Strategy Report', *HM Treasury News Release*, June 11th.

Buchanan, J. (1958) *Public Principles of Public Debt*, Richard D. Irwin: Homewood, Illinois.

Buchanan, J. (1977) 'Why Does Government Grow?' in Borcherding, T., *Budgets and Bureaucrats. The Sources of Government Growth*, Duke University Press: Durham, NC.

Buchanan, J. (1979) 'Politics without Romance: A Sketch of Positive Public Choice Theory and Its Normative Implications', in Buchanan, J. and Tollison, R. (1984) *The Theory of Public Choice – II*, University of Michigan Press: Ann Arbor.

Buchanan, J. M. and Tullock, G. (1962) *The Calculus of Consent. Logical Foundations of Constitutional Democracy*, University of Michigan Press: Ann Arbor.

Buchanan, J. and Wagner, R. (1977) *Democracy in Deficit. The Political Legacy of Lord Keynes*, Academic Press: New York.

Butler, E. (1987) 'The Myth and Reality of Green Belt Policy', in, *An Environment for Growth*, Adam Smith Institute: London.

Caborn, R. (1998) *Speech to the British Council of Shopping Centres Annual Conference*, 5th November.

Callinicos, A. (1991) *The Revenge of History: Marxism and the East European Revolutions*, Polity Press: Cambridge.

Camhis, M (1979) *Planning Theory and Philosophy*, Tavistock: London.

Campbell, H. and Marshall, R. (1996), *Ethical Issues in Planning Practice*, Paper presented to the University of Newcastle 50th Anniversary Conference, 25–27 October.

Campbell, H. and Marshall, B. (1998) 'Acting on Principle: Dilemmas in Planning Practice', *Planning Practice and Research*, 13, 2, 117–28.

Clark, J. and Newman, J. (1997) *The Managerial State: Power, Politics and Ideology in the Remaking of Social Welfare*, Sage: London.

Cloke, P., Philo, C. and Sadler, D. (1991) *Approaching Human Geography. An Introduction to Contemporary Theoretical Debates*, Paul Chapman: London.

Colman, J. (1993) *Planning Education in the 1990s, Australian Planner*, 31, 2, 19–23.

Connor, S. (1997) *Postmodern Culture. An Introduction to Theories of the Contemporary*, Blackwell: London.

Corkindale, J. (1998) *Reforming Land Use Planning: Property Rights Approaches*, Institute of Economic Affairs: London.

Cullingworth, J. B. (1997) 'British Land Use Planning: A Failure to Cope with Change?' *Urban Studies*, 24: 5–6, 945–60.

Davidoff, P. and Reiner, T. A. (1962) 'A Choice Theory of Planning', reprinted in Faludi, A. (1973) *A Reader in Planning Theory*, 11–39, Pergamon Press: Oxford.

Davies, J. G. (1972) *The Evangelistic Bureaucrat*, Tavistock, London.

Dear, M. (1986) *Postmodernism and Planning, Environment and Planning D: Society and Space*, 4, 367–84.

Dear, M. (1988) 'The Postmodern Challenge: Reconstructuring Human Geography', *Transactions of the Institute of British Geographers.* 13, 262–74.

Dear, M. (1995) 'Prolegomena to a Postmodern Urbanism', in Healey, P., Cameron, S., Davoudi, S., Graham, S. and Madani-Pour, A., *Managing Cities. The New Urban Context*, John Wiley: Chichester.

Dear, M. and Scott, A. (1981) *Urbanisation and Urban Planning in Capitalist Society*, Methuen: London.

Denman, D. R. (1980) *Land in a Free Society*, Centre for Policy Studies: London.

Department of the Environment (1980) *Development Control Policy and Practice Circular 22/80*, HMSO: London.

Department of the Environment (1983) *Enquiry into the Planning System in North Cornwall*, HMSO: London.

Department of the Environment (1984) *Industrial Development Circular 16/84*, HMSO: London.

Department of the Environment (1985) *Lifting the Burden. Cmnd 9571*, HMSO: London.

Department of the Environment (1986) *Planning Policy Guidance Note 6 – Retailing and Town Centres*, HMSO: London.

Department of the Environment (1988) *Planning Policy Guidance Note 5 – Simplified Planning Zones*, HMSO: London.

Department of the Environment, Transport and Regions (1998) *The Economic Consequences of Planning to the Business Sector*, HMSO: London.

Department of the Environment, Transport and Regions (1998a) *Modernising Local Government*, HMSO: London.

Department of the Environment, Transport and Regions (1998b) *Modern Local Government. In Touch with the People*, HMSO: London.

Department of the Environment, Transport and Regions (1998c) *Modernising Local Government. Improving Local Services Through Best Value*, HSMO: London.

Department of the Environment, Transport and Regions (1998d) *Guidance on Enhancing Public Participation in Local Government*, HMSO: London.

Department of Trade and Industry (1998) *Competitiveness White Paper*, HMSO: London.

Docherty, T. (1993) *Postmodernism. A Reader*, Harvester Wheatsheaf, Hemel Hemstead.

Donald, J. (1992) 'Metropolis: The City as Text', in Bocock, R. and Thomson, K. (eds) *Social and Cultural Forms of Modernity*, Polity Press: Cambridge.

Downs, A. (1957) *An Economic Theory of Democracy*, Harper and Brothers: New York.

Downs, A. (1967) *Inside Bureaucracy*, Little, Brown: Boston.

Dreyfus, H. and Rabinow, P. (1982) *Michel Foucault: Beyond Structuralism and Hermeneutics*, University of Chicago Press: Chicago.

Drucker, P. (1957) *Landmarks of Tomorrow*, Harper and Row: New York.

Dryzek, J. (1990) *Discursive Democracy. Politics, Policy and Political Science*, Cambridge University Press: Cambridge.

Dunleavy, P. (1985) 'Bureaucrats, Budgets and the Growth of the State: Reconstructing an Instrumental Model', *British Journal of Political Science*, 18, 21–49.

Dunleavy, P. (1998) cited in Gay, O. 'Voting Systems: The Jenkins Report, House of Commons Research Paper 98/112', House of Commons: London.

Eagleton, T. (1981) *Walter Benjamin or Towards a Revolutionary Criticism*, New Left Books: London.

Eagleton, T. (1986) 'Capitalism, Modernism and Postmodernism', in *Against the Grain: Essays 1975– 1985*, Verso: London.

Eagleton, T. (1996) *The Illusions of Postmodernism*, Blackwell: London, Cambridge.

Eccleshall, R. (1984) 'Introduction: The World of Ideology', in Eccleshall, R., Geoghegen, V., Jay, R. and Wilford, P., *Political Ideologies*, Hutchinson: London.

Elster, J. (ed.) (1998) *Deliberative Democracy*, Cambridge University Press: Cambridge.

Evans, A. (1985) *Urban Economics: An Introduction*, Blackwell: Oxford.

Evans, A. (1987) 'Urban or Rural Development?', in, *An Environment for Growth*, Adam Smith Institute: London.

Evans, B. (1993) 'Why We No Longer Need a Planning Profession', *Planning Practice and Research*, 8: 1, 9–15.

Evans, B. (1995) *Experts and Environmental Planning*, Averbury: Aldershot.

Evans, B. (1997) 'From Town Planning to Environmental Planning', in Blowers, A. and Evans, B, *Town Planning in the 21st Century*, Routledge: London.

Faludi, A. (1973) *Planning Theory*, Pergamon: Oxford.

Featherstone, M. (1988) 'In Pursuit of the Postmodern: An Introduction', *Theory, Culture and Society*, 5, 2–3, 195–216.

Feldman, M. M. A. (1995) 'Regime and Regulation in Substantive Planning Theory', *Planning Theory*, 14, 65–95.

Feldman, M. M. A. (1997) 'Can we talk? Interpretive Planning Theory as Comedy', *Planning Theory*, 17, 43–64.

Festenstein, M. (1997) *Pragmatism and Political Theory*, Polity Press: Cambridge.

Filion, P. (1996) 'Metropolitan Planning Objectives and Implementation Constraints: Planning in a Post-Fordist and Postmodern Age', *Environment and Planning A*, 28: 1637–60.

Fischer, F. and Forester, J. (eds) (1993), *The Argumentative Turn in Policy Analysis and Planning*, UCL, London.

Flower, E. and Murphy, M. (1977) *A History of Philosophy in America*, Capricorn Books: New York.

Flyvbjerg, B. (1998a) *Rationality and Power*, University of Chicago Press, Chicago.

Flyvbjerg, B. (1998b) 'Empowering Civil Society', in Douglas, M. and Friedmann, J., *Cities for Citizens*, John Wiley: Chichester.

Forester, J. (1980), 'Listening: The Social Policy of Everyday Life (Critical Theory and Hermeneutics in Practice)', *Social Praxis* 7, no. 3/4, pages 219–32.

Forester, J. (1989) *Planning in the Face of Power*, University of California Press: Berkeley, CA.

Forester, J. (1993), *Critical Theory, Public Policy and Planning Practice*, State University of New York Press: Albany NY.

Forester, J. (1996), 'Beyond dialogue to transformative learning: how deliberative rituals encourage political judgement in community planning processes', in S. Esquith (ed.), *Democratic Dialogues: Theories and Practices*, University of Poznan, Poznan.

Forester, J. (1998) 'Rationality, Dialogue and Learning', in Douglas, M. and Friedmann, J., *Cities for Citizens*, John Wiley: Chichester.

Forester, T. (ed.) (1980) *The Microelectronics Revolution*, Basil Blackwell: Oxford.

Forester, T. (ed.) (1985) *The Information Technology Revolution*, Basil Blackwell: Oxford.

Foucault, M. (1965) *Madness and Civilisation: a History of Insanity in the Age of Reason*, Tavistock: London.

Foucault, M. (1970) *The Order of Things, an Archaeology of the Human Sciences*, Tavistock: London.

Foucault, M. (1972) *The Archaeology of Knowledge*, Tavistock: London.

Foucault, M. (1973) *The Birth of the Clinic, an Archaeology of Medical Perception*, Tavistock: London.

Foucault, M. (1979) *Discipline and Punishment*, Vintage Books: New York.

Foucault, M. (1980) *The History of Sexuality*, Vintage Books: New York.

Friedmann, J. (1987) *Planning in the Public Domain: From Knowledge to Action*, Princeton University Press: Oxford.

Friedmann, J. and Kuester, C. (1994) 'Planning Education in the Late 20th Century: An Initial Inquiry', *Journal of Planning Education and Research*, 14, 1, 55–64.

Fukuyama, F. (1989) *The end of history?*, Washington, DC: National Affairs.

Gamble, A. (1988) *The Free Economy and the Strong State*, Macmillan: London.

Gay, P. (1969) *The Enlightenment: An Interpretation. Vol 1: The Rise of Modern Paganism*, Wildwood House: London.

Giddens, A. (1984) *The Constitution of Society: An Outline of the Theory of Structuration*, Polity Press: Cambridge.

Giddens, A. (1990) *The Consequences of Modernity*, Polity Press: Cambridge.

Gitlin, T. (1998) 'Postmodernism: What Are They Talking About', in Berger, A. A. (1998).

Goffman, E. (1959), *The Presentation of Self in Everyday Life*, Doubleday, New York.

Gordon, C. (ed) *Power/Knowledge: Selected Interviews and Other Writings, 1972–1977*, Harvester: Brighton.

Grant, J. (1994) *The Drama of Democracy. Contention and Dispute in Community Planning*, University of Toronto Press, Toronto.

Grant, J. (1994a) 'On Some Public Uses of Planning "Theory" ', *Town Planning Review*, 65, 1 59–76.

Grant, M. (1998) 'Commentary', in Corkindale, J., *Reforming Land Use Planning: Property Rights Approaches*, Institute of Economic Affairs: London.

Grant, M. (1999) 'Planning as a Learned Profession', *Plans and Planners*, vol 1, Summer 1999, 21–26.

Greed, C. (1996) *Implementing Town Planning*, Longman: Harlow.

Gunder, M. and Fookes, T. (1997) 'In Defence of Planning Praxis, Knowledge and the Profession: Planning Education and Institutions for the New Century', *Planning Practice and Research*, 12, 2, 133–46.

Haber, H. (1994) *Beyond Postmodern Politics*, Routledge: New York.

Habermas, J. (1981) *Modernity versus Postmodernity*, New German Critique, 22, 3–14.

Habermas, J. (1984) *The Theory of Communicative Action, Volume 1: Reason and the Rationalization of Society,* Polity Press: Cambridge.

Habermas, J. (1984) *The Theory of Communicative Action. Reason and the Rationalization of Society.* vol 1, Polity Press: Cambridge.

Habermas, J. (1987) *The Philosophical Discourse of Modernity*, Polity Press: Cambridge.

Haigh, N. (1997) *Manual of Environmental Policy*, Cartermill: London.

Hall, P. (1977) 'The Inner Cities Dilemma', *New Society*, 3: 14–26.

Hall, P., Gracey, H., Drewett, R. and Thomas, R. (1973) *The Containment of Urban England,* Allen and Unwin: London.

Hall, S. (1988) 'Brave New World', *Marxism Today*, October, 24–9.

Hall, S. (1992) 'Introduction', in Hall, S. and Gieben, B., *Formations of Modernity*, Open University Press: Milton Keynes.

Hall, S. and Jaques, M. (eds) (1989) *New Times*, Lawrence and Wishart: London.

Hamilton, P. (1990) 'The Enlightenment and the Birth of Social Science', in Hall, S. and Gieben, B. *Formations of Modernity*, Open University Press: Milton Keynes.

Hamilton, P. (1992) 'The Enlightenment and the Birth of Social Science', in Hall, S. and Gieben, B. *Formations of Modernity*, Polity Press: Cambridge.

Handy, B. (1998) *A Spy Guide to Postmodern Everything*, in Berger, A. A. (1998).

Harper, T. L and Stein, S. M. (1995) 'Out of the Postmodern Abyss: Preserving the Rationale for Liberal Planning', *Journal of Planning Education and Research*, 14, 233–44.

Harrison, A. (1977) *Economics and Land Use Planning*, Croom Helm: London.

Harrison, P. (1998) 'From Irony to Prophecy: A Pragmatist's Perspective on Planning', Paper presented to the 'Once Upon a Planners Day' Conference, University of Pretoria, 22–23rd January.

Harvey, D. (1973) *Social Justice and the City,* Arnold: London.

Harvey, D. (1989) *The Urban Experience,* Blackwell: London.

Harvey, D. (1990) *The Condition of Postmodernity,* Blackwell: Oxford.

Harvey, J. and Bather, L. (1982) *The British Constitution and Politics* (Fifth Edition), Macmillan: London.

Hassan, I. and Hassan, S. (1983) (eds) *Innovation/Renovation: New Perspectives on the Humanities,* University of Wisconsin Press: Madison.

Hayek, F. A. (1944) *The Road to Serfdom,* Routledge and Kegan Paul: London.

Healey, P. (1992), 'A Planner's Day: Knowledge and Action in Communicative Practice', *Journal of the American Planning Association,* Vol 58, 9–20.

Healey, P. (1993), 'The Communicative Work of Development Plans', *Environment and Planning B: Planning and Design,* 20, 83–104.

Healey, P. (1994) 'The Argumentative Turn in Planning Theory and its Implications for Spatial Strategy Formulation, Paper for Conference on Planning Theory and Social Theory' University of Tampare: Finland.

Healey, P. (1996a) 'Collaborative Planning in a Stakeholder Society', *Paper presented to the University of Newcastle 50th Anniversary Conference,* 25–27th October.

Healey, P. (1996b) 'The Communicative Turn in Spatial Planning Theory and its Implications for Spatial Strategy Formulation', *Environment and Planning B: Planning and Design,* 23, 217–34.

Healey, P. (1997) *Collaborative Planning. Shaping Places in Fragmented Societies,* Macmillan: London.

Healey, P. (1998) 'Collaborative Planning in a Stakeholder Society', *Town Planning Review,* 69: 1.

Healey, P. and Hillier, J. (1995) 'Community Mobilization in Swan Valley: Claims, Discourses and Rituals in Local Planning', Working Paper No. 49, Dept. of Town and Country Planning, University of Newcastle.

Healey, P., Purdue, M. and Dennis, F. (1995) *Negotiating Development: Rationales and Practice for Development Obligations and Planning Gain,* Spon: London.

Hebdige, D. (1988) *Hiding in the Light: On Images and Things,* Routledge: London.

Hee-Soh, B. (1986) 'Political Business Cycles in Industrialized Democratic Countries', Kyklos, 39, 31–46.

Held, D. (1987) *Models of Democracy,* Polity Press: Cambridge.

Hillier, J. (1993), 'Discursive Democracy in Action', Paper presented to Association of European Schools of Planning Congress, Lodz, Poland, July.

Hillier, J. (1995) 'The Unwritten Law of Planning Theory: Common Sense', *Journal of Planning Education and Research,* 14: 2, 292–6.

BIBLIOGRAPHY 271

Hillier, J. (1996) 'Beyond confused noise', Paper presented to the Cultural Studies Association of Australia Conference 1996, Freemantle.

Hillier, J. (1996a) 'Deconstructing the Discourse of Planning', in Mandelbaum, S., Mazza, L. and Burchell, R., *Explorations in Planning Theory*, Rutgers University: New Brunswick.

H. M. Government (1998) *Select Committee on Public Administration*, Third Report, HMSO: London.

H. M. Treasury (1998) *Pre-Budget Report*, HMSO: London.

Hoch, C. (1984) 'Doing Good and Being Right – the Pragmatic Connection in Planning Theory', *American Planning Association Journal*, 4, 1, 335–45.

Hoch, C. (1995) *What Planners Do*, Planners Press, Chicago.

Hoch, C. (1996) 'A Pragmatic Inquiry About Planning and Power', in Seymour, J., Mandelbaum, L. and Burchell, R., *Explorations in Planning Theory*, Center for Urban Policy research: New Brunswick.

Hoch, C. (1997) 'Planning Theorists Taking an Interpretive Turn Need not Travel on the Political Economy Highway', *Planning Theory*, 17, 13–64.

Holston, J. (1995) 'Spaces of Insurgent Citizenship, *Planning Theory,* 13, 35–52.

Huyssen, A. (1984) 'Mapping the Postmodern', *New German Critique,* 33, 5–52.

Imrie, R. (1999) 'The Implications of the "New Managerialism" for planning in the Millennium', in Allmendinger, P. and Chapman, M. *Planning Beyond 2000,* John Wiley: London.

Innes, J. (1994) *Planning Through Consensus-Building: a new view of the comprehensive planning ideal*, (University of California IURD: Berkeley, CA).

Innes, J. (1995), 'Planning Theory's Emerging : Communicative Action and Interactive Practice', *Journal of Planning Education and Research*, 14, 3, 183–90.

Irvine, K. (1987) *Question and Answers from An Environment for Growth*, Adam Smith Institute: London.

Isaacson, W. (1998) 'Our Century and the Next One', *Time*, April 13th, 30–5.

Jacobs, J. (1961) *The Death and Life of Great American Cities,* Vintage Book: New York.

Jameson, F. (1984) 'Postmodernism, or The Cultural Logic of Late Capitalism', *New Left Review*, 146, 53–92.

Jameson, F. (1984a) 'Foreword', in Lyotard (1984) *The Postmodern Condition: A Report on Knowledge*.

Jameson, F. (1992) *'Postmodernism, or The Cultural Logic of Late Capitalism',* Verso: London.

Jencks, C. (1977) *The Language of Postmodern Architecture*, Pantheon: New York.

Jencks, C. (1989) *What is Post-Modernism?* (Third Edition), Academy Editions: London.

Jessop, B. (1990) 'Regulation Theories in Retrospect and Prospect', *Economy and Society*, 19, 153– 216.

Jessop, B. (1994) 'Post-Fordism and the State', in Amin, A. (ed.) *Post-Fordism. A Reader,* Blackwell: Oxford.

Johnston, R. J. (1992) *Philosophy and human geography: an introduction to contemporary approaches,* Arnold: London

Jones, P. J., Natter, W. and Schatzki, T. (1993) 'Post-ing Modernity', in Jones, P. J., Natter, W. and Schatzki, T., (eds) *Postmodern Contentions. Epochs, Politics, Space.* Guilford Press: New York.

Jones, R. (1982) *Town and Country Chaos*, Adam Smith Institute: London.

Joseph Rowntree Foundation (1995) *The Scope for Choice and Variety in Local Government*, Joseph Rowntree: York.

Joseph Rowntree Foundation (1996) *Community Identity and Local Government*, Joseph Rowntree Foundation: York.

Kaufman, J. and Escuin, M. (1996), 'A Comparative Study of Dutch, Spanish and American Planner Attitudes', Paper presented to ASP/AESOP Joint Congress, Toronto.

Keeble, L. (1952) *Principles and Practice of Town and Country Planning*, Estates Gazette: London.

Kellner, D. (1989) *Jean Baudrillard. From Marxism to Postmodernism and Beyond*, Polity Press: Cambridge.

Kosko, B. (1994) *Fuzzy Thinking*, Flamingo: London.

Kumar, K. (1995) *From Post-Industrial to Post-Modern Society. New Theories of the Contemporary World*, Blackwell: London.

Labour Party (1991) *Democracy, Representation and Elections*, Labour Party: London.

Labour Party (1996) *Planning for Prosperity: A Review of Planning Issues*, Labour Party: London.

Laclau, E. (1988) 'Politics and the Limits of Modernity', in Ross, A. (ed.) *Universal Abandon*, University of Minnesota Press: Minneapolis.

Laclau, E. and Mouffe, C. (1985) *Hegemony and Socialist Strategy: Towards a Radical Democratic Politics,* Verso Book: London.

Lash, S. and Urry, J. (1987) *The End of Organised Capitalism*, Polity Press: Cambridge.

Lauria, M. (1997) 'Communicating in a vacuum: Will anyone hear?', *Planning Theory*, 17, 40–3.

Lauria, M. and Whelan, R.K. (1995) 'Planning Theory and Political Economy: The Need for a Reintegration', *Planning Theory*, 14, 8–33.

Lechte, J. (1994) *Fifty Key Contemporary Thinkers. From Structuralism to Postmodernity,* Routledge: London.

Lemert, C. (1997) *Postmodernism is not what you think*, Blackwell: Oxford.

Lent, A. (1994) 'Radical Democracy: Arguments and Principles', in Perryman, M., *Altered States*, Lawrence and Wishart: London.

Liggett, H. (1996) 'Examining the Planning Practice Conscious(ness)', in Mandelbaum, S., Mazza, L. and Burchell, R., *Explorations in Planning Theory*, Rutgers University: New Brunswick.

Light, A. and Katz, E., (1996) *Environmental Pragmatism*, Routledge: London.

Lipietz, A. (1997) 'Warp, Woof and Regulation: A Tool for Social Science', in Benko, G. and Strohmayer, U. (eds) (1997).

Lipsky, M. (1978) *Street Level Bureaucracy*, Russell Sage: New York.

Little, J. (1994) *Gender, Planning and the Policy Process,* Pergamon: Oxford.

Low, N. (1991) *Planning, Politics and the State. Political Foundations of Planning Thought*, Unwin Hyman: London.

Lowe, P. and Ward, S. (1998) *British Environmental Policy and Europe*, Routledge: London.

Lyotard, J-F. (1983) 'Answering the Question: what is postmodernism?', in Hassan and Hassan (1983).

Lyotard, J-F. (1984) *The Postmodern Condition: A Report on Knowledge*, University of Minnesota Press: Minneapolis.

Lyotard, J-F. (1984a) 'Interview' with Georges Van Den Abbeele, in *Diacriticis* 3.

Lyotard, J-F. (1985) *Just Gaming*, translated by Wlad Godzich, University of Minnesota Press: Minneapolis.

Lyotard, J-F. (1988) *The Differend: Phrases in Dispute*, University of Minnesota Press: Minneapolis.

McKinsey Global Institute (1998) *Driving Productivity and Growth in the UK Economy*, McKinsey Global Institute: London.

McLaughlin, B. (1994) 'Centre or Periphery? Town Planning and Spatial Political Economy', *Environment and Planning A*, 26, 1111–22.

McLean, I. (1993) *Democracy and Representation*, Blackwell: Oxford.

McNay, L. (1994) *Foucault. A Critical Introduction*, Polity Press: Cambridge.

MacRae, C. D. (1977) 'A Political Model of the Business Cycle', *Journal of Political Economy*, 85, 239– 63.

Mandel, E. (1975) *Late Capitalism*, New Left Books: London.

Mandel, E. (1978) *Late Capitalism*, New Left Books: London.

Marcuse, P. (1995) 'Not chaos but walls', in Watson, S. and Gibson, K. (eds) (1995).

Masselos, J. (1995) 'Postmodern Bombay: Fractured Discourse', in Watson, S. and Gibson, K. (eds) *Postmodern Cities and Spaces*, Blackwell: London.

Masuda, Y. (1985) 'Computopia', in Forester (1985).

Mendip Disrict Council (1994) Report to Planning Committee, 4th October.

Midelfort, E. (1980) 'Madness and Civilisation in Early Modern Europe: a Reappraisal of Michel Foucault', in *After the Reformation: Essays in Honor of J. H. Hexter*, Malament, B. (ed.), University of Philadelphia Press: Philadelphia.

Miller, G. and Real, M. (1998) 'Postmodernity and Popular Culture: Understanding our National Pastime', in Berger, A. A. (ed.) *The Postmodern Presence,* Sage: London.

Mills, C. (1959) *The Sociological Imagination*, Oxford University Press: New York.

Mommaas, H. (1996) Modernity, Postmodernity and the Crisis of Social Modernisation: A Case Study of Urban Fragmentation' *International Journal of Urban and Regional Research* 20, 2, 196–216.

Moore, B. (1989) 'Constructing and deconstructing plausibility', *Environment and Planning D*, 7(3), 313–26.

Moore-Milroy, B. (1989) 'Constructing and Deconstructing Plausibility: Environment and Planning D:' *Society and Space*, 7, 3, 313–26.

Moore-Milroy, B. (1991) 'Into postmodern weightlessness', *Journal of Planning Education and Research*, 10: 3, 181–7.

Morris, J. (1998) 'Forward', in Corkindale, J., *Reforming Land Use Planning: Property Rights Approaches*, Institute of Economic Affairs: London.

Mouffe, C. (1984) 'Towards a Theoretical Interpretation of New Social Movements', in Hanninen, S. and Paldan, L., *Rethinking Marx*, International General/IMMRC: New York and Bagnolet.

Mouffe, C. (1996) 'Radical Democracy or Liberal Democracy?', in Trend, D. (ed.) *Radical Democracy. Identity, Citizenship, and the State*, Routledge: London.

Mouffe, C. (1996a) 'Deconstruction, Pragmatism and the Politics of Democracy', in Mouffe, C., *Deconstruction and Pragmatism*, Routledge: London.

Mounce, H. O. (1997) *The Two Pragmatisms. From Peirce to Rorty*, Routledge: London.

Muller, J. (1998) *Paradigms and Planning Practice*, International Planning Studies, 3, 3, 287–302.

Naisbitt, J. (1984) *Megatrends: Ten New Directions Transforming Our Lives*, Warner Books: New York.

Nino, C. (1996) *The Constitution of Deliberative Democracy*, Yale University Press: New Haven, Conn..

Niskanen, W. A. (1971) *Bureaucracy and Representative Government*, Aldine-Atherton: Chicago.

Norris, C. (1982) *Deconstruction: Theory and Practice*, Methuen: London.

Norris, C. (1985), *The Contest of Faculties: Philosophy and Theory After Deconstruction*, Methuen: London and New York.

Olson, M. (1965) *The Logic of Collective Action. Public Goods and the Theory of Groups*, Harvard University Press: Cambridge, Mass.

Oranje, M. (1996), 'Modernising South Africa and Its Forgotten People Under Postmodern Conditions', Paper presented to the University of Newcastle 50th Anniversary Conference, 25–27 October.

Outhwaite, W. (1987) *New Philosophies of Social Science. Realism, Hermeneutics and Critical Theory*, Macmillan: London.

Outhwaite, W. (1994), *Habermas. A Critical Introduction*, Polity Press: Cambridge.

Parker, K. (1996) 'Pragmatism and Environmental Thought', in Light, A. and Katz, E. (1996).

Pateman, C. (1970), *Participation and Democratic Theory*, Cambridge University Press: Cambridge.

Pearce, et al. (1978) *Land, Planning and the Market*, Cambridge University Dept, Land Economy Paper No. 9.

Pennance, F. (1974) 'Planning, Land Supply and Demand', in Walters, et al., *Government and the Land*, Institute of Economic Affairs: London.

Pennington, M. (1996) *Conservation and the Countryside: By Quango or Market?*, Institute of Economic Affairs: London.

Perryman, M. (1994) *Altered States. Postmodern, Politics, Culture*, Lawrence and Wishart, London.

Philo, C. (1992) 'Foucault's Geography, Environment and Planning D:' *Society and Space*, 10, 137–61.

Pickvance, C. (1977) 'Marxist Approaches to the Study of Urban Politics: Divergence Among some Recent French Studies', *International Journal or Urban and Regional Research*, 1, 2.

Pile, S. and Rose, G. (1992) 'All or Nothing? Politics and Critique in the Modernism–Postmoderism Debate', Environment and Planning D. 10, 123–36.

Piore, M. and Sabel, C. (1984) *The Second Industrial Divide: Possibilities for Prosperity*, Basic Books: New York.

Porter, R. (1990) *The Enlightenment*, Macmillan: London.

Poster, M. (1989), *Critical Theory and Post-Structuralism: In Search of a Context*, Cornell University Press: Ithaca and London.

Poster, M. (1998) 'Postmodern Virtualities', in Berger (1998).

Poulantzas, N. (1978) *State, Power, Socialism*, New Left Books: London.

Pratt, A. (1995) 'Putting Critical Realism to Work: the Practical Implications for Geographical Research', *Progress in Human Geography*, 19, 1, 61–74.

Rabinow, P. (1984) *The Foucault Reader*, Pantheon: New York.

Reade, E. (1987) *British Town and Country Planning*, Open University Press, Milton Keynes.

Richardson, T. (1996), 'Foucauldian Discourse: Power and Truth in Urban and Regional Policy Making', *European Planning Studies*, 4, 3.

Robinson, D., Dunn, K. and Ballintyne, S. (1998) *Social Enterprise Zones*, Joseph Rowntree Foundation: York.

Rorty, R. (1985) 'Habermas and Lyotard on Postmodernity', in Bernstein (1985), 161–75.

Rosenberg, B. and White, D. (1957) *Mass Culture*, The Free Press: Glencoe, Illinois.

Royal Town Planning Institutue (1999) Introduction to web site at http://www.rtpi.org.uk/

Rydin, Y. (1998) *Urban Environmental Planning in the UK*, Macmillan: London.

Sabel, C. (1982) *Work and Politics: the Division of Labour in Industry*, Cambridge University Press: Cambridge.

Sager, T. (1994) *Communicative Planning Theory*, Avebury: Aldershot, Hants.

Sandercock, L. (1995) 'Introduction' *Planning Theory*, 13, 10–33.

Sandercock, L. (1998) *Towards Cosmopolis*, John Wiley: Chichester.

Sarup, M. (1988) *An Introductory Guide to Post-Structuralism and Postmodernism*, Harvester Wheatsheaf, Hemel Hempstead.

Sayer, A. (1993) 'Postmodernist Thought in Geography: A Realist View', *Antipode*, 24, 320–44.

Scott, A. and Roweis, S. (1977) 'Urban Planning Theory in Practice: A Reappraisal', *Environment and Planning*, 9, 1097–111.

Siegan, B. (1972) *Land Use Without Zoning*, Lexington Books: Lexington, Mass.

Smart, B. (1985) *Michel Foucault*, Routledge: London.

Smart, B. (1993) *Postmodernity*, Routledge: London.

Soja, E. (1989) *Postmodern Geographies,* Verso: London.

Soja, E. (1997) 'Planning in/for Postmodernity', in Benko, G. and Strohmayer, U. (eds) (1997).

Soloman, J. (1998) 'Our Decentered Culture: The Postmodern Worldview', in Berger, A. A. (1998).

Somerset County Council (1972) Frome Town Expansion.

Sorensen, T. and Auster, M (1998) 'Theory and practice in planning: further apart than ever?', Paper presented to the Eighth International Planning History Conference, University of New South Wales, 15–18 July.

Steen, A. (1981) *New Life for Old Cities*, Aims of Industry: London.

Stephen, F. (1988) *The Economics of the Law*, Wheatseaf: London.

Stigler, G. (1975) *The Citizen and the State. Essays on Regulation*, University of Chicago Press: Chicago.

Stonier, T. (1983) *The Wealth of Information: A Profile of Post-Industrial Economy*, Thames Methuen: London.

Teitz, M. (1996a) 'American Planning in the 1990s: Evolution, Debate and Challenge', *Urban Studies*, 33, 4–5, 649–71.

Teitz, M. (1996b) 'American Planning in the 1990s: Part II, The Dilemma of the Cities', *Urban Studies*, 34, 5–6, 775–95.

Tewdwr-Jones, M. (1996), 'Reflective Planning Theorising and Professional Protectionism,' *Town Planning Review*, 67, 2, 235–43.

Tewdwr-Jones, M. and Harris, N. (1998) 'The New Right's Commodification of Planning Control', in Allmendinger, P. and Thomas, H. (eds) *Urban Planning and the British New Right*, Routledge: London.

Tewdwr-Jones, M. and Thomas, H. (1997), 'Collaborative action in local plan-making: planners: perceptions of 'planning through debate', *Environment and Planning B: Planning and Design*.

Thomas, H. (1999) 'Planning and the Planning Profession', in Greed, C., *Social Town Planning*, Routledge, London.

Thomas, H. and Krishnarayan, V. (1994) '"Race", Disadvantage and policy Processes in British Planning' *Environment and Planning A*, 26, 1891–910.

Thomas, K. (1997) *Development Control. Principles and Practice*, UCL Press: London.

Thornley, A. (1993) *Urban Planning under Thatcherism: The challenge of the market (Second Edition)*, Routledge: London.

Toffler, A. (1981) *The Third Wave*, Bantam Books: New York.

Trend, D. (ed.) (1996) *Radical Democracy. Identity, Citizenship, and the State*, Routledge: London.

Tufte, E. (1978) *Political Control of the Economy*, Princeton University Press: Princeton.

Tullock, G. (1965) *The Politics of Bureucracy*, University Press of America: New York.

Turner, B. (ed.) (1990) *Theories of Modernity and Postmodernity*, Sage: London.

Turner, B. (1990a) *Periodization and Politics in the Postmodern*, in Turner, B. (ed.) (1990).

Udehn, L. (1996) *The Limits of Public Choice*, Routledge: London.

Underwood, J. (1980) 'Town Planners in Search of a Role' *Occasional Paper No. 6*, School for Advanced Urban Studies: Bristol.

Urban Task Force (1999) *Executive Summary*, HMSO, London.

Vaz, K. (1996) 'Planning for Prosperity', Press Release, Labour Party: London.

Venturi, R. (1966) *Complexity and Contradiction in Architecture*, The Architectural Press: London.

Wagner, R. W. (1977) 'Economic Manipulation for Political Profit: Macroeconomic Consequences and Constitutional Implications', *Kyklos*, 30, 395–410.

Walters, A. (1974) 'Land Speculator – Creator or Creature of Inflation?', in Walters et al. (ed.), *Government and the Land*, Institute of Economic of Affairs: London.

Ward, S. (1994) *Planning and Urban Change*, Chapman: London.

Waters, B. (1987) 'The Need for Planning Flexibility', in *An Environment for Growth*, Adam Smith Institute: London.

Watson, V. (1998) *The 'Practice Movement' As An Approach to Developing Planning Theory – Origins, Debates and Potentials*, Paper presented to the 'Once Upon a Planners Day' Conference, University of Pretoria, 22–23rd January.

Webber, M-J. (1991) 'The Contemporary Transition', *Environment and Planning D*, 9, 165–82.

Webster, F. (1995) *Theories of the Information Society*, Routledge: London.

West, W. A. (1974) *Town Planning Controls – Success or Failure?*, Institute of Economic Affairs: London.

Wilder, C. (1998) 'Being Analogue', in Berger, A. A. *The Postmodern Presence. Readings on Postmodernism in American Culture and Society*, Altamira Press: Walnut Creek.

Williams, R. (1977) *Marxism and Literature*, Oxford University Press: Oxford.

Williams, R. (1996) *European Union Spatial Policy and Planning*, Paul Chapman: London.

Wilson, J. and Banfield, E. (1964) 'Public-Regardingness as a Value Premise in Voting Behaviour', *The American Political Science Review*, 58, 876–87.

Wollen, P. (1993) *Raiding the Icebox: Reflections on Twentieth-Century Culture*, Verso: London.

Yeung, H. W. (1997) 'Critical Realism and Realist Research in Human Geography: a Method or a Philosophy in Search of a Method?', *Progress in Human Geography*, 21, 1, 51–74.

Yiftahcel, O. (1994) 'The Dark Side of Modernism: Planning as Control of an Ethnic Minority', in Watson, S. and Gibson, K., (eds) *Postmodern Cities and Spaces*, Blackwell: Oxford.

Yiftahcel, O. (1998) 'Planning and Social Control: Exploring the Dark Side', *Journal of Planning Literature*, 12, 4, 395–406.

INDEX

Adorno, T. W. 16–18, 35
Allmendinger, P. 96
Allmendinger, P. and Chapman, M. 55, 86
Amin, A. 64, 66
Antonio, R. and Kellner, D. 193
apperceptive mass 140
Archaeology of Knowledge, The 36, 37, 38
Archer, A. 203–4, 216
archive 37
Association of District Councils 114

Barraclough, G. 21
Baudrillard, J. 10, 22, 26, 27, 41–6, 52, 55, 83
Bauman, Z. 13, 18
Beauregard, B. 93–5, 159, 168
Bell, D. 21, 29, 58–64
Berger, A. A. 72–74
Berman, M. 13
Bertens, H. 33, 41
Best, S. and Kellner, D. 21, 22, 36, 38, 40, 43,
    44, 45, 46, 48, 49, 70, 71, 81, 86, 196,
    198–201, 204
Bhaskar, R. 203–4, 216, 221–2
Birth of the Asylum, The 35

Chapman, J. W. 20
collaborative planning 5, 122–37, 142, 153–4,
    190–1
Coming of Post-Industrial Society, The 58
Community Land Act 113
Confederation of British Industry 177
Connor, S. 30
consensus 31, 128–9
Conservatism 116–20, 158, 182
Consumer Society, The 41
Containment of Urban England, The 115
Corkindale, J. 180
critical realism 215
critical social theory 198–204
Cullingworth, J. B. 4

dark side 13–14, 16, 20, 75, 96–8, 156
Davidoff, P. 243–244
Davies, J. 2
Dear, M. 80

deregulation 117
Derrida, J. 22, 26, 29
DETR (Department of the Environment,
    Transport and Regions) 230, 237, 260
Development Land Tax 113
Dewey, J. 122, 138, 139, 142–4
Dialectic of Enlightenment 16
Differend, The 29, 32, 33
Discipline and Punishment 38
discourse 142–3, 154
discursively created subject 51
Dobry Committee 115
Docherty, T. 17–18, 41
Durkheim, E. 15, 123

Eagleton, T. 33, 75, 76, 81, 82, 87, 97
Eco, U. 13
enlightenment 1, 6, 10–19, 27, 30, 38, 41, 76
enterprise zones 182–4
episteme 36, 37, 44, 51
European Union 114
European Commission 242
Evans, A. 178
Evans, B. 2
exististentialism 22

Faludi, A. 94
Festenstein, M 138, 140, 141
Feyerabend, P. 217–218
flexible specialisation 66
Flyvbjerg, B. 8, 96–7, 109–110, 129, 149,
    156
Fordism 6, 60, 64–9, 94
Forester, J. 8, 122, 129, 130, 147–9, 156,
    191
Forget Foucault 45
Foucault, M. 8, 10, 22, 26, 34–41, 43, 44, 45,
    50, 52, 123, 127, 194, 219–21
Frankfurt School 20, 35, 75
French School 19, 21, 27
Frome 100–11, 255
Fukuyama, F. 20, 86, 160

genealogy 38
General Permitted Development Order 243

Giddens, A. 12, 13, 14, 20, 68, 78–80, 97, 122
globalisation 5, 12
Grant, J. 254
Grant, M. 3
Greed, C. 1

Haber, H. 29, 32, 189, 205–9
Habermas, J. 11, 15, 21, 38, 40, 76, 78, 122–5, 150
Hall, S. 65, 86
Harper, T. L and Stein, S. M. 149, 155, 212
Harrison, P. 146, 151, 211–12
Harvey, D. 9, 10, 12, 15, 20, 46, 65, 75, 76, 77
Hayek, F. A. 170
Healey, P. 2, 92, 113, 122, 124–32
Heideggar, M. 22
Henley Centre 13
hermeneutics 213–14
Hillier, J. 214
Hoch, C. 138, 144–146, 151, 212
Horkheimer, M. 16–18, 35
Huyssen, A. 21
hyper-real 43, 44

information society 55
ideal speech 125
Innes, J. 122
ironist 143, 213
Israel 158

Jameson, F. 7, 10, 15–16, 33, 46–8, 77
Jenkins Commission 235
Jenks, C. 27–8
Jessop, B. 67

Kantian ideal 32, 53
Keeble, L. 1, 3
Kellner, D. 41, 42, 43, 44
Kuhn, T. 8, 29, 33, 140, 217
Kumar, K. 20, 21, 26, 61–4

Labour Party 92, 113, 185, 235, 244
Laclau, E. and Mouffe, C. 49–50, 68, 83, 195, 209–10
Language of Postmodern Architecture, The 71
Lash, S. and Urry, J. 67
Le Corbusier 21
L'echange symbolique et la mort 43
Local Government Commission 232

Low, N. 170
Lyotard, J-F. 10, 17, 22, 25, 26, 28, 29–34, 37, 43, 44, 50, 52, 55, 80, 123, 127, 193–4, 205

McKinsey Institute 185–6
McLaughlin, B. 3
McNay, L. 35, 37
Madness and Civilisation 35, 36
Major, J. 117–18
Mandel, E. 47
Marx, K. 15, 48, 50, 189
Marxism 22, 23, 29, 41–7, 49, 69, 76, 127, 158, 197, 219
Masselos, J. 167
Mead, George Herbert 123
Mendip District Council 100
meta-narrative 30, 47, 49, 53
Mirror of Production, The 41
mode of accumulation 65
modernising planning 184, 188
modernity 9, 10, 17–23, 36, 41, 75, 93, 112–20
Moore-Milroy, B. 121
Mouffe, C. 207, 209

National Enterprise Board 113
naturalism 216
Neill Commission 238
neo-liberalism 122, 169–88, 199–200
Nietzsche, F. 16, 21, 22, 29, 38
Norris, C. 41
nihilism 26, 41, 110

Oranje, M. 133, 235
Order of Things, The 36, 37
Outhwaite, W. 127

pagan politics 53
participation 145
participatory democracy 128
Peirce, C. 137
Pennington, M. 174, 178, 188
phenomenology 22, 213
Pickvance, C. 114
planning and the market 173–5
planning and modernity 91, 93
planning for real 123
Planning Policy Guidance Note 6 108
Porter, R. 10, 11, 15
post-Fordism 60, 64–9, 85, 94, 115
post-industrial 19–21, 58–60, 68
Postmodern Condition, The 29, 33

postmodern
    alternatives 198–226
    criticism 74–84, 149
    cultural logic of late capitalism 46
    emergence 19–23
    main themes 88, 225–6
    methodologies 211–26
    new times 27–8, 47, 55
    planning 122, 155–69, 227–56
    science 31
    social theory 25, 27–8, 202
postmodernism 6, 7, 8, 9, 17–23
post-structuralism 20, 29
Poulantzas, N. 40
power 26, 38, 40, 52, 97, 208, 219
pragmatism 5, 122, 137–54, 191–2, 211
prophecy 146
public choice theory 5, 170–3

Rabinow, P. 26
rationality 96
RDA (regional development agency) 261
realism 202–4
regime of accumulation 65
relativism 222–5
relativity 26
Richardson, T. 125
Road to Serfdom, The 170
Rorty, R. 8, 49, 77, 122, 138–41, 143–4
Royal Institute of Chartered Surveyors 241
Royal Town Planning Institute 2, 175, 243
Rydin, Y. 115

Sandercock, L. 7, 90, 95–6, 98, 109, 156,
    162–8, 190
Sarup, M. 41
Saussure, F. 29
Sayer, A. 7, 211, 215, 222–3
Scott Report 239
Scottish Parliament 184
sensibility 69–74
simplified planning zones 182–3, 243

simulacra 44
Single Regeneration Budget 102
Smart, B. 35, 36
Soja, E. 155, 159–62, 168
Somerset County Council 101
Sorensen, T. and Auster, M. 165–6
South Africa 133, 158
special development orders 184
structuralism 22
symbolic exchange 43, 195
System of Objects, The 41

Taylorism 6, 64
Tewdwr–Jones, M. 127
Tewdwr–Jones, M. and Harris, N. 118–20
Thatcher, M. 91, 112, 115, 117, 168
Theory of Communicative Action, Volume 1
    123
Thomas, H. 1, 2, 254
time–space compression 12, 20, 58
Touraine, A. 29
Towards Cosmopolis 162, 165
Toynbee, A. 20
transcendental meaning 51
Turner, B. 7, 19, 71

Udehn, E. 170–1
urban development corporation 182
urban task force 4
use classes order 4, 176

Venturi, R. 70

Weber, M. 16, 78
Webster, F. 57–62
Welsh Assembly 184
Westway Centre 100–11
Williams, R. 231
Wittgenstein, L. 22, 29

Yiftachel, O. 156–9